Washington, Virginia, a History 1735-2018

Maureen I. Harris, PhD, MPH

Independently published through Kindle Direct Publishing (KDP), a subsidiary of Amazon.com

ISBN-13: 9781687007469

Table of Contents

Preface 5

Introduction 7

Chapter 1. Early History of The Land That Became The Town of Washington, Virginia 9

Chapter 2.Establishment of the Town of Washington,1796-1797 17

Chapter 3. Formation of Rappahannock County and Selection of Washington as the County Seat 24

Chapter 4. The Town of Washington in the Early 1800s 31

Chapter 5. Washington in the Later 1800s 45

Chapter 6. Washington in the Early 1900s 69

Chapter 7. Washington in the Later 1900s and the Early 2000s .. 82

Chapter 8. Town Comprehensive Plans, Ordinances, Architectural Review Board, Zoning Board, and Task Forces 117

Chapter 9. The Town Water Supply and Wastewater Systems .. 128

Chapter 10. The Inn at Little Washington 143

Chapter 11. History of the Original Town Lots & Other Homes .. 155

Chapter 12. Schools in the Town of Washington 252

Chapter 13. Churches in the Town of Washington 258

Chapter 14. Roads and Transportation 273

Chapter 15. The Town of Washington in 2018 284

Appendix 1. Land Grant to the Kennerlys, 1735 290

Appendix 2. Petition to Establish the Town, 1796 292

Appendix 3. Petition to Add Porter's Land to the Town, 1797 293

Appendix 4. Franklin Clyde Baggarly and the Legend of George Washington 294

Appendix 5. Mayors of the Town 300

Appendix 6. Population Estimates 301

Appendix 7. Businesses and Organizations in the Town, 2018 .. 302

Index 303

Preface

This book was begun while I was a researcher at the Rappahannock Historical Society in Washington, Virginia. There I discovered that my fourth great-grandfather, George Harris, purchased 120 acres of land along South Poughs (Poes) Road at Hungry Run in 1799 and that his nephew Richard settled along the Rush River in what became known as Harris Hollow. My working career was in medical epidemiology research at the National Institutes of Health, but when I retired to rural Rappahannock County, Virginia, I fell in love with Virginia history. I found that the skills honed as an epidemiology researcher were easily translatable to historical research.

Many individuals helped me in this endeavor. Margaret (Peggy) Ralph, Clerk of the Rappahannock County Court and her two Deputy Clerks, Deidre Vest and Kaitlin Struckmann, helped find the many Court documents that contributed to the book. Laura Dodd, Town Clerk and Administrative Assistant to the Town Council of Washington, gave me access to town documents and provided many insights into the town's history and governance. Peter Luke, former Rappahannock County Commonwealth Attorney and County Attorney, graciously shared with me his extensive research on the legend of George Washington. Judy Tole and Eva Grimsley provided numerous files and documents of the Rappahannock Historical Society. George Walters, Ray Gooch, and John Fox Sullivan provided much-valued support and encouragement. Individuals who reviewed parts of the book and provided helpful comments include Gary Aichele, Fred Catlin, Kees Dutilh, Juliet Del Grosso, Peter Kramer, Joyce Kramer, Andre LeTendre, Aney Massie, Patrick O'Connell, George Walters, and Ruth Welch.

I would like to dedicate this book to all the people who have lived in the town of Washington, Virginia, and created the history that I have tried to share in this book.

Maureen I. Harris, PhD, MPH
Woodville, Virginia

Introduction

Washington, Virginia, is a small town in Rappahannock County in the eastern foothills of the Blue Ridge Mountains, adjacent to Shenandoah National Park. The town was officially established in 1796 by an act of the General Assembly of Virginia. A second Act in 1797 added additional land to form a town with two north-south streets, five cross streets, and 51 one-half acre lots. Four of the cross-streets bear the names of the men who petitioned the General Assembly to form the town and who owned the land on which the town was founded: Wheeler, Calvert, Jett, and Porter. Washington was designated as the county seat of Rappahannock County in 1833. The town was incorporated in 1894, and the town limits were expanded in that year and again in 1985 and 1989. The boundaries of the town encompass a land area of 182.0171 acres. In the U.S. census estimates for 2018, there were 125 people who were residents of the town.

The town is governed by a seven-member elected Town Council composed of a mayor, a treasurer, and five other members who meet in the historic Town Hall. As the legislative authority for the town, the council deliberates and votes on legislation, town programs, and budgets, and approves funding for town services. The town's history and architecture have elevated it to a position on the National Register of Historic Places and the Virginia Landmarks Register. It has been described as perhaps the best preserved of the county seat communities in the Virginia Piedmont.[1] Washington combines a unique blend of rural character and historic significance. It is a mixture of open spaces, village-style commerce, homes, historic structures, and local government activities.

The town's nickname "Little Washington" avoids confusion because of its proximity to Washington D.C. which lies only 70 miles to the northeast. The nickname has standing for, in 1804, Methodist Episcopal Bishop Francis Asbury, the famed traveling circuit rider, noted in his diary: "Took the path to Little Washington ... and met with a kind reception and good entertainment."[2]

---

[1] Calder Loth, editor, *The Virginia Landmarks Register, 3rd edition*. University Press of Virginia, 1986, page 358

[2] *The Journals and Letters of Francis Asbury, II.* London, Epworth Press, 1958, p.447

Chapter 1. Early History of The Land That Became The Town of Washington, Virginia[1]

Native Americans

It has been stated that the land on which the town of Washington is located was once an Indian trading post, but there is no documentation to support this theory. It is possible that Indians may have traded with each other in this vicinity; however, based on the history below, by the time the English settled the area that is now the town of Washington there were no Indians living there.[2]

In the early 1600s the tribes called by the English as Manahoac, which were part of the Siouan confederacy, lived in the area from the falls of the Potomac and Rappahannock rivers to the North Anna River and northwest to the Allegheny Mountains. Their main area of concentration was the upper waters of the Rappahannock and Rapidan rivers. At this time there were several Siouan tribes that comprised the Manahoac; their population is estimated to have been about 1,500. There is no known record of a European having visited a Manahoac village or of having had contact with this group in the upper Rappahannock River. There is also no known description of a Siouan village in the Virginia Piedmont. Information about the existence of the Manahoac and the location of their villages came only from interrogations of Amoroleck, a Manahoac Indian from the village of Hassininga, who had been wounded and taken captive by the English during one of John Smith's explorations of the falls of the Rappahannock River.

Between the Manahoac and the English settlements in the Virginia Tidewater region were the Algonquian groups forming part of the Powhatan confederacy who were hostile to the English and also to their Siouan neighbors to the northwest. They served as a barrier and prevented contact between the English colonists and the tribes living above the falls of the rivers.

The Monacan Indians have also been mentioned as being in the Rappahannock County area, but the tribes constituting this group were located further south, in the area between the North Anna River to the falls of the James River and

[1] This chapter is based on Maureen I. Harris, "History of the Land and People Who Founded the Town of Washington, Virginia, 1735-1833", *Magazine of Virginia Genealogy*, Volume 53, No. 1, 2015

[2] This conclusion and the discussion of Native Americans below is drawn from Ben C. McCary, *Indians in Seventeenth-Century Virginia*, The University Press of Virginia, Charlottesville, 1957; David I. Bushnell Jr., *The Manahoac Tribes in Virginia*, Smithsonian Miscellaneous Collections, Volume 94, Number 8, 1935; and John Smith, "The Generall Historie of Virginia," in *Travels and Works of Captain John Smith*, Edward Arber II, editor, John Grant Publishing Co., Edinburg, 1919

Rivanna River and northwest to the Allegheny Mountains. The Monacans were also Siouan tribes and were confederates of the Manahoac.

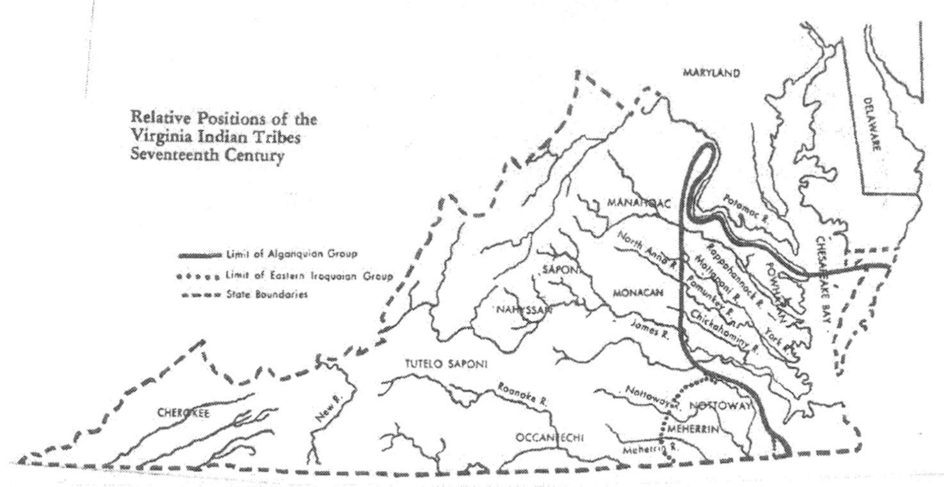

Map of Virginia showing location of Manahoac and other Native American tribes

By the middle of the 1600s most of the Indian settlements in the upper valleys of the James and Rappahannock rivers had been abandoned. A census of Native Americans in 1669 found 725 bowmen in populated regions of the colony of Virginia, among which were only 50 Manahoac living on what was then the frontier of English settlement between the James and Rappahannock rivers.[3] In 1670 the German John Lederer explored what was then a wilderness from the falls of the Rappahannock River to the Blue Ridge; no Indians were mentioned in his journals of this trip.[4] Like other Indian tribes, many of the Manahoac had probably succumbed to diseases introduced by the English and the remainder had either been exterminated by hostile Indians from the north or had left the area.[5] The remaining Manahoac are believed to have migrated in the mid-1670s to unpopulated regions of Kentucky's Big Sandy River.[6]

Some Indians, primarily the Iroquois, still remained in Virginia, although they were substantially weakened in numbers and power. In 1721 an Indian delegation went to Williamsburg and agreed to the basic terms of a treaty with the English. In 1722, Governor Spotswood of the Virginia colony and the governors of the Maryland, Pennsylvania, and New York colonies decided to

---

[3] Eugene M. Scheel, *Culpeper, A Virginia County's History Through 1920*, Green Publishers, Orange, VA, 192, page 4

[4] John Lederer, *The Discoveries of… Begun in March 1669 and Ended in September 1670*, London, 1672, reprint 1902

[5] Information from John R. Swanton, Smithsonian Bureau of American Ethnology, quoted in Darwin Lambert, *The Undying Past of Shenandoah National Park*, Roberts Rinehart Publishers, 1989, page 22

[6] John Smith, "The Generall Historie of Virginia," in *Travels and Works of Captain John Smith*, Edward Arber II, editor, John Grant Publishing Co., Edinburg, 1919, pages 366-377

cooperate in treaty negotiations with the Indians. They met with leaders of the Indian tribes in Albany, New York in 1722. Spotswood achieved his primary objective, which was to obtain the Indians' pledge to stay west of the Blue Ridge mountains and to not cross into the Piedmont south of the Potomac River: "We agree to this Article & faithfully promise not to pass over the great River which the English call Potowmack nor the great Ridge of Mountains which extend along your Frontiers."[7] The treaty also prohibited the Indians from occupying any previous settlements east of the Blue Ridge.[8]

By the mid-1700s, the Indians in the colony of Virginia were scarcely numerous enough to be regarded as a foe. In 1759-1768, three separate lists of Native Americans who were residing independently in the eastern part of North America were compiled by individuals who were knowledgeable of the Indian situation. In none of these lists were the Monacan or Manahoac peoples listed, and there were no other tribes listed who were inhabitants anywhere in the colony of Virginia.[9]

With the Treaty of Albany in 1722 and the significant diminishment of Indians in the colony of Virginia, the way was open to English settlement of the Piedmont.

The 1735 Land Grant to the Kennerlys

The first recorded official document relating to the land that became the town of Washington was a royal land grant in the year 1735 for 1,750 acres from King George II of England to Thomas, James, and Elizabeth Kennerly.[10] This land was called Delameres Forest and it included the land that was to become the town in 1796-1797. A major reason for issuing land grants in the Virginia Colony was to establish English ownership of the land and to protect the land against intrusion by the French and Spanish governments. In this early period of settlement, grants could be issued to any person who qualified as a settler or who supported emigrants who would become settlers. This "headright" system was a major means of distributing land in the early Virginia colony.

Although the Northern Neck, or Fairfax, Proprietary was first established in 1649, its boundaries were not permanently decided until 1745, at which time the land between the Rapidan and the Rappahannock rivers was included in the

---

[7] E.B. O'Callaghan, editor, *Documents Relative to the Colonial History of the State of New York*. Albany, Weed, Parsons and Co., 1855; Volume 5, pages 657-681

[8] Helen C. Rountree, editor, *Powhatan Foreign Relations, 1500-1722*, University Press of Virginia, 1993, pages 195-196; Douglas Southall Freeman, *George Washington, A Biography, Volume One, Young Washington,* New York, Charles Scribner Sons, 1948

[9] Thomas Jefferson, *Notes on the State of Virginia (1787)*, William Peden, editor, University of North Carolina Press, 1954, pages 102-107

[10] Library of Virginia. Virginia Colonial Land Office Patent Book No. 15, 1732-1735, p. 531. See Appendix 1 for full text of the land grant.

Proprietary, which was owned by Thomas Lord Fairfax. Until that time, the Colonial Virginia Land Office issued grants to land in the area, under the imprimatur of the King of England.[11]

Beginning Text of the Land Grant to Thomas, James, and Elizabeth Kennerly from King George II, 19 June 1735

George the Second by the Grace of God of Great Britain France and Ireland King Defender of the Faith To all to whom these presents shall come Greetings. Know ye that for divers goods and considerations but more especially for and in Consideration of the Importation of Six Persons to Dwell within this our Colony and Dominion of Virginia whose names are Samuel Kennerly, Ellin Kennerly, Thomas Kennerly, Elizabeth Kennerly, James Kennerly and Catherine Kennerly As also for and in consideration of the sum of Seven Pounds Five Shillings of good and Lawful money for our aide paid to our Receivor General of our Revenues in this our said Colony and Dominion We have given granted and confirmed and by these presents for us our Heirs and Successors Do Give Grant and Confirm unto Thomas Kennerly, James Kennerly and Elizabeth Kennerly one certain tract or parcel of Land containing One Thousand Seven Hundred and fifty acres commonly known by the name of Delameres Forest Lying and being in the Parish of Saint Mark in the County of Orange between the mountains and the fork of the Rushy River...

The 1,750 acres granted to the Kennerlys was awarded to them for payment of seven pounds five shillings of "good and lawful money," an annual fee of one shilling for every fifty acres of land, and because of "the importation of six persons to dwell within this our Colony of Virginia." These six individuals were Thomas, James, and Elizabeth, their sister Catherine, their mother Ellin Kennerly, and their stepfather Samuel Kennerly.[12] The Kennerlys were probably of Scottish or English origin and were new residents in Virginia. Unlike many people who received land grants in the early 1700s (e.g., Francis Thornton), the Kennerlys lived on their land for many years and were thus some of the earliest settlers in what became Rappahannock County. Indeed, Thomas, James, Catherine, and Samuel received additional land grants near the original 1735 grant.[13] No heirs of the Kennerlys are believed to still be living in the vicinity of Rappahannock County.

---

[11] "The Fairfax Grant," *Virginia Places*, www.virginiaplaces.org/settleland/fairfaxgrant

[12] Relationships are documented in Culpeper County Will Book A, pages 2 and 135

[13] Northern Neck Grants Book G, pages 29, 66, and 261; Land Office Patent Book No. 15, page 530

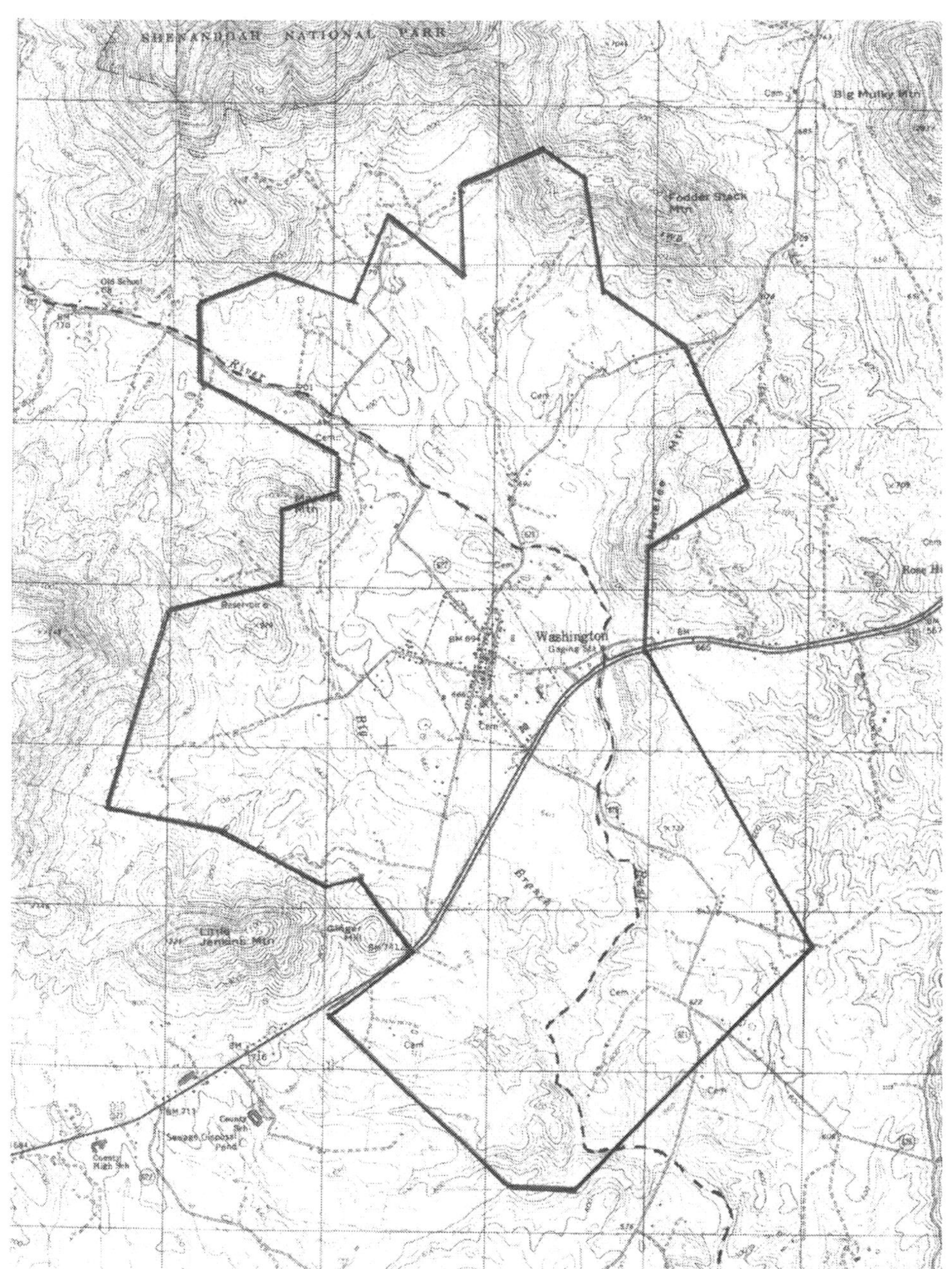

Plat of the Kennerly land grant, 1735. The plat has been drawn on a recent U.S. Geological Survey topographic map which shows modern features, including the town of Washington (which was only formed in 1796-1797) and Route 211. The boundaries and location of the land grant were determined from metes and bounds in the grant document, geographic features (i.e., rivers, streams, mountains), and boundaries of adjacent properties. The Rush River is shown with dashed lines.

The Kennerlys likely farmed their land, as did most settlers in Virginia. They also built a mill on the Rush River, on the site of the current Washington Mill, and constructed a road to the mill on what is now Old Mill Road.[14] In 1745, the three Kennerly grantees divided their land into three parts. Thomas received the central part, adjacent to and south of the Rush River and containing the land that became the town of Washington.[15] Thomas sold his land to Henry Gambill in 1753 and moved to South Carolina.[16] Gambill divided the land: in 1754 he sold the western part, which contained what became the major part of town of Washington, to John Minor;[17] in 1761 he gave the eastern part, which contained what became the northeastern portion of the town, to his son William Gambill.[18]

These two parts were bought and sold multiple times between 1761 and the 1790s.[19] Individuals involved in these sales were Garrett Minor, Anthony Strother, Joseph Pondexter, John Garwood, Robert Shirwood, Benjamin Myers, John Vilett, and Thomas Allen. Most of these men owned the land for only a few years and made no lasting mark on the future town of Washington.

Acquisition of Kennerly Land by William Porter, George Calvert, James Jett Jr., and James Wheeler, 1791-1796

Two important individuals acquired the land in the 1790s. In 1791, William Porter was given 247 acres of the western land by his father-in-law, Samuel Porter, a resident of Fauquier County.[20] Twelve years before, William (born in 1759, died in 1815) had married his first cousin, Samuel's daughter Sarah (born in 1760, died in 1836). In all likelihood, William and Sarah had moved to Samuel's land shortly after their marriage. They built their home there, now called "The Meadows" and owned by a former mayor of the town of Washington, John Fox Sullivan, and his wife Beverly. The Porters raised thirteen children in this home.[21] The home and part of the land remained in the Porter family until 1871.

---

[14] Culpeper County Deed Book B, page 132
[15] Orange County Deed Book 10, p. 278, no date, located between other documents dated 1745
[16] Culpeper County Deed Book B, page 70
[17] Culpeper County Deed Book B, page 132
[18] Culpeper County Deed Book C, page 609
[19] Culpeper County Deed Book E, pages 160, 486, and 591; Deed Book F, page 140; Deed Book G, page 276; Deed Book P, pages 117 and 409; Deed Book Q, page 524
[20] Samuel Porter had acquired 447 acres of the western land from Robert Shirwood in 1773 (Culpeper County Deed Book G, page 276); he gave the northern part of this land to his son-in-law William Porter in 1791 (Culpeper County Deed Book Q, page 387) and the southern part of this land to his son-in-law Edward Burgess in 1795 (Culpeper County Deed Book S, page 194)
[21] Maureen Harris, "The Lost Will of William Porter of Culpeper County, 1815," *Magazine of Virginia Genealogy,* Vol. 50, 2012, pages 320-324

In 1795, George Calvert acquired 230 acres of the eastern land.[22] George was a descendant of the Maryland Calverts, which included the first Lord Baltimore. His father had moved from Maryland to Prince William County, Virginia, and his son George was born there in 1744. In 1764 he married Lydia Beck Ralls, and they had 14 children between 1767 and 1793.[23] In 1777, he purchased 1174 acres of land near today's Flint Hill that became his home, which he named "The Horseshoe." Late in life, George moved to Bourbon County, Kentucky, where he died.[24]

William Porter sold three small parcels on the eastern border of his land during 1792-1794, all of which were located on land that became the town of Washington. He sold two acres to James Wheeler in 1792, on which was located Wheeler's storehouse; two acres to James Jett Sr. and John Jett, who sold this parcel to James Jett Jr. in 1795, on which was located Jett's store; and 6 acres to George Calvert in 1794.[25] Wheeler, Jett, and Calvert were probably acquiring land in anticipation of applying to the Virginia General Assembly in 1796 to create the town of Washington.

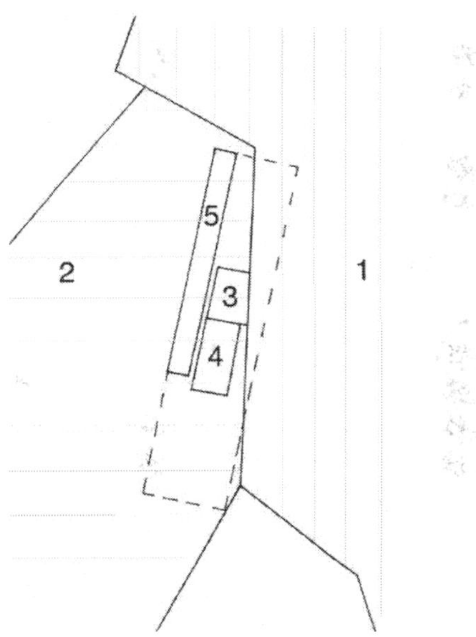

Schematic drawing showing William Porter's land, George Calvert's land, and three parcels of land purchased from William Porter in 1792-1794. Shown with dashed lines are the boundaries of the town of Washington in 1797, after Porter's land was added to the parcels of land owned by Calvert, Jett, and Wheeler. 1 and vertical lines - western part of George Calvert's land; 2 and horizontal lines - eastern part of William Porter's land; 3 - Two acres purchased by James Wheeler from William Porter; 4 - Two acres purchased by James Jett Sr. and John Jett from William Porter; the Jetts sold this parcel to James Jett Jr.; 5 - Six acres purchased by George Calvert from William Porter.

---

[22] Culpeper County Deed Book S, page 170

[23] George's daughter Lydia married George Wheeler, brother of James Wheeler who provided 2 acres of land to form the town of Washington in 1796

[24] Ella Foy O'Gorman, compiler, *Descendants of the Virginia Calverts*, Higgenson Book Co., Salem, Massachusetts, 1947, pages 26-38, 73-74, 91-92

[25] Culpeper County Deed Book R, pages 35 and 333, and Deed Book S, pages 194 and 278

Based on sales of Porter's land during 1792-1845 and of Calvert's land in 1799, it can be calculated that 25 acres of the town of Washington originated from Porter's land and 5 acres from Calvert's land (See Chapter 2).

James Wheeler was a farmer who owned land adjacent to the land of William Porter.[26] He appears to have never married. He died in 1811 and in his will he emancipated seventeen of his slaves and requested that they be removed to the state of Ohio, "where they may enjoy their liberty unmolested." The remainder of his estate was bequeathed to his niece Mariah Bidwell, his brother George, and George's three daughters.[27] James Jett Jr. was born in about 1763, the son of James Jett Sr. and Roxena Duncan.[28] He also appears to have never married. When he died in 1808, he left $500 to each of his brother John's three children and the remainder of his estate to his brother Robert. His will mentioned no wife or children.[29]

It was common at this time for a road to exist as a boundary between two farms, and information from several deeds indicates that the road to Chester's Gap ran along the eastern boundary of William Porter's land (and the western boundary of George Calvert's land) at about the place where Gay Street exists today. A deed for a property sold in 1769 stated that "the main road" was at the border of the property and that this road ran from today's intersection of Main Street with Route 211 and extended northeast for 1221' to Big Branch.[30] This road became the southeastern border of Samuel Porter's land in 1773. When William Porter sold a 6-acre rectangle of land to George Calvert in 1794, the southeast corner was on the "west side of the road leading from Thornton's Gap to Chester's Gap." This deed also specified that "a new road should be cut" along the east side of Calvert's 6 acres; this new road appears to have become today's Main Street.

There were two buildings mentioned in the deeds to Wheeler and Jett, indicating that there was some commercial activity located at the eastern boundary of Porter's land, along the Chester Gap road. These were James Wheeler's storehouse and Jett's store. There was also a schoolhouse on Porter's land at the southeast corner of the Jett purchase from Porter.

There was no mention in deeds or any other documents of any residences at the eastern part of Porter's farm or the western part of Calvert's farm, where the town of Washington would be established in 1796-1797. Indeed, it seems illogical that Porter or Calvert would have permitted houses to have been built on what was their privately-owned land.

---

[26] Culpeper County Deed Book R, page 3
[27] Culpeper County Will Book F, page 263
[28] Lois M. and Ernest C. Jett, *Jett Trails Revisited*, Amundsen Pub. Co., Decorah, Iowa, 1999, pages 18-21
[29] Culpeper County Will Book E, page 289
[30] Culpeper County Deed Book E, page 696

Chapter 2. Establishment of the Town of Washington, 1796-1797

The First Petition and the 1796 Act of the Virginia General Assembly

On 1 November 1796, George Calvert, James Jett Jr., and James Wheeler petitioned the General Assembly of Virginia to "establish a town by the name of Washington on twenty five acres of land of your said petitioners." The three men noted in their petition that they "were possessed of lands within said (Culpeper) County contiguous to each other" and that it would "be of public utility were there a town established on their lands, being situated in a fertile thick settled country, which might induce mechanics[1] to settle therein." They had already "made some improvements" and the town was "to be laid off in lots of half an acre each under such regulations as have been heretofore customary for your honorable house to prescribe in similar situations." The town was to be named for George Washington, who had announced his retirement from the presidency six weeks earlier on 19 September 1796 and who was probably the most revered person in the United States.

Petition from George Calvert, James Jett Jr., and James Wheeler to establish the town of Washington, 10 November 1796

To the Honble Speaker and Gentlemen of the house of Delegates of the Commonwealth of Virginia,

The Petition of George Calvert, James Jett jun & James Wheeler inhabitants of Culpeper County humbly shewith –

That your Petitioners are possessed of lands within the said County contiguous to each other; that they conceive it would be of public utility were there a Town established on their lands, being situated in a fertile thick settled Country, which might induce mechanics to settle therein. They therefore pray that a Law may pass to establish a Town by the name of Washington on twenty five acres of land of your said petitioners in the County aforesaid, and whereas they have already made some improvements, to same to be laid off in Lots of half an acre each, under such regulations as have been heretofore customary for your Honble house to prescribe in similar institutions; And your Petitioners as in duty bound shall pray etc.

Source: George Calvert, James Jett, & James Wheeler, Culpeper County, 10 November 1796, Legislative Petitions Digital Collection, Library of Virginia, Richmond, VA, Record number 000154065; also, Legislative Petitions of the General Assembly, 1776-1865, Accession Number 36121, Box 58, Folder 63.

---

[1] The word "mechanics" is an old term applied to various craftsmen such as carpenters, masons, blacksmiths

The General Assembly responded by passing an act on 14 December 1796 establishing the town of Washington. Eleven other new towns in Virginia were also established by this Act.[2] Washington was only the third town created in Culpeper County. The town of Fairfax (later renamed Culpeper) was created in 1759 and Stevensburg in 1782; the town of Woodville followed Washington in 1798.[3]

Act of the Virginia General Assembly*
Chap. 21. – An ACT to establish several towns.
(Passed December 14, 1796.)

1. Be it enacted by the general assembly,

5. That twenty-five acres of land, the property of John Calvert,# James Jett, junior, and James Wheeler, in the county of Culpeper, shall be, and they are hereby vested in John Strother, James Green, Edward Pendleton, Charles Browning, and John Jett, gentlemen, trustees, to be by them, or a majority of them, laid off into lots of half an acre each, with convenient streets, and establish a town by the name of Washington.

13. So soon as the said lands, where the same hath not already been done, shall respectively be laid off into lots, the trustees thereof ... shall proceed to sell the same, at public auction, for the best price that can be had; the time and place of such sales being respectively advertised for two months successively, previous thereto, in some one of the newspapers within this commonwealth, and to convey the said lots to the purchasers in fee, subject to the condition of building on each, a dwelling house, sixteen feet square at least, with a brick or stone chimney, to be furnished fit for habitation, within seven years from the day of sale, and pay the money arising from such sales, to the proprietors of the said lands, respectively, or their legal representatives.

14. The trustees of the said towns, respectively, or a majority of them, are empowered to make such rules and orders for the regular building of houses therein, as to them shall seem best; and to settle and determine all disputes concerning the bounds of the said lots.

15. If the purchaser of any lot, in either of the said towns, shall fail to build thereon, within the time limited in his deed of conveyance, the trustees of the said town, where the lot has been sold by them, and where such failure happens,

---

[2] These towns were Jonesborough in Grayson County, Mechanic in Orange County, Ca Ira in Cumberland County, Salem in Fauquier County, Ligontown on the Appomattox River, Clementstown in Amelia County, Dickensonville in Russell County, Jamestown in Prince Edward County, Amsterdam in Botetourt County, Pleasantville in Monangalia County, and Bernardsburg in Fluvanna County

[3] Eugene M. Scheel, *Culpeper, A Virginia County's History Through 1920*. Green Publishers Inc., Orange, Virginia, 1982, pp. 77-81

may, thereupon, enter into such lot, and sell the same again, and apply the money for the benefit of the inhabitants of the said town.

17. Vacancies by death, or otherwise, of any one or more of the trustees of the said towns, respectively, shall be supplied in manner prescribed by an act of assembly, passed in the year one thousand seven hundred and seventy-eight, entitled, "An act to empower the freeholders of the several towns, not incorporated, to supply the vacancies of the trustees and directors thereof."

**Eleven other towns were also established by this Act; only the text relating to the town of Washington is quoted.*

 # "John" Calvert is incorrect; The correct name is George Calvert, who acquired land in 1794 and 1795 (above), part of which became land on which the town of Washington was built.

Source: Samuel Shepherd, The Statutes at Large of Virginia, from October Session 1792 to December Session 1806, Inclusive, in Three Volumes, (New Series), Being a Continuation of Hening, New York, AMS Press, Inc., 1836, Volume II, page 29-32

The Second Petition and the 1797 Act of the Virginia General Assembly

One year later, Calvert, Jett, Wheeler, and William Porter sent a second petition to the General Assembly of Virginia. They referred to the 1796 Act establishing the town on 25 acres of land owned by Calvert, Jett, and Wheeler but stated that "the trustees met to lay off said land into lots of half an acre each...but found it could not be done without a part of Mr. Porter's land...With his consent, the trustees marked off 51 half-acre lots with convenient streets as per the plat annexed ...Your petitioners pray that your honorable body will pass an act to annex the land of William Porter to said town." A plan of the proposed streets of the town and 51 lots was attached to the petition; interestingly, four of the streets were named after the four petitioners.

Petition from George Calvert, James Jett, James Wheeler, and William Porter to include the land of William Porter in the Town of Washington, 1 November 1797

To the Honorable the Speaker and Gentlemen of the House of Delegates of the State of Virginia. The Petition of George Calvert, James Jett, James Wheeler and William Porter humbly shewith, That your Honorable Body passed an act the last Session Establishing a Town by the name of Washington on the Lands of George Calvert, James Jett and James Wheeler and condemned Twenty Five acres of Land for the same; in order to fulfill said Act the Trustees met to lay off said Land into Lotts of half an acre each agreeable to said law, but on Examination of the Ground they found it could not be done into Form or

Convenience without including a part of Mr. Porters Land. Therefore with the consent of all Parties the Trustees proceeded to mark and make off Fifty one half acre Lotts with convenient streets as per Platt herewith annexed, and after advertising the same agreeable to Law the whole of said Lotts were sold accordingly. Now your petitioners pray your Honorable Body to Pass an Act to annex the Land of William Porter to said Town, agreeable to the manner and Form Laid off by said Trustees, and your petitioners will ever pray etc.

Culpeper County
1st November 1797

George Calvert
James Jett jun
James Wheeler
William Porter

Source: George Calvert, James Jett Jr., James Wheeler, and William Porter, Culpeper County, 1 December 1797, Legislative Petitions Digital Collection, Library of Virginia, Richmond, VA, Record number 000154073; also, Legislative Petitions of the General Assembly, 1776-1865, Accession Number 36121, Box 58, Folder 71

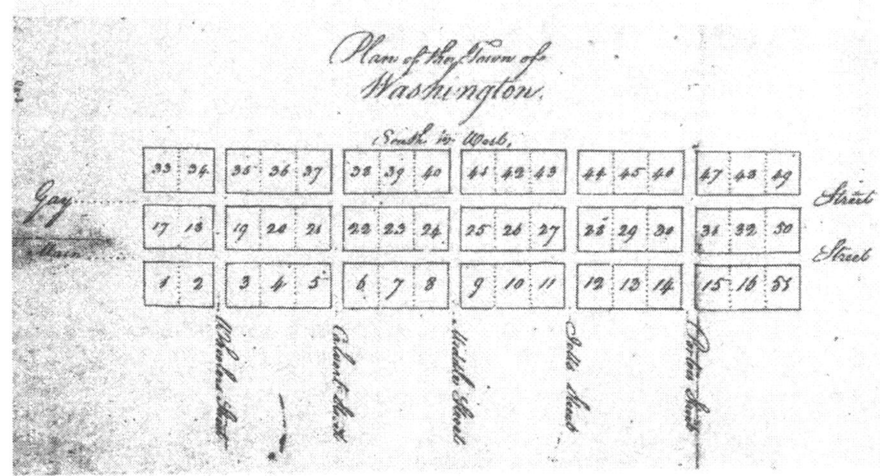

Plan of the Town of Washington Accompanying the Petition of George Calvert, James Jett Jr., James Wheeler, and William Porter, 1 November 1797

On 25 December 1797, the General Assembly passed an act "for adding certain lots to the town of Washington." The act stated that "the lots and streets, as the same are already laid off on the lands of William Porter, contiguous to the town of Washington ... are hereby added to and made a part of said town."

Act of the Virginia General Assembly to Add William Porter's Land to the Town

Chap. 76. – An ACT for adding certain lots to the town of Washington, in the county of Culpeper.
(Passed December 25, 1797.)

1. Be it enacted by the general assembly, That the lots and streets, as the same are already laid off on the lands of William Porter, contiguous to the town of Washington, in the county of Culpeper, shall be, and they are hereby added to and made a part of the said town, to all intents and purposes as if the same had been included in the lands originally laid off for the said town.
2. This act shall commence and be in force from and after the passing thereof.

Source: Samuel Shepherd, *The Statutes at Large of Virginia, from October Session 1792 to December Session 1806, Inclusive, in Three Volumes, (New Series), Being a Continuation of Hening.* Volume II, page 131, New York, AMS Press, Inc., 1836.

Based on later sales of Porter's land during 1792-1845 and of Calvert's land in 1799, it can be calculated that 25 acres of the town of Washington originated from Porter's farm and 5.5 acres from Calvert's farm:

Land of the Town of Washington Derived from the Lands of William Porter, James Wheeler, James Jett Jr., and George Calvert

Area of each lot = 8 poles x 10 poles = 132' x 165' = ½ acre
Width of streets = 30'
Area of town = 30.5 acres

William Porter's Land:	
Sold to James Wheeler, 1792	2 acres
Sold to James Jett Jr., 1793-1795	2 acres
Sold to George Calvert, 1794	6 acres
Remaining part of Porter's land	15 acres
	25 acres
George Calvert's Land	5.5 acres

Sale of Lots in the Town, 1798

Five town trustees had been appointed in the 14 December 1796 Act of the General Assembly of Virginia that established the town. These five men were

John Strother, James Green, Edward Pendleton, Charles Browning, and John Jett. The trustees were directed to sell the town lots at public auction "for the best price that can be had" and to "pay the money arising from such sales to the proprietors of said lands." These proprietors were, of course, George Calvert, James Wheeler, James Jett Jr., and William Porter.

Lot 1 - Richard Jackson, 18 pounds 14 shillings for Lots 1, 33, & 44	LOT 17 - David Lansdown, 31pounds 15 shillings Lots 17, 19, 20, 45, & 46	LOT 33 - Richard Jackson, 18pounds 14 shillings for Lots 1, 33, & 44
LOT 2 - John Ray 7 pounds 15 shillings	LOT 18 - George Yates 5 pounds 15 shillings	LOT 34 - James Yates 6 pounds 1 shilling
	WHEELER STREET	
LOT 3 - David Engler 16 pounds 8 shillings for Lots 3 & 21	LOT 19 - David Lansdown, 31pounds 15 shillings Lots 17, 19, 20, 45, & 46	LOT 35 - Levy Garwood 12 pounds 6 shillings for Lots 35 & 36
LOT 4 - Joseph Ray 8 pounds 1 shilling	LOT 20 - David Lansdown, 31pounds 15 shillings Lots 17, 19, 20, 45, & 46	LOT 36 - Levy Garwood 12 pounds 6 shillings for Lots 35 & 36
LOT 5 - Benjamin Heaton 9 pounds 1 shilling	LOT 21 - David Engler 16 pounds 8 shillings for Lots 3 & 21	LOT 37 - George Wheeler 6 pounds 12 shillings
	CALVERT STREET	
LOT 6 - Edward Bigbee 9 pounds 9 shillings	LOT 22 - John Miller 11 pounds 2 shillings	LOT 38 - Daniel Covington Brown, 13 pounds 8 shillings for Lots 38 & 39
LOT 7 - John Collins 40 pounds	LOT 23 - James Wheeler 174 pounds for Lots 23 & 24	LOT 39 - Daniel Covington Brown, 13 pounds 8 shillings for Lots 38 & 39
LOT 8 - George Calvert 49 pounds for Lots 8, 42, & 43	LOT 24 - James Wheeler 174 pounds for Lots 23 & 24	LOT 40 - Ralls Calvert 10 pounds 19 shillings
	MIDDLE STREET	
LOT 9 - Thomas Thatcher 17 pounds 10 shillings	LOT 25 - James Jett Jr. 185 pounds	LOT 41 - John Farrow 10 pounds 4 shillings
LOT 10 - Nathan Dyke 9 pounds 15 shillings	LOT 26 - Edward Pendleton 18 pounds for Lots 26 & 27	LOT 42 - George Calvert 49 pounds for Lots 8, 42, & 43
LOT 11 - Courtney Norman 7 pounds	LOT 27 - Edward Pendleton 18 pounds for Lots 26 & 27	LOT 43 - George Calvert 49 pounds for Lots 8, 42, & 43
	JETT STREET	
LOT 12 - William Porter, 25 pounds 18 shillings for Lots 12, 13, 14, & 47	LOT 28 - John Strother 20 pounds 10 shillings	LOT 44 - Richard Jackson, 18pounds 14 shillings for Lots 1, 33, & 44
LOT 13 - William Porter, 25 pounds 18 shillings for Lots 12, 13, 14, & 47	LOT 29 - Thomas Estes 9 pounds 18 shillings	LOT 45 - David Lansdown, 31pounds 15 shillings Lots 17, 19, 20, 45, & 46
LOT 14 - William Porter, 25 pounds 18 shillings for Lots 12, 13, 14, & 47	LOT 30 - Thomas Walters 9 pounds 6 shillings	LOT 46 - David Lansdown, 31pounds 15 shillings Lots 17, 19, 20, 45, & 46
	PORTER STREET	
LOT 15 - John O'Neal 8 pounds 2 shillings	LOT 31 - John Wheeler 20 pounds 10 shillings	LOT 47 - William Porter, 25 pounds 18 shillings for Lots 12, 13, 14, & 47
LOT 16 - Henry Menefee 8 pounds 2 pence	LOT 32 - Charles Yates 6 pounds 8 shillings	LOT 48 - William Smith 5 pounds
LOT 51 - John Vince 6 pounds 9 shillings	LOT 50 - Fielding Scandland 6 pounds 15 shillings	LOT 49 - David Johnston 6 pounds 3 shillings

Sale of Washington Town Lots, 1798
Source: Culpeper County Deed Book T, pages 320-407

The five trustees quickly proceeded to sell the 51 lots of the town in 1798.[4] Most lots sold for 5-10 pounds.[5] However, Lots 23 and 24 were purchased by James Wheeler for 174 pounds; these two lots were the location of Wheeler's storehouse on the 2 acres that he had purchased from William Porter in 1792.[6] James Jett Jr. purchased Lot 25 for 185 pounds; this was the location of Jett's store on the 2 acres purchased from Porter in 1792 by James Jett Sr. and John Jett and sold to James Jett Jr. in 1795.[7]

---

[4] Culpeper County Deed Book T, pages 320-407.

[5] The British system of pounds/shillings/pence was in use during the colonial period and for some time after the Revolutionary War. It is estimated that one British pound in the year 1798 was equivalent to about 35 U.S. dollars in the year 2000.

[6] Culpeper County Deed Book R, page 35

[7] Culpeper County Deed Book R, page 333 and Deed Book S, page 278

Chapter 3. Formation of Rappahannock County and Selection of Washington as the County Seat

Washington Becomes the County Seat, 1833

The land that became Rappahannock and Madison counties was part of Culpeper County when the latter was established in 1749. Over time, the western part of Culpeper County became more densely populated, and the difficulty of traveling to Culpeper courthouse for Court sessions and to conduct legal business grew more significant. A trip on horseback or carriage could take a day or more, and the roads were often impassible if rivers and streams were high. Court sessions often took more than a day, and people coming from a distance had to stay overnight and pay for rooms and meals. After many petitions to the Virginia General Assembly, the area around Madison became a new County in 1792, but it was not until 1833 that petitions, counter petitions, and political maneuvering resulted in the creation of Rappahannock County.

On 8 February 1833, an Act passed by the General Assembly of Virginia created the new county of Rappahannock from within the boundaries of the county of Culpeper.[1] The first sessions of the County Court, for the purpose of organizing the new county, were held at the tavern owned by Mrs. Anne Coxe, now the building housing the gifts shops of the Inn at Little Washington at the northwest corner of Main and Middle streets. Six men who were not residents of the new county – Charles Hunton of Fauquier County, John E. Shell of Brunswick County, Charles James Faulkner of Berkeley County, William M. Robertson of Page County, William D. Sims of Halifax County, and James Richards of Culpeper County – were named as commissioners to impartially ascertain the most proper place for holding Court and erecting public buildings, i.e., for establishing the County seat.[2] For rural Virginians of that era, the courthouse was the center of most political, social, legal, and commercial activity.[3] This importance is exemplified by the early County land tax books, which often gave the location of a property in terms of its specified distance and direction from the courthouse.[4] The location of the courthouse was a major issue for the new County government.

Four of the six commissioners met at Mrs. Coxe's tavern in the town of Washington on 16-18 May 1833. They had received twenty-one written statements suggesting places for the County seat. "With all the facts and evidence before them," the commissioners "proceeded to form an opinion of the matters

---

[1] Acts of the General Assembly of the Commonwealth of Virginia, Chapter 73 for the year 1833

[2] Rappahannock County Deed Book A, page 24

[3] John O. Peters and Margaret T. Peters, *Virginia's Historic Courthouses*, University of Virginia Press, 1995

[4] Rappahannock County Land Books, 1834-1847

submitted to them." They concluded that the courthouse should be located in the town of Washington, "a village with a population of 300 souls ... a populous and productive neighborhood already numbering sixty houses ... and a place of some mercantile capital and business. Its advantages of waters, wood, and fuel are unsurpassed by any other place in the County. Although it is not situated on any leading thoroughfares, it is accessible by good public roads from any point of the county."[5]

With this decision, the town of Washington, Virginia, passed from being part of a backwoods undeveloped farm owned by the Kennerly family in 1735 to being the county seat of a thriving new county in 1833.

Immediately after this decision was reached, Jacob and Abigail Nicol sold Lots 44, 45, and 46 to the Justices of Rappahannock County, which lots are the current location of the County courthouse, jail, and administrative offices.[6]

Construction of the Courthouse, Court Clerk's Office, and Jail, 1833-1836

Before the courthouse was constructed, Court was held in the Free Meeting House on Lot 6.[7] Daniel Mason, Alexander Spilman, and William J. Menefee were authorized to spend $25 to repair this building to accommodate the Court meetings.[8] This frame building was demolished in 1904.

On 2 April 1833, the Rappahannock County Court justices appointed William A. Lane, Daniel Mason, and Henry R. Menefee as commissioners to form a plan for the dimensions and construction of the public buildings for the county.[9] Their report described the dimensions and arrangement of and the materials needed to build the courthouse, the Court Clerk's office, and the jail and the jailor's house with estimates for the cost of building these structures. For the courthouse and Clerk's office, the three commissioners had originally believed that a courthouse similar to that in Culpeper would be appropriate, with a detached Clerk's office. However, they believed that this would be too expensive and they suggested a plan similar to that used in Luray in Page County which was 40' square with an attached office measuring 20' by 15' at each of the front ends of the building. An arcade 10' in width would extend along the whole 80' front of the building. The jail and courthouse were to be constructed of brick, with stone foundations 18 inches above ground and slate roofs. The cost of the courthouse and clerk's office was estimated to be $5000. They recommended that a bell not be housed in a cupola because of the cost.[10]

---

[5] Rappahannock County Deed Book A, page 24-29
[6] Rappahannock County Deed Book A, page 18-19
[7] Rappahannock County Minute Book A, page 4
[8] Rappahannock County Minute Book A, page 4-5
[9] Rappahannock County Deed Book A, page 12
[10] Rappahannock County Deed Book A, page 12ff

Some of the commissioners' recommendations for the courthouse were obviously not followed, since the courthouse was constructed during 1834 as a separate building from the Clerk's office and no arcade was built. However, a cupola was built on the top of the building to house a bell.

On 6 May 1833, William Lane, Daniel Mason, Henry R. Menefee, William Slaughter, and Gabriel Parks were appointed as commissioners "for the purpose of contracting for and superintending the erection of the public buildings of this County."[11] An obscure item in the minutes of the January 1835 meeting of the Rappahannock County Court justices, who were administering the new County government, stated that "$1500 is levied as the third and last payment" to Malcolm F. Crawford for construction of the courthouse and adjacent Court Clerk's office.[12] This identifies Crawford as the builder of the courthouse and Clerk's office, but who was Malcolm F. Crawford?

Biography of Malcolm F. Crawford

The story of Malcolm F. Crawford begins with Thomas Jefferson, architect/designer of his own homes, "Monticello" and "Poplar Forest," the Virginia State Capitol building, and the buildings of the University of Virginia. In the early 1800s, there were no "professional" architects as we know the profession today. Jefferson was self-trained, gaining knowledge and experience of architecture from reading, observation, and travel, particularly during his tenure as the American minister to France during 1785-1789. Jefferson came to embrace Palladian and Roman Revival temple forms, developing a style termed "Jeffersonian classicism."[13] Many scholars credit Jefferson with creating America's first fully formed native architectural style.[14]

For the University of Virginia, Jefferson designed a set of buildings comprised of the Rotunda, the pavilions, and dormitories. His plan included two parallel rows 250' apart consisting of five pavilions on each side. The professors would live on the upper floors of the pavilions and give instruction on the ground floor. Between the pavilions were dormitory rooms for the students, resulting in proximity between the students and their teachers and creating an "academical village."

Construction at the University began in 1817, but the immensity of Jefferson's plan soon made it apparent that local labor was totally inadequate for this task.

---

[11] Rappahannock County Minute Book A, page 17 and page 248
[12] Rappahannock County Minute Book A, page 248; Minute Book B, page 3
[13] Richard Guy Wilson, editor, *Buildings of Virginia*, New York, Oxford University Press, 2002
[14] Calder Loth, *Virginia Landmarks Register*, Charlottesville, VA, 1986

James Dinsmore, one of Jefferson's master carpenters, noted in 1819[15] of "the difficulties we labor under here in procuring good workmen." It became obvious that skilled workmen had to be procured from outside the Charlottesville area. Advertisements were placed in newspapers in Staunton, Richmond, and Philadelphia, and over 150 craftsmen were hired from along the eastern United States, including twenty from Philadelphia, and from as far away as Ireland, England, and Italy. Included were carpenters, brickmasons, stonemasons, plasterers, painters, and glazers.

Through their work in construction of the university, many of Jefferson's craftsmen became skilled in the correct use of classical architecture. They also, like Jefferson, learned about designing buildings through books and observation.[16] Armed with their new knowledge, many went on to significant careers. These individuals applied their skills in the design and construction of a wide variety of Jeffersonian classical buildings throughout Virginia. A particularly important group of these works is county courthouses. During the second quarter of the 19th century, more than twenty courthouses exhibiting characteristics of Jeffersonian classicism were built across the state.[17]

One of these craftsmen was Malcolm F. Crawford.[18]

Photograph of Malcolm F. Crawford in 1860. *Source: Mr. Jim Lang of Texas, a descendant of Crawford*

Crawford was of Scottish origin and was born in 1794 in the town of Warren on the southern Maine coast. He was recruited as a young man to work on building the new University of Virginia and was the principal carpenter for twenty-seven of the University student rooms and dormitories. In 1825 Crawford, then living in Albemarle County, Virginia, married Amanda M. F. Craven, the daughter of John H. Craven who owned a mill in the Charlottesville area.

[15] K. Edward Lay, "Charlottesville's Architectural Legacy," *Magazine of Albemarle County History*, Vol. 46, Charlottesville, May, 1988

[16] Richard G. Wilson, editor, *Buildings of Virginia*, New York, Oxford University Press, 2002, p. 22-23

[17] http://blog.classicist.org/?p=5037#sthash.z6d1uTmr.dpuf

[18] Maureen Harris, "Will the Real Courthouse Architect Please Stand Up?", *Rappahannock News*, 4 June 2017 (Part 1) and 17 June 2017 (Part 2)

After his tenure at the University, Crawford continued to work in Virginia, carrying with him the principles of classical Jeffersonian Roman Revival architecture learned through his work at the University. In 1822-1828, he built several large homes in Virginia,[19] including the home "Edgehill" for Thomas Jefferson Randolph, a favorite grandson of Thomas Jefferson.[20] In 1830, he built the Madison County courthouse and several homes in that county and architectural experts have attributed the 1830s Caroline County courthouse in Bowling Green to Crawford.[21]

In 1832, the contract for the new Page County courthouse in Luray was awarded to the talented partnership of Crawford and William Phillips.[22] In 1833, they built the Presbyterian Church in downtown Fredericksburg, the exterior of which looks very much like one of Crawford's courthouses.[23] In 1838, Crawford built the Greene County courthouse.[24] And in 1840 Crawford built the courthouse in Spotsylvania County[25] and the home "West End" in Louisa County.[26]

But, most importantly, in 1834-1835 he built the Rappahannock County courthouse and the Court Clerk's office.

Malcolm F. Crawford and his wife Amanda Craven, whom he married in 1825 in Albemarle County, Virginia, had 14 children. They lived in Albemarle County and he continued to work as an architect and master carpenter in Virginia until 1863. In that year, Amanda died and Malcolm moved to Valdosta, Georgia, to live with their daughter Euphemia and her husband Edward Lang. There, he continued to be a carpenter and he also served as a postmaster. He died in Valdosta on 20 February 1876 at age 81 years.[27]

Architecture of the Courthouse and Court Clerk's Office

Built of brick in 1834, the courthouse was constructed with double front doors

---

[19] K. Edward Lay, *The Architecture of Jefferson Country*, University of Virginia Press, 2000; Richard G. Wilson, editor, *Buildings of Virginia*, New York, Oxford University Press, 2002, p. 129

[20] K. Edward Lay, *The Architecture of Jefferson Country*, University of Virginia Press, 2000; National Park Service, "Journey Through Hallowed Ground" register of Virginia historic places

[21] Calder Loth, "Classical Comments: Jeffersonian Temples of Justice," Institute of Classical Architecture and Art, The Classicist Blog. blog.classicist.org/?p-5037; Richard G. Wilson, editor, *Buildings of Virginia,* New York, Oxford University Press, 2002, p. 353

[22] John O. Peters and Margaret T. Peters, *Virginia's Historic Courthouses*, University of Virginia Press, 1995

[23] Richard G. Wilson, editor, *Buildings of Virginia*, New York, Oxford University Press, 2002, p. 306-307

[24] K. Edward Lay, *The Architecture of Jefferson Country*, University of Virginia Press, 2000; http://spotsylvaniamuseum.org/blog?FeedID=24

[25] John O. Peters and Margaret T. Peters, *Virginia's Historic Courthouses*, University of Virginia Press, 1995

[26] K. Edward Lay, "Charlottesville's Architectural Legacy," *Magazine of Albemarle County History*, Vol. 46, Charlottesville, May, 1988

[27] Genealogical information furnished by Mr. Jim Lang of Texas, 2016; he is a descendant of Malcolm F. Crawford.

and deep recessed windows. Some of the windows were originally false to give the building a more uniform appearance from the outside. The courthouse is described in the 1975 application to the National Register of Historic Places for the Washington Historic District as being a two-story, Flemish-bond brick Jeffersonian-style building with the entrance in the pedimented gable end. In Flemish-bond brickwork, the exposed ends of bricks ('headers') alternate with bricks laid lengthwise ('stretchers') in each course. The building has a lunette window in the gable, as well as a tall one-stage wooden belfry. The facade is ornamented by brick Tuscan pilasters, plastered and painted white.

The Rappahannock County courthouse, built by Malcolm F. Crawford in 1834

Originally, the courthouse's entire first floor was the courtroom. A raised platform spanning the width of the building was the judges' stand. In front of this was a section marked off with railings for the jury, lawyers, and other people participating in the trials. The rest of the room contained benches for spectators. Two stairways, one on each side of the room, led up to a second story interior balcony over the audience and behind this was two rooms used a jury rooms with a fireplace in each for heating. At present the courtroom is on the second story with offices occupying the ground level.

Portion of the courthouse bell, bearing the date 1834. Photograph courtesy of Peter Luke, 2018

On 13 October 1834, William Lane, Daniel Mason, and Henry R. Menefee were authorized to purchase a bell for the courthouse.[28] In 1835 Duff Green was paid $123.60 for the bell.[29] In 2014 during restoration of the exterior of the courthouse, Peter Luke, the former Commonwealth Attorney and County Attorney, had a photograph taken of the bell in the

[28] Rappahannock County Minute Book A, page 221
[29] Rappahannock County Minute Book A, page 316

building's cupola. The bell had the date "1834" on it, indicating that it was the original courthouse bell.

The Clerk's office was built in 1834-1835 adjacent to and north of the courthouse. It is described as a three-bay, one-story building with interior end chimneys and second parapet gable ends. The brickwork was laid in Flemish bond.[30] The building is now the front part of the building that houses the offices of the Rappahannock County Commissioner of Revenue.

The front part of this building was the original Court Clerk's office built by Malcolm F. Crawford in 1834. It served as the Clerk's office until 1979. It is now the office of the Rappahannock County Commissioner of Revenue.

Construction of the Jail, 1835-1836

The Rappahannock County jail was built by Stafford County carpenter John W. Fant. The County Court Commissioners signed a $2,000 contract with him in June, 1833. The next October, the commissioners approved a change from stone to brick for the foundations of the jail. The jail was completed in June of 1836, when the Court appointed Fant as commissioner to procure a stove for the criminal room.[31]

The Rappahannock County jail, built by John W. Fant of Stafford County in 1835-1836 and subsequently enlarged

[30] National Register of Historic Places, Washington Historic District Nomination Form, 15 April 1975

[31] Rappahannock County Minute Book A, pages 26 and 74

Chapter 4. The Town of Washington in the Early 1800s

Origin of the Name "Little Washington"

The town's nickname "Little Washington" can be dated to at least 1804. In that year, Methodist Episcopal Bishop Francis Asbury, the famed traveling circuit rider, noted in his diary: "Took the path to Little Washington ... and met with a kind reception and good entertainment."[1] The name was probably applied to the town to avoid confusion because of its proximity to Washington D.C. which lies only 70 miles to the northeast and was being built as the new capital of the United States at that time. The name continued being used. An envelope postmarked 1840 was addressed to Middleton Miller, Little Washington, Va.; Miller lived in the home that was converted to the Middleton Inn in the 1990s.[2] Many items of military correspondence during the Civil War refer to "Little Washington." For example, Major General Nathaniel Banks whose troops camped near the town used Little Washington as the address on many of his dispatches. Major General John Pope, when his army was near Sperryville, issued orders under the address "HQ., Army of Virginia, Little Washington, Va."[3]

Forfeiture and Resale of Town Lots

The 14 December 1796 Act of the General Assembly of Virginia that established the town also stated that the purchaser of a lot must build "a dwelling house, sixteen feet square at least, with a brick or stone chimney, to be finished fit for habitation, within seven years."[4] Although we do not know exactly what such a structure looked like, it probably resembled the building located at 322 Main Street, which is a chinked log structure with a stone chimney.

Log building located at 322 Main Street, probably one of the early buildings constructed in the town

[1] *The Journals and Letters of Francis Asbury, II*. London, Epworth Press, 1958, p.447
[2] Information from Mary Ann Kuhn, owner of the Middleton Inn
[3] Information from historian Art Candenquist, *Rappahannock News*, 20 September 2018
[4] Samuel Shepherd, *The Statutes at Large of Virginia, from October Session 1792 to December Session 1806, Inclusive, in Three Volumes, (New Series), Being a Continuation of Hening*. New York, AMS Press, Inc., 1836, Volume II, pages 29-32

Thomas Jefferson characterized the private buildings and homes in Virginia. "They are very rarely constructed of stone or brick; much the greatest proportion being of scantling and boards, plaistered with lime. It is impossible to devise things more ugly, uncomfortable, and happily more perishable. There are two or three plans, on one of which, according to its size, most of the houses in the state are built. The poorest people build huts of logs, laid horizontally, stopping the interstices with mud. These are warmer in winter and cooler in summer than the more expensive constructions of scantling and plank."[5]

If the purchaser of a town lot in 1798 failed to build a structure within seven years, the Act of the Virginia General Assembly of 1796 stated that the lot could be forfeited and resold by the Town Trustees. Not all owners of the 51 lots had built a structure on their land within seven years as required by the 1796 Act, and on 9 January 1804 the General Assembly extended this time period.[6] This law applied to seven towns in Virginia.

Act of the Virginia General Assembly to Extend the Time for Building on Town Lots, 9 January 1804*
Chap. 69. – An ACT allowing a further time to the owners of lots in certain towns to build thereon.
(Passed January 9, 1804.)

1. Be it enacted by the general assembly, ... that the further time of seven years, to be computed from the fourteenth day of December, one thousand eight hundred and three, shall be allowed the owners of lots in the town of Washington in the said county of Culpeper ... to build upon the said lots according to law. Provided, That nothing herein contained shall in any manner affect any rights which may have been acquired by others in consequence of the neglect of the owners of any of the said lots to build thereon within the times heretofore prescribed by law.
2. This act shall be in force from the passing thereof.

**Six other towns were also referred to in this Act; only the text relating to the town of Washington is quoted.*

Source: Samuel Shepherd, *The Statutes at Large of Virginia, from October Session 1792 to December Session 1806, Inclusive, in Three Volumes, (New Series), Being a Continuation of Hening.* New York, AMS Press, Inc., 1836, Volume III, page 55

---

[5] Thomas Jefferson, *Notes on the State of Virginia* (originally published in 1787), William Peden, editor, W.W. Norton Co., New York, 1954, page 152

[6] Samuel Shepherd, *The Statutes at Large of Virginia, from October Session 1792 to December Session 1806, Inclusive, in Three Volumes, (New Series), Being a Continuation of Hening*. New York, AMS Press, Inc., 1836, Volume III, page 55

This time limit was extended yet further but the town trustees began seizing and reselling town lots in 1822. Sixteen of the lots were forfeited and resold during 1822-1826 and one was seized and resold in 1833 and another in 1834.[7] These eighteen lots represented fully one-third of the fifty-one lots.[8]

The Rappahannock County Land Book for 1836 indicates that there were no buildings on seventeen of the lots in that year.[9] As late as 1850, seven of the town lots still did not have buildings on them; these were lots 14, 17, 20, 33, 39, 50, and 51. Indeed, lots 17, 50 and 51 appear to have never had any structures on them.

The Town of Washington as Described in 1833

When the commissioners selected Washington as the County seat, they described the town as "a village with a population of 300 souls ... a populous and productive neighborhood already numbering sixty houses ... and a place of some mercantile capital and business. Its advantages of waters, wood, and fuel are unsurpassed by any other place in the County. Although it is not situated on any leading thoroughfares, it is accessible by good public roads from any point of the county."[10] The Rappahannock County Land Book for 1836 shows that there were no houses on seventeen lots; it is likely therefore that the estimate of 300 souls and sixty houses are overestimates of the town's population and housing.

Plan of the Town of Washington in 1833

Only a few of the structures in the town were shown on an 1833 plan of the town.[11] These included Mrs. Calvert's home on Lot 5, Mrs. Coxe's home and tavern on Lot 8, Dr. Drake's home and office on Lot 11, a Meeting House on Lot 18, the jail on Lot 21, and Mrs. Resor's home and tavern on Lot 43. These were apparently buildings that were important at the time. Other buildings in existence, not shown on the plan, were homes and also small commercial establishments iconic to the time such as blacksmith and wagon-maker shops.

---

[7] Culpeper County Deed Book Deed Book OO, pages 50 and 346; Deed Book PP, pages 6, 8, 183, 185, 247, 248, 250, and 433; Deed Book TT, page 408; Rappahannock County Deed Book A, page 85

[8] The eighteen lots were numbers 1, 2, 3, 6, 10, 11, 16, 19, 20, 27, 28, 29, 30, 34, 35, 39, 46, and 51 (excludes courthouse lots)

[9] These lots were numbers 1, 2, 12, 13, 14, 15, 17, 19, 20, 31, 33, 34, 35, 39, 47, 50, and 51 (excludes courthouse lots)

[10] Rappahannock County Deed Book A, page 24-29

[11] Rappahannock County Deed Book A, page 189

Main Street

Gay Street

No 1	No 17	No 33
No 2	Meeting House No 18	No 34
No 3	No 19	No 35
No 4	No 20	No 36
Mrs Calwell's No 5	Present Jail No 21	No 37
No 6	No 22	No 38
No 7	No 23	No 39
Mrs Coale's No 8	No 24	No 40
	Middle Street	
No 9	No 25	No 41
No 10	No 26	No 42
Dr Draken's No 11	No 27	Mrs Reasons No 43
No 12	No 28	No 44
No 13	No 29	No 45
No 14	No 30	No 46
No 15	No 31	No 47
No 16	No 32	No 48
No 17	No 50	No 49

Plan of the Town of Washington in 1833

The Town of Washington as Described in 1835

An 1835 gazetteer contained a description of the town and asserted a population of 350 and 55 dwelling houses. However, this assessment of the town appears to greatly overstate the status of the town. As mentioned above, the Rappahannock County Land Book for 1836, which contains the dollar value of buildings on each of the lots, shows that 17 of the 51 lots had no buildings on them in 1836, and only 34 lots had buildings with a value greater than $0. Nevertheless, the text of the gazetteer is as follows:

In 1835, the town of Washington was described as follows:[12]
"Washington, P.V. [Post Village] and seat of justice, 118 ms [miles] from R.[Richmond] and 81 S. W. of W. C. [Washington City, i.e., Washington D.C.]. It is situated at the southeastern foot of the Blue Ridge, in a fertile country, upon one of the head branches of Rappahannock River (called Rush river) and recently chosen as the seat of justice for the county. It was formerly a P.O. [Post Office] in Culpeper Co. It contains besides the usual county buildings (lately erected), 1 academy, *55 dwelling houses,*[13] 4 mercantile stores, 2 taverns, 1 house of public worship, free for all denominations. The principal mechanics are 4 blacksmiths, 4 carpenters, 2 saddlers, 1 hatter, 1 tanner, 2 wagon makers, 3 tailors, 4 shoemakers, 1 cabinet maker, 1 silversmith, 3 milliners, 1 plaisterer and bricklayer. In the vicinity there is a large and highly respectable female seminary in which are taught all the various branches of English literature, together with the French and Italian languages; and in the immediate neighborhood, are 2 large and extensive manufacturing flour mills. This village is rapidly improving, and is in a flourishing and prosperous condition, being situated in a thickly settled and enterprising neighborhood. Population 350 persons; of whom 4 are attorneys, and 2 regular physicians. County Courts are held on the 1st Monday in every month. Quarterly in March, June, September, and November. Judge Field holds his Circuit Superior Court of Law and Chancery on the 22nd of April and September."

Commercial Licenses

Licenses were required for certain occupations, and fees for these licenses provided income to the State of Virginia. In the early 1830s, merchant's licenses in Washington were issued to Browning & Thorn, Daniel Mason, Henry and John Miller & Jones, and A.R. and S.G. Davis; these were probably the four mercantile

[12]Joseph Martin, compiler, *The 1835 Gazetteer of Virginia and the District of Columbia*, Charlottesville, Moseley & Tomkins, Printers, 1835. Reprinted by Willow Bend Books, 65 East Main Street, Westminster, Maryland, 2000, page 276-277

[13] Italics for author's emphasis. This statement of "55 dwelling houses" seems to be particularly incorrect, because the Rappahannock County Land Book for 1836 indicates that there were no buildings on seventeen of the 51 town lots in that year.

stores noted in the 1835 description of the town (above). Ordinary/tavern licenses were granted to Anne Coxe and George Thorn who each ran taverns in the town, on Lots 8 and 42, respectively.

Plan of the Town of Washington in 1837

A plan of the town in 1837 showed the location of two County buildings and the County jail, built during 1834-1836, on town Lots 44-46 on Gay Street. The courthouse and jail were shown at their current locations; the Court Clerk's

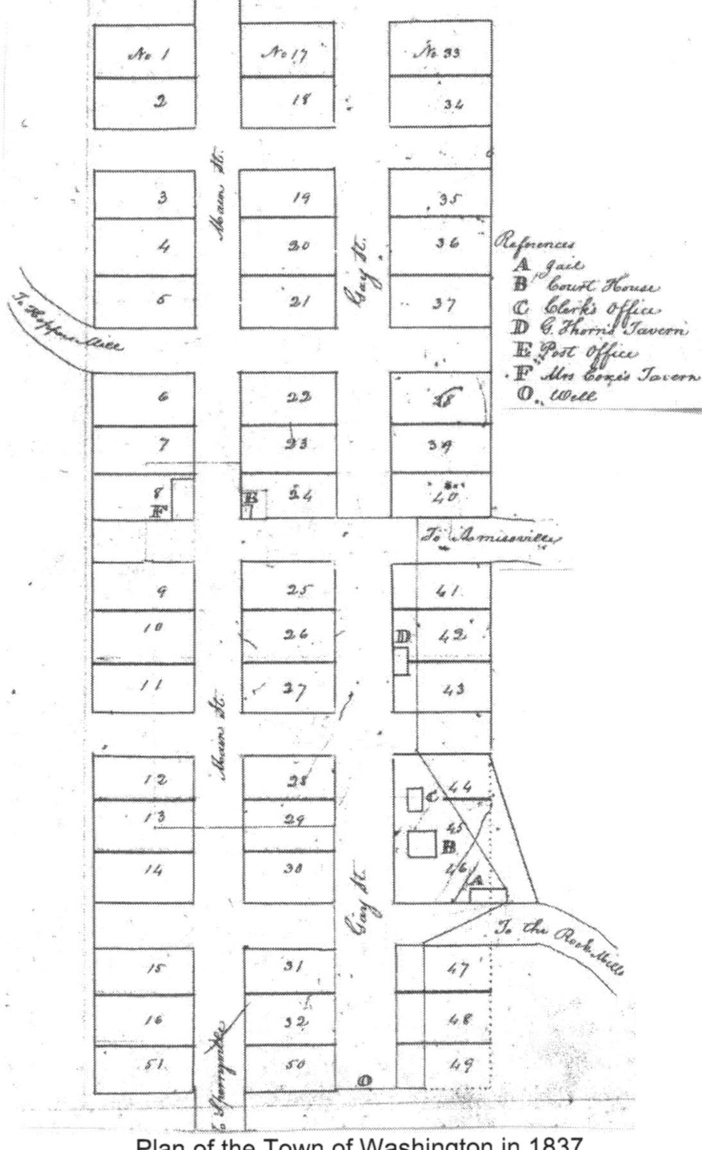

Plan of the Town of Washington in 1837

office was the front section of the building adjacent to and north of the courthouse that currently houses the office of the Commissioner of Revenue.[14] This building served as the Court Clerk's office from 1835 to 1979,[15] when the new Clerk's office was built adjacent to and south of the courthouse.[16]

Also shown is Thorn's Tavern on Gay Street on town Lot 42. A merchant's license had been issued to George Thorn in 1834 and an ordinary license had been issued to him in 1836. This building was formerly owned by the Resor family and was used as their home and as a tavern[17] until it was purchased by John William Jett in 1835;[18] Thorn presumably rented the building from Jett.[19] The Post Office was located on the northeast corner of Main and Middle streets, where the Inn at Little Washington is today. A town well was shown at the south end of Gay Street.

On the plan, roads leading out of the town of Washington were designated by their destinations: Hopper's Mill (next named Blue Ridge Avenue and now Harris Hollow Road), Amissville (today's Warren Avenue), Rock Mills (today's Mount Salem Avenue), and Sperryville (the south end of today's Main Street).

Homes and Other Buildings in the Town[20]

As discussed in Chapter 1, before the town was established in 1796, there is no evidence that there were any buildings on the land that became the town except a storehouse owned by James Wheeler, a store owned by the Jett family, and a school operated by William Porter.[21] Nearby was Porter's home which still exists and is named "The Meadows;" Porter's farm comprised most of the land on which the town would be located in 1796-1797.

As the town prospered and grew in importance as the seat of government of Rappahannock County, homes and businesses were built that were more elaborate than the simple "dwelling house, sixteen feet square at least, with a brick or stone chimney" specified by the Virginia General Assembly in 1796. Buildings that existed before the Civil War include:

---

[14] Rappahannock County Deed Book C, page 71

[15] National Register of Historic Places, Washington Historic District Nomination Form, 15 April 1975

[16] Elisabeth B. and C. E. Johnson Jr., *Rappahannock County, Virginia, A History*, Orange, VA: Green Publishers, 1981

[17] Rappahannock County Chancery Case #5, Resor vs. Resor; Rappahannock County Deed Book A, page 384

[18] Rappahannock County Deed Book B, page 200 and page 249

[19] This building became the home of the Baggerly family in 1866. The building was moved in 1931 to the slope east of the town, above a pond, and was renovated and enlarged and renamed Avon Hall.

[20] See Chapter 11 on History of the Town Lots for details of these structures

[21] Culpeper County Deed Book R, page 35, Deed Book R, page 333, and Deed Book S, page 278

- A building on Lot 1 worth $100 in 1850 owned by Nathaniel B. Ralls
- The Stonestreet house on Lot 2 worth $350 in 1850; Butler Stonestreet lived on this lot and operated his wheelwright shop on Lot 3, and his son James was a blacksmith there
- The Nicol house on Lot 4, worth $235 in 1836 and $400 in 1850
- Mrs. Calvert's house on Lot 5, worth $200 in 1836
- The Free Town Meeting House on Lot 6
- The log cabins on Lot 7, first owned by Lewis Fossett and leased to Robert M. Heterick as his law office, worth $200 in 1836 and $550 in 1850
- Mrs. Coxe's Tavern on the south part of Lot 8, worth $1985 in 1836
- The mercantile store on the north part of Lot 8, owned by James and John Jett, merchants, in 1836 and worth $595
- The building on Lot 9 owned by Daniel Mason worth $600 in 1836 and $1200 in 1850; the building evolved into the tavern and hotel of John Carter
- A house worth $350 in 1850 owned by Henry Johnson, a cabinet-maker, on Lot 10
- Dr. Francis T. Drake's house (and presumably also his office) on Lot 11, worth $300 in 1836 and $500 in 1850 when it was owned by Horatio G. Moffett, an attorney
- The house on Lot 12 constructed by Henry Johnson in about 1837, worth $250 in 1850, owned by Walker and Mary Holland beginning in 1854. Holland was a tailor and maintained his business in his home
- The two-story brick house on Lot 13, constructed by Henry Johnson and sold to J.Y. Menefee, an attorney, in 1841, worth $1200 in 1850
- The wagon-makers house and shop on Lot 15 worth $400 in 1850, owned by John F. Carter
- A building on Lot 16 worth $300 in 1836, probably built by P.W. Fant, owned by George Nicol, a blacksmith, in 1850
- The Old Church meeting house on Lot 18
- A brick house on Lot 19 owned by William J. Menefee, an attorney and Rappahannock County Court Clerk from 1833 to 1858, worth $700 in 1850
- The original town jail and a house on Lot 21 worth $385 in 1836, purchased by James Leake Powers, a carpenter, owned by Dr. Adolphus W. Reid in 1850 worth $950
- The brick Washington Presbyterian Church on the eastern part of Lot 22, constructed in 1856-1858 by James Leake Powers
- The wood frame house on the western part of Lot 22 owned by the Spiller family and worth $285 in 1836 and $250 in 1850
- A building on Lot 23 owned by George Thorn worth $285 in 1836 that was destroyed by fire in 1880
- A log building located at the west part of Lot 24 owned by Tilmon Porter which served as an early post office; also on this lot before the Civil War were a shoemaker shop, a tailor's shop, a sadler's shop, and a cabinet-maker's shop

- A building worth $392 owned by Francis S. Browning in 1836 on the east part of Lot 24
- A building on Lot 25 worth $585 in 1836 owned by Gabriel Smither
- Trinity Episcopal Church on the eastern part of Lot 25, constructed in 1857 by James Leake Powers
- The home of James Brereton Jones on Lot 26, worth $785 in 1836. Jones added the mercantile building, a small log house, and the summer kitchen, and the buildings were valued at $2350 in 1850
- The brick store building on Lot 27 worth $835 in 1836 and $1450 in 1850, owned by Oliver P. Smith
- A building on Lot 28 worth $100 in 1836 owned by Dr. Francis T. Drake
- On Lot 29, the Spilman house facing Main Street worth $700 in 1836, and the home of John Jett Sr. facing Gay Street
- A building on Lot 30 owned by Elijah Amiss in 1836 worth $100 and owned by Thomas Hughes in 1850 worth $50
- A building on Lot 31 worth $60 in 1850 owned by John F. Carter
- A building on Lot 32 worth $135 in 1836 owned by James Stonestreet and in 1850 by John F. Carter
- The Academy ("Rabbit Gum") on Lot 34
- A building on Lot 35 worth $100 in 1836 and 1850 owned by William J. Menefee and Robert M. Heterick, attorneys; Menefee was Clerk of the Rappahannock County Court during 1833 to 1858, and Heterick was Clerk during 1860 to 1881
- A building on Lot 36 worth $265 in 1836 owned by George Connard
- The Calvert home on Lot 37, worth $285 in 1836, which became the home of James Leake Powers in 1844
- The Nicol home on Lot 38, worth $235 in 1836; in 1850, Jacob Nicol was a gunsmith and his son Napolean had a blacksmith shop, shoe shop, and wagon repair shop on the lot.
- The Daniel O'Neale home on Lot 40, worth $435 in 1836 and $550 in 1850
- The home of John Groves and his family on Lot 41 worth $150 in 1836 and $550 in 1850; Groves was the town collector
- Resor's tavern, later Thorn's tavern and the Washington Academy, on Lot 42 and Lot 43, worth $785 in 1836
- The courthouse, Court Clerk's office, and the jail on Lots 44-46
- A building on Lot 47 worth $50 in 1850 owned by Joseph Nicklin
- A building worth $100 and owned by James M. Oder in 1836 on Lot 48
- The Robert Dearing home on Lot 49, worth $235 in 1836

Schools[22]

William Porter established a school on the western edge of his farm in about 1790.[23] When this land became part of the town of Washington, he donated ½ acre adjacent to the northwestern border of the town to erect a school "for educating youth of both sexes" and for "the promotion of science and dissemination of useful knowledge."[24] In 1834, the Academy was established on Lot 34. It was incorporated in 1837 under the supervision of George W. Grayson, assisted by James Dow, a graduate of Union College in New York.[25] The school was housed in a brick building of two rooms with a fireplace in each room. On the front side of the building was a small porch, two doors, and two windows; on the back side of the building were four windows.[26] The building was beloved by students and townspeople, who affectionately called it "the Rabbit Gum" because of its resemblance to a rabbit box, the two-compartment trap used to catch rabbits. The Washington Academy was established in 1849 in the building that had housed Thorn's tavern on Lot 42 and part of Lot 43. This school was founded by George W. Grayson (born in Kentucky) and H. W. Maertens (born in Germany).[27] Needlework and drawing were taught, in addition to the basics; music and language lessons were available for an extra charge. Board was available for a 10-month session at $85 per month.

Churches[28]

There were three churches in the town during the first half of the 1800s. In about 1815, a building was erected on Lot 18 that served as the Old Free Church. It was the center of the community's religious life for many years. The church was nondenominational and was used by the Presbyterians, Episcopalians, Baptists, and Methodists until they built their own separate places of worship.[29] The Washington Presbyterian Church was constructed on Lot 22 in 1856-1858 by James Leake Powers on land that had been given by Tamar Spiller.[30] The 1½-story 5-course American brick building is in the Doric architectural style. Over time, church membership declined and the church closed in 1892.[31] Trinity

---

[22] See Chapter 12 for details

[23] Culpeper County Deed Book R, page 333

[24] Culpeper County Deed Book Z, page 202

[25] Elisabeth B. and C. E. Johnson Jr., *Rappahannock County, Virginia, A History*, Orange, VA, Green Publishers, 1981

[26] *Rappahannock News*, 8 July 1965

[27] Elisabeth B. and C. E. Johnson Jr., *Rappahannock County, Virginia, A History*, Orange, VA, Green Publishers, 1981

[28] See Chapter 13 for details.

[29] Mary Elizabeth Hite, *My Rappahannock Story Book*, The Dietz Press, Richmond VA, 1950, page 177; M. Elizabeth Buntin, *Mission: A Study of the Churches of Bromfield Parish*, pages 43-46, files of Trinity Episcopal Church

[30] Rappahannock County Deed Book J, page 414

[31] Elisabeth B. and C. E. Johnson Jr., *Rappahannock County, Virginia, A History*, Orange, VA, Green Publishers, 1981, page 155

Episcopal Church was constructed on the eastern part of Lot 25 in 1857 on land conveyed by John G. Lane.[32] The builder was James Leake Powers. The church building, constructed in the style known as "country Gothic" with an exterior originally of board and batten, is considered to be one of the finest examples of American village church architecture in Virginia. The Church has remained active since that time.

Taverns and Hotels

In 1802, Mrs. Anne Coxe acquired Lot 8. She was the daughter of George Calvert's brother John Calvert and his wife Helen (Bailey) Calvert and had married Capt. David J. Coxe in 1799. In 1803, she received a license to establish an "ordinary" (an inn or tavern) at this site, so the building that still exists on this site was probably constructed in the very early 1800s. The main floor was used to serve meals; upstairs were several small private rooms that were rented to lady travelers and to more affluent gentlemen and a large common room where lodgers rented space – often just a space on a bed that was shared with other travelers or even space on the floor.[33] In 1850, after Anne's death, the building was sold to Amos Dear and the building became known as Dear's Hotel.[34]

An 1833 plan of the town, shown above, shows that "Mrs. Resor's house" was located on Lots 42-43.[35] Mary Resor resided there and maintained a tavern. In 1837, Thorn's tavern was located in the building.[36] A merchant's license had been issued to George Thorn in 1834 and an ordinary license had been issued to him in 1836. The building later became the Washington Academy and a boarding house before becoming the home of the Baggarly family.

The Washington Post Office

John Strother Jr. was appointed Washington's first postmaster on 1 October 1804 and held this position until 1808 when Jeremiah Strother took office.[37] The next postmaster was Ralls Calvert (born in 1767, died in 1815), the son of George Calvert and Lydia Beck Ralls. He had married Mary Wade Strother in 1790, and they raised a family of twelve children. Their youngest child, Lucy, married James Leake Powers in 1844. Ralls purchased Lot 40 when the Town Trustees sold lots in the town in 1798.[38] In 1815, Tilmon Porter, son of William and Sarah

---

[32] Rappahannock County Chancery Case 2222; Rappahannock County Deed Book 65, page 183
[33] Recollections of Mrs. Edna Walker, owner of "Washington House", in Daphne Hutchinson and Theresa Reynolds, *On the Morning Side of the Blue Ridge*, a compilation of articles published in the *Rappahannock News* in 1983, page 50
[34] Rappahannock County Deed Book H, page 421
[35] Rappahannock County Deed Book A, page 189
[36] Rappahannock County Deed Book C, page 71
[37] Eugene M. Scheel, *Culpeper, A Virginia County's History Through 1920*, Green Publishers Inc., Orange, Virginia, 1982, p. 82
[38] Culpeper County Deed Book T, page 389

Porter, became the fourth postmaster. He inherited town Lots 23 and 24 from his father.[39] A log cabin, located at the southwest corner of Lot 24, was the site of the post office in 1815, with Tilman Porter as postmaster. An 1837 plan of the town shows the post office located at this site.[40]

Physicians in the Town

Dr. Francis T. Drake resided on town Lot 11 in 1833 and, as was the custom of the time, probably had his office in his home. Dr. Joseph Nicklin was a well-known physician and served as a surgeon in the War of 1812. Later, he was a member of the Virginia House of Delegates, and in 1839 and 1843 he was president of the Washington Town Board of Trustees, which managed the town before it became incorporated in 1894.[41] He purchased Lot 6 in 1841[42] and was the first of three physicians to own the building on this lot. One of Nicklin's daughters, Martha Ann, married the architect James Leake Powers in 1837.

The 1850 U.S. census was the first census in which persons were asked to state their occupation. This information permits identification of three physicians who were living in the town in 1850. These were:

- Joseph Nicklin, age 74, who was living with his son-in-law James Leake Powers on town lot 37. Nicklin was retired from medical practice.
- Benjamin F. Kinsey, age 25, who lived at Dear's Hotel on town Lot 8 and later became the County coroner.
- Adolphus W. Reid, age 30, who lived on town Lot 21 and had his medical office on town Lot 6, which he had purchased from Joseph Nicklin in 1850.

Government of the Town, 1833-1861

The Town was governed by a Board of Trustees during this time. The Trustees enacted a Code of Bylaws in the early stages of the town; unfortunately, this document is lost. In 1838, they ordered that part of these Bylaws relating to obstructing the streets be repealed and they ordained that citizens of the town could "keep in the streets not more than three loads of wood at any time."[43] The Trustees also ordained that the town collector should ring the courthouse bell at 10am on every Sabbath to provide notice to nonresident slaves to leave the town. If slaves were found in the town after this time, the town collector had the duty of inflicting a punishment of 10 lashes on the bare back. The town collector was also empowered to inflict 5 lashes on any nonresident slave who was in the town after 9pm each night. Further, not more than three negroes were permitted to

---

[39] Copy of will in Rappahannock County Chancery Case #316 and Case #318
[40] Rappahannock County Deed Book C, page 71
[41] Minute Book, Town of Washington Board of Trustees, 3 June 1839, 14 April 1843
[42] Rappahannock County Deed Book D, p. 232
[43] Minutes of the 9 March 1838 meeting of the Town Trustees

assemble together within the town limits; if more than that, the punishment was 5 lashes.

In June 1839, an election of a 7-member Board of Trustees was held. Those elected were Joseph Nicklin, Horatio G. Moffett, Daniel Mason, William J. Menefee, Daniel O'Neale, James B. Jones, and Henry Johnson. Nicklin was elected President of the Board, for which he was required to take out a bond of $150. Robert M. Heterick was appointed as Clerk of the Board, Absalom Lillard was appointed to be Town Collector, and James Leake Powers was appointed as Supervisor of the Streets.[44]

Certain orders by the Board pertained to financial matters. The Board decreed that the clerk of the Board and the treasurer of the Town would receive a salary of $10 per year. Residents of the town were required to work on maintaining the town's streets on a schedule of days, but could be exempt from this duty by paying 75 cents per day for each day they were scheduled. If a resident obstructed the streets of the town, a fine was levied in the amount of 25 cents per day. Residents of the town were subject to a tax on white males over age 16 years, slaves, and horses.[45]

In June 1842, the individuals elected to serve as Trustees of the Town were Joseph Nicklin, Daniel O'Neale, James B. Jones, Henry Johnson, William J. Menefee, Middleton Miller, and Oliver P. Smith. Nicklin remained as President of the Board. James Leake Powers had resigned the office of Superintendent of the Streets after the death of his wife, and Amos Dear was appointed to this position.[46] The Board of Trustees also changed the amount for being exonerated from working on the streets from 75 cents per day to 50 cents per day.

No minutes of the Board of Trustees are available for the period 1843-1855. The next extant minutes referred to the election of a new Board on 5 August 1855. On this date, Amos Dear, Benjamin Calvert, Robert M. Heterick, Henry Foster, Middleton Miller, Oliver P. Smith, and J. W. Menefee were elected as Trustees of the Town. Minutes between this time and June 1877 are also missing.

In 1852 the General Assembly of Virginia directed that Rappahannock County be divided into districts, with distinct boundaries, and the places for holding elections be determined for each district. The town of Washington was placed in District 3, with the courthouse designated as the place for voting.[47]

---

[44] Minutes of the 3 June 1839 meeting of the Town Trustees
[45] Minutes of the 6 July 1839 meeting of the Town Trustees
[46] Minutes of the June 1842, April 1843, and May 1843 meetings of the Town Trustees
[47] Rappahannock County Deed Book I, page 132

Washington in the Civil War

In 1861, Virginia seceded from the Union. No battles or even skirmishes were fought in Washington during the Civil War, but the War did not bypass the town. A large Union encampment of more than 45,000 soldiers occupied the fields east of the town. Three buildings in Washington are believed to have served as headquarters or hospitals for the opposing armies during the Civil War. The Union army set up a hospital in the circa 1840 home called "Tranquility" on Gay Street (town Lot 19) which would later become the home of French Pendleton Carter who was an officer in Company G, 12th Virginia Cavalry. Diagonally across the street to the northeast, the Union army headquartered and treated ailing soldiers in the circa 1830 Washington Academy ("Rabbit Gum," on town Lot 34). The Meadows plantation, located on Porter Street west of the town core and formerly the home of William Porter, one of the founders of the town, served as a hospital for both Confederate and Union soldiers. Adding to Washington's Civil War history, Middleton Miller of The Maples (now the Middleton Inn) owned Glenn Mills, a woolen mill at Waterloo on the Rappahannock River where he manufactured the "Rebel Grey" worn by Confederate soldiers. Charlie Dear, whose family owned Dear's Hotel on town Lot 8, was a member of the famous Mosby's Raiders.[48]

A Confederate Monument was erected in 1900 at the north end of the courthouse complex through the efforts of the local chapter of the Daughters of the Confederacy, to honor the men from Rappahannock County who served their cause in the Civil War. In 2006, the monument was found to be in poor condition, and the County contracted with Conservation Solutions, Inc., to repair and refurbish it.[49] Two Virginia Civil War Trails markers are located on the courthouse grounds. One deals with the Confederate monument; the other describes the case of Kitty Payne, a freed slave who was kidnapped and held in the jail for her safety while her legal case was being considered by the Court.

[48] Daphne Hutchinson and Theresa Reynolds, *On the Morning Side of the Blue Ridge*, a compilation of articles published in the *Rappahannock News* in 1983, page 76, 77, and 81

[49] *Rappahannock News*, 16 March 2006

Chapter 5. Washington in the Later 1800s

In 1870, Virginia adopted a new constitution. This established the General Assembly as the legislative body for the State. It also dictated that localities should be divided into districts, with distinct boundaries, and the places for holding elections be determined for each district. Rappahannock County was divided into five districts. The town of Washington was included in District 3, the Hampton District, and the voting place was established as the courthouse in the town. This was identical to the pre-war Districts of the County.[1] Commissioners for District 3 were Edward T. Jones (who had served as Clerk of the Rappahannock County Court in 1860), Thomas B. Massie, and Horatio G. Moffett; the elected Supervisor was John G. Lane.

The Rappahannock County Treasurer's Office, constructed in 1874

In 1874, there was a new addition to the courthouse complex. The Treasurer's office, which had formerly been a rented room in the building now housing the Rappahannock Historical Society, was constructed on the courthouse grounds by John J. Hawkins at a cost of $900.[2]

In the 1800s court days were wild, full of people in town for trials, lawyers playing poker, and taverns full of country people who made sure their monthly trip to town coincided with court day.[3] Amos Dear's hotel on Lot 8, formerly Mrs. Coxe's tavern, served as lodgings and provided meals to the influx of people. In 1855 John and Frances Carter acquired Lot 9 and converted the building into a hotel and tavern.[4] The County supervisors had the authority to grant licenses to merchants, and there were strict regulations in regard to selling alcoholic beverages. In 1881, such a license was issued to David Lloyd for Lloyd's Hotel in Washington on Lot 24.[5] John Dulin purchased part of Lot 29 in 1885[6] and turned the building, conveniently located opposite the courthouse on Gay Street, into "Dulin's Saloon." He sold the property in 1897 to George G.

---

[1] Rappahannock County Deed Book I, page 132

[2] Elisabeth B. and C. E. Johnson Jr., *Rappahannock County, Virginia, A History*, Orange, VA: Green Publishers, 1981, page 54

[3] Daphne Hutchinson and Theresa Reynolds, *On the Morning Side of the Blue Ridge*, a compilation of articles published in the *Rappahannock News* in 1983, page 91

[4] Rappahannock County Deed Book R, page 81

[5] Elisabeth B. and C. E. Johnson Jr., *Rappahannock County, Virginia, A History*, Orange, VA: Green Publishers, 1981, page 55

[6] Rappahannock County Deed Book Q, page 426

Bywaters who also maintained a barroom on the property.[7] In the 1890s Washington Clark operated Clark's Tavern, serving meals, on Lot 31; people would line up from the courthouse down to this building to be served.[8]

The Town Bylaws and Ordinances, 1877

The minutes of the Town Board of Trustees for June 1877 recited the names of Trustees elected on 7 June 1877, who were William N. Carter, Richard Morrison, Charles N. Dear, Edward Cary, Napolean B. Nicol, Washington Clark, and James W. Stonestreet. Nicol was elected as President of the Board and Morrison was elected as Treasurer. The Board selected Robert M. Heterick as Clerk of the Board[9] and appointed James A. Wharton as Town Collector and John A. Compton as Overseer of the Streets.[10] The new Board also appointed Carter, Dear, and Morrison to a committee to prepare a code of bylaws and ordinances for the Town.

The set of bylaws and ordinances were discussed, modified, and then adopted by the Town of Washington Board of Trustees at their meetings on 16 June, 12 July, 17 July, and 21 July 1877. The bylaws dealt with the method of collection and reporting of taxes and fees, maintenance of the streets, restraint of animals in the town, arrest of drunk persons, and many other items. There was instituted a tax of 11 cents per $100 assessed value of real and personal property.

A Code of By Laws for the Regulation of the Town of Washington

Section 1st. Be it enacted and ordained by the Trustees of the said Town that it shall be the duty of the Town Collector to collect all the taxes, fines, etc., for the use of the Corporation and pay over the same to the Treasurer at the close of each month taking his receipt for the sum.
2nd. Be it further enacted and ordained that it shall be the duty of the Overseer of the Streets to call out all hands subject to work on the streets, for the purpose of working them according to law not to exceed six days in a year, giving them at least nine days previous notice thereof, and every person warned as aforesaid may be excused from working on the streets by paying to the said Town Collector before such day seventy-five (75) cents for each day, to be appropriated by said Town Collector to the hiring of other hands to work on the streets on such day.
3rd. And be it further enacted and ordained that every person failing to work on the streets is to pay seventy-five cents for each day as provided for in the preceding section (and the oaths of the Overseer of the Streets and the Town Collector shall be evidence of the fact) shall be returned by the said Overseer to

---

[7] Rappahannock County Deed Book U, page 111
[8] Rappahannock County Deed Book S, page 397
[9] Heterick also served as Clerk of the Rappahannock County Court during 1860 to 1881
[10] Minutes of the 9 June 1877 meeting of the Town Trustees

the Trustees of the Town or one of them, as a defaulter. And upon their or his direction the same Collector shall proceed to make the fines without delay.

4th. And be it further enacted and ordained that it shall be the duty of the Town Collector to remove all nuisances which may be found within the Town of which he has any notice or knowledge.

5th. And it is further enacted and ordained that if any person or persons shall suffer his, her or their firewood or other timber other than timber for Building, Boxes, Plows, or Hogsheads etc. or any other obstruction to a free passage upon the sidewalks or streets of the said Town to remain longer than twenty four hours after having been notified by the Town Collector to remove the same, shall upon the conviction thereof before any magistrate pay a fine not exceeding fifty cents for every twenty four hours the same may remain to be collected by the Town Collector and appropriated as other monies belonging to the said Town.

6th. It is further enacted and ordained that it shall be the duty of the said Town Collector to serve all warrants and executions, etc., growing out of any proceeding authorized by the said Trustees, or by observation of law, for which he shall receive such fees as are allowed by law to Constables in similar cases.

7th. And be it further enacted and ordained that it shall be unlawful after the passage of this ordinance for any person on any occasion to exhibit before the Taverns or Court House or lead through the streets of the town any stallion, stud horse or jack ass, and if any person shall offend against the provisions of this section, the person offending shall pay a fine of five dollars for each offense.

8th. And be it further enacted and ordained that no person shall ride a race through the streets or shall strain a horse through the streets, and if any person or persons shall offend against the provisions of this section they shall incur a fine of one dollar for each offence.

9th. And be it further enacted and ordained that no exhibition of animals shall take place within the limits of the said town without first obtaining a license from the Clerk of the Board of Trustees for which the sum of five dollars shall be paid and a fee of one dollar to the clerk for granting such license and no Juglar, Fire Eater, Players or Performers by sleight of hand or otherwise shall perform without first obtaining license for which he or they shall pay the sum of one dollar and a fee of 25 cents to the Clerk for granting such license. If any of the above performances shall be attempted without a license obtained as above provided in this section, the performers or owners of the animals as the case may be shall pay a fine of twice the amount of license to be collected and applied as other fines.

10th. And be it further enacted and ordained that no one shall discharge any kind of firearm, kindle or make any bonfire, throw fire balls or discharge any kind of fireworks whatever, within the limits of the corporation and if any shall offend against the provisions of this section, he or they shall pay a fine of one dollar for each offence.

11th. And be it further enacted and ordained that every person owning a proud slut shall keep her confined to his or her lot while in that condition and the owner failing to confine such proud slut shall pay a fine or one dollar for every twenty four hours she shall be at large or the slut shall be killed under the direction of the Town Collector and there shall not be more than two dogs allowed to any one tenement in the town and any person disposed to keep more shall pay a fine of one dollar for all over that number found upon his or her lot.

12th. And be it further enacted and ordained that it shall be the duty of the Town Collector to report monthly to the Treasurer all monies that may come into his hands – which reports shall be filed by the Treasurer for safekeeping. And all warrants which may be issued to the Town Collector under any of the preceding or subsequent sections of this code of laws shall be brought to the Clerk and registered in a Bank to be kept by the Town Collector and produced (except when filed in the Clerk's office of the County Court of Rappahannock County) upon the settlement of his accounts.

13th. And be it further enacted and ordained that the Town Collector is declared the only person authorized to receive any money due and payable under the act of the Assembly and under the provisions of this Code of Bylaws for the Government and Regulation of the Town of Washington. And it is declared to be his duty to pay any such monies so collected over to the Treasurer forthwith, and take his receipt for the same, and that it be the duty of the Treasurer to report to the Board of Trustees every three months (or oftener if required) the condition of the Treasury.

14th. And be it further enacted and ordained that there shall be a tax of 11 cents on every hundred dollars of the assessed value of all the real and personal property within the limits of the Corporation (the list for that purpose to be made out and furnished the Town Collector by the Clerk) and it is hereby made the duty of the Town Collector to collect all the taxes imposed by this Act and pay the same over to the Treasurer and take his receipt for the same at the same time reporting all delinquents on or before the first day of November in each year.

15th. And be it further enacted and ordained that the Clerk and Treasurer be allowed the sum of (blank) dollars per annum to be paid out of any monies in the Treasury not otherwise appropriated.

16th. And be it further enacted and ordained that the Town Collector be allowed a salary of (blank) dollars per annum and for collecting taxes and levies, fines, etc., six percent upon the amount collected and fifty cents for each arrest made, to be paid out of the fine imposed upon him or them so arrested.

17th. And be it further enacted and ordained that whenever it may be desired by the Town Collector, Treasurer, or any member of the Board that a meeting be called for the transaction of business it shall be the duty of the Town Collector to give immediate notice to the members of the time and place at which they are desired to meet and it shall be the duty of the members to attend accordingly and upon the failure so to attend they shall be fined seventy five cents for each omission unless good cause be shown for such absence, such fines to be collected and accounted for as other fines are by law collected and accounted for.

18th. And be it further enacted and ordained that there shall be no Horse Racks upon any public thoroughfares except in the alleys, but any person may by permission of the Board upon application made to it, erect a horse rack upon the streets for the convenience of customers to new places of business provided that such rack be not erected upon the side walk or the side of the street which has been or may be curbed for the use of foot passengers, and such rack when so erected shall be constructed so as to prevent horses being fastened to it from wetting upon the sidewalk. The location of such rack to be designated in the order of permission under this section. And no horses are to be tied or hitched to the fences or in the streets (except to racks) within the limits of the Corporation.

And if any person tie or hitch a horse to the fences of the lots within the Corporation he shall be fined fifty cents.
19th. And be it further enacted and ordained that it shall be the duty of the Town Sergeant to arrest all persons drunk upon the streets or otherwise disagreeable or quarrelsome and to disperse all unruly and noisy assemblies within the limits of the Corporation.
20th. And be it further enacted and ordained that all the preceding sections shall be in force from this date except section 18 in regard to horse racks.
21st. And be it enacted and ordained that in the event of the Treasurer or Collector failing to comply with 12th section of the Bylaws of the Board the same to be removed after ten days notice.

In regard to Ordinance 18, Richard Morrison was given permission to hitch horses at the platform in front of his store house.[11] Also, W. W. Moffett was granted permission to erect a horse rack for the benefit of the *Blue Ridge Echo* newspaper office.[12] J.B. Cooper was permitted to erect a horse rack to be used by visitors to his house and shop.[13] And the Baptist Church was allowed to erect horse racks on the west side of Gay Street and on the south side of Porter Street near the church.[14] These permissions followed on a Court order that stated "It being represented to the Court that horses are frequently turned into the Court House lot and occasionally tied within the enclosure and the grass trampled up and destroyed, the Court doth order that the Sheriff of this County take such steps as will prevent horses or any sort of such stock from being turned in or suffered to remain in the Court House lot should any be found therein."[15]

In 1880, Dr. Adolphus W. Reid was Chairman of the Board of Trustees; other Board members were H.S. Menefee, J. F. Lillard, Dr. M.F. Hansbrough, William H. Carter, H.F. Stonestreet, and Charles H. Dear. Hansbrough was Treasurer of the Board and John F. Dulin was Town Sergeant and Overseer of the Streets. Apparently there was quite a problem with stock animals running free within the town. The Board resolved that "all stock found running at large within the corporate limits of Washington shall be taken up by the Town Sergeant, and the owner required to pay 25 cents per head for each head of stock and the same amount for each offence."[16] The Board also ordered that the lot fenced off in the alley between the courthouse lot and Baggarly's lot be used by the Town Sergeant for the safekeeping of any stock that he may have to restrain;[17] this alley is located at the east end of Jett Street. The Board warned that "on and after the

---

[11] Minutes of the 21 July 1877 meeting of the Town Trustees
[12] Minutes of the 17 July 1880 meeting of the Town Trustees
[13] Minutes of the 27 July 1880 meeting of the Town Trustees
[14] Minutes of the 10 June 1881 meeting of the Town Trustees
[15] Quoted in Elisabeth B. and C. E. Johnson Jr., *Rappahannock County, Virginia, A History*, Orange, VA: Green Publishers, 1981, page 85
[16] Minutes of the 17 July 1880 meeting of the Town Trustees
[17] Minutes of the 27 July 1880 meeting of the Town Trustees

20th day of June the law in relation to stock would be rigidly enforced and offending persons would be punished or fined accordingly."[18] If the owner of the stock did not pay the fines, the Town Sergeant could sell the stock at public auction. The Sergeant, J.A. Compton, was to be paid $1.50 for capturing "offending stock."[19] Also, hog pens were prohibited to be located "near enough to any street to render them offensive to passers by."[20]

The Board fixed the rate of taxation in 1880 at 7½ cents per hundred dollars of real and personal property.[21] The 16 November 1880 meeting of the Board of Trustees was held at the Hansbrough Drug Store in the town; most prior meetings had taken place at the courthouse building. At this meeting, the Board ordered that all persons trespassing through any church lot could be fined 50 cents for each offence.[22] In May 1881 the Board agreed to pay the expense of having the well near Mrs. Dear's hotel (now the Inn Tavern Shops) covered over "with a good and substantial frame."[23] There are no extant minutes of the Board of Trustees for the period from 2 October 1881 through 1893.

In 1892, a commission composed of Robert Heterick, W. Williamson, and Joseph Nicklin was asked to inspect the jail and to give a report. They found that the condition was good. The jail was properly secured by bolts, bars, and locks. Two rooms each about 10' by 16' were for prisoners charged with a felony, and two rooms each about 12' by 18' were for debtors. Heating was by fireplaces and stoves. The jailors were furnishing the prisoners with sufficient wholesome food and the building was kept clean. The commissioners made only one suggestion for change, i.e., that the debtors have an outdoor space into which they could go during the daytime.[24]

Church Construction

Five churches were built in the town during the second half of the 1800s. The Presbyterian Church, built during 1856-1858 under the direction of James Leake Powers, was constructed on Lot 22. It was built of brick in the Doric architectural style. The minister during 1853-1866 was Thomas S. Witherow but after that time it appears that only lay individuals ministered to the congregation, which was declining in numbers. The Church continued until 1891, when only two

---

[18] Minutes of the 17 July 1880 meeting of the Town Trustees
[19] Minutes of the 25 June 1881 meeting of the Town Trustees
[20] Minutes of the 24 September 1880 meeting of the Town Trustees
[21] Minutes of the 24 September 1880 meeting of the Town Trustees
[22] Minutes of the 16 November 1880 meeting of the Town Trustees
[23] Minutes of the 13 May 1881 meeting of the Town Trustees
[24] Daphne Hutchinson and Theresa Reynolds, *On the Morning Side of the Blue Ridge*, a compilation of articles published in the *Rappahannock News* in 1983, page 92

active church members remained,[25] and the church building was officially closed the following year.

In 1857, John G. Lane purchased the eastern part of Lot 25[26] which he conveyed to Trinity Episcopal Church. The cornerstone of the church was laid on 30 May 1857, by the Masonic Lodge of Washington, Virginia, and construction by James Leake Powers was completed within the year at a total cost of $1,800. The original facade was board and batten and the style is Country Gothic.

In 1874 Mary Long of Baltimore, Maryland, purchased Lot 47 and deeded part of the lot to the trustees of the Baptist Society of Christians and the Washington Masonic Lodge 78 for the purpose of erecting a Baptist church.[27] Since both the Baptists and the Masons were looking for places to meet at the time, they collaborated on constructing a building, with the Masons owning the top floor and the Baptists owning the rest.[28] The Washington Baptist Church was built in 1874-1875 by Corbin L. Proctor, a carpenter from Shenandoah County, Virginia.[29] It is an impressive example of Renaissance revival style architecture.

The First Washington Baptist Church is historically significant for its construction for the African-American religious community and for the Oddfellows use of the second floor. The church was organized in 1876 by Reverend George W. Horner. In 1880 the congregation purchased a small lot of land on Main Street, just north of the original boundaries of the town. The cornerstone was laid in 1881 and church construction was soon started, with one-third of the cost being borne by the Rising Hope Lodge Grand Order of Odd Fellows who maintained an Assembly hall above the church sanctuary.[30]

In 1889, Baldwin B. Baggarly and his wife Emma gave a parcel of land measuring 61' x 37' located at the southwest corner of Lot 43 to the Washington Methodist Episcopal Church South, to be used as a place of divine worship, subject to authorizations by the General Conference of the Church.[31] Through many fundraisers and solicited contributions, $4,000-$5,000 was raised for construction of the church. The cornerstone of the church was laid by Washington Lodge No. 78, Ancient Free and Accepted Masons, in the northeast corner of the foundation, as required by Masonic tradition. The inscription on the stone reads "M. E. Church South, September 5, 1889." The building was

---

[25] Elisabeth B. and C. E. Johnson Jr., *Rappahannock County, Virginia, A History*, Orange, VA, Green Publishers, 1981, page 155
[26] Rappahannock County Deed Book K, page 301
[27] Rappahannock County Deed Book N, page 268 and page 434
[28] Elisabeth B. and C. E. Johnson Jr., *Rappahannock County, Virginia, A History*, Orange, VA, Green Publishers, 1981, page 172
[29] National Register of Historic Places, 2006 resurvey, Section 8, page 31
[30] Elisabeth B. and C. E. Johnson Jr., *Rappahannock County, Virginia, A History*, Orange, VA, Green Publishers, 1981, page 174
[31] Rappahannock County Deed Book R, page 475

erected by John A. Cannon of Manassas, Virginia, and was completed during 1890.

Buildings and Residents in the Town

Washington was little impacted by the urban-industrial development of the 1800s. It remained a town of residences, commercial establishments iconic to the time, five churches, and the courthouse complex. Only a few buildings are believed to have been constructed after the Civil War through the end of the 1800s. These included the five churches discussed above.

The Stonestreets lived on Lot 2 and 3, and in the 1880s Haden Stonestreet operated a blacksmith shop there.[32] On Lot 4, Lucy and Mary Nicol are believed to have operated a millinery shop from their home. The physician, Dr. Adolphus W. Reid, had his office in the building on Lot 6 and lived on Lot 21. In the 1880s Reid was chairman of the Town of Washington Board of Trustees.[33] In 1890 Dr. Lyle J. Millan had his offices in the building on Lot 6. The building on Lot 7 was owned by Lewis Fossett, who leased it to Robert M. Heterick who used the building as his law office.[34] Heterick had been clerk of the Town of Washington Board of Trustees in 1839 and was a member of the Board of Trustees in 1855;[35] during 1860 to 1881 he served as Clerk of the Rappahannock County Court. On Lot 8 was located Dear's Hotel, the former Mrs. Coxe's Tavern, acquired by Amos and Phebe Dear in 1850.[36] A mercantile store that had been built for Mrs. Coxe's nephew, located adjacent to and north of the tavern, was owned by the Jett family and by James W. Stonestreet during this period.[37] Saintie (Carter) Dudley and her husband Francis Dudley lived in the house on Lot 9. In 1880 through 1910, John and Lucy Cooper were the owners of Lot 11; he is believed to have had a saddler shop on the lot.[38]

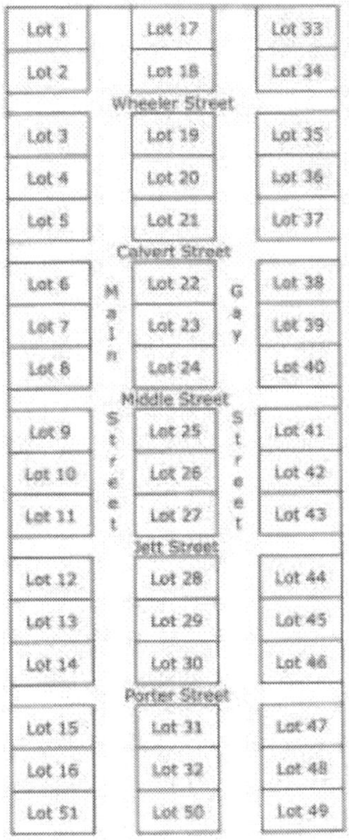

[32] Rappahannock County Deed Book R, page 276
[33] Minute Book, Town of Washington Board of Trustees, 15 July 1880
[34] Rappahannock County Deed Book D, page 138
[35] Minute Book, Town of Washington Board of Trustees, 3 June 1839 and 5 August 1855
[36] Rappahannock County Deed Book H, page 421
[37] Rappahannock County Deed Book N, page 321, and Deed Book R, page 165
[38] Rappahannock County Land Records

From 1854 to 1907 the house on Lot 12 was owned by Walker and Mary Holland.[39] He was a tailor and maintained his business in his home. He was also the Washington postmaster, and the post office was located in a small one-room building on the property. J.Y. Menefee had acquired Lot 13 in 1841 and Lot 14 in 1857[40] and for the next 70 years these two lots were the home of the Menefee family and their descendants. He was a distinguished lawyer, the county Commonwealth Attorney in the 1850s, and a member of the Town of Washington Board of Trustees in 1855.[41] The Menefees raised eleven children in their home. John A. Compton purchased Lots 16 and 51 in 1863 for $450.[42] The two lots remained in the Compton family for the next 85 years.

In 1815, James Yates and John Miller had purchased town Lot 18 for "the benefit of the public and on which is erected a house for public worship."[43] The 1833 plan of the town of Washington shows that a meeting house was located on this lot.[44] Apparently the building was abandoned and deteriorated, and the trustees of "Old Church" relinquished all claim to the lot. In 1880 they gave the lot, known as "the Old Church Lot" to the Reformed Episcopal Church.[45] In 1914 the trustees sold the lot to Eugenia Dudley.[46]

The attorney William J. Menefee had purchased Lot 19, on which there was a brick house, in 1841.[47] He was a member of the Washington Town Board of Trustees in 1839 and 1843.[48] It is believed that the house was used by Union forces during the War Between the States. In 1879 "Tranquility," as it was then known, was purchased by French Pendleton Carter. He brought his bride Judith Terrier Miller of Poplar Shade to this home, and they raised a family of seven children. He was born in Washington in 1845 and died there in 1920. He was a member of Company G, 12th Regiment, Virginia Cavalry, became an attorney and served as Commonwealth's Attorney from 1870-1879 and as Examiner of Records for the 26th Judicial District, and was a representative of the Senatorial District in the Virginia State Senate.[49]

Dr. Adolphus Reid and his wife Mary lived on Lot 21.[50] Dr. Reid was retained in a medical capacity annually for a stipulated sum by local families. He was also chairman of the Washington Board of Trustees in the 1880s.[51]

---

[39] Rappahannock County Deed Book I, page 451
[40] Rappahannock County Deed Book H, page 501, and Deed Book K, page 154
[41] Minute Book, Town of Washington Board of Trustees, 5 August 1855
[42] Rappahannock County Deed Book L, page 283
[43] Culpeper County Deed Book HH, p. 288
[44] Rappahannock County Deed Book A, page 189
[45] Rappahannock County Deed Book Q, page 327
[46] Rappahannock County Deed Book 27, page 204
[47] Rappahannock County Deed Book D, page 233
[48] Minute Book, Town of Washington Board of Trustees, 3 June 1839, 14 April 1843
[49] Mary Elizabeth Hite, *My Rappahannock Story Book*, The Dietz Press, Richmond, Virginia, 1950, page 177
[50] Rappahannock County Deed Book Q, page 443; 1850 Rappahannock County Land Records
[51] Minute Book, Town of Washington Board of Trustees, 27 July 1880

In 1880 Lot 23 was owned by William A. Lillard. The buildings on the lot had been destroyed by fire in about 1890,[52] and a substantial house valued at $700 in 1900 was constructed by Lillard on the lot. A storehouse was located on the eastern part of Lot 24, possibly James Wheeler's storehouse located on the 2 acres of land he acquired from William Porter in 1792[53]. The Cary family owned this property from 1873 until 1903.[54] On the western part of Lot 24 was Henry Foster's shoe-maker shop in a log house at the northeast corner of Main and Middle streets and Albert Holland's cabinet-maker shop. Foster was a member of the Washington Town Board of Trustees in 1855. In 1870 David Lloyd, a mulatto, purchased the property and converted the log house into Lloyd's Hotel.[55]

James Brereton Jones and his wife Eliza lived in the large home on Lot 26, which is now called "The Parsonage" and is owned by the Inn at Little Washington. Jones also constructed a mercantile building fronting on Gay Street and three dependencies to the home on land he owned that was part of Lot 27.

Early photograph of the home of the Jones family. The entrance fronted on Main Street. Photo courtesy of the Inn at Little Washington.

---

[52] Notation from the 1890 Rappahannock County Land Book

[53] Culpeper County Deed Book R, page 35

[54] Rappahannock County Deed Book P, page 161, and Deed Book W, page 150

[55] Rappahannock County Deed Book M, page 285

The three dependencies of the Jones family home: the exterior kitchen, dairy, and smokehouse-root cellar. Photo by Peter Kramer in the early 1970s.

On the southeastern part of Lot 27 was a brick store acquired by Oliver P. Smith in 1848;[56] he was a member of the Town of Washington Board of Trustees in 1843 and in 1855.[57] Smith sold the property in 1870 to James Wayman, N.B. Wayman, and James A. Templeman, merchants and partners, trading under the name of Wayman and Templeman.[58] The small log building now at 322 Main Street is probably what some of the original buildings in the town of Washington looked like in the early 1800s.

Lots 28, 29, and 30 (except a small part of Lot 29) were owned by Benjamin F. Kinsey at his death in 1870. In 1877, a contract for sale of the property by his wife Ann V. Kinsey to the trustees of St. Paul's and Trinity Episcopal Churches described several commercial buildings on the lots. A blacksmith shop operated by Ben Cliffen was located at the southeast part of Lot 30 and a stable was located on the northeast part of Lot 28; a drug store was located along Gay Street on the northeast part of Lot 29, in the house that had belonged to John Jett Sr.[59] The lots were acquired by Trinity Church for use by the ministers of St. Paul's and Trinity Episcopal Churches, located in Woodville and Washington, respectively.[60] The property was known as "the Rectory Lots" and the Spilman/Kinsey house on Lot 29, fronting on Main Street and originally built in the 1830s, was used by the ministers of the churches. Reverend Tellinghest and Rev. Claybrook lived in this house.

---

[56] Rappahannock County Deed Book F, page 133 and Book G, page 376
[57] Minute Book, Town of Washington Board of Trustees, June 1843, and 5 August 1855
[58] Rappahannock County Deed Book M, page 466
[59] Rappahannock County Chancery Case 728
[60] Rappahannock County Deed Book P, page 303

On the northwestern part of Lot 31, facing Main Street, was a large three-story building with front porch galleries purchased by Howard Compton in 1855.[61] Through 1890, the property was owned by Elias Compton, and in 1893 John W. Clark purchased Lot 31.[62] The building was known as Long House, where Washington Clark and then his son John operated Clark's Tavern. Meals were served in the late 1800s for 50 cents and on court days people would line up, from the courthouse down to this building, to be served.[63]

The Academy, also called "Rabbit Gum," was a school located on Lot 34. This academy existed as a private institution before public education was instituted. With the formal establishment of the public school system in 1871, it became Washington's public school. The building may have been used by Union forces during the War Between the States. James Leake Powers owned and lived in the house on Lot 37 with his third wife, Margaret Cary. They remained on Lot 37 until his death in 1889 at the age of 89 and her death in 1900. The family of Jacob Nicol lived in the home on Lot 38. Napolean Nicol was a blacksmith and had his blacksmith shop, shoeshop, and wagon repair shop on Lot 38 until his death in 1892. Another blacksmith shop, owned by Ben Cliffen, an African American, was located on Lot 41.

Lots 39 and 40 were owned by the family and descendants of Daniel O'Neale, including Catherine Cary, a daughter of Daniel O'Neale and wife of George M. Cary.[64] (Three of Daniel O'Neale's daughters married Carys.) In the northeast corner of Lot 39 is located a graveyard containing the graves of Susan Ellen Cary (born 1835, died 1903), Edward Cary (1827-1898), George Michael Cary (1823-1894), and Daniel O'Neale Cary (1873-1875).[65] The building that had housed Thorn's Tavern and later the Washington Academy on Lots 42 and 43 was purchased by Baldwin Bradford Baggarly in 1866, who converted the old tavern and school building into his home.[66]

Lots 44, 45, and 46 were occupied by the courthouse complex, with its new addition of the Treasurer's office in 1874. A home was constructed on Lot 48 in the late 1800s and the property was purchased by Thomas Hayward, Clerk of the Rappahannock County Court.[67] In 1848, Middleton Miller had acquired Lot 49 and Lot 50 from John S. Hughes, together with adjoining land to the south on which he built the home "The Maples."[68] He is believed to have lived in the log

[61] Rappahannock County Deed Book J, page 309
[62] Rappahannock County Deed Book S, page 397
[63] Daphne Hutchinson and Theresa Reynolds, *On the Morning Side of the Blue Ridge*, a compilation of articles published in the *Rappahannock News* in 1983, page 113
[64] Rappahannock County Deed Book P, page 92
[65] Rappahannock Historical Society cemetery records
[66] Rappahannock County Deed Book L, page 464; Jett also sold property to the east of the lots to Baggarly
[67] Rappahannock County Deed Book T, page 210
[68] Rappahannock County Deed Book G, page 468

cabin built on Lot 49 by Robert Dearing in the 1820s while he was constructing "The Maples." Miller remained the owner until his death in 1893.

Physicians in the Town

Dr. Adolphus W. Reid had his office in the building on Lot 6 and lived on Lot 21. In the 1880s Reid was chairman of the Town of Washington Board of Trustees.[69] Dr. M.F. Hansbrough was treasurer of the Town Board of Trustees in that year and later opened a drug store on Gay Street on Lot 29. In 1890 Dr. Lyle J. Millan had his medical offices in the building on Lot 6. In 1900, three other physicians were living in the town: Dr. Henry DeJarnette, age 27; Dr. Theodore L. Booten, age 37; and Dr. Edward W. Brown, age 40.[70] Booten was selected as the first mayor of the town when it was incorporated in 1894; Brown was appointed to the new Town Council as a councilman. Brown was the son of Whitfield Brown, owner of Brown's Store in Culpeper County. He received his M.D. degree from the University of Virginia, married Rappahannock County native Elizabeth Eastham, and practiced medicine in Rappahannock County for over 60 years. He lived on town Lot 38 and his office was located in a small building at the southwest corner of the lot. Brown was an active Mason and a member of the Baptist church. He died on 2 June 1950 at the age of 92 years.

Newspapers

In 1877 the first newspaper in Rappahannock County, *The Rappahannock News*, was started by J.R. Grove but survived for only one year. *The Blue Ridge Echo* quickly followed, published from 1878 until 1882 by Rappahannock Judge W.W. Moffett. This was followed by *The Call* which had a brief existence and then by *The Blue Ridge Guide*, started in 1886 by W.B. Settle who published *The Guide* until his death in 1889. The business was then sold by the Settle estate to George E. Cary, who had been Settle's printer. The Blue Ridge Guide continued under the capable management of Cary until his health failed and the newspaper closed its offices in 1936.[71]

Activities and Entertainment

Entertainment was simple in this era. Croquet was very popular, as was riding horses and just walking around the town of Washington.[72] The Academy on Lot 34 ("Rabbit Gum") served as somewhat of a town hall for the community, a place

---

[69] Minute Book, Town of Washington Board of Trustees, 15 July 1880
[70] U.S. census for 1900
[71] An excellent history of Rappahannock County's newspapers from 1877 to 1983 can be found in Daphne Hutchinson and Theresa Reynolds, *On the Morning Side of the Blue Ridge*, a compilation of articles published in the *Rappahannock News* in 1983, pages 123-124
[72] Daphne Hutchinson and Theresa Reynolds, *On the Morning Side of the Blue Ridge*, page 31

for dances, prayer meetings, lectures, and parties.[73] One large affair occurred on 5 September 1882. This was a "Basket Picnic, Tournament and Dance" sponsored by "the young men of Washington and vicinity." There was riding near Miller's Grove at 2pm and dancing at Washington House on town Lot 8 at 8pm. The Committee of Invitation included Charles Green, James Jett, George W. Kinsey, John F. Lillard, A.G. Miller, and Byrd Willis. The Committee of Arrangement included Charles C. Eastham, Thomas F. Hayward, W.A. Jordan, and H.M. Miller.[74] In 1897, a concert was held to benefit the construction of the Confederate monument on the courthouse grounds.[75]

Incorporation of the Town, 1894

Until 1894, the town was still managed by a Board of Trustees, as directed by the original 1796 legislation that created the town. This changed in early 1894, when the town of Washington was incorporated.

On 12 February 1894, the General Assembly of Virginia passed an act "to incorporate the town of Washington in the county of Rappahannock." The act stated that the town would become a municipal corporation" and that government of the town "shall be vested in a council of seven." The Act described elections of the town council, taxation of real and personal property, and various other matters pertaining to management of the town. It also enlarged the town such that the boundaries of the town "shall extend three hundred yards on every side beyond the boundaries of the said town, as described in the original charter of the said town."

Acts of the General Assembly of Virginia, Chapter 228. An act to incorporate the town of Washington, in the county of Rappahannock. Approved February 12, 1894.

1. Be it enacted by the general assembly of Virginia, That the territory contained within the limits set forth and described in section two of this act be deemed and taken as the town of Washington, and the inhabitants of the town of Washington, for all purposes for which towns are incorporated in this commonwealth, shall be a body politic, in fact and in name, under the style and denomination of the town of Washington, and as such shall have, exercise and enjoy all the rights, immunities, powers and privileges, and be subject to all the duties and obligations incumbent upon and pertaining to said town as a municipal corporation.

---

[73] Recollections of William E. Compton, articles in *The Rappahannock News* in 1956
[74] Daphne Hutchinson and Theresa Reynolds, *On the Morning Side of the Blue Ridge*, page 53
[75] Daphne Hutchinson and Theresa Reynolds, *On the Morning Side of the Blue Ridge*, page 114

2. The boundaries of the said town shall extend three hundred yards on every side beyond the boundaries of the said town, as described in the original charter of the said town.*

3. The government of the said town shall be vested in a council of seven, to be elected by ballot on the first Saturday in June, eighteen hundred and ninety-five, and every two years thereafter.

4. Any person entitled to vote in the county of Rappahannock, and residing within the corporate limits of the said town thirty days previous to any election, shall be entitled to vote at all elections under this act of incorporation.

5. The mayor shall appoint two members of the council, who, with the clerk of the council, shall hold said election between the hours of one in the afternoon and sunset, and they shall decide any contest with reference to the right of any individual to vote, and shall count the ballots. In case it is impossible to decide the seven who have the highest number of votes by reason of a tie, the said clerk shall decide in the presence of the two councilmen aforesaid by lot. Said clerk shall immediately thereafter make out and deliver to each one of the councilmen elected a certificate of his election.

6. The following named persons are hereby appointed to fill the following offices until the first day of July, eighteen hundred and ninety-five, and until their successors are elected and qualified – namely: Theodore L. Booton, mayor; E. W. Brown, Clarence J. Miller, John F. Lillard, James F. Strother, junior, H. M. Dudley and C. E. Johnson, councilmen. The said council, which includes the mayor as president thereof, shall have the power to appoint a sergeant, treasurer, commissioner of the revenue, and such other officers as may be necessary, who shall be elected by the qualified voters of said town on the first Saturday in June, eighteen hundred and ninety-five, their term of office to begin on the first day of July following, and the said officers shall be elected biennially thereafter.

7. The mayor and councilmen shall qualify by taking an oath of office before any person qualified to administer oaths, and if the mayor or any of the above appointed councilmen should fail to qualify for the days after four of those above named shall have qualified, they shall be deemed to have declined said office, and those who have qualified shall proceed to fill the vacancies thus existing. All the officers of the corporation shall serve without compensation, except as hereinafter provided, and except that they receive the fees allowed by law for acting as justice in any case. Any of the said officers may be removed from office by the unanimous vote of the council for good cause. The council at its first regular meeting shall elect a mayor pro tempore, who shall have all the powers of the mayor in his absence, or when from any cause the mayor is unable to discharge his duties as such. The mayor shall be the presiding officer of the council, but shall have no vote except in case of a tie. The mayor shall and may exercise all jurisdiction, civil and criminal, now by law conferred upon justices of the peace; shall preserve peace and good order in said town, and to this end shall be a conservator of the peace, with all the powers of the same, and shall be entitled to the same fees as a justice of the peace.

8. That for the purpose of maintaining the police regulations of said town under the authority of this act, the jurisdiction of the corporate authorities thereof shall be and the same is hereby, made to extend one mile beyond the limits of the said town.

9. The sergeant of said town shall have the same power and discharge the same duties as constable within the corporate limits of said town, and to the distance of one mile beyond the same. He shall have power to arrest in said town, or anywhere within Rappahannock county, upon a warrant issued by the mayor or a justice of the peace, any person charged with a violation of the laws of this commonwealth or ordinances of said town, and where the same are committed in his presence within the limits of said town, he shall have authority and power to attest forthwith, without warrant, the offender and carry him before the mayor or some conservator of the peace of said town, to be dealt with according to law. The council may appoint him as collector of taxes and levies, allowing him a certain per-centum for collecting the same.

10. The person whose duty it is to collect town levies, taxes and fines shall have the same power to distrain therefor as tax collectors have in similar cases.

11. The council may impose a tax on the real and personal estate in said town, which shall not exceed thirty cents on the one hundred dollars of the assessed value thereof. The council may also impose a license tax for the privilege of doing any business within the corporate limits, to be half as much as now imposed by law in this state, and it may impose a poll tax not to exceed fifty cents per capita on every male inhabitant of said town over the age of twenty-one years. In case a liquor license should be granted, the license tax for keeping a bar-room shall not be less than fifteen dollars nor more than thirty dollars per annum, to be determined by a majority of the council, and for selling liquor not be drunk on the premises, not less than ten dollars nor more than twenty-five dollars per annum, to be determined likewise by a majority vote of the council.

12. The council shall have power to make accurate bounds of existing streets, to compel the removal of obstructions therefrom, and to lay off and have new streets, alleys, sidewalks, and to provide and protect shade trees thereon. The council of said town shall have the same jurisdiction for condemning lands for streets, alleys, and sidewalks of said town as the county court has for condemning land for road purposes. The council shall have power to provide against and prevent the running at large of hogs, dogs, horses and other animals; to prevent the cumbering of streets, sidewalks and alleys; to make sanitary regulations in reference to contagious or other diseases; to regulate the building of houses, stables, privies, hog-pens and slaughter-houses; to abate nuisances at the expense of those who cause them; to restrain and punish drunkards, vagrants and street-beggers; and to make, pass and ordain such ordinances, rules, regulations and by-laws as they may deem necessary for the general good.

13. The council shall keep in order the streets, alleys and walks of said town; and it may require the male inhabitants over sixteen years of age to work on the same. The inhabitants of the said town shall not be required to work on the county roads, nor shall the real and personal property in said town be subject to taxation for county road purposes.

14. The said town shall be allowed the use of the jail of Rappahannock county for the safe-keeping and confinement of all persons who shall be sentenced to imprisonment under the general laws or ordinances of said town; and when any judgment shall be rendered against a person for any fine or penalty under an ordinance of said town, and the same be not immediately paid, the person or persons so in default may be required, by order of the court passing sentence, to work out such fine or penalty on the public streets or other public

improvements, at fifty cents a day, under the direction of the sergeant, and under such rules and regulations as may be deemed proper by the council.

15. This act shall be in force from its passage.

*The "original charter" is the act of the Virginia General Assembly that established the town on 14 December 1796.

The First Washington Town Council and the Ordinance Adopted by the Council, 1894

The following individuals were appointed to fill the office of Town Councilmen when the town was incorporated in 1894: Dr. Theodore L. Booten, Mayor; Dr. E. W. Brown, Dr. C. E. Johnson, Judge H. M. Dudley, James French Strother, Clarence J. Miller, and John F. Lillard. Baldwin B. Baggarly was Treasurer of the Town, James L. Oden was Town Sergeant, and J. F. Lillard was Sheriff. The Town Council adopted an ordinance on 15 March 1894, shortly after the town's incorporation act was passed.

ORDINANCE
of the
Town of Washington, Virginia,
Adopted March 15th, 1894.

1. The tax levy shall from time to time be laid by the Council and until changed shall be as follows: On each one hundred dollars in value, twenty-five cents on each titheable.

2. The annual tax on licenses shall be as provided in the following

SCHEDULE

On merchants, attorneys, physicians and dentists, and all persons engaged in any occupation not herein specifically mentioned, liable to be taxed by the town, an amount equal to one-third of the State tax.
Peddlers, $2.50
Auctioneers, $2.50
Common Criers, $1.00
Junk Dealers, $5.00
Daguerrean artists or photographers, $2.50
Houses of private entertainment, $2.50
Boarding houses, $2.50
Eating houses, $2.50
Billiard tables, etc., $10.00
Circus shows, etc., each exhibition, $10.00
Theatrical performance where admittance more than 25 cents, $2.50

Same where under 25 cents, $1.50
Hobby horses, 2.50 first day and each day or part of day, $1.00
Livery stables, $2.50
Standing Stallion or Jackass, $2.50
On liquor dealers for barroom license, $25.00
Retail liquor, $20.00

3. It shall be the duty of the Assessor to make the above-named assessments and return them to the town Treasurer on or before the first day of May in each year, and if the same be not paid by the 15th day of May the Treasurer shall make out a ticket therefor with five percent added, and collect the same in the manner provided by law, and all taxes upon licenses for business commencing after the first of May shall be payable immediately upon assessment and if not so paid it shall be the duty of the Treasurer to collect the same according to law with five per cent added.

4. No person shall within the corporate limits of the town of Washington, or within one mile of the boundary of said town, sell wine, ardent spirits, either by wholesale or retail, or to be drunk at the place where sold or in any manner, without having obtained a license therefor. The tax on these licenses shall be as follows:
On a retail liquor dealer, $20.00
On a bar room liquor dealer, $25.00.
On a license to a bar-room dealer or to a retail dealer who sells only malt liquor the tax shall be $25.00 for both privileges.
Any ordinary keeper, $30.00, and he may also obtain a license as a retail liquor dealer by the payment of an additional tax of $20.00.
Any druggist who desires to do so may obtain a retail liquor dealers license, and he shall be subject to and governed by the provisions of Section 13 of an act of the General Assembly approved March 3, 1880.

5. The Mayor of the town for the time being shall be the head of the police and subject to such provisions as the Council may prescribe; shall have full control over them and may suspend for cause any member thereof.

6. The Mayor may when from peculiar circumstances he shall believe it necessary to appoint special policemen to the extent the public necessity shall require, provided he shall report such appointment to the Council at its next meeting.

7. The Sergeant shall report to the Mayor every day all that he is bound to notice in the discharge of his duty. At least twice in every week he shall make personal inspection of all the streets and alleys of the town and give information to the Mayor of any violation of the laws of the State or ordnances of the town concerning any matter of police regulation.

8. The Sergeant shall report to the Mayor every nuisance or obstruction that he may find on or in any alley, sidewalk, creek, gutter or drain, in any house or on any land within the corporate limits, and he shall execute the order of the Mayor

in regard thereto. He shall report to the Mayor every violation of any ordinance, and give such other notice and information as may be useful in the enforcement of any ordinance. Whenever in his opinion repairs are required to any street or public alley he shall without delay report the same to the Committee on Streets.

9. The town shall provide for keeping its streets and alleys in good repair.

10. All pavements and sidewalks now in existence or hereafter to be made shall be kept in repair, and when necessary reconstructed at the expense of the town.

11. It shall not be lawful for any person to place or cause to be placed any goods, wares, merchandise, wood, coal, plank, boxes or other property more than two feet from the wall of his building, or in or upon or on the side of any street, alley or sidewalk of the town and permit the same to remain longer than is actually necessary for its removal. Nor shall it be lawful for any person to permit any goods, wares, merchandise, wood, coal, plank, boxes, barrels or other property to remain on the sidewalks or alleys of said town in front of his premises between sunset and sunrise, and any person violating this ordinance shall be fined not less than one nor more than five dollars for each offence. Provided that any owner or occupant of property may erect a mounting block on the outer edge of the sidewalk not more than three feet in length and eighteen inches in width.

12. Snack stands, cake and lemonade stands, and other stands of like description occupying any street or sidewalk are hereby declared to be nuisances without permission of the Mayor.

13. It shall not be lawful for any person to deposit the sweepings of his store house, dwelling, shop or other building, or any paper, ashes, damaged fruit, or to allow chips or trash from wood cutting to remain upon any street, alley or sidewalk or in any drain, creek or sewer in the town. Any person violating any provision of this section shall be fined one dollar for every offence.

14. It shall not be lawful for any person to loaf or loiter upon any pavement or sidewalk in the town to the annoyance of the occupant of any property along the same. Any person found so loafing or loitering shall upon complaint of any such occupant be arrested by the police and upon conviction before the Mayor shall be fined not more than one dollar for each offence.

15. It shall not be lawful for any persons to congregate on any sidewalk or crossing in such a manner as to hinder or obstruct any person walking along the same, and it shall be the duty of the Sergeant to keep the crossings clear and the sidewalks open for the passage of persons using the same. Any person violating this ordinance shall on conviction be fined not exceeding one dollar. This ordinance, at the discretion of the Mayor, may be suspended on public occasions.

16. If any person shall leave his horse, mule or team unhitched and unattended or shall willfully gallop or recklessly drive the same or suffer the same to run at

large in any street or alley of the town he shall be fined not less than one nor more than ten dollars for every such offence.

17. No horse shall be allowed to stand upon any sidewalk or pavement under a penalty of fifty cents to be paid by the owner or person having charge of such horse – one-half to go to the Sergeant.

18. It shall not be lawful for any person to obstruct any street or sidewalk within the town by playing ball or by playing bandy or at marbles or at any other game or occupation. Any person violating this ordinance shall be fined not exceeding one dollar for each offence.

19. For the more perfectly securing of such prisoners as may be compelled to work on the streets, the Mayor may have provided a ball and chain for each prisoner so worked on the streets, to be affixed to his leg before leaving the jail and not to be taken off until his return to the jail.

20. Whenever any person shall be imprisoned for the nonpayment of a fine or other penalty or costs of prosecution and shall be compelled to work on the streets as herein provided, he shall be credited on his fine or penalty and costs such sum for each day's labor as may be prescribed by the Council, and until further order the said compensation is fixed at fifty cents per day.

21. All vagrants or persons without visible means of support found within the limits of the town shall be at once arrested by the Sergeant, and upon conviction of said offence shall be punished at the discretion of the Mayor by fine, by confinement in jail not exceeding thirty days, or by labor upon the streets for a like period.

22. If any person shall, without permission of the Mayor, set off or discharge any torpedo, pop-cracker or any fire-works or any combination of gunpowder or other combustible or dangerous material within the limits of the corporation, he shall be fined at the discretion of the Mayor not exceeding ten dollars.

23. Any person who shall sell without license any wine, ardent spirits, malt liquors or a mixture of any of them within the corporate limits, he shall be fined the sum of twenty dollars for every such offence, one-half of which shall go to the informer.

24. If any person licensed to sell wine, ardent spirits, malt liquors or any mixture of any of them to any intoxicated person, or permit any intoxicated person to drink any intoxicating spirits at his bar-room or other place of business, or shall permit any drunken person to stop in his bar-room or other room connected therewith, he shall forfeit to the town not less than one nor more than twenty dollars.

25. If any person licensed to sell as aforesaid shall permit any person notoriously incapable of controlling his appetite for intoxicating spirits to drink at his place of business or room connected therewith, or shall sell to any such person any intoxicating spirits, he shall forfeit to the town not less than ten nor more than twenty dollars. And if he knowingly sells any wine, ardent spirits, malt liquor or

any mixture of any of them to a third party for the use of such person so incapable of controlling his appetite, he shall forfeit the sum of twenty dollars, one-half of which shall go to the informer.

26. If any person licensed as aforesaid shall permit any minor to enter his bar-room or other room connected therewith or to stop therein he shall forfeit to the town not less than one nor more than ten dollars. And if he permits such minor, without such permission of parent or guardian, to drink any intoxicating spirits at such place he shall forfeit to the town an additional sum of five dollars. And if any retail liquor merchant shall sell or give to any such minor or any wine, ardent spirits or malt liquor, or any mixture of any of them, he shall forfeit to the town not less than one nor more than ten dollars.

27. The Mayor, or in his absence the Mayor pro tempore, may, whenever in his opinion the good order of the town requires it, notify all persons so licensed to close the bar rooms or other places of business, and any person so licensed who shall thereupon refuse or neglect to close his bar room or other place of business, shall be fined five dollars and the further sum of twenty dollars for every fifteen minutes thereafter that he shall continue to keep open his bar room or other room connected therewith.

28. It shall not be lawful for any person to discharge any gun or other firearms within the limits of the corporation. Any person violating this ordinance shall be fined not less than one nor more than five dollars for each offence. Provided that the occupant of any lot may discharge such firearms into the ground on his lot for the purpose of unloading and cleaning the same, and may shoot at rats or other noxious animals or birds on his premises.

29. Any person who shall be guilty of riot, rout or unlawful assembly or assault and battery, or any offence which would amount to a breach of the peace and any person who shall in any public place contend with angry words or use indecent or profane language, shall be fined for each offence not less than one nor more than twenty dollars.

30. Any person who shall willfully disturb any assembly of persons met for the worship of God, whether he be in or outside of said assembly, shall be fined for every such offence not less than two nor more than twenty dollars.

31. If any person shall be found guilty of willfully obstructing the officers or agents of the town in the discharge of their duties he shall be fined not less than five nor more than twenty dollars for each offence.

32. If any person shall suffer his cow or ox to run at large between the hours of dusk and sunrise in the streets or alleys of the town, or shall permit his cows or oxen to run at large in the streets in the day time, such person so offending shall be fined not less than one nor more than five dollars for every such offence. This law to take effect from May 1st, 1894.

33. No hog shall be suffered to run at large within the corporate limits. It shall be the duty of the Sergeant to take up every hog so found running at large and report the same to the Mayor.

34. If at any time the Mayor has cause to apprehend the existence of hydrophobia or madness among the dogs of the town it shall be lawful for him to require, by proclamation placarded in conspicuous places, that all the dogs be confined to the lots of their owners for such time as he may prescribe, and all dogs found going at large contrary to such requirement be killed in such manner as he may direct. The owner of any such dog so found going at large shall forfeit $2.50 for every such offence.

35. Any person having in his possession any proud slut and suffering the same to run at large within the corporate limits in that condition, or allowing it to remain on his premises to the annoyance of the neighborhood, shall be fined one dollar for every day said animal shall run at large or so annoy the neighborhood.

36. All householders are hereby required to clean their privies and hog-pens thoroughly and keep them in good order. Any person failing to do so after twenty-four hours notice by the Sergeant shall be fined two dollars for every day he shall fail to comply with this regulation.

37. All privies and hog-pens that open for the escape of filth on any street or public alley of the town, or into the channel of any creek or drain or any sewer and also any privies and hog-pens that stand within five feet of the margin of any street, alley, channel, creek, drain or sewer (having their openings for the escape of filth toward such street, alley, etc.) are hereby declared to be nuisances and the owners or occupants of the premises on which such are situated, shall be fined not less than one dollar for each day they shall remain after notice from the Sergeant to remove them.

38. If any person shall in the day time bathe in any creek or stream within the limits of the corporation, or in any manner indecently expose his person, he shall be fined not exceeding five dollars for every such offence.

39. If any person shall pollute the water of any of the public springs, pumps or wells, he shall be fined not less than one nor more than five dollars for every such offence.

40. If any person shall tear down or deface any bill or advertisement so long as the same may be of benefit to the party causing it to be posted he shall upon conviction be fined not less than one nor more than ten dollars, one-half of which shall go to the informer; provided, that nothing herein shall prevent anyone from tearing down advertisements posted on his own premises.

41. If anyone shall be found guilty of injuring any shade trees upon any of the streets, alleys or public grounds of the town, he shall be fined not less than one nor more than five dollars for each tree so injured.

42. If any person shall willfully tear down or deface any stake, post or other landmark erected as a guide for curbing or other purposes he shall be fined not less than one nor more than five dollars for each offence.

43. If any person shall be found guilty of breaking or defacing any of the lamps, either public or private, or other property of any description he shall be fined for each offence not exceeding twenty dollars.

44. The foregoing ordinances shall take effect from and after the first day of April, 1894 (except Nos. 32 and 33) which shall take effect from and after May 1st, 1894.

Authorization to Impose Property Taxes and Fees, 1898

In an act of the Virginia General Assembly passed on 28 February 1898, the Town Council was authorized to impose a property tax and other fees, with a further provision prohibiting the granting by the court of a license for the sale of liquor without the consent in writing of the majority of the electors of the town qualified to vote.

Acts of the General Assembly of Virginia, Chapter 584. An act to amend and re-enact section 11 of an act entitled an act to incorporate the town of Washington, in the county of Rappahannock, approved February 12, 1894, with license to sell liquor in said town. Approved February 28, 1898.

1. Be it enacted by the general assembly of Virginia, That section eleven of an act entitled an act to incorporate the town of Washington, in the county of Rappahannock, approved February twelfth, eighteen hundred and ninety-four, be amended and re-enacted so as to read as follows:

"11. The council may impose a tax on real and personal estate in said town, which shall not exceed thirty cents on the one hundred dollars of the assessed value thereof. The council may also impose a license tax for the privilege of doing any business within the corporate limits of said town, to be half as much as may be imposed by the existing laws of the state on such business, for state purposes, and may also impose a full tax not to exceed fifty cents per capita on every male inhabitant of said town over the age of twenty-five years. In case a liquor license should be granted the license tax to sell by retail as now provided by law shall not be less than twenty-five dollars nor more than fifty dollars, to be determined by a majority vote of the council; provided, however, that no license to sell wine, ardent spirits, malt liquors, or any mixtures thereof, alcoholic bitter, or fruit preserved in alcohol by wholesale or retail, or in any other way, in the corporate limits of said town or within one mile thereof shall be granted by the county court of the county of Rappahannock nor by any other authority to any person or persons, clubs, firms, or corporations, unless and until the applicant for such business shall file before the court the consent in writing of a majority of the electors of said town as to the number of such electors shall be accepted as prima facie correct."

2. This act shall be in force from its passage.

Sheriff Lillard planted young shade trees on the courthouse green in 1889, producing "one of nicest shadiest lawns in the State."[76] At the turn of the century, Washington was a charming rural town, its dusty streets lit by gas lights and shaded by towering trees.[77]

---

[76] *Blue Ridge Guide*, 18 April 1889

[77] Caption to an "Out of the Attic" photograph published in the *Rappahannock News*, 12 August 1982

Chapter 6. Washington in the Early 1900s

At the beginning of the 1900s, the town population was almost 300 persons. A Confederate Monument was erected in 1900 at the north end of the courthouse complex through the efforts of the local chapter of the Daughters of the Confederacy, to honor the men from Rappahannock County who served their cause in the Civil War.[1] Recovery from the Civil War and the country-wide depression of the 1870s had been slow, but times were becoming more prosperous by the turn of the century.

Telephones were being introduced. The first ones were in stores, as they were considered to be business tools. Later, the telephone became a social instrument when the party line was established. The *Blue Ridge Guide* was being published by George E. Cary and served as a weekly source of information. Automobiles began to appear shortly before World War I, but roads through the town were still quite primitive.

Government

The Virginia Constitutional Convention of 1901-1902 resulted in legislation that abolished monthly Court days in the town (and in other County seats) and created 24 circuit courts for the State. The legislation also instituted a poll tax of $1.50 for all voters.

An Act of the General Assembly in 1903 contained stringent regulations for saloons in towns with less than 500 population, and all saloons in the town were forced to close. In 1914, prohibition was adopted. During prohibition, a law was passed designed to punish drinkers. In addition to a fine for drinking in public, there was a $10 fee paid to the law official who arrested the offender. The law was designed to encourage the arrest and prosecution of those found drunk.[2]

In about 1910, the County Supervisors discovered that no county taxes had been collected from the town residents for several years past, and the Commonwealth Attorney was instructed to take steps such that "the inhabitants of the said Town may bear their proper proportion of the taxation."[3] Further, because of the more complex budgeting and financial obligations of the town, the Town Treasurer

---

[1] In 2006, the monument was found to be in poor condition, and the County contracted with Conservation Solutions, Inc., to repair and refurbish it (*Rappahannock News*, 16 March 2006).

[2] Recollections of Aubrey Keyser, son of Hubert Keyser who was sheriff during 1919-1941, in Daphne Hutchinson and Theresa Reynolds, *On the Morning Side of the Blue Ridge*, a compilation of articles published in the *Rappahannock News* in 1983, page 90-91

[3] Elisabeth B. and C.E. Johnson Jr., *Rappahannock County, Virginia, A History*, Green Publishers, Orange, VA, 1981, p. 60

became more and more unable to accomplish his duties. Finally, an emergency situation arose when the Town Treasurer resigned and a considerable amount of taxes were still unpaid. To rectify this situation, the Virginia General Assembly passed an Act on 15 March 1915 whereby the Rappahannock County treasurer took over the former duties of the treasurer of the Town of Washington. The County Treasurer was to collect all property, license, and capitation taxes due to the Town and disburse the Town's funds according to the direction of the Town Council.

Acts of the General Assembly of Virginia, Chapter 96. An act to amend and re-enact an act entitled an act to incorporate the town of Washington, in the county of Rappahannock, approved February 12, 1894, as amended by an act approved February 28, 1898, by adding thereto an additional section, to be known as section 16. Approved March 15, 1915.

1. Be it enacted by the general assembly of Virginia, That an act entitled an act to incorporate the town of Washington, in the county of Rappahannock, approved February twelfth, eighteen hundred and ninety-four, as amended by an act approved February twenty-eighth, eighteen hundred and ninety-eight, be amended and re-enacted by adding thereto an additional section, to be known as section sixteen, and to read as follows:

Sec. 16. The treasurer of the county of Rappahannock and his successors in office, by virtue of this act shall be treasurer of the town of Washington, and as such shall provide a separate account, and proceed to collect by such process as other taxes are now collected by law, all property, license and capitation tax that are now due and as the same shall hereafter become due said town, and the said treasurer and his sureties, shall be accountable to said town for same as for other funds now committed to him by law as treasurer of Rappahannock county; and said treasurer shall disburse such funds in his possession belonging to said town according to orders from the town council, and he shall render statements of his receipts and disbursements to said town council when so requested by them, and said treasurer shall settle his accounts with said town council annually. As treasurer of the town of Washington said treasurer shall receive for his services such fees as are now allowed him by law as county treasurer, to be paid out of the town fund.

All acts or parts of acts inconsistent with this act are hereby repealed.

An emergency existing by reason of the fact that the town treasurer has resigned and a considerable amount of the taxes are now unpaid, thereby necessitating the immediate execution of the provisions of this act, the same shall be in force from its passage.

On 29 September 1917, the Washington Town Council enacted an ordinance affirming the names of the streets and lot numbers in the town to be the same as those then in use. Although the Town Council was not aware of this in 1917, these street names and lot numbers were the same as those in the plan of the town submitted to the Virginia General Assembly by Calvert, Wheeler, Jett, and Porter in 1797.[4] The 1917 ordinance was readopted and affirmed by the Town Council on 17 May 1930.[5]

Mud was a problem in the early 1900s. The streets were unpaved. To cope with the mud, wooden and brick sidewalks were installed in front of the courthouse buildings; the first cement sidewalks were poured in the town in the 1920s.[6] In 1924, W.C. Campbell was contracted with to construct a cement walk and fence in front of the courthouse yard at a cost of $388.80 for the walk and $282.80 for the fence.

Newspapers

The *Blue Ridge Guide* newspaper was serving the town in this era. The first newspaper, *The Rappahannock News*, had started in 1877 and survived for one year. The *Blue Ridge Echo* followed and was published from 1883 to 1888. The *Blue Ridge Guide* was started in 1888 and survived for 47 years under the capable management of George Cary until 1936 when his health failed and the newspaper closed its offices. There was no paper published until 1949 when *The Rappahannock News* was reopened by Lucy Catherine Bowie and her brother Bruce Bowie. The offices of this newspaper were first located on the west side of Lot 25 where the Trinity Church parking lot is today, and then moved to a new building on Lot 13. This newspaper published many articles about the town, as well as summaries of the minutes of the Town Council and the town's budgets. Although ownership of this paper changed several times, in 2018 it was still being published weekly from offices that were still located in the town of Washington.

The Post Office

Until about 1909, the Washington Post Office was located on Lot 12, owned by Walker and Mary Holland. Walker was a tailor and maintained his business in his home, as well as the post office for which he was postmaster. After Holland's death in 1909, the post office was moved to Luther Partlow's large 3-story brick mercantile store on the southeast corner of Gay and Jett streets on Lot 27. From about 1915 until 1956, the post office was located in the former site of the Rappahannock National Bank on the northeast corner of Main and Jett streets. Postmaster Jay West Brown is stated to have blown a fox horn when the mail

---

[4] See Chapter 2; George Calvert, James Jett Jr., James Wheeler, and William Porter, Culpeper County, 1 December 1797, Legislative Petitions Digital Collection, Library of Virginia, Richmond, VA, Record number 000154073; also, Legislative Petitions of the General Assembly, 1776-1865, Accession Number 36121, Box 58, Folder 71.

[5] Rappahannock County Deed Book 36, page 1

[6] Town of Washington Comprehensive Plan, 2017, page 5

was ready for pickup.[7] In 1934, W. Arthur Miller was appointed as postmaster and served in this capacity for 31 years, retiring in 1965. Miller was a native of Rappahannock County and was the son of Senator and Mrs. John Miller. He and his wife Emily Brent Miller lived at Mount Prospect. After his retirement, he was active in foxhunting and organized the Rappahannock Hunt, the first hunt club in the County.[8]

Banks

The town had three banks in the early part of the 1900s. In 1900, a two-story frame building on Gay Street across from the courthouse, that had been a saloon, was purchased by C.J. Rixey who converted the building into a branch of the Farmers and Merchants Bank.[9] This bank was short-lived, as Rixey sold the property in 1903 to the Rappahannock National Bank.[10] The president of this new bank was H.M. Dudley, and the bank had received authorization to commence business the prior year.[11] The frame building on the property was the site of the bank for several years, until the building was moved to the northeast corner of Jett and Main streets on Lot 27; there it continued to serve as the bank until a new bank building made of brick was constructed in 1914-1915 on the original parcel of land on Gay Street.[12]

A drawing of the Rappahannock National Bank used on bank checks in the 1900s

The third bank was in Stuart's Store, constructed in 1908 on the southwest corner of Main and Calvert streets (Lot 6). William M. Stuart operated a merchandise store in the building; he also loaned money from an enormous safe in the rear of the building. Stuart was forced by the federal government to close the bank in

---

[7] Statement by Joan Culmer Platt, *Rappahannock News*, 13 September 2018

[8] *Rappahannock News*, 23 December 1965, quoted in the 28 June 2018 edition of the newspaper

[9] Rappahannock County Deed Book V, page 62; this property became Tax Map 20A-3-89

[10] Rappahannock County Deed Book W, page 95

[11] Treasury Department certificate No. 6443 authorizing the bank to commence business, dated 29 September 1902, copy in Rappahannock Historical Society files

[12] Cover photograph, Kathryn Lynch, *Images of America, Rappahannock County*; postcard cancel-stamped in 1906 showing 'Bank' above the Main Street door of the building, Rappahannock Historical Society files; the construction date of 1914-1915 is based on information from Rappahannock County Land Books which show that the value of the building on the Gay Street property increased from $380 in 1914 to $1950 in 1915.

the 1920s because the government no longer recognized private banks. It is believed to have been the last private bank in the United States.

A few days after President Roosevelt took office in 1933, he ordered all banks in the U.S. to close. Those that were in sound financial shape, such as the Rappahannock National Bank, were closed for only four days but many banks did not reopen for 30 days or more.[13] The Rappahannock National Bank remained in the town through the 1900s but moved out of town to a location on Route 211 in 2003, leaving the town with no financial institution.

Electricity and Telephones

During the 1920s, the use of electric power was becoming increasingly more important. Page Power Company, later Northern Virginia Power Company, strung lines along the roads with outlets going to individual houses and stores.

Telephones operated through a switchboard were introduced to the town in the 1920s. The first switchboard was operated by Daisy Fox Partlow and the central telephone office was located in her home on Lot 21. For thirteen years from 1936 until dial telephones were installed in 1949, Mrs. Alfred Verner and her daughters Phyllis and Mary operated the switchboard from their home in Washington, first at the Stone House, then at the Carter-Dudley House on Lot 9, then at the Bywaters House on Middle Street. The switchboard provided 24-hour service for residents of Washington, Sperryville, and Flint Hill and connected to Front Royal and Culpeper.[14] Callers would crank their phones, causing a light to blink on the switchboard, and one of the operators would connect the caller to the desired person. Round-the-clock phone service meant that someone had to be attending the switchboard at all times.

The switchboard operators performed other services. The fire siren was in their home and when the operators received notification of a fire they set off the siren. After a fire siren, there would be a flurry of calls to the switchboard asking where the fire was, who was involved, and how much damage was done. The operators usually knew where everyone was, not only because they placed calls from various places but also because people would ring up and tell the operators where they were so that calls could be directed there. It was an accepted fact that the operators knew everything that was going on. In addition to completing calls, it was customary for the operators to dispense up-to-the-minute reports on birth, deaths, and marriages and offer information about who had been where with

---

[13] Interview with Giles Miller, who worked at Culpeper's Central Fidelity Bank, in Daphne Hutchinson and Theresa Reynolds, compilers, *On the Morning Side of the Blue Ridge*, articles from the Rappahannock News of 1983, page 15

[14] Theresa Reynolds, "Old-fashioned switchboard served Rappahannock Callers," *Rappahannock News*, 6 January 1983; Information from Marilyn (Merrill) Bailey, November 2015

whom and when they were likely to return. The operators even arranged dates for the local boys.

The switchboard in the Verner home was also a center of information for out of-town visitors, as the only pay telephone was located in there. In the late 1940s dial telephones were installed in homes and businesses and there was no longer a need for telephone operators to connect callers.[15] This was the bittersweet end of an era.

Stores and Other Commercial Buildings

In the early 1900s, a building on Lot 31 was a stage coach stop and John Clark's blacksmith shop and livery stable. These were destroyed by fire in 1916; F. Downing Wood purchased the property in the 1920s and constructed an apple packing facility. (The Wood family owned the farm called "Sunnyside" adjacent to the town of Washington on which there were extensive apple orchards.)

Luther T. Partlow's General Store was located on the southeastern part of Lot 27, at the corner of Jett and Gay Streets, in the early part of the 1900s. It was a large brick building constructed in about 1820 with one story that fronted on Gay Street and a lower level along Jett Street. The building had a varied and colorful career having contained the mercantile store, a barroom, drug store, Felbert Green's barber shop, and a restaurant in the basement owned by Lucy "Jennie" Roberts, a member of a local African-American family. The restaurant served a delicious meal for 25 cents (35 cents on special days).[16] There was also a Delco electric plant in the basement of Partlow's store which furnished electricity to many of the residents of the town. The building was destroyed by fire in the 1930s.

In 1908 William M. Stuart acquired Lot 6 on the southwest corner of Main and Calvert streets after the old building on this property was torn down. There he constructed his merchandise store (and bank) which he operated until the 1920s. Lit by gas lights, Stuart's Store supplied most of the needs of the townspeople. In 1928 T.C. Lea opened his Lea Bros Store in the building, but moved his store to Lot 27 in 1935 when he constructed a new building there on the northwest corner of Gay and Jett streets.[17] In the 1940s the building on Lot 6 became the Washington Cash Store.

---

[15] Elisabeth B. and C.E. Johnson Jr., *Rappahannock County, Virginia, A History*, Green Publishers, Orange, VA, 1981, p. 67-74; Laura A. Matthews, *A Ramble Through Rappahannock*, Scribblers Inc., Warrenton, Virginia, 2000, page 24

[16] Caption for a 1909 photograph of Partlow's store in 1909, Rappahannock Historical Society files

[17] *Rappahannock News*, 3 March 1966, quoted in the 26 July 2018 edition of the newspaper

Stuart's Store in the early 1900s
Source: Website of the Friends of the Former Washington Cash Store

Attorney T.C. Lea constructed a new store on the site of the former Partlow's Store in 1935.[18] The building contained one story on Gay Street and a basement level along Jett Street. Lea came from a family of storekeepers; his father J. P. Lea and his two uncles W. B. Lea and L. L. Lea were in the mercantile business. From 1938 to 1941, T. C. Lea served as the fire chief of the Rappahannock Volunteer Fire Department. In 1942 he served as chairman of the Panel War Price and Ration Board of the county and in the late 1940s he served on the school board. Lea began the Rappahannock Insurance Agency in 1941 by purchasing the Rappahannock Realty Company. He served on the Washington Town Council for a number of years and was treasurer of the Rappahannock Red Cross.[19]

In about 1900, John Edward Thornton built a one-story garage on the northeast corner of Main and Middle streets (Lot 24) opposite his hotel (Washington House) on the northwest corner. He appears to have moved the log "Corner house" on this site to the east, where it later became the Middle Street Gallery. Thornton's Garage complemented his hotel business by providing parking space for carriages and, later, for motorcars while offering the additional convenience of servicing the latter with gas, tires, and repairs. He added an additional 1½ stories, reportedly to appease his wife who wanted rowdy card games, partying, and dancing removed from Thornton's hotel.[20]

---

[18] *Rappahannock News*, 3 March 1966, quoted in the 26 July 2018 edition of the newspaper; National Register of Historic Places, Washington Historic District, 2006 Update

[19] *Rappahannock News*, 19 January 1950, quoted in the 3 March 2016 edition of the newspaper

[20] Recollections of Mrs. Edna Walker, owner of "Washington House", in Daphne Hutchinson and Theresa Reynolds, *On the Morning Side of the Blue Ridge*, a compilation of articles published in the *Rappahannock News* in 1983, page 50-51, and in *Rappahannock News*, 1 July 1982

In the 1930s, George E. Cary constructed a two-story frame building at 307 Main Street (Lot 11) that had a poolroom and a place for dances, with apartments above.[21] In 1945, the building housing Merrill's Motor Company was constructed on the southwest corner of Main and Middle streets (Lot 9). And in 1947-1948 the theater located at the southwest corner of Gay and Jett streets was constructed by B.R. Armel.[22] It was originally used as a movie theater and also as a venue for community plays by local citizens and schoolchildren.

Entertainment

In the early 1900s there were few opportunities for organized social entertainment. People spent time playing baseball, riding horses, buggy riding, and sleigh riding in winter. Dances were popular. The whole upstairs of the Washington School could be converted to a dance hall, and dances also took place on the second floor of Thornton's garage on Lot 24. The expansive upper space in Thornton's building evolved into the town's first community entertainment and recreational center. Over time, there was a barroom, poolhall, poker and card games, dance hall, basketball court, and a theater to show movies. This venue saw the birthplace of basketball in Rappahannock County in the early 1920s. Both boy's and girl's teams played there until the gymnasium was constructed at the Washington High School. Poker playing was a major social event for men in Washington. One favorite spot was "Buzzard's Roost," the upstairs of the butcher shop across Main Street from Washington House; table stakes might go as high as $400-$500.

Washington had a reputation because of its drinking and gambling. The people in Flint Hill called the town "the hell hole of Rappahannock County."[23] Court days were a high point on the calendar. In the early 1900s, there was a saloon on Gay Street across from the courthouse. In 1885, John Dulin had purchased the property and turned the building there into "Dulin's Saloon."[24] After moving to California, he sold the property to George G. Bywaters who also maintained a barroom on the property.[25] People would flock to this establishment. "Everybody would get drunk, fight, and run their horses around town." In the 1930s to the 1950s, J.A. Swan of Culpeper owned much of Lot 28, and on March

---

[21] Elisabeth B. and C.E. Johnson Jr., *Rappahannock County, Virginia, A History*, Green Publishers, Orange, VA, 1981, p. 144

[22] Rappahannock County Deed Book 53, page 271; information from Rappahannock County Land Books show the value of buildings on the lot increased from $0 in 1947 to $3500 in 1948

[23] Recollections of Jack Miller, who lived in the town of Washington all his life, in Daphne Hutchinson and Theresa Reynolds, *On the Morning Side of the Blue Ridge*, a compilation of articles published in the *Rappahannock News* in 1983, page 100-101

[24] Rappahannock County Deed Book Q, page 426

[25] Rappahannock County Deed Book U, page 111

court days he would bring his new machinery, tools, and wares to the empty lot for people to see. Children were even let out of school for this event.[26]

In addition to these somewhat raucous activities, however, there was also a tea room in the town, "The Cherry Tree and Hatchet," operated by Mrs. Ruth Meigs, wife of Acton Meigs, and her daughters. In the 1930s one could purchase a chicken dinner for 75 cents; with the chicken came potatoes, vegetables, salad, hot rolls, preserves, and dessert. The economy breakfast was 40 cents and included fruit, cereal, eggs, ham or bacon, toast, preserves, and coffee.[27] The Washington House hotel and tavern, operated by the John Edward Thornton family, was located on town Lot 8 as the successor to Mrs. Coxe's tavern and Dear's hotel. In the 1930s, George E. Cary constructed a two-story frame building on the southern part of Lot 11 for recreational purposes. A poolroom serving beer was in the basement. The private Rappahannock Club had Saturday night dances, dancing lessons, and children's parties on the main floor; there were apartments above.[28]

The Depression and Economic Recovery

Rappahannock County had struggled through the chesnut blight, the loss of many apple crops from frost, and the stripping of the mountains whose woods had provided the major income for many families. The brutal drought of the early 1930s and the national depression were two more blows to this rural population. The town of Washington benefitted from the projects initiated at this time by Roosevelt's New Deal. The Civilian Conservation Corps began constructing Skyline Drive, as a result of which tourists began flocking to the town for food and lodging in the late 1930s following economic recovery. Home demonstration agents employed local women to make clothing for the poor; one of the sewing rooms was in the old mercantile building on Lot 8.[29] In the mid-1930s, the Town obtained a grant from the WPA and issued $20,000 in bonds to construct the Washington Water Works, consisting of a piping system from a spring in the mountains to a reservoir and then to the town.[30]

The Fire Department

---

[26] Recollections of Jack Miller, who lived in the town of Washington all his life, in Daphne Hutchinson and Theresa Reynolds, *On the Morning Side of the Blue Ridge*, a compilation of articles published in the *Rappahannock News* in 1983, page 100-101

[27] Daphne Hutchinson and Theresa Reynolds, *On the Morning Side of the Blue Ridge*, a compilation of articles published in the *Rappahannock News* in 1983, page 114

[28] Elisabeth B. and C.E. Johnson Jr., *Rappahannock County, Virginia, A History*, Green Publishers, Orange, VA, 1981, p. 144

[29] Daphne Hutchinson and Theresa Reynolds, compilers, *On the Morning Side of the Blue Ridge*, articles from the Rappahannock News of 1983, page 13

[30] The history of this complex project is detailed in Chapter 9

In 1935, a volunteer fire department was organized as a result of the new waterworks system providing potable water to the town. Franklin Clyde Baggarly was elected chief of the new department and was asked by the Town Council to develop a constitution and by-laws.[31] Having a functioning fire department and water supply were essential to the town for obtaining fire insurance. The Washington Volunteer Fire Department was incorporated in 1939. Its officers at that time were T.C. Lea, president; L.V. Merrill and D.C. Updike, vice-presidents; L.J. Turner, secretary-treasurer; and W.A. Miller and George J. Davis Jr. as additional trustees.[32] In 1940, Warner Miller sold part of town Lot 29 to the Town of Washington.[33] On this lot was constructed the cinderblock Washington Fire Department building, which was set back from the street and had large bays for entrance and exit of the firetrucks. The fire department remained in this building until the 1970s when it moved to a new larger building on Warren Avenue. The old firehouse was renovated as an office building and in 2018 it housed the offices of the Commonwealth Attorney and the County Attorney.

Description of the Town in 1936

The federal Works Projects Administration (WPA) funded a historical inventory of the town in 1936. The project was researched and written by Margaret Atkins of Sperryville. Her description of the town included the following:
"Washington is one of the delightful small towns of the Virginia Piedmont. Its residents are composed of happy, contented people, maintaining a pleasing social life among each other, and never at any time too much "hurried," yet still having their own pleasures. The town is incorporated and has shaded macadamized streets. It is well supplied with five churches, two auditoriums, a National bank, a hotel, two wayside restaurants, ten tourist homes, County Court buildings, a Masonic Hall, the Washington High School with over 200 pupils, a barber shop and other business places and professional offices. The town is situated on the Lee Highway sixty-five miles from the nation's capital, to and from which three motor stage coaches operate daily. Other motor lines traverse the town on a regular schedule providing connections (via railroads) to all parts of the United States. The Post Office operates six daily mails to and from the town. It is a delightful place in which to spend a quiet vacation amidst beautiful and agreeable surroundings."[34]

---

[31] *Culpeper Exponent*, 3 October 1935

[32] Elisabeth B. and C.E. Johnson Jr., *Rappahannock County, Virginia, A History*, Green Publishers, Orange, VA, 1981, p. 379

[33] Rappahannock County Deed Book 43, page 139

[34] Margaret E. Atkins, "Washington, Virginia, the County Seat of Rappahannock County," Works Progress Administration Historical Inventory Project, sponsored by the Virginia Conservation Commission under the direction of the Division of History. Sources of information were George Cary, editor of the Blue Ridge Guide, and Franklin Clyde Baggarly, former town attorney. The document contained the disclaimer that "this information had not been checked for accuracy."

Roads and Transportation

Automobiles began to appear on Rappahannock County roads shortly before World War I. With the advent of the automobile many roads were tarred and graveled during the 1920s. U.S. Highway 21 (today's Route 211) was improved and rebuilt as a macadam road through the town of Washington during this time.[35] In the 1920s, Trinity Episcopal Church purchased an automobile for the rector's use; in 1925 the Church purchased a new Ford coupe for the rector. Multiple vestry minutes mention dollar outlays for repairs.

For those who did not have automobile transportation, John W. Clark began a jitney service named the Front Royal & Washington Motor Transportation Company that was chartered in 1916. Busses ran between Washington and Front Royal, and the route connected the town of Washington with the Southern Railway trains at Front Royal which permitted people to travel by railroad to Washington D.C., Harrisonburg, Hagerstown, or Roanoke. Clark sold the company to Walker B. Jenkins in 1920,[36] and Jenkins renamed the company as the Walker B. Jenkins Bus Line. It provided daily roundtrip bus service from Winchester and Front Royal, through Washington, and then south to Culpeper and Fredericksburg, until the mid-1950s. The bus routes also connected with railroad service in Richmond and the Shenandoah Valley.[37] Jenkins made two round-trips a day, giving Rappahannock residents without transportation a chance to spend a day shopping or meeting appointments. The bus service also aided those who were unable to do errands in person; the drivers would have a list of notes and pick up medicine, groceries, and supplies for those on their list. In the mid-1950s Jenkins sold the line to the Virginia Trailways Bus Company and the service was discontinued shortly thereafter.[38]

The Commonwealth of Virginia took over maintenance of all primary and secondary roads in the 1930s. The State Highway Commission was constructing Lee Highway and the Town Council requested that the highway be run through the town. Presumably, this request was to create a better road through the town, with maintenance of the road being the responsibility of the State rather than the Town. The request was probably also in anticipation of the benefits to the town of increased tourism from the planned new Shenandoah National Park.

---

[35] Elisabeth B. and C.E. Johnson Jr., *Rappahannock County, Virginia, A History*, Green Publishers, Orange, VA, 1981, pages 59-60 and pages 140-141; Rappahannock County Deed Book 30, page 357

[36] Rappahannock County Deed Book 30, page 357

[37] Daphne Hutchinson and Theresa Reynolds, compilers, *On the Morning Side of the Blue Ridge*, articles from the Rappahannock News of 1983, page 28

[38] See Chapter 14 for more details

During construction of the highway through the town, Main Street was macadamized and widened. Unfortunately, some of the town's residences were severely weakened by this construction. One of these was the two-story brick home built in the mid-1800s by J.Y. Menefee, a distinguished lawyer. The building, located on the west side of Main Street between Jett and Porter streets on town Lot 13, had porches on the first and second floor and was often described as one of the most beautiful homes in the town of Washington. It was valued at $1000 in 1900.[39] The highway construction weakened the house, large cracks appeared, and the house was dismantled in the 1940s. Another damaged building was Clark's Tavern on the southeast corner of Main and Porter streets (Lot 31); the front porches and second and third stories of this building had to be removed because of structural instability.

In the later 1930s there was economic recovery from the Depression, and caravans of tourists began visiting the town of Washington on their way to Skyline Drive. In addition to Thornton's garage on town Lot 24, gas stations were constructed on the western part of Lot 25 in the 1930s and on Lot 13 in the 1940s, as well as Critzer's Service Station built in the 1940s on the north side of Middle Street. During the Second World War, rationing was instituted throughout the nation to ensure that items in short supply would be available for the war effort. Gasoline was one of the rationed commodities.[40]

L.V. Merrill came to the town from Wisconsin in the 1920s and rented Thornton's garage on town Lot 24. After World War II he purchased town Lot 9 at the southwest corner of Main and Middle streets, in 1945.[41] At that time, the Carter-Dudley house was located there. Merrill hired a Richmond company to move the house to the southern part of Lot 9. "It was quite an interesting thing to everybody within the town because nothing like that had ever happened in their memory, a large house being removed and pushed down the street."[42] Merrill converted the house into a four-unit apartment building and constructed a new brick building at the corner of Main and Middle streets. Merrill's Motor Company, housed in the new building, was a Ford dealership with a car display window in the front. The Company thrived until its closing in 1979.[43]

---

[39] 1900 Rappahannock County Land Records

[40] Daphne Hutchinson and Theresa Reynolds, *On the Morning Side of the Blue Ridge*, a compilation of articles published in the *Rappahannock News* in 1983, page 88

[41] Rappahannock County Plat Book 3, page 13

[42] Recollections of Marilyn Merrill Bailey, daughter of L.V. Merrill, in an interview conducted by the Rappahannock League for Environmental Protection, 2018

[43] Rappahannock County Deed Book 193, page 199

Construction of New Homes

There was considerable construction of new residential structures during the first half of the 1900s. In 1908, Phelbert Scott Green purchased a parcel of land at the south end of Lot 41 and constructed a house on his property and also a small building at the rear of the land which served as Green's Barbershop.[44] This house eventually became "Trinity House." In about 1910, John W. Clark constructed his home and bus station on Lot 15. The Moffett home at 537 Gay Street (Lot 20) was constructed by Rappahannock native Charles Hawkins in 1929. The home at 577 Main Street (Lot 3) was built during 1930-1940. The 1½-story frame home at 525 Main Street (Lot 5) was built in about 1940, and the two-story frame building at 307 Main Street (Lot 11) was constructed in about 1937. Stonehaven, the 2½-story stone home at 218 Main Street (Lot 30) was constructed in 1930. The 1½-story Dorothy Hawkins house at 225 Wheeler Street and its exact duplicate, the home at 309 Wheeler Street (Lot 18), were both constructed in about 1927.[45] Almost all of the homes on Mt. Salem Avenue as well as the Washington high school were constructed during this time, through subdivision of Middleton Miller's farm on the west and Bartow Brown's property on the east.

In 1950, a Mr. Barnhill came to the town of Washington as a concession owner for the Keystone Attractions carnival that was performing near the town. Barnhill had first visited the town in 1929. On his return visit, he stated that he "can see very little change in the town."[46]

---

[44] Rappahannock County Deed Book Y, page 30

[45] National Register of Historic Places, 2006 amendment to the 1975 application for the Washington Historic District

[46] *Rappahannock News*, 14 September 1950, reprinted in the 21 February 2019 edition of the newspaper

Chapter 7. Washington in the Later 1900s and the Early 2000s

The Election of an All-Women Town Council

A major event heralded the beginning of the second half of the 20th century, with the election on 13 June 1950 of seven women to serve as the Town Council of Washington. "A revolution occurred in the Old Dominion," according to NBC commentator Morgan Beatty in his coast-to-coast "News Events of the World" broadcast the following evening. Though not a "battle of the sexes," the revolution comprised "an all-woman slate which defeated an all-male ticket" for the offices of mayor and six council members. This, according to Mr. Beatty, constituted "a revolt of the women at Washington, Virginia."

The All-Woman Town Council: Mayor Dorothy Davis and her six co-council members – Elizabeth Racer, Dorothy Hawkins, Louise Price, Achsah Miller, Bobbie Critzer, and Ruby Jenkins. Source: 1950 Colliers Magazine photograph, reprinted in the *Rappahannock News*, 13 March 2014 and 29 November 2018

Elected as mayor was Dorothy Cox Davis, age 28, mother of three children - Mary age 10, George age 9, and Dorothy age 4 - and wife of George H. Davis Jr., an attorney with the Department of Justice. The six council members elected were Achsah Dudley Miller, age 55, mother of two children - Frances age 23 and Louise age 21 - and wife of Clarence Jackson Miller Jr., a banker and farmer; Louise Miller Price, age 55, a teacher and mother of three sons - Daniel age 29, John age 27, and Clarence age 24 - and widow of John W. Price; Robbie Critzer, age 54, mother of one son, J. Wallace age 24, and wife of J.W. Critzer, sheriff of Rappahannock County; Ruby Jenkins, age 30, secretary to the County Agent of Rappahannock County; Nellie Elizabeth Racer, age 26, beauty parlor operator in the town of Washington; and Dorothy B. Hawkins, age 25, mother of one son, Ronald age 3, and wife of Milton M. Hawkins, an employee of the American

Viscose Corporation. All of these women were Rappahannock County natives.[1] They were installed as the Town Council on 1 September 1950.

The election is believed to have evolved from a conversation that included trial justice Brooke M. "Snippy" Miller in which town residents were complaining about conditions in the town, including weeds growing along the streets, trash, dogs running loose, the condition of the fire department, and burned-out street lamps. Indeed, as early as 1892 the *Blue Ridge Guide* newspaper had reported that "The sanitary condition of our town [Washington] is bad and should be attended to at once."[2] When the blame was laid on the all-male town council, someone quipped, "Why not elect women instead?" Judge Miller followed up on this conversation, recruited the seven women, and served as their campaign manager. The women were reticent to run at first, and the all-woman ticket was not completed until three days before the election. By the day of the election, excitement was running high, and 99 out of a possible 122 voters turned out.[3] When the votes were counted, all seven women had been elected. They had defeated the six men who were also on the ballot.[4]

As a result of the election, nationwide publicity was given to the election and to the town of Washington through the press, radio, and television. The inauguration ceremony was covered by representatives of national magazines and news media. The newly-elected women were featured in *Life* magazine and were televised on WBAL's newsreel, "Women in the News," which was carried on almost all east coast television stations. The *Evening Star* newspaper in Washington, D.C. carried the story on its front page with the headline "Women sweep men from all offices in town council vote." Most of the leading daily newspapers in the nation carried the story including, for example, those in Washington, New York, Philadelphia, St. Louis, and Kansas City. Locally Dr. John Snead, a county physician, erected a sign at Washington's corporate limits: "Caution, You are now entering She-Town." It was reported that some men forbade their wives from setting foot in the town, fearing they might get "uppity" ideas.[5]

The town in the 1950s has been described by town resident Fran Eldred, grand-daughter of J.E. Thornton who purchased the Dear's Hotel in 1903: "The Town was dead, I mean everything but grass growing up in the streets, houses unpainted. It was a disaster area. When I left here to go away to school, I swore

---

[1] Program for the installation of the all-women town council, 1 September 1950
[2] *Blue Ridge Guide*, 29 September 1892
[3] Elisabeth B. and C.E. Johnson Jr., *Rappahannock County, Virginia, A History*, Green Publishers, Orange, VA, 1981, p. 142
[4] Program for the installation of the all-women town council, 1 September 1950
[5] *Rappahannock News*, 29 November 2018

I'd never come back."[6] However, the all-women Town Council, over the next several years, accomplished a great deal to improve the quality of the town such as planting dogwood trees, replacing burnt-out street lights, and efficiently dispatching stray dogs and waist-high weeds along the town's streets. Prior to their election, trash accumulating in the town's alleys was picked up once a month by horse and wagon; the women saw to it that collection was modernized with trucks and increased to three loads monthly. They also freed the town water system from a long-held debt, repaired the reservoir, and enacted the town's first zoning ordinance.[7] Women dominated the Town Council for many years thereafter. The mayor's salary was $10 per month; that of council members was $5 per month.

Items from the Minutes of the All-Women Washington Town Council Meetings, 1953-1958

The Town Council instituted an annual "Clean-Up Week" in April of each year for the purpose of collecting and disposing of trash in the streets and alleys, trimming trees, cutting weeds, and stimulating private property owners to "clean-up/paint-up/fix-up." A committee was formed to address the burned-out lights and a man was hired to keep the streets clean and the weeds down. Laws were passed designed to keep stray dogs off the streets, mileage signs were installed, and the Civil War monument was repaired. The Council created a finance committee to study town expenses and drafted a budget each year. In 1953, town income came primarily from Alcoholic Beverage Control Board receipts and a tax on sale of Rappahannock National Bank stock shares (80 cents per $100); this income amounted to $1,831. Town expenses were for cutting weeds, trash removal, street cleaning, water rent, electricity, and the mayor's salary of $60; these expenses amounted to $1,413. In 1954, the five fire hydrants in the town were painted bright red, a resolution was sent to Richmond opposing integration, and the speed limit through the town was changed to 35 mph. In 1955 a town booklet was prepared with drawings and maps by Christine Johnston and text by Alice Verner and Ruby Jenkins, the telephone company agreed to place a telephone booth in the town, the Virginia Department of Transportation resurfaced the streets in the town, yellow lines were painted to deter people from parking in front of stores and houses, eight public benches were placed in the town, and the alley adjacent to the Merrill Motor Company, which was unsightly and full of old cars and discarded tires, was cleared. In 1956, an evergreen tree was planted near the Rappahannock National Bank to serve as the town Christmas tree; there was much discussion given to the idea of trying to encourage industries to come to the town as a means of providing employment,

[6] Quoted from Tim Sayles, "Virginia's Little Washington," *Mid-Atlantic Country Magazine*, December 1988, page 22

[7] Town of Washington Comprehensive Plan, 1986, page 7; Laura A. Matthews, *A Ramble through Rappahannock*, Scribblers Inc., Warrenton, page 8

increasing revenue, and enlarging the population of the town; there was considered to be a severe problem of traffic from tourists driving through the town. In 1957 a lease was established with Mr. A.H. Keyser to permit the town trash to be deposited at the dump on his property; this lease was extended through 1961. In April 1958, the Rappahannock County Board of Supervisors requested that the Town of Washington move its flagpole to the center of the courthouse grounds so that a Confederate flag could be placed near the Confederate monument; this request was granted unanimously by the Town Council.

The Town Budget

A television commentary by Bill Monroe in August 1975 noted that the federal government, facing a $70 billion deficit, might take a lesson from the town of Washington: "The town council has set a tentative budget for next year of $9,157, about the same as last year. The spending items range from a high of $1,350 for trash removal and street cleaning to a low of $25 for telephone calls for official business. Mayor Peter Kramer, a cabinet-maker by trade, gets paid $10 per month and other members of the Town Council get $5. But they have to reckon with a Catch 22: if they don't attend the monthly Council meetings, they don't get paid."[8]

By comparison, the Town Council approved the town's budget for FY 2019 that totaled $852,250, with town expenses being $364,700, Washington Water Works being $112,050, and the Washington Wastewater system being $375,500.[9] Much of the town's income is from its meals and lodging tax. This is set at 2.5%, whereas the county's is 4.5%. Other income is from water and sewer usage fees and sewer connection fees.

Businesses in the Town

There were few businesses in the town in the 1950s. T.C. Lea operated his Lea Brothers Store in a building he had constructed on Lot 27, fronting on Gay Street, in 1935.[10] He came from a family of storekeepers, including his father J. P. Lea and his two uncles W. B. Lea and L. L. Lea. T.C. Lea operated his store until his death in 1957, after 38 years of doing mercantile business in the town. His widow continued the business until 1964 and then sold it to her son T. Carlyle Lea Jr. who was an attorney and judge for the Rappahannock County Court.[11] On 19 December 1968 an IGA food store opened in the building; the store was operated by Mr. and Mrs. Wayne Sophia.[12] However, this enterprise was short-lived; the

---

[8] *Rappahannock News*, 28 August 1975

[9] Minutes of the Washington Town Council, May 2018

[10] *Rappahannock News*, 3 March 1966, quoted in the 26 July 2018 edition of the newspaper; National Register of Historic Places application for the Washington Historic District, 2006

[11] *Rappahannock News*, 3 March 1966, quoted in the 26 July 2018 edition of the newspaper

[12] *Rappahannock News*, 12 December 1968, quoted in the 20 April 2017 edition of the newspaper

building housing the store and the contents of the building were sold at public auction in 1970.[13] The concrete block building constructed in 1955 on the southern part of Lot 14 was used by the W.A. Miller-John Caskie Real Estate Firm on the south side of the building and the Washington Post Office, from April 1956 to 1981, on the north side. The Rappahannock County Health Department was also located in the building and, later, Mrs. John M. Barber Jr. opened a beauty shop in the building.[14] The Washington Cash Store was located on Lot 6 and was the town's all-purpose general merchandise store established in 1946, where you could buy anything from a pair of gum boots to a sirloin steak.

The Washington Cash Store. Photo from the Friends of the Former Washington Cash Store website

Fran Eldred, granddaughter of J.E. Thornton who purchased the Dear's Hotel in 1903, had left the town in the 1950s vowing never to return to the town she grew up in, which she described as "a disaster area." However, she returned with her husband and three children in 1975 to launch the business named the Washington House of Reproductions, selling custom lighting, gifts, and antiques in the old mercantile shop on Lot 8. Eldred became a magistrate in Rappahannock County in 1976 and was Chief Magistrate of the Twentieth Judicial Circuit Court for 10 years until her retirement in 1995.[15] In her estimation, Washington was beginning to recover from its malaise in the late 1970s. Eldred credited the business upturn to the opening of an antiques shop and then The Country Store, which sold antiques, crafts, food, and country items in the building on Lot 24 on

[13] Auction sale advertised in *Rappahannock News*, 12 February 1970; plat recorded in Deed Book 80, page 631, 9 January 1964
[14] *Rappahannock News*, 12 April 1956
[15] *Rappahannock News*, 15 November 1995

the northeast corner of Main and Middle streets that had been her grandfather's garage.[16]

Merrill's garage converted in the late 1960s to the Washington Antiques store. Photo courtesy of the Inn at Little Washington

Also in the town in the 1970s the Fodderstack Pottery on Lot 7 containing the studio and showroom of June Jordan; the Merrill Motor Company on Lot 9, a Ford sales and service station; Nature's Foods and Ice House Crafts on Lot 12, selling homemade bread, gifts, furniture, and Christmas decorations; the Washington House Sandwich Shoppe on Lot 24, and the Cherry Tree and Hatchet restaurant on Lot 25.[17] On Lot 27 were the Rush River Company selling antiques, clocks, artisan ware, natural foods and a wide range of regional crafts; Country Cupboards owned by Gene Lyman, who had moved to the town from Alexandria, Virginia and who reproduced period furniture, restored antiques, and created custom built cabinets and furniture; and Jenkins Auction House which carried antiques and used furniture and held auctions on the 2nd and 4th Thursdays each month. Washington Antiques on Warren Avenue sold antiques, collectibles, and bric-a-brac, and Peter Kramer, cabinetmaker, was located on Lot 31.[18] In 1973, Kramer had purchased the old apple packing building constructed by F. Downing Wood in the 1920s, renovated the building, and converted it to be used as a business office for his building

---

[16] Quoted from Tim Sayles, "Virginia's Little Washington," *Mid-Atlantic Country Magazine*, December 1988, page 22

[17] Daphne Hutchinson and Theresa Reynolds, *On the Morning Side of the Blue Ridge*, a compilation of articles published in the *Rappahannock News* in 1983, page 22

[18] 1976 Washington Business Council flyer, Rappahannock Historical Society files

company and as a shop for his original woodworking creations and furniture restoration.[19] Many of these businesses continued into the 1980s.[20]

Peter Kramer became renowned in the town of Washington for his exquisite renovation and restoration of town buildings, including Thornton's garage, the Clopton House, the dependencies to the Clopton House, the Jones mercantile building, the Packing Shed, the IGA store, the Geneva Welch Gallery, and the Gay Street Inn and initiating the process of designating the town as an Historic District while he was mayor of the town. In 1979, the Rappahannock League for Environmental Protection awarded him with their "Conservation Award for 1979."[21]

L.V. Merrill, owner and operator of Merrill Motor Company, was a legend in his time. With his trademark stubby unlit cigar protruding from the corner of his mouth, he was a permanent fixture sitting behind the plate glass windows of his motor company. Along with his cars, he dealt in "helping hands." For every person who purchased an automobile from him, there were probably two more who received assistance of some kind from this good Samaritan. For example, back when a family was lucky to have a car, Merrill lent automobiles for people to use if tragedy struck such as sickness and especially a death in the family.[22] His daughter said, "My father was so conscientious. If a truck was loaded with apples but was having mechanical problems, he would stay there till 3 or 4 o'clock in the morning and personally work on the truck for it to be ready to go. For out-of-state people, if he didn't have the parts to repair their cars, I was sent to DC to pick up parts and the people stayed with us until they got repaired and went on their way."[23]

Business activities in the 1980s and 1990s included Country Heritage Antiques and Crafts which sold many regional craft items including quilted pillows, patchwork pieces, dried flower arrangements, and handmade pottery. Charles and Fran Eldred continued their successful business Washington House of Reproductions through a contract with Oklahoma State University to create reproduction gas lighting fixtures.[24] The building where Merrill's car dealership was located was purchased by Werner Krebser, M.D., in 1979, and he renovated the building and rented it to four businesses – Nature's Foods, Hayseed Antiques, the Beauty Box, and photographer Pali Carolyn Delevitt.[25] Douglas Baumgardner purchased the building located on the southern part of Lot 14 in

---

[19] *Rappahannock News*, 15 February 1973, quoted in the 24 January 2019 edition of the newspaper
[20] *The New York Times*, 12 June 1983; *Southern Living magazine*, 1986
[21] Personal communication from Peter Kramer, 2019
[22] *Rappahannock News*, 12 April 1979, quoted in the 29 November 2018 edition of the newspaper
[23] Recollections of Marilyn Merrill Bailey in an interview conducted by the Rappahannock League for Environmental Protection, 2018
[24] *Rappahannock News*, 1 July 1982
[25] Rappahannock County Deed Book 133, page 607; *Rappahannock News*, 26 November 2015

1982 for his law office and added ground and upper levels in the rear. Dr. W. Neal Mayberry of Luray opened a dental office in the rear ground level on 3 June 1982, seeing patients on Thursdays.[26] In 1987, the rear lower level was the site of Washington Video Rentals, owned by Susan Kauffman and Rae Haase, which sold and rented video tapes. Formerly in the old Apple Packing Shed on Lot 31, Mostly Yesteryear relocated for business in the Clopton House on Lot 26 as a two-room shop filled with quality mahogany and walnut furniture from the mid-1800s, Oriental rugs, unusual glassware and porcelain, and nostalgic collectibles. Also located in the Clopton House was the Rappahannock County Health Department, the realty firm of Eileen Day, and the Rappahannock Mental Health Clinic, the county's first full-time mental health facility.[27] The business called Country Heritage, managed by Nan Thomasson, was also located here. In 1991 Piedmont Fine Arts opened in the Clopton House; this business sold an eclectic mix of painting, photography, sculpture, and furniture. Ochs Delikatessen (sometimes called the "Ochs Box") was also located on Lot 26. A bookstore called Cabin Fever Books was established in June Jordon's former pottery shop on Lot 7, and the Rush River Company on Lot 27 also sold books; featured in these bookstores in 1995 was "The Rappahannock River," by Walter Nicklin, who was later to become publisher of the *Rappahannock News*.[28]

Photo courtesy of Peter Kramer 1

Edmund Kavanagh opened his shop titled Jewelry by Kavanagh in the log cabin on Lot 27 in 1997.[29] The craft and antique store named Rare Finds was located in a house on Lot 41, and in the early 1990s Mountainside Market was located there. This shop sold gourmet and natural foods including a wide assortment of specialties from fruit juices and vitamins to kitchen gadgets and toiletries and imported and Virginia wines.

---

[26] *Rappahannock News*, 27 May 1982
[27] *Rappahannock News*, 3 August 1978 and 4 February 1988
[28] *Rappahannock News*, 1 March 1995
[29] *Rappahannock News*, 17 December 1997

Over time, many businesses relocated out of the town or went out of business. The Washington Cash Store which had existed on Lot 6 since 1946 was closed in 1988, renovated, and leased to the Rappahannock County Health Department, with three apartments upstairs.[30] Lot 7 formerly housing June Jordan's pottery business was converted to overnight accommodations for guests of the Inn at Little Washington.[31] The Inn's gift shop on Lot 8 was created from the building that had been Mrs. Coxe's Tavern and then Dear's Hotel and then Washington House, together with the adjacent mercantile building of John Jett that had become the Washington House of Reproductions.[32] Merrill's car dealership on Lot 9 became the Country Cafe and the U.S. Post Office. On Lot 24, the Country Store (formerly Thornton's and then Merrill's garage) became the restaurant of the Inn at Little Washington and the adjacent Washington House Sandwich Shoppe was destroyed by fire. Multiple small businesses had existed on the western part of Lot 25 including the Cherry Tree and Hatchet restaurant,[33] the Washington Cafe, and a gas station; these buildings were cleared to make way for the Trinity Church parking lot in 1962.[34] Businesses that had been located in the Clopton House on Lot 26 ceased when the building was converted to overnight lodging for Inn guests and renamed "The Parsonage."[35] The building housing the Rush River Company and, later, the Stoneyman Gourmet Farmer on Lot 27 fronting on Gay Street was converted to the Gay Street Gallery and the studio of Kevin Adams.[36] The small log building on the northwestern part of Lot 27 that had housed Country Heritage Antiques and Crafts and Edmunds Jewelry shop was converted to a real estate office. Gene Lyman's cabinet and restoration shop on the southwestern part of Lot 27 was converted to the offices of the *Rappahannock News*.

The T.C. Lea building on Lot 27 which had briefly housed an IGA food store became the Washington Arts Building in the 1990s. The property had been purchased by Peter Kramer who added 1½ stories to the building and remodeled the interior. It contained several businesses: Peter Kramer, cabinetmaker, who created hand-crafted furniture; Talk of the Town, a shop filled with imaginative gifts and accessories, such as hand-crafted jewelry and puppets; The Buyers Agency, which specialized in representing the buyers in real estate transactions; Minuteman Printers, the Washington office of Bob Naylor Sales & Graphics;

---

[30] *Rappahannock News*, 4 February 1988; in June 2019 the Rappahannock County Health Department was moved from 491 Main Street to Dr. Jerry Martin's former medical office at 338-A Gay Street (*Rappahannock News*, 27 June 2019)

[31] Rappahannock County Deed Book 230, page 372

[32] Rappahannock County Instrument 020000388; *Washington Post*, 16 October 2002

[33] Daphne Hutchinson and Theresa Reynolds, *On the Morning Side of the Blue Ridge*, a compilation of articles published in the *Rappahannock News* in 1983, page 22

[34] Photograph and caption for the western part of Lot 25, *Rappahannock News*, 13 December 1962, reprinted in the 4 September 2008 edition of the newspaper

[35] Rappahannock County Instrument 120000273

[36] Rappahannock County Instrument 150000150 and Instrument 150000328

Tree Works, the office of forester and arborist Lyt Wood offering all kinds of tree care; and Hospitality Design, which designed commercial interiors for hotels and restaurants. Mazie's Daisies, a full-service florist shop managed by Patricia Bartholomew, opened in the lower level of the building in 1998.[37] The property was sold in 2015 to 311 Gay Street LLC (attorney Mark Allen and journalist John McCaslin, editor of *The Rappahannock News*).[38] Businesses in the building in 2018 were the restaurant Tula's Off Main, the realty firm of Rappahannock Real Estate Resources Inc., owned by Louis G. (Butch) Zindel, several telework "virtual" offices, and the Rappahannock County Zoning office, the Building Inspector's office, and the Emergency Services office.

The Rappahannock National Bank on Lot 29 was moved out of town in 2003 and the building became the site of several law offices. The Washington Fire Department was located in the adjacent building on Gay Street until the 1970s; it became the offices of the Commonwealth Attorney and the Rappahannock County Attorney. On Lot 31 the old Packing Shed Gallery deteriorated and in 2018 housed only the business JPC Designs Woodworking. The First Washington Museum, on the west part of Lot 31, was dismantled and abandoned. The craft and antique store called Rare Finds was located in a frame house on Lot 41, and in the early 1990s Mountainside Market was located there. In 1998 the house and land were sold to Trinity Episcopal Church;[39] the Church converted the house to the church office, "Trinity House."

New businesses came into town, many of them appealing to tourists and to the clients of the Inn at Little Washington, such as the high-end stores on Main Street including "Wine Loves Chocolate" on Lot 10, "R. H. Ballard Shop and Gallery" on Lot 11, and Little Washington Spa on Lot 13; the shop Rare Finds returned to town on Lot 14. A list of businesses in the town in 2018 is contained in Appendix 7.

In December 2018, the *Rappahannock News* awarded the honor of Citizen of the Year to Louis G. (Butch) Zindel, a real estate broker and builder who owns Rappahannock Real Estate LLC located on Gay Street in the town.[40]

Restaurants and Lodging

A few restaurants existed in the town in the 1970s and 1980s. Charles and Frances Eldred operated a restaurant in Washington House on Lot 8; Frances was the daughter of Edna (Thornton) Walker and the granddaughter of John Edward and Margaret Thornton who established "Washington House" in the tavern

---

[37] *Rappahannock News*, 11 November 1998, quoted in the 26 July 2018 edition of the newspaper
[38] Rappahannock County Instrument 100000095 and Instrument 150000856
[39] Rappahannock County Instrument 980001684
[40] *Rappahannock News*, 20 December 2018, p. A1

constructed by Anne Coxe. Breakfast and lunch were served Monday through Saturday at Nature's Foods and Cafe located first on Lot 12 and then on Lot 9. The Black Kettle Motel off of Warren Avenue served food on Thursday through Sunday from 11am to 9pm. In 1978, the Inn at Little Washington was established as a new restaurant in the Country Store building on Lot 24, and this grew to become an internationally recognized establishment drawing patrons from around the world.[41] A series of short-lived restaurants occupied the southern part of the brick building on Lot 9 from March 1985 to December 1989. These were the Brambles Cafe, operated by John and Ilene Shipman; a renovated Brambles Cafe operated by Richard and Elaine Vigurie, who lived on Gay Street, serving "good healthy food" under the management of Mel Davis; and the Village Cafe managed by Marque and Ann Kolack and Lois and Arthur Neufeld.[42] Finally, in December 1989 the restaurant was reopened as The Country Cafe managed by David Huff.[43] In the 1990s the Cherry Tree and Hatchet restaurant was located on Lot 25 and Ochs Delikatessen (sometimes called the "Ochs Box") was located on Lot 26.

In 2018, there were four restaurants in the town. These were the Inn at Little Washington on Lot 24, the Country Cafe on Lot 9, Tula's Off Main which was opened on Lot 27 on Gay Street by Mark Allen and John McCaslin, and the Foster Harris House Bed & Breakfast on Lot 16 which served five-course dinners on weekends to its overnight guests as well as to the public in a 10-seat dining room.

There was no commercial lodging in the town before the 1970s except at Washington House on Lot 8 and at the Black Kettle Motel east of town on Warren Avenue. However, the many tourists coming through the town on their way to Shenandoah National Park created a huge need for overnight lodging. Edna Walker, owner of Washington House, recollected that "This was a tourist town. We had hordes of people coming out to see Skyline Drive. Every house in town but three took tourists. Everybody in town was in business."[44] The nature of commercial lodging changed in the 1980s when three bed and breakfast establishments were created – the Foster-Harris House, the Gay Street Inn, and Heritage House;[45] in 2014, Heritage House was sold and renamed The White Moose Inn.[46] In 1984-1985, the Inn at Little Washington renovated the second floor of the main Inn building and opened its first guest rooms in what had once been a basketball court and movie theater. Two bi-level suites were created on

---

[41] See Chapter 10 for the history of the Inn at Little Washington

[42] *Rappahannock News*, 28 March 1985, 22 May 1986, and 10 December 1987

[43] *Rappahannock News*, 7 December 1989

[44] Recollections of Edna Walker and her daughter Francis Eldred, owners of "Washington House", in Daphne Hutchinson and Theresa Reynolds, *On the Morning Side of the Blue Ridge*, a compilation of articles published in the *Rappahannock News* in 1983, page 51

[45] Tim Sayles, "Virginia's Little Washington," *Mid-Atlantic Country Magazine*, December 1988, p.22; *Rappahannock News*, 19 April 1984

[46] Rappahannock County Instrument 120000812

the top floor of the building in 1986. The Inn created additional lodging by converting the Guy Burke-Byrd Jones house (Lot 39), the Morehouse home (Lot 7), the Carter-Dudley house (Lot 9), and the Jones-Clopton house (Lot 26) to overnight guest rooms. Each of these properties was carefully renovated and restored to meet guidelines of the town's Architectural Review Board and to create buildings that complemented the historic nature of the town. In 1994, the home constructed by Middleton Miller was purchased by Mary Ann Kuhn, who converted the residence into a bed and breakfast establishment and renamed it The Middleton Inn.[47] This Inn has received AAA's Four Diamond Award, and the building is listed on the Virginia Landmarks Register.

Buildings in the Town

A number of buildings have been constructed since 1950. These include the buildings housing the Geneva Welch Gallery at 341 Main Street, Wine Loves Chocolate at 353 Main Street, the Little Washington Spa at 261 Main Street, Rare Finds at 211 Main Street, the Theater at Washington Virginia at 291 Gay Street, the CenturyLink telephone building at 320 Gay Street, the Rappahannock Medical Clinic at 338 Gay Street, the Department of Social Services at 354 Gay Street, Country Places Realty at 360 Gay Street, and the Inn's Claiborne House at 456 Gay Street. It also includes a vacant building at 249 Main Street, a 6-unit apartment building at 233 Main Street, the Buntin home at 191 Main Street, the small brick house on Lot 32, the log home at 171 Gay Street, the home owned by Skippy Giles at 532 Gay Street, the Comp home at 639 Main Street, and the Rappahannock County Clerk's office at 238 Gay Street.[48]

Some of the homes that existed in 1950 have been converted to commercial establishments or other nonresidential uses. These include the Morehouse home on Lot 7, the Carter-Dudley home on Lot 9, the Clopton House on Lot 26, and the Byrd Jones house on Lot 39, which were converted to overnight lodging by the Inn at Little Washington. Others are the Compton home on Lot 16 which became the Foster-Harris House bed and breakfast; the Oden home on Lot 22, the Lillard-Sisk home on Lot 23, and the Bywaters-Verner house on Lot 24 which were purchased by the Inn; the Mary Lea residence on Lot 27 which housed the *Rappahannock News* offices in 2018; the Phelbert Green home on Lot 41 which became the offices for Trinity Church; and the home on Lot 48 which became the Gay Street Inn.

Since 1950, there has also been renovation of many buildings in the town, both by businesses and by private homeowners. The Town estimated that $12-$14 million had been spent on renovation of up to 35 buildings in the town.[49] Some

---

[47] Rappahannock County Deed Book 189, page 537 (plat), and Deed Book 208, page 582 (deed)
[48] National Register of Historic Places for the Washington Historic District, 2006 Update
[49] Town of Washington Comprehensive Plan, 2017, page 16

of these were buildings owned by the Inn at Little Washington and the Clopton House LLC and included the main Inn building (formerly a garage and the Country Store on Lot 24), the Inn Tavern Shops (formerly Mrs. Coxe's tavern on Lot 8), The Parsonage (formerly the home of James Brereton Jones and his descendants on Lot 26), The Claiborne House (formerly the site of the home of Guy Burke on Lot 39), and the Carter House (formerly the home of the family by this name on Lot 9). Two large homes that were renovated by their owners were Mount Prospect and Avon Hall. These renovations were guided by the Historic District Ordinance and the Architectural Review Board.

The Town conducted an inventory of buildings in the town for the 2017 Comprehensive Plan. It was estimated that there were 45 owner-occupied units, 9 vacant residential units, 28 rental units, 50 commercial units, and 7 vacant lots. In 2010, the estimated household size for owner-occupied homes was 1.74 and that for rental dwellings was 1.92.[50]

The Washington Post Office

From about 1910 until 1956, the two-story frame building on the northeast corner of Main and Jett streets housed the Washington Post Office. In 1955, Lot 14 at the northwest corner of Main and Porter streets was sold to W. Arthur Miller, and in April 1956 the Washington Post Office was relocated to a new cinderblock building that Miller constructed on the southern part of this lot.[51] The Post Office was housed in the northern part of the new building, with the W.A. Miller-John Caskie Real Estate Firm on the south side.[52] Miller was the postmaster at that time.[53] A mailbox was requested by the Town to be located outside the Post Office.[54] In about 1961, Carol Miller became Washington's postmaster; she retired in April 1991 after 30 years in this position.[55] In 1981 the Washington post office was relocated from Lot 14 to the northern part of the brick building on Lot 9 at the southwest corner of Main and Middle streets (389B Main Street)[56] and remained there through 2018. Lot 9 was sold by Werner Krebser to Patrick O'Connell and Reinhardt Lynch in 1992.[57]

In 2018, the U.S. Postal Service announced that the Washington Post Office, which had been located in the town of Washington since at least 1804, would be moved to a site on Route 211 between Bank Road and Schoolhouse Road.[58] Attempting to keep the post office within the town, the Town Council passed a

---

[50] Town of Washington Comprehensive Plan, 2017, page 27-28
[51] Rappahannock County Deed Book 64, page 299; Minutes of the Washington Town Council, March 1956
[52] *Rappahannock News*, 12 April 1956
[53] *Sunday Star, Washington D.C.*, 20 May 1956, page A-15
[54] Minutes of the Washington Town Council, March 1955
[55] *Rappahannock News*, 4 April 1991
[56] Personal communication from Carol Miller, former postmistress, 2018
[57] Rappahannock County Deed Book 193, page 199
[58] *Rappahannock News*, 6 September and 13 September 2018

resolution in December 2018 authorizing sale of a half-acre property on Warren Avenue at Leggett Lane to Mid Atlantic Postal Properties, which proposed to build the postal facility and lease it to the Postal Service.[59]

Newspapers Serving the Town and the County

Until 1936, George Cary had published *The Blue Ridge Guide* newspaper in a small frame building fronting on Main Street adjacent to Cary's home on Lot 11. This newspaper was the successor to the original *Rappahannock News*, published in 1877-1878; *The Blue Ridge Echo*, published in 1878-1882; and *The Call*, published in about 1883-1885.[60] Publication of *The Blue Ridge Guide* ceased in 1936 because of Cary's poor health and there was no local newspaper until 1949, when Lucy Catherine Bowie and Bruce Bowie started publishing the *Rappahannock News*. Their office was located on the western part of Lot 25 at the southeast corner of Main and Middle streets. In 1950, Lucy purchased the southern part of Lot 13, which had been the site of the Menefee family home.[61] A plain 1½-story concrete block building was constructed on this land, and this became the *Rappahannock News* office. With the help of their sole employee, John M. Barber, the Bowies brought to their office a used Linotype machine and other equipment purchased in Scottsville, Virginia.[62] In 1956 Lucy sold the business to Madison County Judge Basil Burke.[63] Judge Burke and printer John Barber were joined by R.E. Many and Sarah Latham, the latter of whom was employed by the newspaper for the next 25 years.[64] In 1962, the newspaper was sold to Green Publishers of Orange; in 1972 it was sold to Fauquier Publishing Company; and in 1977 it was sold to Fauquier Times Democrat Company of Warrenton, Virginia, with Arthur Arundel as President. In 2013, the newspaper moved to the 2-story stuccoed building on the northeast corner of Main and Jett streets (309 Jett Street) that had formerly housed the Rappahannock National Bank, the Post Office, a residence, and several businesses. In 2018, the *Rappahannock News* was an independent newspaper, owned by Rappahannock Media, with Dennis Brack as publisher and journalist John McCaslin as editor.

Sheriff William Buntin

The only recent sheriff of Rappahannock County to live in the town of Washington was William Buntin. In 1950 William A. and Elizabeth Buntin

---

[59] *Rappahannock News*, 13 December 2018, p. A6; discussions about the location of the Washington post office continued into 2019 and finally resulted in development of the half-acre property as the new post office facility (*Rappahannock News*, 15 August 2019)

[60] An excellent history of Rappahannock County's newspapers from 1877 to 1983 can be found in Daphne Hutchinson and Theresa Reynolds, *On the Morning Side of the Blue Ridge*, a compilation of articles published in the *Rappahannock News* in 1983, pages 123-124

[61] Rappahannock County Deed Book 54, page 127

[62] Daphne Hutchinson and Theresa Reynolds, *On the Morning Side of the Blue Ridge*, page 123

[63] Rappahannock County Deed Book 59, page 141 and Deed Book 65, page 68

[64] Daphne Hutchinson and Theresa Reynolds, *On the Morning Side of the Blue Ridge*, page 124

purchased the northern part of Lot 16, containing 0.3445 acre (195 Main Street) and the Buntins built the brick home that is located on the property.[65] William was appointed sheriff of Rappahannock County in 1976 and retired in 1984. There was a tale that errant teenage boys, driving without a license and having managed to acquire beer from a country store, were spotted by Sheriff Buntin. The teenagers took flight and thought they had eluded the sheriff by speeding and taking numerous back roads through the county. However, when the boys arrived home a few hours later they found Sheriff Buntin waiting for them on their front porch. Some Rappahannock County men recall that the worst fear of their miscreant youth was to be apprehended by Buntin and then be hauled before Judge Rayner Snead at the courthouse. Elizabeth taught at the high school, was a social worker for 33 years, served as director of Rappahannock County Social Services, authored the scripts for the Trinity Church house tours, and wrote a book on the history of Bromfield Parish."[66] After William's death, Elizabeth and their daughter Nancy continued to live in the family home on Main Street. In 2018, she had lived in the town of Washington for 68 years and she celebrated her 102nd birthday with her daughter Nancy on 1 November 2018.

Activities, Entertainment, and Recreation

In 1946, Harold C. Geest and his wife Hester, residents of Culpeper County, had acquired town Lot 14 at the northwest corner of Porter and Main streets.[67] There were no buildings on the lot, and in 1951 Geest leased the western part of the lot to the Town of Washington for use as a recreation area for a period of five years.[68] The town's playground equipment had been stored in the basement of Lea's store on Lot 27, and it was reinstalled on the leased land.[69] The playground was located on this property until 1956 when Geest sold the property to W. Arthur Miller.[70]

The building on town Lot 11 on the northwest corner of Main and Jett streets also provided recreational facilities. It had been built in the 1930s and contained a pool room serving beer in the basement. The private Rappahannock Club had Saturday night dances, dancing lessons, and children's parties on the main floor. There were apartments on the second floor.[71] Another place for entertainment was the fire hall; in 1954, the Town Council agreed to let teenagers use this building for parties.[72] It was also reported in 1983 that "locals hung out on

---

[65] Rappahannock County Deed Book 54, page 250

[66] *Rappahannock News*, 8 November 2018; M. Elizabeth Buntin, *Mission: A Study of the Churches of Bromfield Parish*, files of Trinity Episcopal Church

[67] Rappahannock County Deed Book 48, page 20

[68] Rappahannock County Land Books showed no dollar value for buildings; Rappahannock County Deed Book 56, page 448

[69] Minutes of the Washington Town Council, November 1958 and May 1962

[70] Rappahannock County Deed Book 64, page 229

[71] Elisabeth B. and C.E. Johnson Jr., *Rappahannock County, Virginia, A History*, Green Publishers, Orange, VA, 1981, p. 144

[72] Minutes of the Washington Town Council, October 1954

weekends at the Washington Cash Store, the town's all-purpose general store, where you could buy anything from a pair of gum boots to a sirloin steak."[73] In 1951, a group of people led by attorney George Davis, husband of mayor Dorothy Davis, sponsored the summer music concert of the Blue Ridge Musical Festival Association at Avon Mill, on Old Mill Road. Over 600 people attended.[74]

The Trinity Episcopal Church women instituted their 2-day fall house tour, dried flower sale, and afternoon tea in 1956. Headquarters for the event were located in the Church's parish hall on Gay Street. For many years, this was the only fall event in Rappahannock County and the entire community worked to present the best of Rappahannock County homes. The dried flower sale was discontinued in 2016, but the house tour occurred annually through 2018. Almost 200 homes were showcased during the 62-year tenure of this event.[75] The Church sponsors an annual Halloween party that many hundreds of children attend.

For many years beginning in 1968, William and Ramona Carrigan graciously permitted the lawn in front of their home, Avon Hall, to be used for 4th of July festivities, including an afternoon of fun and games and entertainment and an evening fireworks display.[76] This event was open not only to town residents, but to all who wished to view the celebration of the country's independence. Carrigan was the *Rappahannock News'* "Man of the Year" in 1981. Although he and Ramona were only part-time residents of the town, he gave his second home full-time dedication. He played an instrumental part in creation of the Rappahannock County library and the Rappahannock Historical Society in the 1960s. He purchased the old garage at the northeast corner of Main and Middle streets and restored the building, initiating the revitalization of the town.[77] After the Town of Washington purchased Carrigan's Avon Hall property in 2002,[78] the 4th of July celebration was discontinued for several years and then was recreated by the Sperryville Volunteer Fire Department on Bill Fletcher's field on Route 522 and then on the Ben Venue farm near Route 211.

The town celebrated its bicentennial in December 1996, commemorating 200 years since its establishment in 1796 by the Virginia General Assembly. Many activities occurred, including walking tours of the town, carriage rides through the town, a Christmas Bazaar benefitting the Child Care and Learning Center, a bake sale for the Rappahannock League for Animal Welfare, a parade through the town, the Piedmont String Ensemble presentation, a Toy Soldiers Christmas

---

[73] *The New York Times*, 12 June 1983

[74] Daphne Hutchinson and Theresa Reynolds, *On the Morning Side of the Blue Ridge*, a compilation of articles published in the *Rappahannock News* in 1983, page 51-52

[75] Helen Williams, "The final House Tour," *Rappahannock News*, 4 October 2018

[76] Minutes of the Washington Town Council, July 1968; Rappahannock County Deed Book 169, page 362

[77] *Rappahannock News*, 31 December 1981, quoted in the 24 January 2019 edition of the newspaper.

[78] Rappahannock County Instrument 020001760

musical, a "birthday party" and tree planting ceremony at the Town Hall, and a presentation of the Shepherd's Play at the Ki Theater.[79]

Many social activities were sponsored by the Baptist and Episcopal churches. For example, in February 2010, the Washington Baptist Church sponsored its 14th Annual Variety Show at the Theatre in Washington. A free chili/soup supper at the church preceded the family-oriented show, which included the singing group Immersed and the Church's Praise Team, the Ma and Brother routine, skits, drama, jokes, and youth presentations.[80]

The southwest corner of Jett and Gay streets is the location of The Theatre at Washington, Virginia (291 Gay Street). The theater was constructed by Buford Roy Armel in 1947-1948. It was originally used as a movie theater and also as a venue for community plays by local citizens and schoolchildren. During the early film years, the theater was packed almost every night of the week, hot dogs and hamburgers were sold from what is now the box office, and what is now the office section of the building was an apartment lived in by the building's owner and his family.[81] At that time, the building was segregated; African Americans were permitted only in the balcony and not downstairs.[82] The theater and lot were owned and managed beginning in 1983 by Patricia W. Weinberg.[83] She developed the theater into a venue for a wide variety of musical and dramatic performances, usually on weekends and often for one or two performances only. The Rappahannock Association for the Arts and the Community (RAAC), a local nonprofit volunteer organization promoting local artists, also used the theater before relocating their performance venue to the former Methodist Church building on Lot 43 although the Friday night film series remained in the Theatre. The Theatre became known for its professional musical performances, including the noted Smithsonian at Little Washington chamber music series, and featured many well-known classical instrumental and vocal artists. The Theatre also presented professional chamber music, recitals, jazz, and a variety of other light music, humor and drama. In 2014, Weinberg sold this enterprise to The Theatre at Washington, Virginia LLC (Nancy Raines), which continued the tradition of high-quality performances developed by Weinberg.[84]

The Rappahannock Association for the Arts and the Community (RAAC) was a major force in community-based entertainment. It was a focal point for the arts in Rappahannock County and it fulfilled its mission to create the opportunity for all residents of the County to enrich their lives through exposure to the arts. The

---

[79] *Rappahannock News*, 11 December 1996

[80] *Rappahannock News*, 8 February 2010

[81] Personal communication from Wendy Weinberg, 2019

[82] Recollections of J. Stewart Willis in an interview conducted by the Rappahannock League for Environmental Protection, 2018

[83] Rappahannock County Deed Book 143, page 593

[84] Rappahannock County Instrument 140001081

nucleus of this organization began in 1982 when it sponsored films in the theater located on town Lot 28 on Gay Street that was then called "The Gay Street Theater." RAAC also sponsored community Christmas celebrations on the courthouse lawn in the 1980s. RAAC grew to became a local nonprofit volunteer organization promoting local artists and presenting such cultural activities as quality films, theater, concerts, poetry readings, and dance. In 1991 the RAAC offices were located in the Packing Shed building on town Lot 31 and the performing venue was the Ki Theater on Lot 43 on Gay Street. This latter building had been the Methodist Church; it was purchased by Rappahannock County in 1990 for use as a public facility.[85] As RAAC developed, the theater became the RAAC Community Theater. In this venue were presented plays, readings, and poetry coffee houses. RAAC also sponsored workshops, dances, programs, concerts, school events, cinema, and other activities that enhanced the community's artistic well-being. A novel event was the presentation of oral biographies by local residents, called "No Ordinary People" which celebrated its 20th anniversary in 2018.[86] RAAC also sponsored the "First Friday Movie" at the Theatre at Little Washington, featuring recent films; the "Second Friday Talk" at the Rappahannock County library, with guest speakers on a variety of topics; the Fall Art Tour of the Artists of Rappahannock; and Soup and Soul, a monthly potluck dinner where artists discussed their work. RAAC was given money through a bequest by Claudia Mitchell in 2011, and this fund served as the organization's primary channel for offering financial support to the arts in Rappahannock County. As of June 2018, the Claudia Mitchell Fund had given away $209,000 in grants to 56 different artists and organizations in the community.[87]

A new feature occurred in 2016-2018, that of the Inn at Little Washington sponsoring a Saturday morning open-air market in the courtyard next to The Parsonage, where local farmers brought their produce and local artisans displayed their wares. Civic celebration of the Fourth of July returned to the town in 2017 and 2018, when the new owners of Avon Hall -- Bill Fischer and Drew Mitchell -- sponsored a celebration for all on the grounds of their property. Festivities were highlighted by an American Festival Concert, led by conductor John Bourgeois.[88] In September 2018, "Innstock Culinary Festival" was held on the lawn west of the Inn's Tavern Shops. This was an outdoor food and music festival featuring a 'family reunion' of Inn employees over the past 40 years, attended by over 1,000 persons. Former Inn sous chefs returned to cook signature dishes for attendees. There was also live music and fireworks. There was a charge for admission to the festival, but all of the town's residents were granted

[85] Rappahannock County Deed Book 179, page 774
[86] *Rappahannock News*, 20 September 2018
[87] *Rappahannock News*, 2 June 2018
[88] *Rappahannock News*, 30 June 2017

complimentary admission; the Town Council had voted to provide $5,000 to the Inn in support of this event.[89]

The Town's Christmas Celebrations

For many years, the town erected and decorated a town Christmas tree. An elaborate ceremony was held to decorate and light the tree annually.[90] There was also a home decoration contest at this time, with a vigorous competition for the most beautifully decorated house. A Christmas party for children was held in the old Fire Hall building on Gay Street, and carolers walked the streets and rode in wagons serenading the town citizens.[91] During 1980-1985, the Rappahannock Association for Arts and the Community (RAAC) sponsored a community Christmas celebration on the courthouse lawn. This involved decoration and lighting of the town Christmas tree, caroling, cookies and cider at the Gay Street theater, a children's Christmas dance, Christmas plays, and live instrumental music.[92]

Beginning in 1986 the Town government, its citizen Christmas Committee, and the Washington Business Council organized the town's "Colonial Christmas" to celebrate the Christmas holidays by reenacting colonial traditions. The Council was a nonprofit organization dedicated to promoting tourism and business in the town. Many activities occurred for this event during the first weekend of December. These included strolling carolers dressed in colonial costumes, tours of the town by costumed colonial tour guides, colonial dance performances in the Town Hall by women in period ballgowns and men in frock coats accompanied by chamber music, Christmas plays at the theater, craft demonstrations in shops, Santa's Bakeshop, a children's Christmas bazaar and puppet show, Christmas tree trimming on the courthouse lawn, bonfires, a living nativity scene, and colonial meals served at local restaurants.[93] Colonial Christmas dinners were also sometimes served at the Fire Hall, at a cost of $10 for adults and $5 for children. In 2000-2002, candlelight dinners were held at the Washington Baptist Church for a cost of $15 for adults and $5 for children.[94] The Church has also sponsored a Christmas eve candle-lighting service with special music, a time for children, and a retelling of "The Story of Christmas" from the Gospel accounts, concluding with the singing of "Silent Night."[95] In some years, the

---

[89] Minutes of the Washington Town Council, February, April, and May 2018; *Rappahannock News*, special supplement, September 2018; *Rappahannock News*, 6 September 2018

[90] Minutes of the Washington Town Council, December 1963, provides an example of documentation for this

[91] Recollections of Ruby Jenkins and Mrs. Arthur Miller published in *Rappahannock News*, 23 December 1982

[92] *Rappahannock News*, 30 December 1982; *Culpeper Star-Exponent*, 21 December 1984

[93] *Rappahannock News*, 11 December 1986, 1 December 1988, 30 November 1989, 6 December 1990; 2 December 1992; *Culpeper Star-Exponent*, 25 November 1989, 26 November 1990; announcement brochures in the Rappahannock Historical Society files

[94] Colonial Christmas brochures, Rappahannock Historical Society files

[95] *Rappahannock News*, 13 December 2018

Rappahannock County High School Culinary Arts class sponsored a Christmas Sweet Shoppe featuring handmade truffles and Christmas candy at the Town Hall.

In recent years, the Town sponsored its annual Christmas parade through the town, consisting of the United States Army fife and drum corps, vintage automobiles, parade presentations by local businesses and community organizations, and vehicles carrying the Mayor, Town Council and, of course, Santa Claus. The year 2018 was the 14th annual celebration. Local businesses sold hot food and drinks, and stores and shops were open. The Town also sponsored the Town Christmas Party. This was a potluck covered dish dinner and party in the Town Hall, open to all residents and persons who worked in the town and their families.[96]

The Methodist Church

The Methodist Church located on the southeast corner of Gay and Jett streets on Lot 43 was purchased by the Town from the trustees of the Church in 1980.[97] It became the Washington Town Hall. The Washington Fire Department Ladies Auxiliary Thrift Store also operated in the building. However, the building had no heat or restrooms and was used only sporadically. In 1990 the Town sold the lot and building to Rappahannock County for use as a public facility.[98] In the 1990s it became the Ki Theater and then the theater of the Rappahannock Association for the Arts and the Community (RAAC).

The County Library and the Washington Town Hall

The Presbyterian Church on Lot 22 had been unused since the 1890s. The property was purchased in 1939 by Franklin Clyde Baggarly, the owner of the Avon Hall property adjacent to the town and a former attorney for the town.[99] After he was declared incompetent in 1959, his wife Frances Trott Bagggarly sold the eastern part of the lot in 1960 to the trustees of the County Free Library System, who were Q. D. Gasque (who was Superintendent of Public Schools), Elisabeth Johnson, Freer Wilson, T. J. Pillar, and Virginia Miller.[100] William M. Carrigan was elected chairman of the library's Board of Trustees.[101] This group of dedicated Rappahannock County residents rescued the old building and turned it into a public library, which officially opened on 19 September 1963. The town,

[96] Invitations to the Town of Washington Christmas Party, Town files; *Rappahannock News*, 13 December 2018, p. B2

[97] Rappahannock County Deed Book 136, page 710

[98] Rappahannock County Deed Book 179, page 774

[99] Rappahannock County Deed Book 44, page 177

[100] Rappahannock County Chancery Case #2292, Baggarly vs. Baggarly; Rappahannock County Deed Book 71, page 595

[101] *Rappahannock News*, 29 July 1965, reprinted in the 7 February 2019 edition of the newspaper

and the County, thus had its first public library. The collection of books was accrued primarily by donations, and the library was initially open to patrons on Wednesday afternoons between 2pm and 5pm.[102] In 1983 a 100-year time capsule in the shape of a pyramid was constructed by Edward Bailey and installed on the grounds of the library. A sealed copper box containing artifacts and messages was placed in a concrete water-tight vault in the stone-faced capsule. The vault was sealed in a special ceremony on July 4, 1983 to be opened on July 4, 2083. The library remained in the old church building until the end of 1990, when it was moved into a newly erected building on Lee Highway just outside of the town.

The building and land were sold by the library Board of Trustees and Rappahannock County to the Town of Washington in 1989[103] and it was converted to serve as the Washington Town Hall, which had been located in the former Washington Methodist Church building on Lot 43 since 1980.[104] Pews from the Methodist church were moved to the building, and ladder-back chairs from an early stage of the Inn at Little Washington were donated to the building.[105] Eve Willis, an interior decorator and spouse of Mayor J. Stewart Willis, created the cushions and draperies for the building.[106] Many books were donated by Mayor John Fox Sullivan to fill the former library shelves. An office for the Town's administrative assistant was created in the former church balcony.

The Rappahannock Historical Society

In 1964, over fifty people met at the Rappahannock County courthouse to organize the Rappahannock Historical Society. Judge Raynor Snead chaired the meeting, and William Carrigan and Dorothy Davis helped run the meeting and explain the reasons for the formation of the Society.[107] In 1965, the Virginia Telephone and Telegraph Company was occupying a very old building on town Lot 43 that had been one of the outbuildings to the Baggarly manor house. This brick two-story building is believed to be one of the earliest brick structures in the town of Washington. The Telephone Company planned to raze the building, but Carrigan argued that it should be preserved and the Company agreed to give it to the Rappahannock Historical Society, providing that the building be moved. There was no lot to move onto, so they agreed to donate 2250 square feet of their land to the Society in 1965.[108] Shortly thereafter, a moving contractor was engaged, a basement dug, foundation poured, and the building was placed on the

---

[102] *Rappahannock News*, 19 September 1963, reprinted in the 5 January 2017 edition of the newspaper
[103] Rappahannock County Deed Book 175, page 298, and Deed Book 181, page 454
[104] Rappahannock County Deed Book 136, page 710
[105] Information from Laura Dodd, the Town's administrative Assistant, 2018
[106] Information from J. Stewart Willis in an interview given to the Rappahannock League for Environmental Protection, 2018
[107] *Rappahannock News*, 15 November 1995
[108] Rappahannock County Deed Book 86, page 519

donated lot, at a cost of $2750 for moving and an additional $2750 for landscaping. In 1974, the building underwent renovation, including repairs to the foundation, roof, and floors at a cost of $7419.[109] In 2000 the building was moved closer to Gay Street and an addition was constructed at the back that approximately doubled the size of the building.

During the 1970s the society was not very active, but when Howard and Helen Holschuh came to the County they were influential in bringing the society back to life.[110] Catherine Knuepfer, Arland Welch, Lucia Kilby, and Misty Hitt were some of the devoted volunteers. Donna Fisher was employed as an administrative assistant to manage the society offices and answer historical and genealogical inquiries until her death. After that, Judy Tole became the executive director, with her husband John Tole as president of the Society's board of directors. The Rappahannock Historical Society & Museum building now houses the Society's offices, research library, museum, and gift shop. Many visitors enter the doors of this building to learn more about the town of Washington and about Rappahannock County. The Society collects, preserves, and interprets the unique history and heritage of this area. The museum contains artifacts of the county donated by descendants and benefactors. The gift shop features books, historical maps, memorabilia, and products from Rappahannock County.

An important task of the Society is assisting individuals doing genealogical research. Material on about 1,000 Rappahannock County families has been gathered. Early volunteers abstracted Rappahannock County birth, marriage, and death records, wills, and chancery records to have information readily on hand. Part of the collections are Rappahannock County censuses and a large amount of information on the surrounding counties. The Society's Cemetery Project has investigated graveyards in the county and identified thousands of individuals buried there. The Society also collects and maintains historical information on county churches, schools, houses, mills, businesses, wars, towns, and many other topics. The Society has obtained oral histories from many County residents to supplement published information. Another project of the Society is conducting research on the history of specific homes and properties in the County, tracing the land and its owners back to when Rappahannock was still part of Culpeper County and even back to the original land grants from Thomas Lord Fairfax and King George II. The Society has also undertaken on-line digitization of the Society collections, with visual interface to the digitized information accessible through the Society's website.

---

[109] Elisabeth B. and C. E. Johnson Jr., *Rappahannock County, Virginia, A History*, Orange, VA, Green Publishers, 1981, page 73

[110] *Rappahannock News*, 15 November 1995

The First Washington Museum

This museum was located on the remaining first floor of what had been an old 3-story tavern on Lot 31. When Main Street was widened and paved after World War I, it was necessary to remove both the front porch and the second-story porch of the tavern. Subsequently, the two top floors were also removed, leaving only a single-story structure. The museum was created by Miss Ruby Jenkins in 1975; Ruby had been a member of the all-women Town Council elected in 1950. The museum was filled with her private collections and with donations by Rappahannock County citizens. One room of the museum was a reproduction of an 18th century kitchen, with copper kettles, kerosene lamps, and samplers. Another room was a recreation of one-room schoolhouse, and a third was a large historic room filled with the history of Rappahannock County and the town of Washington.[111] When Ruby died, her heirs disbanded the museum and sold the contents.

The Middle Street Gallery, the Packing Shed Gallery, and the Gay Street Gallery

In 1981 Dan Lewis, a native of Washington D.C., founded a for-profit art gallery featuring local artists in the basement of the Clopton House on town Lot 26. He added picture framing and massage therapy to his art business, which he moved in 1983 to the log building on Middle Street adjacent to the Inn at Little Washington on town Lot 24. The art gallery was not profitable, so in 1987 he converted it to a non-profit artist's cooperative.[112] The Middle Street Gallery celebrated its seventh anniversary on 6 November 1988.[113] It remained in the building through 2013 and featured museum quality painting, photography, and sculpture. In 2014 the Gallery moved out of the building, and the building was occupied by the store called "Antiques At Middle Street." In the winter of 2017-2018, the Middle Street Gallery returned and occupied the back part of the

Drawing by Dan Lewis, 1985.
Rappahannock News, 13 December 2018

[111] The museum was featured in an article in *Southern Living*, February 1978, page 64; *The New York Times*, 12 June 1983; also, an excellent description of the museum can be found in Daphne Hutchinson and Theresa Reynolds, *On the Morning Side of the Blue Ridge*, a compilation of articles published in the *Rappahannock News* in 1983, pages 113-114

[112] *Rappahannock News*, 29 August 1991 and 13 December 2018

[113] *Rappahannock News*, 3 November 1988

Middle Street building.[114] The 24-member artists cooperative celebrated its 35th anniversary in December 2018. It has maintained its non-profit status because all the artists share responsibility and through conducting a variety of community activities including showing the works of talented high school artists, joining with the community in painting a joint canvas, and offering lectures and learning opportunities.[115]

The studio and gallery of local artist Kevin Adams has been situated in two historic buildings. The first was located on the northeastern part of Lot 31 where, in the 1920s, F. Downing Wood had constructed an apple packing facility. Multiple businesses were located in the building subsequently, including serving as the studio for Adams and as the art gallery named "the Packing Shed Gallery." The second historic building was the mercantile store of James Brereton Jones. In 1836, Jones purchased the one-half acre town Lot 26 from his father-in-law and also purchased the northern part of Lot 27.[116] On this property he built his home, which came to be known as the Clopton House when it was inherited by his granddaughter, Annie Washington Jones Clopton.[117] Jones also built a mercantile building on the part of his property that fronted on Gay Street. In 2012-2015, The Clopton House LLC purchased the property and the mercantile building was sold to Bradams Ridge LLC which, after extensive renovation, became the Gay Street Gallery and the studio of Adams.[118]

Medical Facilities

The town had been without a resident physician for many years. This changed in 1974 when Werner Krebser M.D. and Jerry Martin M.D. purchased 0.871 acre consisting of town Lot 42 and part of Lot 43.[119] In that year, Krebser and Martin obtained permission from the Washington Town Council to build a full-time medical clinic on the property and, in January 1975, the new brick building housing the Rappahannock Medical Clinic was opened.[120] It was estimated to have cost $65,000 and was a modern building by town of Washington standards of the time. Martin was born in Unionville in Orange County, grew up in southern Delaware, graduated from the University of Virginia Medical School, and did post-graduate training at the U.S. naval hospital in San Diego. He returned to Virginia to practice medicine at Culpeper Hospital where he met Krebser.[121] In 1999, Krebser retired and Martin became sole owner of the

[114] *Rappahannock News*, November 23, 2017, page A1
[115] *Rappahannock News*, 13 December 2018
[116] Rappahannock County Deed Book C, page 51
[117] Rappahannock County Will Book H, page 378
[118] Rappahannock County Instruments 120000273, 150000150, and 150000328
[119] Rappahannock County Deed Book 87, page 65; Rappahannock County Deed Book 111, page 190
[120] *Rappahannock News*, 9 January 1975, quoted in the 20 January 2019 edition of the newspaper
[121] *Rappahannock News*, 24 January 2019

medical practice at 338-A Gay Street.[122] He was joined in the practice by Dr. John McCue who later established his own practice in a separate facility.[123] In the rear lower level of the Medical Clinic building at 338-B Gay Street was the office of Capital Metro Physical Therapy, Thomas Papke, P.T.

The Washington Historic District

With the widening of the highway through the town in the 1930s, some of the town's historic buildings were severely compromised and were dismantled in the 1940s. These included, for example, the 3-story building housing Clark's Tavern on the original town Lot 31, of which only the first floor was able to be retained, and the Menefee home on Lot 13 which was considered to be one of the most beautiful homes in the town and which had to be demolished. In the 1950s four commercial cinderblock/masonry buildings were constructed on Town Lots 13 and 14 that were uncharacteristic of the historic buildings in the town. These events may have been the beginning of an awareness by residents and the Town Council of the special historic nature of the town. As a result, efforts began to recognize and preserve the Town's historic buildings.[124]

In the 1970s Peter Kramer, then mayor of the Town, held discussions with the Virginia Historic Landmarks Commission about designating the Town as a historic district.[125] This came to fruition on 15 April 1975 when the "Washington Historic District" was listed on the Virginia Landmarks Register and on 28 May 1975, when the "Washington Historic District" was listed on the National Register of Historic Places.[126] The National Register, established in 1966, is the U.S. government's official list of districts, sites, buildings, structures, and objects deemed worthy of preservation for their historical significance. In both the Virginia Register and the National Register, the Washington Historic District encompassed the entire town and many properties were considered as contributing to the historic nature of the town, but no individual building was so designated.

On 14 August 1985, the Town Council passed a Historic District Ordinance and created an Architectural Review Board with the stated purpose of protecting the style and historic character of the town, to help protect and maintain the

[122] Rappahannock County Instrument 990000074

[123] *Rappahannock News*, 27 January 1999; Martin retired from active medical practice in early 2019; in June 2019 the Rappahannock County Health Department was moved from 491 Main Street to Martin's former medical office at 338-A Gay Street (*Rappahannock News*, 27 June 2019)

[124] Town of Washington Comprehensive Plan, 2017, page 5

[125] Minutes of the Washington Town Council, 11 March 1975

[126] Calder Loth, editor, *The Virginia Landmarks Register*, University Press of Virginia, Charlottesville, 1986, page 358; dhr.virginia.gov/historic-registers/322-0011/ and nps.gov/nr

architectural integrity of the historic district, and to restore and preserve the architectural structures in the town.[127]

In July 2004 the Washington Town Council approved funding for a survey of the town's buildings in response to prior questions about the validity of its Historic District Ordinance.[128] The study cost $20,000 and was conducted by Cheryl H. Shepherd of Millennium Preservation Services in Warrenton, Virginia. She toured the town with officials from the Virginia Department of Historic Resources, and they concluded that the town had great historically significant architecture and strong historic associations.[129] Shepherd's findings led to a reapplication for the Washington Historic District. On 6 September 2006, the Virginia Historic Landmarks Commission again recognized the historic significance of the Town by approving an amendment to the town's Historic District designation. This amendment extended the period of historic significance to 1945 and included many additional buildings located within the corporate limits of the town and constructed up to that year. The National Register of Historic Places was also updated, on 21 November 2006.[130]

Over time, many of the town's neglected building have been rescued from deterioration in an effort to preserve the town's early character. Private owners, the Inn at Little Washington LLC, and the Clopton House LLC have spent millions of dollars renovating properties within the town and returning them to the beauty and character of their origins.

Rechartering of the Town by the Virginia General Assembly, 1985

The Town of Washington was rechartered by the Virginia General Assembly on 14 March 1985.[131] The new town charter had been drawn up by the Washington Town Council in 1984.[132]

1985 SESSION

Virginia Acts of Assembly - Chapter 172

An Act to provide a charter for the Town of Washington, in the County of Rappahannock and to repeal Chapter 226 of the Acts of Assembly of 1893-94, which provided a charter for the town.

Be it enacted by the General Assembly of Virginia

Washington, Town Charter

Chapter 1. Incorporation and Boundaries

---

[127] Town of Washington Comprehensive Plan, 1986, page 22; Comprehensive Plan, 1988, page 22; Comprehensive Plan, 2006, page 7

[128] *Rappahannock News*, 14 August 2004

[129] *Rappahannock News*, 16 September 2004

[130] National Register of Historic Places, Washington Historic District (#322-001) Updated Nomination, 2006

[131] Virginia Acts of the Assembly, 1985 Session, Chapter 172

[132] *Rappahannock News*, 17 January 1985, quoted in the 3 January 2019 edition of the newspaper

1.1 Incorporation -- The inhabitants of the territory comprised within the present limits of the Town of Washington, as such limits are now or may hereafter be altered and established by law, shall constitute and continue to be a body politic and corporate, to be known and designated as the Town of Washington, and as such shall have perpetual succession, may sue and be sued, plead and be impleaded, contract and be contracted with, and may have a corporate seal which it may alter, renew, or amend at its pleasure by proper ordinance.
1.2 Boundaries -- The boundaries of the town until altered, shall be as recorded in the Clerk's Office of the Circuit Court of Rappahannock County, Virginia, in Plat Book 4, at page 68.

Chapter 2. Powers

2.1 General Grant of Powers -- The town shall have and may exercise all powers which are now or hereafter may be conferred upon or delegated to towns under the Constitution and laws of the Commonwealth of Virginia, as fully and completely as though such powers were specifically enumerated herein, and no enumeration of particular powers in this charter shall be held to be exclusive, and the town shall have, exercise, and enjoy all rights, immunities, powers, and privileges and be subject to all the duties and obligations now appertaining to and incumbent on the town as a municipal corporation.
2.2 Adoption of Powers Granted by the Code of Virginia -- The powers granted in 2.1 of this charter include specifically, but are not limited to, all powers set forth in the Code of Virginia, 1950, 15.1-837 through 15.1-907, including subsequent amendments thereof.

Chapter 3. Treasurer, Mayor and Council

3.1 Election, Qualification and Term of Office for the Treasurer, Mayor and other members of the Council -- The town shall be governed by a seven-member town council composed of five council members, the treasurer, and the mayor, all of whom shall be qualified voters in the town and shall be elected by the qualified voters of the town in the manner provided by law from the town at large. The five council members, the treasurer and the mayor in office at the time of adoption of this charter shall continue in office until the expiration of the terms for which they were elected or until their successors are elected and qualified. An election for five council members, the treasurer and the mayor shall be held on the first Tuesday in May, 1986. Elections shall be held on the first Tuesday in May every four years thereafter. The five council members, the treasurer and the mayor shall serve for terms of four year. The term of each person elected under this section shall begin on July 1 next following their election.
3.2 Vacancies -- Vacancies on the council, including the treasurer and the mayor, shall be filled for the unexpired term from among the qualified voters of the town by a majority vote of the remaining members of council.
3.3 Council, a Continuing Body -- The council shall be a continuing body, and no measure pending before such body nor any contract or obligation incurred shall abate or be discontinued because of the expiration of the term of office or removal of any council members.
3.4 Mayor -- The mayor shall be the chief executive officer of the town. He shall have and exercise all the privileges and authority conferred by general law not inconsistent with the charter. He shall preside over the meetings of the town

council and shall have the right to speak therein as a member of the council. He shall have a vote as a member of council but shall have no veto power. He shall be the head of the town government for all its ceremonial purposes and shall perform such other duties consistent with his office as may be imposed by the town council. He shall see that the duties of the various town officers are faithfully performed and shall authenticate his signature on such documents or instruments as the council, this charter or the laws of the Commonwealth shall require.

3.5 Vice Mayor -- The town council, by a majority of all its members, shall elect a vice mayor from its membership at its first meeting to serve for a term of four years in the absence of or during the disability of the mayor; and the vice mayor shall possess the powers and discharge the duties of the mayor when serving as mayor.

3.6 Town Treasurer -- The town treasurer's duties shall be to receive all money belonging to the town, to keep correct accounts of all receipts from all sources and of all expenditures, to be responsible for the collection of all license fees, taxes, levies and charges due to the town, to disburse the funds of the town as the council may direct, and other such duties as prescribed by the council. The treasurer may be compensated for his duties as such, in addition to his compensation as a member of council, as shall be determined by the mayor and the remaining members of council. He shall be a member of council with the same rights and privileges as other members of council.

3.7. Meetings of Council -- The council shall fix the time of its regular meetings, which shall be at least once each month, and, except as herein provided, the council shall follow Robert's Rules of Order, latest edition, for rules of procedure necessary for the orderly conduct of its business except where inconsistent with the laws of the Commonwealth of Virginia. Minutes shall be kept of its official proceedings, and its meetings shall be open to the public unless an executive session is called according to law. Special meetings may be called at any time by the mayor or any four members of the council, provided that the members of the council are given reasonable notice of such meetings. No business shall be transacted at the special meeting except for which it shall be called. If the mayor and all the members of the council are present, this provision requiring prior notice for special meetings is waived.

3.8. Compensation -- Compensation for the treasurer, mayor, and other members of council shall be set by the council subject to any limitations placed thereon by the laws of the Commonwealth of Virginia. Increases in the salaries of the treasurer, mayor and the other members of council shall not be effective until July 1 following the next local election after the council approves such increase. This section does not apply to any compensation paid to the treasurer for the performance of his duties as treasurer.

Chapter 4. Appointive Officers

4.1. Appointments, Duties, Compensation, etc. -- A. The town council may appoint a town superintendent, a town attorney, a police chief and other police personnel and prescribe their qualifications, place of residence, duties and compensation. B. Other Officers. -- The council may appoint any other officers that the council deems necessary and proper and prescribe their qualifications, place of residence, duties and compensation.

4.2. Term of office -- Appointees under this chapter shall serve at the pleasure of the council. The council may fill any vacancy in any appointive office.

Chapter 5. Financial Provisions

5.1. Fiscal year. --- The fiscal year of the town shall begin on July 1 of the year following.

Chapter 6. Miscellaneous

6.1. Ordinances Continued in Force. -- All ordinances now in force in the town, not inconsistent with this chapter, shall be and remain in force until altered, amended, or repealed by the council.

6.2. Severability of Provisions. - If any clause, sentence, paragraph, or part of this charter shall for any reason be adjudged by any court of competent jurisdiction to be invalid, such judgment shall not affect, impair, or invalidate the remainder of the charter but shall be confined in its operation to the clause, sentence, paragraph or part thereof directly involved in the controversy in which such judgment shall have been rendered.

2. That Chapter 226 of the Acts of Assembly of 1893-94 is repealed.
3. That the town council acting as the Board of Zoning Appeals before the effective date of this act is ratified.
4. That an emergency exists and this act is in force from its passage.

By this new charter, the Town was granted much broader powers and increased responsibilities than it had had previously, including all powers "delegated to towns under the Constitution and laws of the Commonwealth of Virginia."[133] In response to this mandate, the town adopted its first Comprehensive Plan in August 1986, ordinances were brought up to date, and a Planning Commission and a Board of Zoning Appeals were established.[134] The Town significantly revised the Zoning Ordinance in 1986, dividing the town into four zones from the prior single zone.[135]

Establishment of the Boundaries of the Town

In the 1796 Act of the General Assembly establishing the town of Washington, 25 acres of land were authorized to be incorporated into the town.[136] One year later, land owned by William Porter was added to this, and the petition to the General Assembly to add Porter's land was accompanied by a plan showing a

[133] Town of Washington Comprehensive Plan, 2006, page 6 and page 15

[134] Town of Washington Comprehensive Plan, 2006, page 15

[135] *Rappahannock News*, 28 August 1986, page A1; Town of Washington Comprehensive Plan, 2017, page 6

[136] Samuel Shepherd, *The Statutes at Large of Virginia, from October Session 1792 to December Session 1806, Inclusive, in Three Volumes, (New Series), Being a Continuation of Hening*, New York, AMS Press, Inc., 1836, Volume II, page 29-32

town of 51 lots with two north-south streets and five cross streets.[137] Based on later deeds of sale, it was determined that the lots measured 132' by 165' (one-half acre), the streets were 30' wide, and the area of the town was 30.5 acres.[138]

On 12 February 1894, when the town was incorporated, the act of the General Assembly provided that the boundaries of the town "shall extend 300 yards on every side beyond the boundaries of the town, as described in the original charter." Then, on 22 January 1985, the County of Rappahannock and the Town of Washington entered into an agreement establishing boundary lines between the two entities. A survey and plat were prepared by James G. Butler delineating the new boundaries, which were approved by the Rappahannock County Court on 6 June 1985. By this enactment, the area of the town became 179.7526 acres.[139]

Finally, in 1999 the Town and Rappahannock County enacted a joint resolution changing the boundaries of the town again. A new survey and plat were prepared by James G. Butler, and the boundaries were extended slightly at two places along the northwest boundaries. The area of the town became 182.0171 acres. This was approved by the Rappahannock County Court on 8 June 1999.[140]

The Avon Hall Property

The Avon Hall house began its recorded history in 1821 as the home of John and Mary Resor and their six children, located on Gay Street on Lot 42 and Lot 43.[141] After John died in 1833, Mary continued to reside there and also had a tavern in the building.[142] John William Jett purchased the property in 1835 and rented it to George Thorn who continued the tavern business.[143] Beginning in about 1849, it served as the Washington Academy and as a boarding house, and in 1866 it was purchased by Baldwin Bradford Baggarly and converted to his home.[144] His only surviving child, Franklin Clyde Baggarly, inherited the property in 1913.[145] In 1931 Franklin Clyde Baggarly moved the house from Gay Street to the hill east of the town above a pond, enlarged the building, added a two-story portico with full height columns, and renamed it Avon Hall.

---

[137] George Calvert, James Jett Jr., James Wheeler, and William Porter, Culpeper County, 1 December 1797, Legislative Petitions Digital Collection, Library of Virginia, Richmond, VA, Record number 000154073; also, Legislative Petitions of the General Assembly, 1776-1865, Library of Virginia Accession Number 36121, Box 58, Folder 71.
[138] Maureen Harris, *History of the Town of Washington, 1735-1833*, Rappahannock Historical Society, 2015
[139] Rappahannock County Deed Book 150, page 721 and Deed Book 152, page 276; Plat Book 4, page 68; Rappahannock County Chancery Case No. 3261
[140] Rappahannock County Instrument 990001042
[141] Rappahannock County Deed Book A, page 189
[142] Rappahannock County Chancery Case #5, Resor vs. Resor; Rappahannock County Deed Book A, page 384
[143] Rappahannock County Deed Book C, page 71
[144] Rappahannock County Deed Book L, page 464
[145] Quoted from Rappahannock County Will Book Q, page 245

The property on which the Avon Hall house is sited was acquired by the Baggarly family during 1866-1954 in multiple parcels, totaling 12.452 acres.[146] In 1959, Franklin Clyde Baggarly's wife Frances Trott Baggarly successfully petitioned the Rappahannock County Court to permit her to take over her husband's business affairs because of his mental incompetence.[147] She sold the 12.452 acres of land containing the Avon Hall house and pond to William and Ramona Carrigan in 1960 for $40,000.[148] In 1968 and 2001, the Carrigans purchased additional land adjacent to their 1960 purchase, such that the total acreage became 19.0097 acres.[149]

In 2002, the Town of Washington purchased the Avon Hall property from the executors of Carrigan's will for $920,000.[150] The land contained the Avon Hall house and extended from Warren Avenue on the north to the property lines of homes and of land owned by the Child Care and Learning Center on Mt. Salem Avenue on the south. The next year, the Town and the Child Care and Learning Center exchanged several small parcels at the southeast part of the Avon Hall property, and in 2006 the Town sold 4.0 acres to Rappahannock County for $400,000.[151] The latter land, designated as Tax Map 20A-1-115B, was a rectangle abutting the east side of the courthouse complex and extending from Warren Avenue to the northern property lines of the Mount Salem Avenue homes. In 2009-2010, the Town constructed the Wastewater Treatment facility on the southern part of the property (Tax Map 20A-1-80), with access to this via a 50' right-of-way from Warren Avenue along Leggett Lane.

Over time, the town was feeling increased pressure to sell the remaining Avon Hall property as it attempted to remain solvent while paying down the debt of the $4 million wastewater treatment plant. Several plans for sale of the property were considered by the Town Council, aided by the Avon Hall Study Group composed of cochairs Gary Aichele and Mary Ann Kuhn, with members Fred Catlin, Judy DeSarno, Allan Comp, and Ray Gooch, aided by land planner Milton Herd. The plans included selling the remainder of the Avon Hall estate as a single parcel; dividing the land into small-lot, reasonably priced homes; selling a ½-acre commercial lot on Warren Avenue; and a combination of these and other options. The Town Council also convened an Avon Hall Property Study Group to consider potential uses for the buildings and for the land. In

---

[146] Rappahannock County Deed Book L, page 464, Deed Book V, page 294, Deed Book Y, page 85, Deed Book Z, page 281, Deed Book Z, page 282, Deed Book 28, page 377, Deed Book 28, page 478; Deed Book 29, page 254; Deed Book 42, page 459, and Deed Book 61, page 107

[147] Rappahannock County Chancery Case #2279 and Case #2286, Baggarly vs. Baggarly; Rappahannock County Bond Book 10, page 100

[148] Rappahannock County Deed Book 72, page 378

[149] Rappahannock County Deed Book 92, page 319, and Rappahannock County Instrument 010000043

[150] Rappahannock County Instrument 020001760

[151] 9 October 2002 resolution by the Town Council; Rappahannock County Instrument 010001263, Instrument 020001778, Instrument 030001778, and Instrument 060001175

January 2016 the Town Council approved a resolution in which the Council would give serious consideration to offers to (1) purchase the entire 15.92-acre property; (2) subdivide the property to create lots to facilitate sale of existing structures on the property; (3) subdivide the property to create a 6-acre lot to include the Avon Hall house and the pond; (4) subdivide the property to create a half-acre lot at the corner of Leggett Lane and Warren Avenue; and (5) develop all or parts of the property to increase the number and diversity of residential homes in the town.[152] The resolution was the culmination of a comprehensive review and planning process that began in 2013. The Avon Hall property was then put on the market for sale.

Two months later, Town attorney John Bennett was engaged in negotiations with a potential buyer, and on 5 July 2016 the Town completed sale of two adjacent parcels of the property to Avon Hall LLC (William Fischer and Andrew Mitchell) for $750,000.[153] The first parcel, designated as Tax Map 20A-1-115, was 7.5584 acres and contained the Avon Hall mansion, the pond, a two-story cottage, and a small frame building. The second parcel, designated as Tax Map 20A-1-116 and located east of the first parcel, was 1.5289 acres and contained a frame building. Certain restrictions were included in the deed, including that the Avon Hall mansion should be preserved in its current appearance and be used only for a single-family residence, that the two parcels could not be subdivided, and that a 50-foot wide wooded buffer zone be maintained to separate the first parcel from view of the wastewater treatment facility. These restrictions were to be in place for a period of 40 years.

The sale addressed several town problems, including the town's ability to pay down the debt on the wastewater treatment system, which was $178,000 per year. The proceeds of the sale were specifically earmarked toward this debt.[154] In 2018, the Town still owned two parcels of the original Carrigan property: 0.5853 acre located adjacent to Warren Avenue (Tax Map 20A-1-119) and 5.2824 acres on which was located the wastewater treatment plant (Tax Map 20A-1-80).

Water, Wastewater, and Trash

A major accomplishment was establishing a safe and reliable water supply and facilities to deal with wastewater. Town water is obtained from two wells located in Harris Hollow constructed in the 1980s and 1990s. In 2010, the Town completed construction of the Washington Wastewater System to deal with the problem of deteriorating septic systems. These issues are described in Chapter 9.

---

[152] Minutes of the 11 January 2016 meeting of the Washington Town Council
[153] Rappahannock County Instrument 160000598
[154] *Rappahannock News*, 17 May 2016

The Town initiated a recycling program in 1976. Mayor Peter Kramer appointed June Jordan, a professional potter who lived on Lot 7 and who was then a member of the Town Council, to start and operate a recycling center. L.V. Merrill permitted land behind his car dealership to be used. In 1977 the recycling center, run by volunteers, collected $550 from selling newspapers and aluminum, which was donated to the Washington Volunteer Fire Department to aid in construction of a new firehouse.[155] Although this effort stopped after several years, the Town re-initiated a recycling program with monthly pickups in 1990.[156] This was also heavily dependent on volunteer efforts and was eventually abandoned. Subsequently, the two Rappahannock County recycling centers in Amissville and at Flatwoods were established and were available to town residents and businesses for trash and recycling.

The Town Relinquished Ownership of the Jett Street and Middle Street "Stub Streets"

In February 1990, the Town Council enacted an ordinance in which the Town vacated the part of Jett Street located east of Gay Street. This was enacted because the Council felt that it was in the public interest to change this land to have no status as a public street or public right of way.[157] The Town also vacated the part of Middle Street located west of Main Street. In 2013 Patrick O'Connell, owner of the Inn at Little Washington, had made it known to the Washington Town Council that the Inn would like to take over ownership of this small property. This parcel of land was owned by the Town and was a public right of way but was unsightly and in disrepair. The land was located between properties of the Post Office/Country Cafe building on the south and the Inn Tavern Shops on the north, both of which were owned by the Inn. The Washington Town Council held a public hearing on this matter on 15 July 2013 at which the Council found that the stub street served only the properties owned by the Inn and that maintaining the stub street "would be a burden on the Town, as no public access is now served." The Council voted to vacate the property to the Inn and to incorporate it into the property of the Inn Tavern Shops (Tax Map 20A-1-18).[158] The Inn and the Town were sued over this transfer of property by David Konick, an attorney in Rappahannock County, who claimed that the transfer was unlawful, but this suit was dismissed by the Circuit Court.[159] On 11 May 2015 the Town Council again voted to vacate the stub street to the Inn; the southern part the parcel was incorporated into Tax Map 20A-1-37 and the northern part was incorporated into Tax Map 20A-1-18.[160] The Inn then considerably

---

[155] *Rappahannock News*, 16 March 1978, quoted in the 13 September 2018 edition of the newspaper

[156] Minutes of the Washington Town Council, 13 June 1990

[157] Rappahannock County Deed Book 178, page 763, 13 February 1990

[158] Rappahannock County Instrument No. 130000836

[159] Rappahannock County Instrument No. 150000269; *Rappahannock News*, 10 December 2013 and 14 May 2015; Rappahannock County Instrument Nos. 150000504 and 150000805

[160] Rappahannock County Instrument No. 150000512

improved the appearance of the property with hardscaping and landscape plantings.

The Middle Street stub street after renovation by the Inn at Little Washington

The Trinity Church Parking Lot

In 1962, 0.15 acre of the western part of Lot 25 was sold by Quarles Oil Company to Trinity Church.[161] Multiple small buildings on this property were torn down, and a parking lot for the Church was constructed on the land.[162]

The Trinity Church parking lot before it was cleared

In 1994 a fountain was installed at the southeast corner of Main and Middle streets at the edge of the Trinity church parking lot. This sculptural fountain, donated to the Church by The Inn at Little Washington, was 6' tall with a bottom container that was 5' wide.[163] In 2014, The Inn again collaborated with Trinity Church to improve the church's parking lot which the Inn leased from the Church

---

[161] Rappahannock County Deed Book 77, page 48

[162] Photograph and caption for the western part of Lot 25, *Rappahannock News*, 13 December 1962, reprinted in the 4 September 2008 edition of the newspaper

[163] *Rappahannock News*, 27 April 1994

and which was adjacent to one of the entrances of the Inn's newly renovated building named "The Parsonage." The Inn paid for improvement to the parcel, including paving the parking lot and installing hardscaping and landscaping.[164] It was estimated to cost $180,000, and the Town contributed $20,000 towards this cost.[165] In 2015, the Town, the Inn, and Trinity Church were sued by local attorney David Konick, who claimed that the Town violated laws governing church-state separation, but the Circuit Court dismissed his initial suits; the Supreme Court of Virginia also rejected Konick's appeal.[166] The Town incurred significant legal costs defending against these suits.[167]

[164] Rappahannock County Instrument 140000455
[165] *Rappahannock News*, 26 March 2015
[166] *Rappahannock News*, 26 March 2015, 14 January 2016, and 16 June 2016
[167] Washington Town Council meeting, April 2016

Chapter 8. Town Comprehensive Plans, Ordinances, Architectural Review Board, Zoning Board, and Task Forces

Early Bylaws and Ordinances and Changes in Government of the Town

When the town was established in 1796, it was to be governed by a 7-member Town Board of Trustees.[1] This body enacted a Code of Bylaws in the early stages of the town; unfortunately, this document is lost.

A second major document enacted by the Town Trustees was the "Code of Bylaws for the Regulation of the Town of Washington" adopted by the Trustees at their meetings in July 1877.[2] The Bylaws contained twenty-one items and dealt with the method of collection and reporting of taxes and fees, maintenance of the streets, restraint of animals in the town, arrest of drunk persons, discharge of firearms, and other items. There was instituted a tax of 11 cents per $100 assessed value of real and personal property.

Until 1894, the town was still managed by a Board of Trustees, as directed by the original 1796 legislation that created the town. This changed on 12 February 1894, when the General Assembly of Virginia passed an act "to incorporate the town of Washington in the county of Rappahannock." The act stated that the town would become a municipal corporation" and that government of the town "shall be vested in a council of seven." The Act described elections of the town council, taxation of real and personal property, and various other matters pertaining to management of the town.[3] The Town Council adopted an ordinance on 15 March 1894, shortly after the town's incorporation act was passed. This 44-item ordinance established a tax of 25 cents per $100 of property; a schedule of fees on multiple occupations, boarding and eating houses, theatrical performances, liquor sales, and others; policing of the town; maintenance of the streets, alleys, and sidewalks; loitering and vagrancy; confinement of horses, mules, cows, hogs, and oxes; maintenance of privies and hog-pens and pollution of public water; discharge of firearms; breach of the peace; and other items.[4]

The Town of Washington was rechartered by the Virginia General Assembly on 14 March 1985.[5] By this new charter, the Town was granted much broader

---

[1] Source: Samuel Shepherd, *The Statutes at Large of Virginia, from October Session 1792 to December Session 1806, Inclusive, in Three Volumes, (New Series), Being a Continuation of Hening*, New York, AMS Press, Inc., 1836, Volume II, page 29-32

[2] See full text of this Code of Bylaws in Chapter 5

[3] See full text of the Act in Chapter 5

[4] See full text of the Ordinance in Chapter 5

[5] Virginia Acts of the Assembly, 1985 Session, Chapter 172; see Chapter 7 for full text of the charter

powers and increased responsibilities than it had had previously, including all powers "delegated to towns under the Constitution and laws of the Commonwealth of Virginia." In response to this mandate, a Planning Commission and a Board of Zoning Appeals were established, ordinances were brought up to date, and the town adopted its first Comprehensive Plan in August 1986. The Town also significantly revised the Zoning Ordinance in 1986, dividing the town into four zones from the prior single zone.[6]

Comprehensive Plans and the Town Planning Commission

Section 15.1, Chapter 11, of the Code of Virginia relates to planning, subdivision of land, and zoning. Section 15.1-446.1 states that every governing body in the Commonwealth of Virginia should adopt a Comprehensive Plan for the territory under its jurisdiction. Article 4 of Chapter 11 of Section 15.1 contains authority and direction for the matters to be considered in developing the Comprehensive Plan, the method of adoption of a Plan, and guidelines for amendment and review of a Plan. The Code's Section 15.2-2223-2230 requires the local planning commission to review the Plan at least once every five years to determine whether it is advisable to amend the Plan. The Plans are for the purpose of "guiding and accomplishing a coordinated, adjusted, and harmonious development of the territory which will, in accordance with present and probable future needs and resources, best promote the health, safety, morals, order, convenience, prosperity, and general welfare of the inhabitants."

Multiple Comprehensive Plans have been prepared by the Town. After the Town was rechartered in 1985, the town's Planning Commission was directed to prepare a Comprehensive Plan specifically for the town, rather than being a part of the Comprehensive Plan for Rappahannock County. The first Plan was adopted by the Town Council, with Dean F. Morehouse as Mayor, on 21 August 1986; much of the Plan dealt with the town's history and an assessment of the current status of the town. Findings were that there were low taxes, no public sewer system, tourism was important, parking was inadequate, litter and trash should be avoided, and groundwater should be protected from contamination.[7] Following adoption, the ordinances which implement the Plan were reviewed and amended. Several amendments to the Plan were made on 10 February 1988.

In the Plan adopted on 8 September 1999 under Mayor J. Stewart Willis, a salient sentence was "Without an up-to-date Comprehensive Plan, public officials who make decisions have no guide other than their own personal opinions as to the public interest." The goals and objectives stated in this Plan included protecting the unique character of the town, preserving natural features, protecting historic resources, providing adequate services and facilities including a safe water

---

[6] *Rappahannock News*, 28 August 1986, page A1; Town of Washington Comprehensive Plan, 2017, page 6
[7] Town of Washington Comprehensive Plan, adopted 21 August 1986

supply, addressing the problem of inadequate sewage disposal systems, supporting recycling programs, and ensuring sufficient funds to support operations in the town.[8]

The Plan adopted on 12 April 2006 dealt extensively with the need for infrastructure, particularly the issue of water and sewer services.[9] Construction of the town's wastewater treatment system began in January 2009 and was completed in April 2010.[10] The 70-page Plan adopted on 10 September 2012 contained an extensive inventory and analysis of the current status of the town, including its history, buildings and housing, commercial activities, finance, land use and zoning, and community facilities and services. Major planning issues were those of the town's water supply, the Avon Hall property investment, attracting new businesses to increase the vitality of the town, and fostering tourism. Goals included preserving the historic character of the town, providing adequate services and facilities to support the needs of the town's inhabitants, and providing adequate funding to support the governing and operation of the town.

The most recent Comprehensive Plan was adopted on 11 September 2017 under Mayor John Sullivan. This Plan was created by the Town Planning Commission with input from professional planners and from the community in numerous ways. The Commission involved the public through forums, letters of update, public meetings, open work sessions, written letters, and interviews. The involvement of the Town's near neighbors and Rappahannock County citizens was also sought through these public discussions and work sessions, and the Plan was coordinated with Rappahannock County officials.[11]

The purpose of the 2017 Plan was "to set forth the findings, goals, and decisions regarding the future land use and development of the Town and to provide criteria to guide decisions, not only with respect to land use but also with respect to planning for the provision of services, capital expenditures, and financial considerations." Further, the purpose was that "these findings, goals, and criteria are attuned to the trends of change, are reflective of them, and at the same time are mindful of the value of the Town's history, so that the Town can have a future that is safe, healthy, non-discriminatory, and economically sound." The Plan was oriented to anticipate where the Town (and the County) might be in the near future and to assess every possible need. The goals and objectives included continuing to be an attractive destination with a culture of hospitality welcoming to visitors; retaining current businesses, building a more diverse mix of businesses and a more diverse employment base; protecting the historic character

[8] Town of Washington Comprehensive Plan, adopted 8 September 1999
[9] Town of Washington Comprehensive Plan, adopted 12 April 2006
[10] See Chapter 9 for details
[11] Town of Washington Comprehensive Plan, adopted 11 September 2017

of the town while encouraging a diversity of housing options; and optimizing town expenses and identifying alternate resources to ensure financial stability of the town.

Historic District Ordinance, the Architectural Review Board, and the Historic District Design Guidelines

The town's historic character was recognized in 1975 by the Commonwealth of Virginia's Historic Landmarks Commission, and the town is listed on the Virginia Landmarks Register and the National Register of Historic Places as the "Washington Historic District."[12] In both the Virginia Register and the National Register, the Washington Historic District encompassed the entire town and many properties were considered as contributing to the historic nature of the town, but no individual building was so designated.

On 14 August 1985, the Town Council passed a Historic District Ordinance and created an Architectural Review Board with the stated purpose of protecting the style and historic character of the town, to help protect and maintain the architectural integrity of the historic district, and to restore and preserve the architectural structures in the town.[13]

The duties of the Architectural Review Board were specified as reviewing plans for all new buildings and plans for changes to existing structures to ensure that exterior color, style, and building textures and materials were compatible with buildings constructed in the town during earlier time periods. The first public meeting of the Board occurred on 21 November 1985 when the Board members considered an application from Werner Krebser and Jerry Martin to construct an office building on the northern part of town Lot 42.[14]

In 1991 the Historic District Ordinance was revised. The new ordinance was based on a draft by John McCarthy, the Rappahannock County Administrator, and modifications recommended by Ann Miller, a certified local government coordinator for the Virginia Department of Historic Resources, and was reviewed by the Town's Planning Commission and Architectural Review Board.[15] The 18-page document followed fairly closely the 1985 ordinance but allowed for more flexibility. For example, the older ordinance stated that no materials may be used in construction that were not in use in 1900 in the town, while the new document stated materials used "in Virginia." Also, construction along Mount Salem Avenue stipulated materials had to be those used up to 1945, whereas the new

---

[12] Calder Loth, editor, *The Virginia Landmarks Register*, University Press of Virginia, Charlottesville, 1986, page 358; www.dhr.virginia.gov/historic-registers/322-0011/ and www.nps.gov/nr

[13] Town of Washington Comprehensive Plan, 1986, page 22; Comprehensive Plan, 1988, page 22; Comprehensive Plan, 2006, page 7

[14] *Rappahannock News*, 28 November 1985

[15] *Rappahannock News*, 29 August 1991

document stated materials could be used that have been used "up to the present." The new ordinance also spelled out procedures for marketing a property when the owner wanted to tear down the buildings and sell only the land.

The Historic District Ordinance was severely challenged in 2002-2004 when Sidney and Mary Catherine Worley presented their plans to the Architectural Review Board in August 2002 to build a new house on town Lot 33 and the adjacent Lot 17. Seven months later the Board denied their request to build the home using the materials they presented, and a public hearing before the Town Council was held on 14 May 2003.[16] Points of contention were the modern composite materials that the Worleys planned to use in construction of the house, which apparently the Architectural Review Board found to be not in keeping with the historic nature of the town. Also, the house was felt to be architecturally incompatible with other properties in the town. The Worleys sued the town.[17] During the ensuing 13 months of litigation, thirteen closed sessions of the Town Council, and many hours of negotiations, an agreement was reached. The Worleys were awarded a $75,000 settlement payment and had up to 5 years to build their house.[18] The town's insurance coverage paid for about two-thirds of the settlement payment as well as the town attorney's fees. The Worleys never built their house in the town; instead they purchased and renovated a house in Flint Hill.

During this litigation, the presiding judge came close to declaring the Historic District Ordinance invalid. As a consequence, the Town paid $20,000 for an architectural preservationist to help revise the Ordinance.[19] The goal was to write a new Historic District Ordinance that would establish, within legal limits, design review standards for development in the town that were compatible with Washington's historical small-town character. The study was conducted by Cheryl H. Shepherd of Millennium Preservation Services of Warrenton, Virginia. She surveyed and inventoried most of the buildings within the incorporated town limits. Officials from the Virginia Department of Historic Resources indicated that the town had great historically significant architecture and strong historic associations.[20] Shepherd's findings led to a reapplication for the Washington Historic District. On 6 September 2006, the Virginia Historic Landmarks Commission again recognized the historic significance of the Town by approving an amendment to the town's Historic District designation. This amendment extended the period of historic significance to 1945 and included many additional buildings located within the corporate limits of the town and constructed up to

[16] *Rappahannock News*, 22 May 2003
[17] Worley v. Town of Washington; *Rappahannock News*, 14 August 2003; *Washington Post*, 18 October 2003
[18] *Rappahannock News*, 20 April 2004 and 23 September 2004
[19] *Rappahannock News*, 22 July 2004
[20] *Rappahannock News*, 16 September 2004

that year. The National Register of Historic Places was also updated, on 21 November 2006.[21]

The Historic District Ordinance was approved by the Town Council on 14 November 2007 with the purposes to protect the historic significance and integrity of the properties within the town, preserve and improve the quality of life for residents, promote tourism and support local businesses, stabilize and improve property values, educate people about the local cultural and historic heritage, promote local preservation efforts, promote harmony of style among buildings of historic design, develop the historic areas as a vital area, and encourage sound stewardship of the town's heritage. The Historic District Ordinance was incorporated into the town's Zoning Ordinance which was approved on 14 May 2008.[22] Because the Washington Historic District encompassed the entire town, regulations in the Zoning Ordinance pertaining to the Historic District were in addition to the regulations pertaining to the underlying zoning districts of the town.

The ordinance reaffirmed the existence of the Architectural Review Board. This Board is composed of five members, appointed by the Town Council, who have demonstrated an interest in preserving the architectural integrity of the town and who may have experience in historic preservation, history, architecture, or construction. The major purpose of the Board is to review, and approve or deny, applications by property owners. The ordinance states that no building, fence, structure, or sign shall be erected, reconstructed or substantially altered until an application has been approved as being architecturally compatible with the historic landmarks, buildings, or structures in the Historic District.

An application approved by the Architectural Review Board receives a Certificate of Appropriateness which is then reviewed by the Town Council. Normal repair and routine maintenance and other minor actions that do not affect the character of the Historic District are exempt from this requirement, and the Architectural Review Board has no authority over the interior of buildings.

The Historic District Ordinance also addressed the issue of minimum maintenance required of property owners. Specifically, no contributing building or structure within the Historic District may be neglected such that irreparable deterioration of the building would result. Razing or demolition of a building also requires an application to and approval from the Architectural Review Board.

The ordinance delineated the considerable amount of information required in an application. The Architectural Review Board is to consider many factors, stated

---

[21] National Register of Historic Places, Washington Historic District (#322-001) Updated Nomination, 2006

[22] washingtonva.gov/ordinances/20140522 TOW Zoning Ordinance.pdf

in the Historic District Ordinance, in determining the appropriateness of any erection, exterior alteration, or restoration. The Board is also to be guided in its decisions by the standards and guidelines established in the town's Historic District Design Guidelines.

These new Town of Washington Historic District Design Guidelines were approved by the Town Council on 22 September 2008, and were amended on 13 February 2012. The Guidelines are based on The Secretary of the Interior's Standards for Rehabilitation & Guidelines for Rehabilitating Historic Buildings.[23] The Town's guidelines are designed to identify and preserve the form and detailing of the architectural materials and features that are important in defining the historic character of the town's buildings. The guidelines are not absolutely specific for each case. They encourage preservation through repair of deteriorated materials or replacement by matching the original in design, color, texture, and materials to maintain the original historic integrity.

Sections of the very lengthy Guidelines deal with alterations and additions to existing buildings; new construction; signs on commercial and other nonresidential buildings; light fixtures, vending machines, and arbors/trellises/pergolas; neglected buildings; relocation of existing buildings; and demolition of structures considered historically significant.[24]

Property owners of buildings within the Washington Historic District are eligible to apply for significant economic benefit of up to 45% combined state and federal rehabilitation tax credits for rehabilitation complying with the Secretary of the Interior's Standards for Rehabilitation.

Town Zoning Ordinance

A zoning ordinance was passed by the Town Council in 1970 in which the entire town was zoned residential, with four "by right" uses: single and two-family dwellings, churches, libraries, and signs advertising businesses in the town. All other property uses were either "grandfathered in" as a nonconforming use or had been granted special-use permits by the Council. Twenty-two specific uses were listed as permitted under the 1970 ordinance.[25]

During 1986, the Town Council adopted a significantly revised Zoning Ordinance, breaking down the town's single zone into four zoning districts: village residential, village mixed use, village services, and rural residential.[26] In this new ordinance, the by-right uses in the village residential zone were

[23] www.cr.nps.gov/hps/alphaindex.htm
[24] Washingtonva.gov/ordinances/HistDistDesGuidelines2008.pdf
[25] *Rappahannock News*, 28 August 1986
[26] Town of Washington Comprehensive Plan, 2006, page 7, and Comprehensive Plan 1999, page 14

expanded to include single family residences, libraries, home occupations, orchards, gardens, vineyards, noncommercial bee-keeping, fowl, and signs. By right uses in the village mixed use zone included all those listed in the village residential zone plus retail uses of less than 700 square feet or craft uses in an existing retail space. In the village services zone, all of the above uses were permitted, plus public buildings and office buildings of not more than two stories with not more than 1000 square feet on the ground floor. By right uses in the rural residential zone were the same as the village residential zone, with the addition of agricultural and forestry uses and structures, including the making of cider and wine and the keeping of farm animals, except swine and except for chicken houses larger than 2000 square feet. As in the 1970 ordinance, nonconforming uses in existence prior to passage of the ordinance were grandfathered in.

The 1986 ordinance also included a list of uses in each of the four zones that could be established by a special permit issued by the Town Council. Special permit uses in the village residential zone included two-family residences, public utilities, and keeping of more than three dogs. In the village mixed use zone, these uses were apartment houses, museums, retail space of less than 700 square feet on the ground floor of new construction or converted residential structure, retail space of 700 to 2000 square feet in an existing retail space, bed and breakfasts, hotels, restaurants, schools, parks, playgrounds, and commercial signs. In the village services zone, the uses by special permit were clubs, lodges, offices in buildings not more than two stories and not more than 1600 square feet on the ground floor, and craft occupations in other than existing retail space. In the rural residential zone, the uses were home industries, private agricultural production, dog kennels, wayside markets, and fairs and carnivals lasting one week or less.

According to Frank Reynolds, an attorney and member of the town's Planning Commission, the 1986 ordinance restricted special use permits in residential areas more than in nonresidential areas, because the 1970 ordinance had not guaranteed the residential character of the residential areas.[27] "The very definite object is the protection of residential areas."

On 14 May 2008, a new Zoning Ordinance was approved, with amendments on 11 October 2010 and 12 August 2013.[28] In this lengthy document of 118 pages, five zoning districts were specified, which were village residential, village mixed use, village services, rural residential, and governmental services.

The village residential zone is essentially a residential district and comprises approximately one-third of the town. The village mixed use zone is also mainly

---

[27] Frank Reynolds, quoted in *Rappahannock News*, 28 August 1986

[28] washingtonva.gov/ordinances/20140522 TOW Zoning Ordinance.pdf

a residential district but contains existing retail spaces in addition; it comprises about 7% of the town. The village services zone contains retail establishments, small office buildings, and offices of Rappahannock County and the state government and comprises about 5% of the town. The rural residential zone is essentially a residential district with a wider range of permitted agricultural activities; about half of the town is in this zone. The governmental services zone comprises about 4 acres that serves as parking lot for government employees, maintenance sheds, and open land.

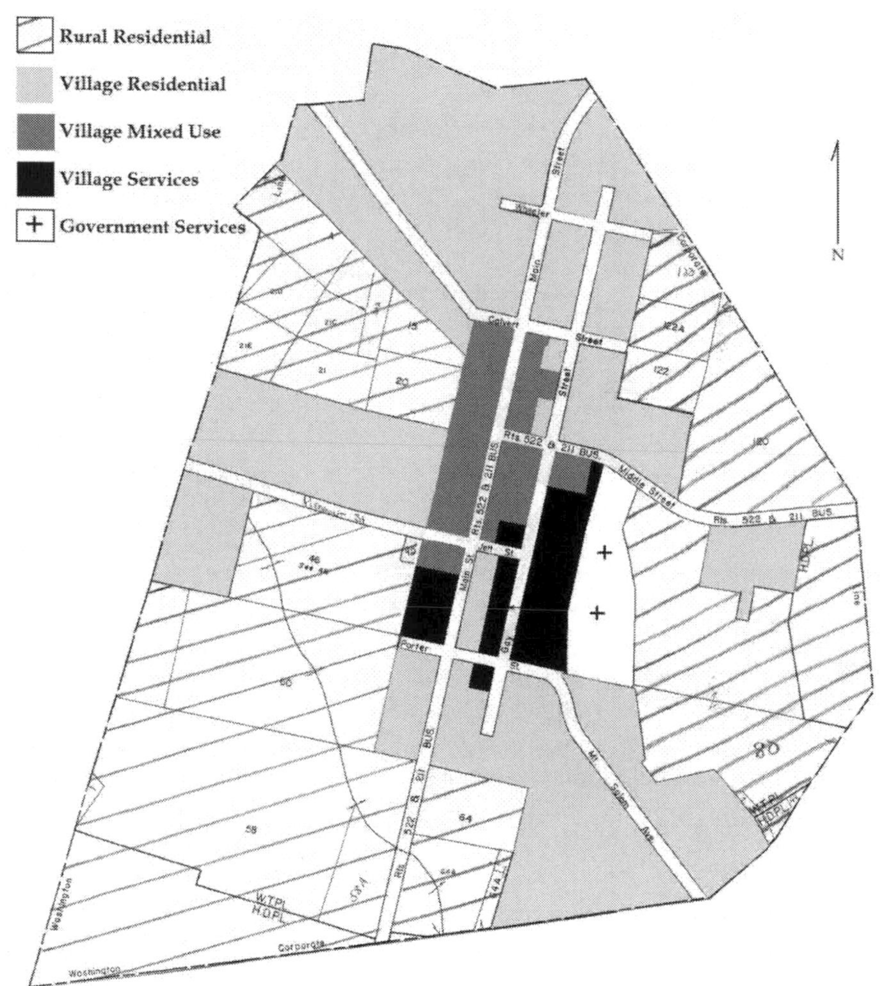

Zoning Districts of the Town of Washington, 2018

Five uses were permitted by right in each of the five zoning districts: single-family residences, noncommercial beekeeping, orchards/gardens/vineyards, making of cider or wine, and keeping three or fewer dogs per dwelling unit. In each district except Governmental Services, temporary and noncommercial signs no larger than six square feet were also permitted. The Village Mixed-Use zone and Village Services zone could contain such signs up to 15 square feet, retail establishments of less than 1000 square feet, and craft occupations in an existing retail space.; the latter zone could also contain public buildings and offices in buildings of not more than two stories above ground with not more than 1000 square feet on the ground floor. The Rural Residential zone could have agricultural and forestry uses and structures, including keeping farm animals except swine and except for structures exceeding 2000 square feet for poultry. The Governmental Services zone could contain governmental offices, public buildings, emergency communications facilities, public safety facilities, parking lots, public parks, and stormwater management facilities. Prohibited within the town corporate limits were mobile homes, travel trailers, recreational vehicles, and temporary structures used as a dwelling.

The Zoning Ordinance document specified a number of uses in each zoning district that could be allowed by special permit, which requires review by the Board of Zoning Appeals. This body consists of five individuals who are residents of the town. They are appointed to the Board by the Rappahannock County Circuit Court judge. They serve for a term of five years, but a member may be reappointed to the Board. The role of the Board is to hear and decide appeals of a zoning violation and applications for special exceptions and variances. The Town receives assistance in administering its Zoning Ordinance from the Town's Interim Zoning Administrator, John Bennett, who also serves as the Town's attorney.

The 2008 Zoning Ordinance and its amendments also delineated extensive special requirements for nonresidential uses; nonconforming uses; general provisions including area, setback, height, density, accessory structures, building permits, and parking. Ordinances related to the Flood Plain District and the Historic District Zoning were also included in the 2008 Zoning Ordinance document.[29]

Other Town Ordinances

A number of other ordinances have been enacted by the Washington Town Council in recent years. These include, for example, the Community Waterworks Cross Connection Control Ordinance in 2006 which was mandated by the Safe Water Drinking Act and was intended to prevent contamination

[29] In late 2018 and early 2019, the Town Council considered and then approved an ordinance to amend the Zoning Ordinance of the town to allow, by special permit, planned unit development in any zoning area.

backflowing into the town's waterworks; the Water Service Ordinance of 1999 which established policies and charges for the provision of water service within the town; the Water Policy Resolution of 2005 which established a tap fee of $5000 for single family residences; and the Subdivision and Site Plan Ordinance of 1992 and the combined ordinance definitions enacted on 14 May 1997, which established regulations for subdivision and development of land within the town's corporate limits.[30]

Town Task Forces, 2018

Several committees composed primarily of town residents were operating in 2018 to address issues and concerns related to the Town. These included the Tourism Task Force, the Business Task Force, the Finance and Administration Task Force, the Infrastructure Task Force, and the Housing Task Force.[31]

---

[30] washingtonva.gov/ordinances/CrossConnectionOrd.pdf; washingtonva.gov/ordinances/WaterPolicyResolution.pdf; washingtonva.gov/ordinances/SubdivisionOrdinance.pdf

[31] Minutes of the 13 August 2018 meeting of the Washington Town Council

Chapter 9. The Town Water Supply and Wastewater Systems

Early History

A plan of the town in 1837 showed that a town well was located at the south end of Gay Street.[1] Other locations for town wells were on the courthouse grounds, dug in 1839; adjacent to Mrs. Coxe's tavern on Lot 8; and between Lots 22 and 23.[2] These were public wells; as needed, owners of the town lots probably dug their own private wells. With regard to wastewater, the original half-acre lots of the town were adequate to meet the requirements for privies.

In May 1881 the Town Board of Trustees agreed to pay the expense of having the well near Mrs. Dear's hotel (now the Inn Tavern Shops) covered over "with a good and substantial frame."[3] In 1892 the *Blue Ridge Guide* newspaper reported that "The sanitary condition of our town [Washington] is bad and should be attended to at once."[4] Apparently this was recognized for, on 15 March 1894, shortly after the town was incorporated, the first Washington Town Council adopted an ordinance that included several items related to the town's water and sewerage "system":

#36. All householders are hereby required to clean their privies and hog-pens thoroughly and keep them in good order. Any person failing to do so after twenty-four hours notice by the Sergeant shall be fined two dollars for every day he shall fail to comply with this regulation.
#37. All privies and hog-pens that open for the escape of filth on any street or public alley of the town, or into the channel of any creek or drain or any sewer and also any privies and hog-pens that stand within five feet of the margin of any street, alley, channel, creek, drain or sewer (having their openings for the escape of filth toward such street, alley, etc.) are hereby declared to be nuisances and the owners or occupants of the premises on which such are situated, shall be fined not less than one dollar for each day they shall remain after notice from the Sergeant to remove them.
#39. If any person shall pollute the water of any of the public springs, pumps or wells, he shall be fined not less than one nor more than five dollars for every such offence.

---

[1] Rappahannock County Deed Book C, page 71; see Chapter 4 for plan of the town in 1837
[2] Rappahannock County Minute Book for 1839
[3] Minutes of the 13 May 1881 meeting of the Town Trustees
[4] *Blue Ridge Guide*, 29 September 1892

The early genesis of the town's water and sewer system probably mimicked changes in the courthouse and adjacent County buildings that are recorded in the minutes of the County government:

-In 1837, Commissioners were appointed by the Court to contract for construction of a privy on the jail lot.

-In 1839, a well was dug on the courthouse grounds. In 1879, a windlass was purchased for the well for $2. In 1900, a pump was installed in the well. In 1932, an electric pump was installed in the well.

-In 1897, the Sheriff was instructed to have a blind erected in the lower corner of the courthouse lot near the stable of B. B. Baggarly for the purpose of urinating behind.

-In 1900, Thomas Heywood, Clerk of the Court, was instructed to have the privy moved and blinds put around it.

-In 1932, a lavatory was installed in the Clerk's office and the Treasurer's office.

-In 1934, a septic tank was installed for the jail.

-In 1935, a sanitary drinking fountain was installed on the courthouse lot.

-In 1936, a sewer system was installed in the jail and toilets were installed in the courthouse through use of Works Project Administration (WPA) labor.

-In 1947, toilets were installed for the Clerk and for the Treasurer.

-In 1949, an electric water cooler was installed in the courthouse.

-In 1957, the courthouse well had been abandoned; because the top of the well was rotting, a concrete top was installed. There was a public drinking fountain in the courthouse yard (as well as one at the corner of Middle and Main streets).

Establishment of The Washington Water Works

In 1935, the Washington Water Works was established to provide treated water to town properties. This project was conducted by the Works Progress Administration (WPA), which was created on 6 May 1935 as the vehicle for overseeing public works projects mandated by the federal Emergency Relief Appropriations Act. This was one of Franklin Roosevelt's many programs intended to deal with the Great Depression in the United States. Renamed the Works Projects Administration in 1939, the program employed mostly unskilled men to carry out public works infrastructure projects. Among other works, they laid roughly 9,000 miles of storm drains and sanitary sewer lines.

The town's new water distribution system originated from a spring at Black Branch where a concrete springhouse was built. Water ran through new water pipes to a 50-foot diameter reservoir and from there to Piedmont Avenue and the town.[5] The pipes were laid in a trench that was 3 feet wide and 3 feet deep on a slope of sufficient grade to permit gravity flow of the water.[6]

---

[5] Rappahannock County Deed Book 39, pages 275 and 315-321

[6] "Plan of Washington Waterworks," exhibit plat in Common Law Case 162, Town of Washington versus Bessie J. Huff et al.

The Town Council needed to acquire right of way easements for laying the pipes from the spring to the reservoir, and from the reservoir to the town.[7] One of the properties on which 1260' of this right of way was to be situated, located about one mile west of the town, was owned by Bessie J. Huff. Huff refused to permit the right of way, and the Town was forced to bring the matter to Court. On 29 May 1935 the Town petitioned J.R.H. Alexander, judge of the Circuit Court of Rappahannock County, to authorize the Town to take the right of way across Huff's land "for the purpose of supplying water to the general public and inhabitants of said Town" and to determine what would be a just compensation to Huff.[8] The Court determined that condemnation of the land was necessary and appointed John A. Keyser, C.E. Johnson, Wade H. Massie Jr., and J. Frank Jones as commissioners to assess the land and to estimate compensation.[9] They determined that $15 would be just compensation.[10]

Apparently, other landowners realized that refusal to grant the right of way would be fruitless and no other suits were brought to the Court. The Town obtained "the perpetual right, privilege, and easement of right of way for the purpose of laying a pipe line and maintaining the same on, over, through, and across the lands" of Annie Jones Wood and her husband William G. Wood (130'), Louemma C. Moffett and her husband William F. Moffett and Frances Carter Smith and her husband Vincent Smith (4132'), Bessie J. Huff (1260'), Lena A. Wayland (891'), James L. Pullen and his wife Dora Pullen (1897'), and the Rappahannock National Bank and the Shenandoah Valley National Bank (935'). From the property owned by the two banks the Town also obtained the site for the concrete springhouse and 2 acres surrounding Black Branch.[11]

To provide for payment of the cost in excess of a grant made to the Town by the U.S. Government, the Town Council proposed to issue bonds.[12] A special election was held in the town on 26 March 1935 to obtain the residents' approval of the project. The vote was 74 in favor, none against, and one vote void.[13] Forty coupon bonds of $500 each, with an interest rate of 4% per year payable semiannually, were executed and delivered; one bond would mature on 1 December of each year beginning in 1938. The bondholders were: Peoples National Bank of Charlottesville, 18 bonds, $9000; Second National Bank of Culpeper, 4 bonds, $2000; Reconstruction Finance Corporation, 4 bonds, $2000; Flora M. Zinn, 8 bonds, $4000; J.S. Galban, 4 bonds, $2000; and J.C. Metcalf, 2

---

[7] Minutes of the Washington Town Council, 16 May 1935
[8] Common Law Case 162, Town of Washington versus Bessie J. Huff et al.
[9] Common Law Order Book H, page 343
[10] Rappahannock County Deed Book 39, page 275
[11] Minutes of the Washington Town Council, 16 May 1935; Rappahannock County Deed Book 39, pages 315-321
[12] Minutes of the Washington Town Council, 17 January 1935
[13] Information from Chancery Case 1913

bonds, $1000.[14] The bonds were payable from the income and revenues of the waterworks system after payment of the costs of operating and maintaining the system, and the Town established charges for water service to provide for payment.[15]

After completion, a Virginia Department of Health publication described the town's water system: "The supply is obtained from an infiltration gallery located on a mountain 2 miles west of the town. Water is piped to a 100,000-gallon covered concrete reservoir located 2 miles west. Hypochlorite solution is added to the water as it enters the reservoir by a gravity-type solution feeder. Water is conveyed to the pipe system in town through a 6-inch line."[16]

In 1935, a volunteer fire department was organized as a result of the new waterworks system in the town. Franklin Clyde Baggarly was elected chief of the new department and was asked by the Town Council to develop a constitution and by-laws.[17] The fire department was incorporated in 1939. In 1940, a parcel of land on Lot 29 on Gay Street was purchased by the Town of Washington.[18] On the lot was constructed the cinderblock Washington Fire Department building, which was set back from the street and had large bays for entrance and exit of the fire trucks. Having a functioning fire department and water supply were essential to the Town for obtaining fire insurance.

Unfortunately, the year after completion of the new water supply system, the springs that were the source of the water went dry due to drought conditions. The springs were supplemented by a well in 1939. However, water shortages continued during the dry summer months. The 1930s drought dealt all of Rappahannock County a severe blow because almost everyone depended on water for agriculture.

The Water Works Goes Into Receivership

According to the bond issuance in 1935, bondholders owned the waterworks system.[19] Over time, revenues from sale of water did not meet the principle and interest on the bonds. The Town defaulted in payments to bondholders, and the bondholders forced the system into receivership in 1942.[20] James W. Fletcher was appointed as receiver, whose duties were to take possession of the water

---

[14] Rappahannock County Chancery Case 1913; presentation by the bondholders at the 24 June 1954 meeting of the Washington Town Council
[15] Minutes of the Washington Town Council, 11 April 1935
[16] Virginia Department of Health, Bureau of Sanitary Engineering, *Public Water Supplies in Virginia, Descriptions and Chemical Analyses*, Publication 125, 1939
[17] *Culpeper Exponent*, 3 October 1935
[18] Rappahannock County Deed Book 43, page 139
[19] Town of Washington Comprehensive Plan, 2012, page 34
[20] Common Law Order Book 9, page 104; Chancery Order Book 9, page 174; Rappahannock County Chancery Case 1913

system, operate it under the direction of the Court, collect all revenues, and investigate whether water meters could be installed, what rates should be charged for water usage, and what steps would be necessary to put the system on a sound financial basis and would result in payment of the bonds' principle and interest. Financial difficulties still followed. Meter installations were completed in July 1944, but the water system was dry during several weeks in the summer of 1944; no collections were made when there was no water provided. Fletcher had the opportunity to use a well drilled by the Virginia Agricultural Extension Service on land owned by the Cloptons west of the town near the community called Blacksburg. This well was to drilled to serve itinerant fruit pickers, and a contract was negotiated between Fletcher and Clopton to lease the well for five years at $100 per year, renewable for up to 20 years.

Fletcher resigned in June 1945, and Rayner V. Snead was appointed as receiver in 1946.[21] No interest had been paid to bondholders for several years.[22] In 1953, the Town petitioned Rayner Snead, in his capacity as judge of the Rappahannock County Court, requesting him to abolish the town's monthly rent on fire hydrants and drinking fountains.[23] The next year, the Town Council discussed using the water rent money, then being held in escrow for fire hydrant rent, to purchase some of the bonds from the 1935 bond issuance.[24]

A public meeting was held at the courthouse in 1954 to hear a presentation by the bondholders regarding selling the bonds to the Town.[25] They proposed converting the bonds from revenue bonds to obligation bonds. This proposal was roundly disapproved by citizens present at the meeting.

After this, many of the Town's requests for repairs were ignored by the bondholders. These requests included, for example, a new chlorinator to replace an antiquated one that was resulting in contaminated water.[26] This contamination was particularly severe after hard rains.[27] A new pump was needed for the water system. In 1957, both of the town's water fountains were inoperable; these were located at the corner of Main and Middle streets and on the courthouse grounds.[28] It was believed that, in case of a major breakdown, the bondholders would not pay for the needed repairs and the town would be out of water. The bondholders were obligated to make no repairs exceeding $1000. Guy Burke, who maintained the system, estimated that 4,000-5,000 feet of galvanized pipe, which was 20 years old, would need to be replaced within a few years, and the chlorinator

---

[21] Snead was followed by J. Rodes Brown Jr., John W. Price, Martha Critzer, and T.C. Lea during 1955-1962
[22] Information from Rappahannock County Chancery Case 1913
[23] Minutes of the Washington Town Council, 8 September 1953
[24] Minutes of the Washington Town Council, 13 April 1954
[25] Minutes of the Washington Town Council, 24 June 1954
[26] Minutes of the Washington Town Council, 12 April and 10 May 1955
[27] Minutes of the Washington Town Council, 13 November 1956
[28] Minutes of the Washington Town Council, 9 July and 13 August 1957

needed to be replaced.[29] In 1956-1958, the Bureau of Sanitary Engineering of the Virginia Department of Health found that 30% of water samples showed contamination. Finally, in 1958, a hypochlorinator was installed. There was much discussion in Town Council meetings about whether the Town should purchase the water supply system.[30]

The Town's water supply was described in 1964 as follows: Water is obtained from an infiltration gallery and a drilled well. Water from the gallery is piped to a 100,000-gallon ground storage reservoir and from this point flows by gravity to the distribution system. The well water is pumped to the reservoir. The water supply is chlorinated and about 85 metered connections are served by the system.[31]

The Town Acquires the Water Works

By December 1966, the Town Council had prevailed on the Court to allow the Town to purchase the Water Works. The Court ordered the Town to pay interest on the bonds, required that $1000 be kept in reserve as an emergency fund, and set the minimum cost for 2,500 gallons of water at $3.00. The Court order required that an initial payment must be made of $50 for each bond plus interest for the prior six months. The Town took out 30-year bonds to finance the purchase, and by this the Town would have full ownership of the waterworks by 1 January 1996. The Rappahannock National Bank agreed to accept payments of water bills for a fee of $10 per month; the Town had responsibility for sending out the water bills to property owners.[32] Later that year, a plan was put into place to remove water meters from inside buildings and locate them outside for ease of reading.[33]

Maintenance of the Town Water System

The Town was now in charge of maintaining the water supply to properties in the town. Guy Burke was employed to read the water meters, maintain the water pumps, add chlorine to the water, and other maintenance jobs. Minutes of the Town Council meetings detail issues with the water system, such as an inoperative chlorinator, lack of water samples being tested for contamination, inadequate water pressure or no water pressure at all, and failure of water pumps. The latter issues affected the Town's ISO fire insurance rating, issued by the Insurance Services Office (ISO) of Virginia, located in Richmond. The ISO

---

[29] Minutes of the Washington Town Council, 12 March, 18 March, and 8 April 1958

[30] Minutes of the Washington Town Council, March 1958

[31] "Rappahannock County, Land, People & Facilities," Governor's Office, Commonwealth of Virginia, Division of Industrial Development and Planning, May 1964

[32] Minutes of the Washington Town Council, 9 November and 14 December 1965 and 8 February and 8 March 1966

[33] Minutes of the Washington Town Council, 13 December 1966

rating depended on the town having a water supply that could deliver 500 gallons per minute and a modern pumper able to pump 800 gallons per minute. At inspection, the town's fire truck would not start and was in poor condition, and the fire hydrant tested would deliver only 240 gallons per minute.[34]

In 1971, the spring-fed reservoir that held the water supply for the town underwent extensive repairs. The 90,000-gallon concrete tank was drained and the entire interior was sandblasted, sealed at the seams, and washed out before being refilled. The town was without water for several days during the process of repair.[35] By June 1971, all bonds for the Water Works had been retired and ownership became solely that of the Town.

In June through October 1977, there was a shortage of water to the town that was deemed "critical;" town residents were pleaded with to use less water.[36] In response, the Town purchased 1 acre of land from Edward Jones Clopton and Eliza Clopton Anderson (Tax Map 19-73) in 1977.[37] Edward and Eliza were the children of Annie Jones Clopton Wood and had acquired the land from their mother.[38] The Town also acquired from them a 50' wide easement extending 250' southeast along an unimproved road from the 1-acre parcel to Route 626 (Piedmont Avenue). The deed stated that the sole purpose of this purchase was for use by the Town for its water system, including "the ability to drill a new well in the future." The Town constructed a well and a pumphouse on this property.[39] In October 1978 the town well on the former Clopton property was almost dry, although the reservoir was "holding its own."[40] In 1980, a well was drilled on the site to a depth of 600' but no water was found; the springs were thought to be a secure water source for the near future.[41] But, on 9 January 1981, town residents turned on their taps and discovered that there was no water.[42]

The three springs on Jenkins Mountain that normally supplied the town were dry during July 1980 through January 1981. Charlie Jenkins, a Town Councilman who was also in charge of the water system, reported that there was only 5' of water in the reservoir and that the well, a backup source, was practically depleted. Usually water was pumped from the well only in the summer months when the springs ran dry, but the springs had been dry for 7 months. The lack of precipitation in 1980 and the lack of winter snowfall had created a serious deficiency in the water table. In the face of the water deficit, water was being

---

[34] Minutes of the Washington Town Council, 9 February 1971, 11 July 1972, 5 June 1974, and 13 April 1976; 5 June 1974 letter to the Town Council from Insurance Services Office
[35] *Rappahannock News*, 20 May 1971
[36] Minutes of the Washington Town Council, June 1977
[37] Rappahannock County Deed Book 126, page 389; Plat Book 2, page 73
[38] Rappahannock County Will Book K, page 498
[39] Rappahannock County Deed Book 138, page 605
[40] Minutes of the Washington Town Council, October 1978
[41] Minutes of the Washington Town Council, May 1980
[42] *Rappahannock News*, 15 February 1981

provided to the town by 3500-gallon tanker trucks. The fire department brought 100 one-gallon containers of drinking water and distributed them at Trinity Church. The Town enlisted the help of a professional dowser, Donald Turner of Front Royal, who had identified several water sources on the Eldon Farms property in Rappahannock County and on his own farm. Together with Charlie Jenkins and Mayor Newbill Miller, Turner explored the town's well site and, with his "water witch," found what he described as a large underground cave. "There's a whole lot of water here," he said.[43]

In response to these conditions, in 1981 the Town purchased 1.0381 acres adjacent to the well lot acquired from the Cloptons and adjacent to Piedmont Avenue (Tax Map 19-72A) from Sidney B. Berry and his wife Anne Hayes Berry.[44] The deed stated that "this property may be used only for the purpose of a well lot and as a source of water by the Town."[45] A new well was drilled to a depth of 410' at the place directed by the dowser, but this produced only 4 gallons per minute, whereas the town required 15 gallons per minute.[46] Then, it rained, and rained, and rained. By mid-February, the reservoir was almost full. Charlie Jenkins also managed to repair leaks in the town's 50-year old water pipes.[47]

Still seeking a more permanent solution, the Town acquired a parcel of 10,000 square feet of land from Clara Updike in 1981. This deed was signed by all members of the Town Council, who were J. Newbill Miller (mayor), Dorothy P. Clater, C.E. Giles Jr., Bradford Fisher, Charles Jenkins, Dorothy Hawkins, and H.T. Updike.[48] The property was adjacent to Route 622 (Harris Hollow Road) where it turns to meet the Rush River (Tax Map 20-11E). A new well was dug on this property, at a cost of $50,000, that yielded 150 gallons per minute. The Town also acquired a 20' wide by 2842' long easement across Updike's property adjacent to Route 622 leading toward the town, according to a survey and plat by Fanning Baumgardner, Professional Engineer, and a geological investigation by Dick McKay of the Division of Mineral Resources. On this easement was constructed a water pipeline. One month later, the Town was granted a 20' wide by 2513' long easement by the Cloptons, extending from the well lot obtained in 1977 and intersecting with the waterline easement obtained from Clara Updike along Route 622.[49]

The town's water system was inspected annually and, in August 1988, the system was deemed deficient. Mayor Dean Morehouse received a letter from the

---

[43] *Rappahannock News*, 15 January 1981
[44] This property and the property obtained from the Cloptons in 1977, totaling 2.0575 acres, were conveyed by the Town to Sidney and Anne Berry in 2004. The Town reserved easements 5' on either side of the existing pipes. Rappahannock County Instrument 040002083
[45] Rappahannock County Deed Book 138, page 605
[46] Minutes of the Washington Town Council, January 1981
[47] *Richmond Times-Dispatch,* 15 February 1981
[48] Rappahannock County Deed Book 139, page 624
[49] Rappahannock County Deed Book 139, page 815

Culpeper Regional Health Department citing the system for failure to submit monthly monitoring reports, lack of a backflow prevention system, a broken automatic chlorinator, lack of a disinfection system for the spring-supplied water, and lack of required documentation for the second of the town's two wells.[50]

In 1990 Water Authority chairman Brad Fisher reported that, in the month of May, 1,134,600 gallons of water were produced from the spring, 52,000 gallons from well #1, and 78,830 gallons from well #2, for a total of 1,265,430 gallons. Of that production, 694,470 gallons were metered to users; the substantial difference between production and use was due to overflow of the reservoir during what Fisher described as a "hyperactive" spring during the month of May.[51]

Because of limitations placed by the federal Environmental Protection Agency, the Town discontinued use of the spring as a public water source in December 1991.[52] A new well was drilled in 1991 to ensure an adequate water supply to

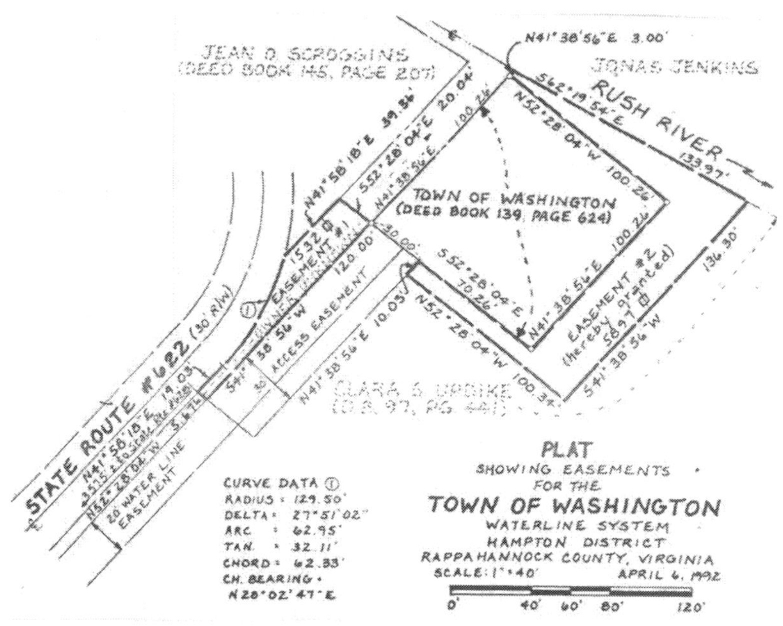

Plat showing the original 10,000 square foot well lot obtained from Clara Updike in 1981 and three easements obtained from her in 1993. Source: Rappahannock County Deed Book 199, page 400

[50] *Rappahannock News*, 22 September 1988

[51] Minutes of the Washington Town Council, 13 June 1990

[52] Rappahannock County Instrument 150000986 contains a plat showing the spring boxes and site of the well lot on Black Branch that were abandoned

the town.[53] In 1993, three easements were obtained from Clara Updike at a cost of $4000.[54] These were a 5897 square foot enlargement of the 10,000 square foot parcel for the purpose of installation of a well house and wells for the public water supply; an adjacent 1532 square foot parcel for access to the well lot; and a 20' wide by 1388' long easement extending along Route 622 for laying waterline pipes adjacent to and parallel with the as-built water line. The distance from the end of this easement to Main Street was 1050'.

By the 1990s, the water pipes leading to the town had become degraded and were leaking, causing a significant loss of water and requiring a continuous maintenance program.[55] A major upgrade to the water system occurred that was financed through the Rural Development Administration of the U.S. Department of Agriculture. A loan-grant package was obtained that consisted of $439,500 in low-interest loans and $424,100 in grant funds. The loans were repaid by the year 2012. In addition, the water treatment process was upgraded to meet State and federal standards.[56]

In 2001, the Town needed to upgrade its water system reservoir and infrastructure to provide adequate reserve for firefighting demands and future water needs. The existing reservoir was located on land owned by Nels Parson (Tax Map 19-62), adjacent to land owned by Sidney Berry (Tax Map 19-62A). Berry granted a 50' diameter easement for construction of a new reservoir and a 25' wide by 1055' long easement from the new reservoir to the well lot that Clopton had conveyed in 1977, adjacent to Piedmont Avenue (Tax Map 19-73).[57] Both Parson and Berry had placed their lands in conservation easements with the Virginia Outdoors Foundation. The Town obtained consent from this organization to construct the reservoir and the new water lines.[58] In 2006, the waterline from the reservoir for a distance of 323.97' was relocated.[59] In that year, the Town installed a new larger capacity water storage reservoir of 225,000 gallons adjacent to the old reservoir that held 100,000 gallons.[60] In 2010 the Town Council budgeted $12,500 to assess a longstanding water system leakage problem originating in the cast-iron water pipes located between Harris Hollow and Piedmont Avenue.[61]

In 1975, the cost for water usage had been set by the Town Council at $3 for the first 2000 gallons, 15 cents per 100 gallons up to 5000 gallons, and above that 20

[53] Town of Washington Comprehensive Plan, 2006, page 29, and 2012, page 35
[54] Rappahannock County Deed Book 199, page 400
[55] Town of Washington Comprehensive Plan, 2012, page 35
[56] Town of Washington Comprehensive Plan, 2006, page 17; 2012, page 35; and 2017, page 20
[57] Rappahannock County Instrument 010001390
[58] Rappahannock County Instrument 010001391
[59] Rappahannock County Instrument 060000325
[60] Town of Washington Comprehensive Plan, 2017, page 30; *Rappahannock News*, 6 July 2006
[61] Minutes of the Washington Town Council, September 2010; *Rappahannock News*, 16 September 2010

cents per 100 gallons; the cost of installing a water meter was $100.[62] A Water Policy Resolution and Water Service Ordinance was adopted by the Town Council in November 1999 which established policies and charges for provision of water service in the town. This permitted the Town Council to modify the charges for supplying water and other charges, such as tap connection fees and minimum monthly usage charges. In October 2005, another Water Policy Resolution was passed, stating that the Town had spent $131,000 in professional fees and construction costs to upgrade the town's water system to provide adequate reserve capacity for firefighting needs; the Town anticipated spending an additional $350,000 to $425,000 to complete the water upgrade project. The resolution established a water tap fee of $5,000 per single family residence, and the Town took responsibility for maintenance of the water meter and the line leading from the meter to the public supply system.[63] In October 2015, faced with a need to increase the town's revenues and after months of study, the Washington Town Council voted to double its rates for usage of the town water (and sewer) systems.[64] This was the first time in more than a decade that usage rates were increased.

In 2018, the sources of drinking water for the town of Washington were two wells located near Harris Hollow Road.[65] The drinking water was monitored on a regular basis and information was entered into the Safe Drinking Water Information System of the Environmental Protection Agency. On 10 July 2018, the town of Washington system (Water System ID VA6157400) was reported to be a community water system, to have ground water as the primary water source, to serve a population of 198 persons, to have no health-based violations, and to have no violations regarding monitoring and reporting of drinking water samples.[66]

The Washington Wastewater System

The method of sewage and wastewater treatment for town properties in the modern era was septic systems maintained by individual property owners. However, a particular problem arose at the southwest end of the town, where a stream flowed and impaired the ability of the land to support septic systems. In addition, multiple subdivisions of the original half-acre lots resulted in inadequate sewage disposal capacity. Because of malfunctioning septic systems, with the potential to contaminate surface and ground water as well as unpleasant odors, the Town Council began discussing the establishment of a municipal wastewater collection and treatment system. In 1994, the Town Council

[62] Minutes of the Washington Town Council, February 1975
[63] Water Policy Resolution for the Town of Washington, passed on 12 October 2005
[64] Minutes of the Washington Town Council, October 2015; *Rappahannock News*, 15 October 2015
[65] 2017 Water Quality Report for the Town of Washington, PWSID #6157400, Rappahannock Historical Society files
[66] Website of the Safe Drinking Water Information System of the Environmental Protection Agency

approved a Wastewater Study Committee to address the problem and to investigate and develop a solution. The town's Comprehensive Plan of 1999 recommended investigating the feasibility of constructing a town wastewater treatment facility, financing for such a project, and acquisition of land for this facility.[67]

In 2002, the Town purchased the Avon Hall property and adjacent land owned by the estate of William and Ramona Carrigan, containing 19.0097 acres, for $920,000 as the probable site for construction of a wastewater treatment facility.[68] In December 2006 the State Water Control Board of the Department of Environmental Quality (DEQ) approved the Town for a $4 million loan at 0 percent interest for 20 years. An environmental assessment report was prepared by the Town and submitted to DEQ in March 2007.[69] In January 2009, the Town instituted construction of a municipal wastewater collection system and a wastewater treatment facility to serve properties within the Town's corporate boundaries. Companies involved in construction of the system were WW Associates, Charlottesville, consulting engineer; Littleton & Associates, Covington, general contractor; Franklin Mechanical, Kilmarnock, general contractor; and Environmental Systems Service, Culpeper, wastewater consultant.

During 2009 the Town obtained permanent easements from owners of town properties to allow the Town to install and maintain the necessary equipment for a sanitary wastewater collection system, including sewer lines, grinder pumps, and storage tanks.[70] Underground pipes were laid that led from each home and business in the town to a wastewater treatment plant constructed on town-owned land that had been part of the Avon Hall property, located on the east side of the town, with access to the plant via a road located on a 50' right of way from Warren Avenue along Leggett Lane. Homeowners and businesses were required to obtain the services of electrical and plumbing contractors to connect their buildings to the grinder pumps installed at their properties. They were also required to abandon their old septic systems.[71] Town-financed contractors installed boxwood shrubs to conceal the above-ground control box for grinder pumps.

The Town received a $489,500 grant from the DEQ when the town agreed to discharge a cleaner-than-normal outflow from the treatment plant into the Rush River. In early March 2010, a five-day test of the system was completed

[67] Town of Washington Comprehensive Plan, 1999, pages 19 and 23
[68] Rappahannock County Instrument 020001760
[69] *Rappahannock News*, 1 March 2007
[70] A typical example of an easement document can be found in Rappahannock County Instrument 100000374
[71] *Rappahannock News*, 11 March 2010 and 16 September 2010

successfully and the Town applied to DEQ for a permit to operate the treatment plant; this permit was received on 16 April 2010.[72]

On 19 April 2010 this system went online, at a cost of about $3.7 million. The project was about $300,000 under-budget, primarily because the underground pipes leading to the treatment plant required almost no expensive blasting or cutting through rock. Within three weeks, 17 customers were connected to the new system; by early September, 94 of the 107 properties were connected and the treatment plant was processing between 20,000 and 25,000 gallons per day. The quality of treated water effluent was better than DEQ standards. The design peak capacity was 60,000 gallons per day; the average use during the first two years was 16,000 gallons per day and peak use was 22,000 gallons per day.[73]

The Town of Washington Wastewater Treatment Plant in 2018

Initial fees for connecting to the wastewater system helped fund the first few years of the system. However, in October 2015, after months of study, the Washington Town Council voted to double its rates for usage of the wastewater system to increase Town revenue.[74] The Town was feeling increased pressure to sell the Avon Hall property as it attempted to remain solvent while paying down the debt of the $4 million wastewater treatment plant loan. In 2002, the Town had purchased the Avon Hall estate and adjacent land from the heirs of William Carrigan as the site for construction of the wastewater treatment facility.[75] Several plans for sale of the property were considered by the Town Council during many months of deliberations and proposals put forward by the Avon Hall Study Group composed of cochairs Gary Aichele and Mary Ann Kuhn, with Fred

[72] *Rappahannock News*, 11 March 2010, 15 April 2010, and 13 May 2010
[73] Town of Washington Comprehensive Plans of 1999, page 35; 2012, pages 16-17 and page 35; and 2017, page 21; *Rappahannock News*, 15 April 2010, 13 May 2010, and 16 September 2010
[74] Minutes of the Washington Town Council, October 2015; *Rappahannock News*, 15 October 2015
[75] Rappahannock County Instrument 020001760

Catlin, Judy DeSarno, Allan Comp, and Ray Gooch, aided by land planner Milton Herd. The plans included selling the remainder of the Avon Hall estate in a single parcel; dividing the land into small-lot, reasonably priced homes; and a combination of these and several other options. In 2016 the Town sold two adjacent parcels of the land, containing 9.09 acres, to Avon Hall LLC (William Fischer and Drew Mitchell) for $750,000.[76] The first parcel, designated as Tax Map 20A-1-115, was 7.5584 acres and contained the Avon Hall mansion, the pond, a two-story cottage, and a small frame building. The second parcel, designated as Tax Map 20A-1-116 and located east of the first parcel, was 1.5289 acres and contained a frame building. This sale addressed several town problems, including the Town's ability to pay down the debt on the wastewater treatment system, which was $178,000 per year. The proceeds of the sale were specifically earmarked toward this debt.[77]

Budgets of the Washington Water Works and the Washington Wastewater System

In 2018, the town's drinking water facilities were funded under a proprietary fund called the Washington Water Works. Revenues came from connection fees and water sales which were estimated to be $112,050. Estimated expenses were for administration ($4,550), capital programs ($25,500), maintenance ($20,000), and operations ($62,000). The wastewater facilities were also funded under a proprietary fund called the Washington Wastewater Fund. Revenue was expected to be $375,500. Expected expenses were for administration ($6,500), capital expenses ($178,000), maintenance ($25,000), operations ($165,500), and professional services ($500).[78]

Eugene Leggett

During his nearly eight-year tenure as mayor of the Town of Washington, Eugene Sheldon Leggett II worked with the Town Council to finance and build the wastewater treatment system, "a project that had been fought over for 20 years by three or four town councils."[79] Another accomplishment was the rebuilding of the town reservoir that more than doubled the size of the town's water supply. To accomplish this, "he won over a divisive Town Council with trust, compromise and consensus after he became mayor in February 2003." Leggett was in earlier years an emergency medical technician and firefighter with the Washington Volunteer Fire and Rescue Company and was its president starting in 1981. He was also chairman of the Rappahannock County Water and Sewer

---

[76] Rappahannock County Instrument 160000598

[77] *Rappahannock News*, 17 May 2016

[78] *Rappahannock News*, 3 May 2018

[79] Mary Ann Kuhn, "The town's hats off to you, Gene Leggett," *Rappahannock News*, 14 June 2012

Authority and had managed the construction of the Sperryville sewage treatment system.

In May 2012, the Town Council named the road leading to the wastewater treatment plant as “Leggett Lane.” He died on 8 June 2012, at age 86 years.

Chapter 10. The Inn at Little Washington

One of the most important events in the modern history of the town of Washington is the opening, on 28 January 1978, of a small restaurant by Patrick O'Connell and Reinhardt Lynch. The two men had been operating a catering business in an old farmhouse nearby and were encouraged by their clients, among them James J. Kilpatrick the noted political commentator, to open a restaurant.

For $200 per month, they rented the downstairs half of a building that originated in about 1906 at the northeast corner of Middle and Main streets on town Lot 24. Over time, the building had been enlarged and had formerly housed a barroom, pool hall, dance hall, movie theater, Merrill's garage, and the Country Store. There they built a kitchen and set about transforming the old building into a restaurant.

The restaurant opened during one of the worst blizzards of the decade, with no liquor license, insufficient electrical power, and a staff of three. The menu was small but elegant, at a cost of $4.95 per person.[1] Some weeks afterwards, John Rosson, a Washington D.C. restaurant reviewer, dined at the restaurant and wrote that it was "the best restaurant in a radius of 150 miles of the nation's capital." Thus began the remarkable history of the Inn at Little Washington.

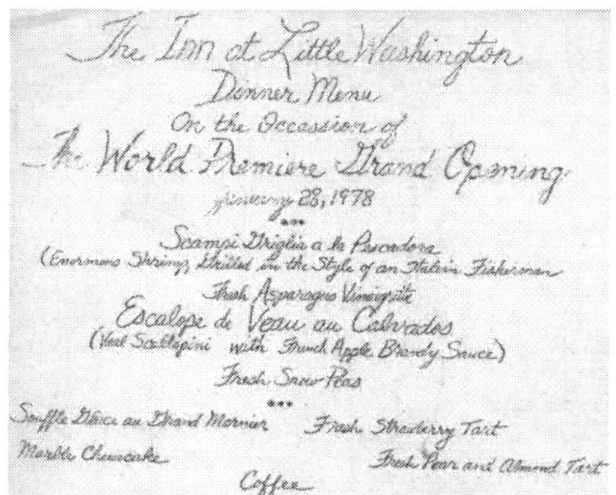
The Inn at Little Washington
Dinner Menu
On the Occasion of
The World Premiere Grand Opening
January 28, 1978
***
Scampi Griglia a la Pescatora
(Enormous Shrimp Grilled in the Style of an Italian Fisherman
Fresh Asparagus Vinaigrette
Escalope de Veau au Calvados
(Veal Scallopini with French Apple Brandy Sauce)
Fresh Snow Peas
***
Soufflé Glacé au Grand Marnier   Fresh Strawberry Tart
Marble Cheesecake   Fresh Pear and Almond Tart
Coffee

Menu for the first dinner served by The Inn at Little Washington, 28 January 1978

O'Connell and Lynch met with considerable resistance at the beginning of their venture. For example, in 2014 the Town Mayor John Sullivan was quoted as saying "For the most part, people today are on the same page. There's not the same viciousness or meanness that there was."[2] Much of this was occasioned by homophobia and an aversion to "come-here's" making changes in the town. One

[1] www.Theinnatlittlewashington.com; *Rappahannock News*, 9 February 2017, page A1
[2] *Washington Post*, 8 June 2014, page G1

issue was the name chosen by O'Connell and Lynch, i.e., "The Inn at Little Washington." Some town residents felt that the word "Little" was disparaging of their town.[3] Soon afterward, Mayor Newbill Miller charged that the tree planters flanking the entrance to the Inn encroached on the public right of way. Locals were irritated because they could no longer hang out on the front porch of the County Store, the establishment that preceded the Inn. Another source of tension was the fact that O'Connell and Lynch lived together and, reportedly, "had a condescending attitude toward locals."[4] There were also difficulties between O'Connell/Lynch and the Sagalyns from whom they rented the Inn building, resulting in a court injunction and an ugly dispute. Congregants of the Trinity Episcopal Church objected when Reverend Jennings Hobson agreed to lease the church parking lot to the restaurant. Teenagers would issue catcalls to the female patrons of the Inn; this was quashed by the sheriff.

Over time, an easy truce was created between the town and the Inn. Writing in 1985, Phyllis Richman of the Washington Post stated that, before the Inn opened in 1978, "there was no restaurant in town and only one place to stay -- a third-rate motel. Now there are bed-and-breakfasts, a cafe, a farmer's market-health food store, and new crafts and souvenir shops. Even greater though, is the change in agricultural life."[5] Indeed, chef O'Connell acquired much of his innovative dinner fare from local agriculture, encouraging people to plant and grow fruits, herbs, and vegetables for his dinners and flowers to decorate his tables and guest rooms.[6] Some residents made specialty cheeses and breads for the Inn. Fish, chickens and ducks, hams and pork, beef, rabbits and even crayfish were procured locally by the Inn. Mattie Ball Fletcher, famous for her secret recipe for candied grapefruit peel, began to provide the Inn with it.[7]

Patrick O'Connell and Reinhardt Lynch circa 1986 (photo courtesy of the Inn)

[3] *Rappahannock News*, 9 February 1978, page 1
[4] Tony Horwitz, *The New Yorker*, 29 March 1999, page 80
[5] *Washington Post*, 2 October 1985, page E1
[6] *The New York Times*, 12 June 1983, page A1
[7] *The Washington Post Magazine*, 4 July 1982, page 11

O'Connell and Lynch purchased the former garage in 1979[8] and the building was extensively remodeled in 1981 into a reception area, hall, service bar, lounge, dining rooms, and kitchen.[9] The goal was to create the ambiance of a French country inn within a historic rural Virginia town. Local talent was extensively used. Castleton contractor Francis Hutchinson did the actual construction, together with painter Louie Bywaters of Rixeyville and stonemason Steve Sealock of Flint Hill. Local resident Josephine Aylor created decorative medallions. Lighting fixtures were procured from the shop across Main Street owned by Charles Eldred. Seamstress Ann Whitcomb of Warrenton created pillows, drapes and banquettes. In 1984-1985, the Inn renovated the second floor of the main Inn building and opened its first guest rooms in what had once been a basketball court and movie theater. Two bi-level suites were created on the top floor of the building in 1986.

In 1990, the Inn proposed a major expansion along Main Street, with buildings to be constructed from the main Inn building at Middle Street north to Calvert Street. The purposes were to add 18 lodging rooms because of the high demand for overnight accommodations, an indoor swimming pool, and a landscaped formal garden between Main and Gay streets. This major expansion created significant rancor in the town and did not occur.[10] Only the landscaped garden was created, on what had been a junkyard in the 1970s; this garden is open to the public. The Inn eventually satisfied its need for additional lodging by converting the Guy Burke-Byrd Jones house (Tax Map 20A-2-131), the Morehouse home (Tax Map 20A-1-17A), the Carter-Dudley house (Tax Map 20A-1-37A), and the Clopton house (Tax Map 20A-1-107) to overnight guest rooms. Each of these properties was carefully renovated and restored to meet Architectural Review Board guidelines and to create buildings that complemented the historic nature of the town.

In 1993, in a story about the Colonial Christmas celebrations in the town, it was stated that "Advance reservations are required for a gourmet dinner at the Inn at Little Washington, where dinners cost $75 to $95 per person."[11] The Inn was assuredly a success.

A new state-of-the-art dream kitchen was installed in the main Inn building in 1998. It reportedly cost $2.5 million and contains a 15' by 7' double-sided European-style range, walls of hand-painted ceramic tiles, and a fireside dining area for guests.[12] From the Inn's garden, one can see into the busy kitchen through large glass windows.

---

[8] Rappahannock County Deed Book 132, page 93

[9] *Rappahannock News*, 19 March 1981, page 1

[10] *Rappahannock News*, 18 January 1990, page A1, and 25 January 1990, page A1; *The Wall Street Journal*, copy of undated article in 1990, page B2; *Richmond Times-Dispatch*, 18 February 1990, page D1

[11] *Fredericksburg Free Lance Star*, 18 December 1993

[12] *The Washington Post*, 23 September 1998, page E1

The Inn at Little Washington at Christmastime (photo courtesy of the Inn)

In 2003 the Inn celebrated its 25th anniversary with a gala 10-course dinner. The cost per person was $1978, representing the year in which the Inn was founded, and the proceeds were used to benefit Share Our Strength, a Washington D.C. based anti-hunger organization. Each course of the dinner was a retrospective, noting the year in which each course was first served, e.g., Sweet Red Bell Pepper Soup with Sambuca Cream (1978).[13]

Patrick O'Connell and Reinhardt Lynch dissolved their business relationship in 2007 by transferring all their properties to Inn at LW Real Estate Holdings LLC, with O'Connell as sole owner of their properties. The LLC had been registered with the Virginia State Corporation Commission on 13 December 2006. Immediately thereafter, the properties were transferred to Inn at LW LLC, with Patrick O'Connell as Managing Member.[14]

In 2013, the Inn made it known to the Washington Town Council that it would like to take over ownership of the "stub street" at the west end of Middle Street. This was a rectangle measuring 30' wide by 170' long and containing about 0.12 acre. This parcel of land was owned by the Town and was a public right of way but was in disrepair. The land was located between the Post Office/Country Cafe building on the south and the Inn Tavern Shops on the north, both of which were owned by the Inn. The Washington Town Council held a public hearing on this matter on 15 July 2013 at which the Council found that the stub street served

[13] *The Washington Post*, 30 January 2003, page C1

[14] Rappahannock County Instrument 070000154; *Culpeper Star Exponent*, 14 February 2007, page A1; *Rappahannock News*, 25 January 2007, page A1

only the properties owned by the Inn and that maintaining the stub street "would be a burden on the Town, as no public access is now served." The Council voted to vacate the property to the Inn and to incorporate it into the property of the Inn Tavern Shops (Tax Map 20A-1-18).[15] The Inn and the Town were both sued over this transfer of property by David Konick, an attorney in Rappahannock County, who claimed that the transfer was unlawful, but this suit was dismissed by the Circuit Court.[16] On 11 May 2015 the Town Council again voted to vacate the stub street to the Inn; the southern 15' by 170' of the parcel of land was incorporated into Tax Map 20A-1-37 and the northern 15' by 170' was incorporated into Tax Map 20A-1-18.[17] The Inn then considerably improved the appearance of the property with hardscaping and landscape plantings.

The Middle Street "stub street" after refurbishment by the Inn

The Inn also collaborated with Trinity Church to improve the church's parking lot located at the southeast corner of Main and Middle streets (Tax Map 20A-1-108), which was adjacent to the entrance of the Inn's newly renovated "The Parsonage." This building had been the home of the Jones family in the 1800s but was used for commercial purposes beginning in about 1940. The Inn paid for improvement of the parking lot, including paving the lot and installing hardscaping and landscaping, costing about $200,000.[18] The Town of Washington contributed $20,000 to this endeavor. In 2015, the Town, the Inn, and Trinity Church were sued by local attorney David Konick, but the Circuit Court dismissed his initial suits; the Supreme Court of Virginia also rejected Konick's appeal.[19] In 1994, the Inn had donated to the Church the 6' tall fountain that is located at the southeast corner of Main and Middle streets.[20]

---

[15] Rappahannock County Instrument No. 130000836

[16] Rappahannock County Instrument No. 150000234 and No. 150000269; *Rappahannock News*, 10 December 2013 and 14 May 2015; Rappahannock County Instrument Nos. 150000504 and 150000805

[17] Rappahannock County Instrument No. 150000512

[18] Rappahannock County Instrument 140000455

[19] *Rappahannock News*, 14 January 2016 and 16 June 2016

[20] *Rappahannock News*, 27 April 1994

In the 40 years since its opening, the Inn at Little Washington has garnered national and international awards. In 1986, the Inn became a member of the Paris-based luxury hotel association, Relais & Chateaux.[21] In 1989, it became the first inn ever to receive the Mobil Travel Guide's 5-Star award. Now known as the Forbes Travel Guide, the Inn has retained this 5-Star rating for both the inn lodging and the inn restaurant for 27 years. In 1992, the James Beard Foundation named O'Connell as the Best Chef in the Mid-Atlantic region. In 1993, the Inn was recognized as the Outstanding Restaurant in America and won national awards for service and wine service. In 2001, O'Connell was given the prestigious Outstanding Chef in America Award. In 2002 O'Connell was bestowed the rank of Maitre D'honneure by the U.S. branch of Chaine des Rotisseurs.[22] The Inn has received the highest possible rating from the American Automobile Association (AAA), 5 diamonds for its restaurant and 5 diamonds for its lodging, for 28 years.[23] The International Herald Tribune chose the Inn as one of the ten best restaurants in the world, and Travel and Leisure Magazine rated the Inn as Number 1 in North America and Number 2 in the world in their World's Best Awards. In 2016 the Michelin Guide to Washington D.C. awarded two stars to the Inn, one of only three restaurants in the D.C. area to earn this distinction and the highest rating in the D.C. guide.[24] In 2018 the Michelin Guide awarded three stars to the Inn, the first and only restaurant in the national capital region to achieve this prized honor, and "La Liste," the French guide to the world's best restaurants, ranked the Inn as the fifth highest rated restaurant in the world and the third highest in North America.[25],[26]

In addition to its national and international fame, the Inn is a valuable member of the town of Washington and the Rappahannock County community. Reinhardt Lynch and, later, Patrick O'Connell have served on the Washington Town Council and the Architectural Review Board. O'Connell has donated countless dinners at the Inn to community organizations seeking to raise money for their activities. For the Washington Christmas celebrations, he has provided baked Christmas treats for sale at Santa's Bakeshop in the Town Hall with the proceeds being donated to the Child Care and Learning Center.[27] O'Connell personally brought lunch to Mattie Ball Fletcher, who lived a block away from the Inn, for many years before her death.[28] He presented an educational cooking

---

[21] *Rappahannock News*, 4 December 1986, page 3; *Bon Appetit*, September 1989, page 79

[22] *The Daily Progress*, 8 March 2002, page D1

[23] *Richmond Times Dispatch*, 12 November 2005; Press release, The Inn at Little Washington, 2016

[24] Press release, The Inn at Little Washington, 2016

[25] *Rappahannock News*, 20 September 2018 and 13 December 2018

[26] The Inn and Chef O'Connell continued to acquire awards in 2019, including 3 stars in the Michelin Guide, the James Beard Lifetime Achievement Award, rank of #3 in the US and #5 in the world by La Liste, 5 stars in the Forbes Travel Guide for accommodations and the Inn restaurant, 5 diamond award from AAA, induction into the DC Restaurant Hall of Fame, and the Wine Spectator Award.

[27] *Rappahannock News*, 2 December 1992

[28] *Rappahannock News*, 2 March 1994

demonstration to the Rappahannock Extension Homemakers in 1991.[29] The Inn sponsored a tea during the Christmas in Little Washington celebrations and cooking classes during this event to benefit the Rappahannock Association for the Arts and the Community.[30] In 1990, the Inn sponsored a tour of its guest rooms, dining room, and gardens to benefit the Episcopal Churchwomen of Bromfield Parish; over 1000 people attended.[31] The Inn also sponsored the annual Christmas card contest for local children age 12 years and younger.[32] In 1991, the Inn recycled over 2000 pounds of glass and aluminum each month at the local recycling center.[33] O'Connell transformed a junkyard on Main Street, north of the Inn building, into the beautiful Inn gardens which were opened to the public.

The Inn continued to perform charitable work for the town and the County, work that has characterized its full existence. O'Connell collaborated with Trinity Episcopal Church to refurbish and beautify the church's parking lot at the southeast corner of Main and Middle streets, installing hardscaping and landscape plantings. He made the same improvements and beautification of the stub street at the west end of Middle Street that he acquired in 2015.[34] A new feature occurred in 2016-2018, that of sponsoring a Saturday morning open-air market in the courtyard next to The Parsonage, where local farmers brought their produce and local artisans displayed their wares. O'Connell launched a charitable foundation in 2018 the focus of which was on historic preservation, culinary arts, and scholarships.

The Inn contributed to bringing increased attention to the need to maintain the historic integrity of the town as a Historic District of the National Register of Historic Places and to implementing the important role of the Architectural Review Board. Largely due to the influence of the Inn and its patrons, the town developed a flourishing bed and breakfast industry and many businesses catering to tourists. The Inn was also the largest private employer in Rappahannock County and the leading employer in the town. It was also the largest source of tax revenue for the town through the 2.5% meals and lodging tax.

Patrick O'Connell and Reinhardt Lynch were honored as Citizens of the Year for 2002 for their significant contributions to the local economy, generous support of local fundraisers, donation of numerous dinners at the Inn to benefit local charities, and service on town organizations. At the time of this award, Lynch had been a member of the Town Council for 14 years, and O'Connell had been

---

[29] *Rappahannock News*, 20 June 1991

[30] *Washington Post*, 16 October 2002; Brochure announcing the Washington Christmas celebrations, Rappahannock Historical Society files

[31] *Rappahannock News*, 20 September 1990

[32] *Rappahannock News*, 14 December 2006

[33] *Culpeper Star Exponent*, 12 January 1991

[34] Rappahannock County Instrument No. 150000512

a member of the Architectural Review Board for 12 years.[35] O'Connell continued his service to the Town government by being an elected member of the Town Council.

Patrick O'Connell published three books -- *The Inn at Little Washington: A Consuming Passion* (Random House, New York, 1996), *Patrick O'Connell's Refined American Cuisine: The Inn at Little Washington* (Bullfinch Press, New York, 2004), and *The Inn at Little Washington: A Magnificent Obsession* (Rizzoli International Publishers, New York, 2014).

Patrick O'Connell, Chef and Owner of the Inn at Little Washington (photo courtesy of the Inn)

The year 2018 marked the 40th anniversary of that first dinner of The Inn at Little Washington. O'Connell arranged for a unique set of 40th anniversary celebrations. These began with an "intimate" cocktail reception in the Inn's Tavern building for many of the long-time friends and clients of the Inn. A garden party was held on the grounds of Mount Vernon to recreate the experience of being a guest at George Washington's table, with chefs from around the country present, the French Ambassador as honorary chair, and fireworks over the Potomac after dinner. In September "Innstock Culinary Festival" was held on the lawn west of the Inn's Tavern Shops. This was an outdoor food and music festival featuring a 'family reunion' of Inn employees over the past 40 years, attended by over 1,000 persons. Former Inn sous chefs were reunited to cook their signature dishes for attendees. There was a charge for admission to the festival, but all of the town's residents were granted complementary admission; the Town Council had voted to provide $5,000 to the Inn in support of this event. Proceeds from the event benefited the nonprofit foundation 'Real Food for Kids.'[36] Finally, there was "Vaux-le-Vicomte -- A Spectacular Soiree" held in a

[35] *Rappahannock News*, 2 January 2003

[36] Minutes of the Washington Town Council, February, April, and May 2018; *Rappahannock News*, special supplement, September 2018; *Rappahannock News*, 6 September 2018

French chateau with a feast for 150 invited guests followed by a grand fireworks display. The U.S. Ambassador to France, Jamie McCourt, served as honorary chair of this event.[37]

In 2018, the Inn at Little Washington LLC and Clopton House LLC were the owners of twelve properties within the original town boundaries.[38] These are:
- Tax Map 20A-1-16, part of Town Lot 6 and containing 0.5601 acre, acquired in 1990.[39] This property was a gravel parking lot shielded by tall shrubbery and wooden fencing.
- Tax Map 20A-1-17A, 437 and 443 Main Street, part of Town Lot 7 and containing 0.2628 acre, acquired in 1998.[40] The building on this property is composed of three log cabins. The part facing Main Street is called "The Mayors's House" because it was owned by Dean Morehouse, a former mayor of the Town. The attached log building at the rear, facing the pasture to the west is called "The Gamekeeper's Cottage." Both serve as overnight accommodations for Inn guests.
- Tax Map 20A-1-18, 439 Main Street, Town Lot 8 and containing 0.5426 acre, acquired in 2002.[41] The property was augmented by 0.0586 acre in 2015 when the Town of Washington transferred ownership of the northern half of the Middle Street "stub street" to the Inn.[42] Located on this property, at the northwest corner of Middle and Main Streets, is a large, authentic early 1800s structure housing The Inn at Little Washington Tavern Shops, originally known as Mrs. Coxe's Tavern in the early 1800s. Anne Coxe acquired Town Lot 8 in 1802 from her uncle, George Calvert, one of the founders of the Town of Washington. She obtained a tavern license in 1803, so the building was probably constructed shortly thereafter. A mercantile store attached to the north side of the tavern was built later for Mrs. Coxe's nephew.[43] In addition to the Inn Tavern Shops, the building contains The Ballroom, a meeting room remodeled by Annapolis, Maryland, architect Wayne Good, that can accommodate 30 persons and has state-of-the-art audiovisual equipment. The top floor of the building is used as storage and offices.
- Tax Map 20A-1-37, 389A Main Street and 389B Main Street, northern part of Town Lot 9 and land to the west and containing 1.4332 acres, acquired in 1992.[44] The brick building fronting on Main Street was built by L.V. Merrill in 1945 to house his Merrill's Garage and car dealership.[45] In 2018 it was the location for

---

[37] *Rappahannock News*, 25 January 2018 and 11 October 2018
[38] For fuller descriptions of these properties, see the section titled "History of the Original Town Lots." See also Rappahannock County Instrument 070000155 for a description of each property.
[39] Rappahannock County Deed Book 179, page 512
[40] Rappahannock County Deed Book 230, page 372
[41] Rappahannock County Instrument No. 020000388
[42] Rappahannock County Instrument 150000512
[43] *Rappahannock News*, 20 May 1976, quoted in the 30 July 2015 issue of this newspaper; also, testimony by Fran Eldred, granddaughter of John Edward Thornton
[44] Rappahannock County Deed Book 193, page 199
[45] Rappahannock County Deed Book 45, page 45; Rappahannock County Plat Book 3, page 13

the U.S. post office and the Country Cafe. The property was augmented by 0.0586 acre in 2015 when the Town of Washington transferred ownership of the southern half of the Middle Street “stub street” to the Inn.[46]

Properties Owned by the Inn at Little Washington, 2018 (gray areas)

- Tax Map 20A-1-37A, 371 Main Street, the southern part of Town Lot 9 and land to the west and containing 0.4199 acre, acquired in 2005.[47] This home was built in about 1850 and was the former home of the Carter and Dudley families. It was first located at the southwest corner of Main and Middle streets, but was moved to its present location in about 1945. In 2017, the Inn instituted a major restoration of this house.[48] It currently serves as overnight lodging for Inn visitors.
- Tax Map 20A-1-107, 360 Main Street, Town Lot 26 and the northern part of Town Lot 27, containing 0.5415 acre, acquired in 2012 and 2015.[49] The building

[46] Rappahannock County Instrument 150000512
[47] Rappahannock County Instrument 050000068
[48] *Rappahannock News*, 21 December 2017
[49] 0.3576 acre (Rappahannock County Instrument 120000273) plus 0.3115 acre (Instrument 150000150 minus 0.1276 acre (Instrument 150000328)

on this property became the home of James Brereton Jones and his wife Eliza in 1836[50] and remained in the Jones family and their descendants until 1944. In 2014, The Inn instituted extensive interior renovations and exterior improvements, costing $4 million, to convert the 6000 square foot Victorian house for use as overnight lodging.[51] The building was named "The Parsonage" because of its location adjacent to Trinity Episcopal Church. Also on this property are three structures called dependencies that were originally associated with the Jones' home. The owner in 2018 was The Clopton House LLC.

- Tax Map 20A-2-131, 456 Gay Street, part of Town Lot 39, containing 0.3838 acre and acquired in 1990.[52] The property was owned by the O'Neale family for many years, and then by the Cary family after three of the O'Neale daughters had married Carys. A Cary graveyard is located in the northeast corner of the property. The small building adjacent to the graveyard serves as the main wine cellar for the Inn; it was the office of Dr. E.W. Brown in the early 1900s. In the 1950s Guy Burke constructed a small house on the property which was enlarged by the next owner, Byrd Jones.[53] In 1991 the deteriorated building was virtually demolished and a new house was built on the property.[54] For a time, this served as the home of O'Connell and Lynch. In 2007 the exterior and interior of the house were remodeled and the building was converted to an elegant overnight residence for guests of the Inn. The house was renamed "The Claiborne House" in honor of Craig Claiborne, food journalist for the New York Times newspaper.
- Tax Map 20A-2-132, 430 Gay Street, part of Town Lot 40, containing 0.3013 acre and acquired in 1992.[55] This property contains a small log house covered with siding used by the Inn for storage, work space and a maintenance shop.
- Tax Map 20A-1-133, 335 Middle Street, the eastern part of Town Lot 24, containing 0.2197 acre and acquired in 2001.[56] The building on the property is a two-story frame house with a side porch constructed in about 1830.
- Tax Map 20A-1-134, 309 Main Street, the northeast corner of Main and Middle streets, the western part of Town Lot 24, containing 0.3151 acre and acquired in 1979.[57] The main Inn building is located on the property; this building houses the restaurant and a total of 11 overnight accommodations (7 guestrooms and 5 suites). The building began in 1906 as a one-story weatherboarded frame garage; a second story was added that served as the town's first community entertainment and recreational center. In 1976, it was the home of The Country Store before becoming the Inn's restaurant in 1978.

---

[50] For a more complete description of this property see "History of the Clopton House," Rappahannock Historical Society, 2013

[51] *Washington Post*, 8 June 2014, page G1

[52] Rappahannock County Deed Book 182, page 30

[53] Rappahannock County Deed Book 132, page 635; Records of the Commissioner of the Revenue for Tax Map 20A-2-131

[54] *Rappahannock News*, 14 November 1991

[55] Rappahannock County Deed Book 191, page 634

[56] Rappahannock County Instrument 010000531

[57] Rappahannock County Deed Book 132, page 93; added to this was 0.0411 acre acquired in 1989 in Deed Book 172, page 551

- Tax Map 20A-1-135, 448 Main Street, Town Lot 23, containing 0.4417 acre, acquired in 1989.[58] The Inn gardens and a house adjacent to the north side of the main Inn building are located on this property. The house was constructed in about 1880 by William Lillard after a fire had destroyed the original house; the Sisk family owned the property before the Inn purchased it.
- Tax Map 20A-1-137, 492 Main Street, the western part of Town Lot 22, containing 0.2568 acre and acquired in 1984.[59] The property, which contains a wood frame house built in about the 1830s, was owned by the Nicol, Resor, and Spiller families in the 1800s and by the Oden family, Annie Miller Almond, and Judge Raynor Snead in the 1900s.

The Inn at Little Washington LLC also owns ten properties adjacent to and west of the original town boundaries. These are:
Tax Map 20A-1-15, acquired in 1990 and containing 1.5104 acres.[60]
Tax Map 20A-1-20, acquired in 2002 and containing 1.6999 acres.[61]
Tax Map 20A-1-21, acquired in 1990 and containing 1.5990 acres.[62]
Tax Map 20A-1-21A, composed of 1.5009 acres acquired in 1999[63] and 0.8960 acres of the adjacent land acquired in 2006.[64]
Tax Map 20A-1-21B, composed of 1.5000 acres acquired in 1997[65] and 0.6041 acres of the adjacent land acquired in 2006.[66]
Tax Map 20A-1-21D, acquired in 1997 and containing 1.5549 acres.[67]
Tax Map 20A-1-21E, acquired in 1990 and containing 1.5316 acres.[68]
Tax Map 20A-1-33, acquired in 2002 and containing 2.8388 acres.[69]
Tax Map 20A-1-33C, acquired in 1993 and containing 1.0055 acres.[70]
Tax Map 20A-1-34, acquired in 1980 and containing 0.7079 acre.[71]

---

[58] Rappahannock County Deed Book 172, page 551
[59] Rappahannock County Deed Book 148, page 202
[60] Rappahannock County Deed Book 179, page 512
[61] Rappahannock County Instrument 020000388
[62] Rappahannock County Deed Book 179, page 512
[63] Rappahannock County Instrument 990001957
[64] Rappahannock County Instrument 060001028; Instrument 170000012 for boundary adjustment
[65] Rappahannock County Deed Book 227, page 794
[66] Rappahannock County Instrument 060001028; Instrument 170000012 for boundary adjustment
[67] Rappahannock County Deed Book 227, page 794
[68] Rappahannock County Deed Book 179, page 512
[69] Rappahannock County Instrument 020000387
[70] Rappahannock County Deed Book 198, page 701
[71] Rappahannock County Deed Book 135, page 691

Chapter 11.History of the Original Town Lots and Other Homes

The names and layout of the streets and location of the lots in the core part of the town have not changed from the original plan of the town presented in 1797 in the second petition to the Virginia General Assembly by George Calvert, James Jett Jr., James Wheeler, and William Porter in which they requested that Porter's land be added to the town.[1] However, most of the original 51 lots have been subdivided and are now described by a Tax Map number.

As discussed in Chapter 1, there is no evidence that there were any buildings on the land that became the town prior to sale of the town lots in 1798, with three exceptions. These are James Wheeler's storehouse, located on the 2 acres that he purchased from William Porter in 1792; Jett's store, located on the 2 acres that the Jetts purchased in 1792; and a schoolhouse located on Porter's property at the southeast corner of Jetts' purchase.[2] William Porter's home was nearby; it is now the home called "The Meadows," located west of the original town land.

The Act of the Virginia General Assembly that established the town in 1796 required the purchaser of a lot to build "a dwelling house" within seven years or the lot would be confiscated by the Town Trustees and resold. This time limit was extended, but the Trustees began seizing and reselling town lots in 1822. Sixteen of the lots were forfeited and resold during 1822-1826 and two were seized and resold in 1833-1834.[3] These eighteen lots represent fully one-third of the fifty-one lots. The Rappahannock County Land Book for 1836 indicates that there were no buildings on seventeen of the lots in that year.[4] As late as 1850, there were still no buildings on seven of these lots.[5] Indeed, Lots 17, 50, and 51 appear to have never had any structures on them.

In this chapter, information about the history of lots in the town was derived primarily from Culpeper County deeds for the period 1796-1833 and from Rappahannock County deeds for the period 1833-2018. These deeds describe sales and purchases of properties. Occasionally these have statements about houses on the lots, but generally they refer only to the land, using terms such as lot, parcel, or actual acreage. A main source of information about buildings on the lots was the annual Rappahannock County Land Books, used for tax

[1] George Calvert, James Jett Jr., James Wheeler, and William Porter, Culpeper County, 1 December 1797, Legislative Petitions Digital Collection, Library of Virginia, Richmond, VA, Record number 000154073; Legislative Petitions of the General Assembly, 1776-1865, Accession Number 36121, Box 58, Folder 71.

[2] Culpeper County Deed Book R, page 35; Book R, page 333; Book S, page 278; Book S, page 194

[3] Culpeper County Deed Book Deed Book OO, page 50 and 346; Deed Book PP, 6, 8, 183, 185, 247, 248, 250, and 433; Deed Book TT, page 408; Rappahannock County Deed Book A, page 85

[4] These lots were numbers 1, 2, 12, 13, 14, 15, 17, 19, 20, 31, 33, 34, 35, 39, 47, 50, and 51

[5] These lots were numbers 14, 17, 20, 33, 39, 50, and 51

purposes, which provide information on the dollar values of the land and dollar values of buildings on the land. The building value includes all buildings on the lot, e.g., a house, a store, and outbuildings such as a shed or garage; a value of $0 implies that there were no buildings on the property. The earliest Rappahannock County Land Book is from 1836; there are no Land Books in Culpeper County for 1833, the year that Rappahannock County was created from Culpeper County, or earlier. A third source of information was the files of the Rappahannock County Commissioner of Revenue which, since about 1952, contain details about each property in the town.

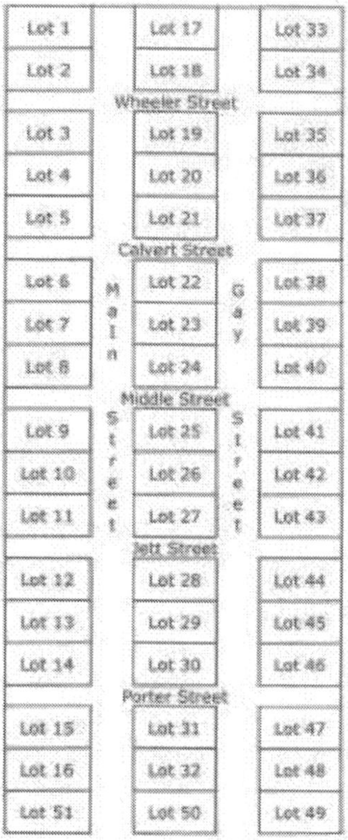

The street grid and original lot numbers of the town of Washington

The National Register of Historic Places nomination, whereby the town of Washington was designated as a Historic District in 1975, and an amendment in 2006 that included additional properties in the Historic District provide fuller descriptions of the architectural aspects of buildings that existed on the town lots in those two years.[6] In these two documents, however, the dates at which a residence or other building was stated to be constructed are often incorrect.

Lot 1 - Tax Map 20A-1-5 (639 Main Street)[7]

The first owner of Lot 1 in 1798 was Richard Jackson. He purchased three lots – 1, 33, and 44 – for which he paid 18 pounds, 14 shillings.[8] Jackson did not live on Lot 1. Rather, his home was at "Homeland" located about 0.75 mile from the

[6] Virginia Department of Historic Resources, National Register of Historic Places, Washington Historic District, #322-0011

[7] For an extensive discussion of the history of Lot 1, see Maureen Harris, "History of 639 Main Street," Rappahannock Historical Society, 2014

[8] Culpeper County Deed Book T, page 381

town on the Fodderstack Road, between Peak Mountain and the Rush River.[9] Jackson was the first absentee owner in the town of Washington.

Apparently, Jackson did not build on Lot 1 as required by the 1796 Act forming the town, and the lot was forfeited to the town trustees. In 1823, the trustees sold the lot, together with forfeited Lots 2 and 3, to Washington and Butler Stonestreet for $18.[10] In 1835, Butler Stonestreet sold Lot 1 to George L. Kendall.[11] There was still no house on the lot at this time. Kendall went deeply into debt and was forced to forfeit the lot to the Rappahannock County sheriff.[12] At a public auction sale in 1837, Nathaniel B. Ralls was the highest bidder and purchased the property for $208.[13]

Ralls was still the owner of Lot 1 in 1850. The lot was valued at $50; the building on the lot was valued at $100, so a small house had been built sometime between 1837 and 1850. Ralls died in 1856 and the property was inherited by his son Samuel, who was Deputy Clerk of the Rappahannock County Court.[14] In 1866, Phoebe Dear brought suit against Ralls for nonpayment of debts.[15] The Rappahannock County Court ordered the sale of "Town Lot 1 containing a house and one-half acre of land known as 'Cabin Hill' located near the house of Butler Stonestreet." The Court directed that Town Lot 1 be sold to James Banks for the sum of $350.[16]

James Banks and his descendants owned Lot 1 and one acre of land adjacent to the north until 1945. Based on information in U.S. censuses, this family was African-American. Banks was born as a slave in 1839. He was the son of Jarett Banks and Nancy Sweny. He "married" Sally Lloyd when they were both slaves (as slaves, they were not permitted to marry), and in 1866/1869 after emancipation, his marriage to Sally was certified. They had one known child, Victor Hugo. James was listed on the U.S. census of 1870 as being a bookkeeper. In 1893, he married Mattie Sloan and they had one child, James Douglass, before James' death in 1896. In 1900, the lot was valued at $50 and the building on the lot was valued at $200.

---

[9] Jackson had purchased the 585-acre property called "Homeland" from Henry Miller. He raised a family of four boys and four girls. Three of the boys emigrated to Kentucky; the fourth son and the four girls married into local families: Daniel Jackson married Mary Corder; Abigail Jackson married David Miller; Jane Jackson married John Miller III, of the Miller family who built "The Maples," now the Middleton Inn; Nancy Jackson married Alfred Dearing of "Fountain Hill," now Caledonia Farm; Phoebe Jackson married Braxton Eastham and they remained at "Homeland" after Richard Jackson died in 1820.

[10] Culpeper County Deed Book PP, page 183

[11] Rappahannock County Deed Book B, page 142

[12] Rappahannock County Deed Book C, page 85

[13] Quoted from Rappahannock County Deed Book C, page 124

[14] 1850 U.S. census of Rappahannock County

[15] Rappahannock County Chancery Case #521, Dear's Administratrix vs. Ralls

[16] Rappahannock County Deed Book L, page 387

Because of Banks' debts, the Court ordered the sale of his property,[17] and the land was sold to Banks' son Victor Hugo Banks and his wife Mary M. Banks.[18] They sold the property to Helen Douglas and Langston G. Carter in 1925.[19]

Carter was the son of Sallie Ann Banks and Amos Alvin Carter; Sallie was the daughter of Victor Hugo and Mary Banks and the granddaughter of James Banks and his first wife Sally. In 1930 the house was valued at $450. In 1934, the property was purchased by Della M. Phillips, a daughter of Victor Hugo Banks.[20] The lot and the attached acreage were purchased by multiple owners from 1945 to 1957, when Clabert E. Smoot and his wife Helen acquired it.[21]

In 2014, Allan T. Comp and Selma Thomas purchased Lot 1, designated as Tax Map 20A-1-5 (639 Main Street) and adjacent land; the property contained 1.10 acres.[22] Comp and Thomas made extensive renovations and additions to the house on the lot during 2013-2014. They remained the owners in 2018.

Lot 2 - Tax Map 20A-1-8 (609 Main Street)

The first owner of Lot 2 in 1798 was John Ray who paid 7 pounds 15 shillings for the lot.[23] Apparently Ray did not build on Lot 2, as required by the 1796 Act forming the town, and the lot was forfeited to the town trustees. In 1823 the trustees sold the lot, together with forfeited Lots 1 and 3, to Butler Stonestreet for $18.[24] There were no buildings on Lot 2 in 1836, but Stonestreet built a house on the lot in about 1840.

In an 1843 deed, Stonestreet indicated that he was living on Lot 2.[25] In 1850, the lot was valued at $50 and the buildings on the lot were valued at $350. Stonestreet was age 55 years in 1850 and was a wheelwright.[26] He was living on Lot 2 together with seven other people whose surname was Stonestreet: Lucinda,

[17] Rappahannock County Chancery Case #1095, Totten and Eshmore vs. Banks
[18] Rappahannock County Deed Book X, page 285
[19] Rappahannock County Deed Book 33, page 86
[20] Rappahannock County Deed Book 39, page 57
[21] Rappahannock County Deed Book 66, page 389
[22] Rappahannock County Instrument 120001092
[23] Culpeper County Deed Book T, page 402
[24] Culpeper County Deed Book PP, page 183
[25] Rappahannock County Deed Book E, page 277; Stonestreet had become burdened with debts and had to mortgage the lot in this deed, but he retained ownership of the property
[26] 1850 U.S. census

age 44; James, age 22, a blacksmith; Elizabeth, age 20; Catharine, age 17; Mary B., age 16; Thomas V., age 11; and Freeman H., age 9. These individuals were probably his wife and children.

Members of the Stonestreet family continued to live in the home on Lot 2 for many years, including descendants Betty, Mary, and Lucy Stonestreet. In 1923, H. F. Stonestreet sold Lot 2 (and Lot 3) to James L. Oden[27] and John W. Oden.[28] The Oden family had married into the Stonestreet family. The lot was owned by the Odens until 1943, when it was purchased by G. Dewey Jenkins and his wife Sadie.[29] It was owned by Clyde Jenkins in 1957, was purchased by Frances Stewart in 1986,[30] by J. Stewart and Evelyn Willis in 1987,[31] and by William Hise in 1989.[32]

In 2018, the owner of Lot 2, designated as Tax Map 20A-1-8 (609 Main Street), was Megan S. Smith. The lot was 0.5503 acre and contained a 2½ -story frame house.

Lot 3 - Tax Map 20A-1-9 (577 Main Street)

The first owner of Lot 3 in 1798 was David Engler who paid 16 pounds 8 shillings for Lots 3 and 21.[33] Lot 3 was forfeited to the town trustees and in 1823 the trustees sold the lot, together with forfeited Lots 1 and 2, to Washington and Butler Stonestreet for $18.[34] In 1823, Butler Stonestreet sold a small part of Lot 3 at its southern end to Michael Nicol, who owned and resided on Lot 4.[35] His son David Nicol had a blacksmith shop on this small part of Lot 3; Stonestreet had a wagonmaker's shop on the main part of Lot 3.[36] In 1850, Stonestreet's portion of the lot was valued at $50 and the buildings on the lot were valued at $100, which were probably his commercial buildings. In 1882, the blacksmith

[27] James L. Oden was town sergeant for the first Washington Town Council in 1894. He married Sallie B. Cary, sister of George Cary who for many years was the editor of *The Blue Ridge Guide*.
[28] Rappahannock County Deed Book 32, page 72
[29] Rappahannock County Deed Book 119, page 259
[30] Rappahannock County Deed Book 160, page 560
[31] Rappahannock County Deed Book 164, page 125
[32] Rappahannock County Deed Book 175, page 274
[33] Culpeper County Deed Book T, page 379
[34] Culpeper County Deed Book PP, page 183
[35] Culpeper County Deed Book PP, page 185
[36] Rappahannock County Deed Book E, page 277

shop on Nicol's part of Lot 3 was occupied by Haden Stonestreet.[37] In 1902, the Nicol's part of Lot 3 was sold to John W. Oden for $75. The property was described as "the land north of the long line between the Stonestreet property and the Nicol property and contains only about 20 or 30 feet".[38] The main, northern part of Lot 3 remained in the Stonestreet family until 1923.

In 1923, H. F. Stonestreet sold the Stonestreet part of Lot 3 to John W. Oden and James L. Oden.[39] The Odens thus owned all of Lot 3. Two years later, James sold his part of Lot 3 to John, and in 1928 John sold all of Lot 3 to Lena M. Tobin.[40] Between 1930 and 1940, the value of the buildings on Lot 3 went from $50 to $1000, so the house that was on the lot in 2018 was probably constructed during this period. The property was sold to Lena and Bernard Moore for $1400 in 1942 and to Minnie Brown Weakley for $3500 in 1943.[41]

Minnie died in about 1955 and her will directed that the properties should be bequeathed to her husband, Upton G. Weakley.[42] In 1968, Upton conveyed the properties to Kermit Ashford Weakley and his wife Mary.[43] In 1995, Kermit made his will and described himself as living at 577 Main Street, Washington, Virginia.[44] Mary inherited the property at her husband's death in 1995. She died the next year at age 75 years. Her executor sold the property to Brandon Fowler in 1999.[45] In 2018, the owners of Lot 3 (577 Main Street), designated as Tax Map 20A-1-9, were Justin and Gail Swift. The lot was 0.5214 acre and contained a 2½-story frame house.[46]

Lot 4 - Tax Map 20A-1-10 (537 Main Street)

The first owner of Lot 4 in 1798 was Joseph Ray who paid 8 pounds 1 shilling for the lot.[47] In 1836, the buildings on the lot were valued at $235, so either Ray

---

[37] Rappahannock County Deed Book R, page 276
[38] Rappahannock County Deed Book V, page 518
[39] Rappahannock County Deed Book 32, page 72
[40] Rappahannock County Deed Book 32, page 420 and Deed Book 34, page 541
[41] Rappahannock County Deed Book 44, page 284 and page 285
[42] Rappahannock County Will Book Q, page 20
[43] Rappahannock County Deed Book 91, page 439
[44] Rappahannock County Will Book 45, page 759)
[45] Rappahannock County Instrument 990002005
[46] In 2019, the Swifts sold the property to Thomas and Constance Bruce for $455,000
[47] Culpeper County Deed Book T, page 401

or the next owner, Michael Nicol, built the 2½-story log house that still existed on this lot in 2018; the logs are covered in weatherboard cladding.

In 1819, Lot 4 was sold to Michael Nicol, who also owned a small part of the adjacent Lot 3 and part of Lot 5. Nicol was married to Sarah Miller, the daughter of Henry Miller II, and they raised a family of 10 children: Achsah A., wife of Thompson Shultz; Elizabeth, wife of Thomas Withers; Henry M., died in Missouri before 1874, widow Eliza; William F., administrator of his father's and mother's estates; Sarah, wife of Thomas Holtzman; David; Aylette; Samuel W.; Mary J.; and Lucy M.[48] Michael Nicol died without a will in about 1840.[49] The house and lot of ¾ acre, composed of Lot 4 and the small part of Lot 3, were inherited by Michael's widow, Sarah. In 1850, the lot was valued at $50 and the buildings on the lot were valued at $400.[50]

Sarah Nicol died in 1873 at age 86 years. A suit was instituted to settle her estate, and the Rappahannock County Court directed that the lot should be sold.[51] Lot 4, together with a small part of Lot 3 and part of Lot 5, was sold to Lucy and Mary Nicol, daughters of Michael and Sarah Nicol, for $735 in 1882.[52] Lucy and Mary are believed to have operated a millinery shop here. In 1900, Lot 4 was valued at $50 and the building on the lot was valued at $350.[53] In 1901, Lucy was a resident of Philadelphia, Pennsylvania, and she sold Lot 4, together with the small parts of Lot 3 and Lot 5, to Lucy Hayward of Rappahannock County for $1,050.[54]

In 1902, Lucy Hayward and her husband Thomas F. Hayward, Clerk of the Rappahannock County Court from 1892 to 1902, sold the eastern half of Lot 4 to Henrietta Peyton for $1200.[55]
Subsequent owners were Thomas H. Huff, Lena Wayland, Rosa Bishop, Lenora Kendall, Alice Reid Wood, Mary Wood Bailey, and J. Newbill and Carol

[48] Rappahannock County Chancery Case No. 767, Nicol vs. Nicol
[49] Rappahannock County Chancery Case No. 101, Nicol vs. Nicol, 1845-1849).
[50] 1850 Rappahannock County Land Records
[51] Rappahannock County Chancery Case No. 767, Nicol vs. Nicol, 1874-1882).
[52] Rappahannock County Deed Book R, page 276
[53] 1900 Rappahannock County Land Records
[54] Rappahannock County Deed Book V, page 364
[55] Rappahannock County Deed Book V, page 534

Miller.[56] The Millers sold the property to Kim and Janice Abraham in 2002[57] and they remained the owners in 2018. The property, designated as Tax Map 20A-1-10 (537 Main Street) contained 0.2467 acre and a 2½-story log house.

Lot 5 - Tax Map 20A-1-11 (525 Main Street) and Tax Map 20A-1-12 (509 Main Street)

The first owner of Lot 5 in 1798 was Benjamin Heaton, who paid 9 pounds 1 shilling for the lot.[58] In 1809, Heaton sold Lot 5 to George Calvert. The 1833 map of the town shows that "Mrs. Calvert's house" was located on Lot 5;[59] in 1836 this house was valued at $200. The northern half of the lot was acquired by Michael Nicol, who lived on Lot 4. The southern half of Lot 5, containing the Calvert house, stayed in the Calvert family until 1853.

The northern part of Lot 5 was inherited by Michael Nicol's wife Sarah at her husband's death in 1840.[60] The property was acquired by the Nicol's daughters Lucy and Mary Nicol in 1873.[61] In 1901, Lucy sold this northern part of Lot 5 to Lucy Hayward and her husband Thomas who was Clerk of the Rappahannock County Court from 1892 to 1902.[62] In about 1940, a 1½-story frame house was built on the property.[63] In 1996, the owner of this northern part of Lot 5 was Elizabeth C. Bennett; in 2018, the owners were Kim and Janice Abraham. The property contained a frame house on 6513 square feet of land and was designated as Tax Map 20A-1-11 (525 Main Street).

In 1850, the owner of the southern part of Lot 5 was the estate of George Calvert, deceased. This portion of the lot was valued at $25 and the building on the lot was valued at $150. The building valuation remained at $150 through 1950. In 1900, the owner was William M. Stuart; he was still listed as the owner in 1950.[64] The owner in 1996 was Pamela Lynn. In 2018 the owner was Lisbeth Sabol; the

[56] Rappahannock County Deed Book W, page 437; Deed Book 40, page 394; Deed Book 40, page 394; Will Book 39, page 607; Deed Book 217, page 521; Instrument 010001314

[57] Rappahannock County Instrument 020000226

[58] Culpeper County Deed Book T, page 400

[59] Rappahannock County Deed Book A, page 189

[60] Rappahannock County Chancery Case No. 101, Nicol vs. Nicol, 1845-1849

[61] Rappahannock County Deed Book R, page 276

[62] Rappahannock County Deed Book V, page 364

[63] National Register of Historic Places, the Washington Historic District, 2006 Update

[64] 1950 Rappahannock County Land Records

property contained a stucco and brick house on 10,546 square feet of land and was designated as Tax Map 20A-1-12 (509 Main Street). The house appeared to be made of two distinct parts, with a brick exterior on one part fronting on Main Street and stucco on the other part extending along Harris Hollow Road. The speculation is that it is made up of two distinct buildings, one that originally served as a farrier and the other as a stable. Inside, the division can be seen in the flooring. One part, perhaps the farrier's, has original worn brick floors, now highly polished; the other, with old wide planked pine flooring, was the stable.[65]

Lot 6 - Tax Map 20A-1-16A (491A Main Street) and Tax Map 20A-1-16

The first owner of Lot 6 in 1798 was Edward Bigbee who paid 9 pounds 9 shillings for the lot.[66] His wife was Lydia Calvert, daughter of George and Ann (Crumper) Calvert. Apparently Bigbee did not build on Lot 6, as required by the 1796 Act forming the town, and the lot was forfeited to the town trustees. In 1822 the trustees sold the lot to Peter Priest for $50.20.[67] Priest sold the lot to Ferdinand Gourdon of Baltimore, Maryland, who sold the lot to Daniel Mason in 1833.[68] On this lot stood the Free Town Meeting House, a frame building. Before the courthouse was constructed on Gay Street, court was held in this building.[69] In April 1833, Daniel Mason, Alexander Spilman, and William J. Menefee were authorized to spend $25 to repair this building to accommodate the court meetings.[70] Menefee was the Court Clerk from 1833 to 1858.

When Daniel Mason went bankrupt in 1840, all his properties were sold at public auction.[71] This included Lot 6 which was sold for $110 to Dr. Joseph Nicklin[72] who was the first of three physicians to own the building. Nicklin's mother, Elizabeth (Calvert) Nicklin, was the third daughter of John and Helen (Bailey) Calvert. Joseph Nicklin was a well-known physician and served as a surgeon in the War of 1812. Later, he was a member of the Virginia House of Delegates,

[65] *Rappahannock News*, 25 September 2008
[66] Culpeper County Deed Book T, page 369
[67] Culpeper County Deed Book PP, page 6
[68] Rappahannock County Deed Book B, page 5
[69] Rappahannock County Minute Book A, page 4
[70] Rappahannock County Minute Book A, page 4-5
[71] Rappahannock County Deed Book C, page 506 and Book D, page 62
[72] Rappahannock County Deed Book D, p. 232

and in 1839 and 1843 he was president of the Washington Town Board of Trustees, which managed the Town before it became incorporated in 1894.[73] One of Nicklin's daughters, Martha Ann, married the architect James Leake Powers in 1837.

In 1850, Lot 6 owned by Joseph Nicklin was valued at $50 and the building on the lot was valued at $100. In that year, Nicklin sold the property to Dr. Adolphus W. Reid.[74] The building served as Dr. Reid's office. In the 1850 U.S. census, Reid was age 30 years and was listed as a physician. His wife was Mary Amanda Wood and they had three children. In the 1880s, Reid was chairman of the Town of Washington Board of Trustees.[75]

Reid sold Lot 6 in 1885 to Dr. Lyle J. Millan, a physician who had his offices in the building.[76] Lucy M. Stuart acquired the property in 1895[77] and the Stuart family owned the property until 1957. The building on the lot was valued at $150 from 1860 to 1900. The building was torn down in 1904, and a new building was constructed in 1908 for William M. Stuart who operated a merchandise store and bank in the building until the 1920s. Lit by gas lights, Stuart's Store supplied most of the needs of the townspeople. He also loaned money from an enormous safe in the rear of the building. It is believed that the last private bank in the United States was the Stuart Bank in the merchandise store. Stuart was forced by the federal government to close the bank in the late 1920s because it no longer recognized private banks. In 1928 T.C. Lea opened his Lea Bros Store in the building, but moved his store to Lot 27 in 1935 when he constructed a new building there on the northwest corner of Gay and Jett streets.[78] In the 1940s the building on Lot 6 became the Washington Cash Store. In 1950 the lot was valued at $100 and the buildings on the lot were valued at $1400. In 1957 the Stuart heirs sold the property to Clarence E. and Rena Mae Giles; the store was owned and managed for many years by Clarence, who was born and raised in Nelson County, and then by his son, Clarence (Skippy) Giles Jr., who inherited the northern part of Lot 6

[73] Minute Book, Town of Washington Board of Trustees, 3 June 1839, 14 April 1843
[74] Rappahannock County Deed Book H, page 203
[75] Minute Book, Town of Washington Board of Trustees, 15 July 1880
[76] Rappahannock County Deed Book Q, page 443
[77] Rappahannock County Deed Book T, page 169
[78] *Rappahannock News*, 3 March 1966, quoted in the 26 July 2018 edition of the newspaper

in 1975.[79] In 1988, Giles petitioned the Washington Town Council for permission to close the Washington Cash Store, renovate it, and lease it to the Health Department, with three apartments upstairs.[80] Giles remained the owner of the northern part of Lot 6, designated as 491A Main Street (Tax Map 20A-1-16A) in 2018. The building on this land, located at the southwest corner of Main Street and Harris Hollow Road, housed the Rappahannock County Health Department on the first floor and three apartments on the second floor in 2018.[81] The Rappahannock Free Clinic also used the building.

In 1990, Reinhardt Lynch and Patrick O'Connell acquired the southern part of Lot 6 (Tax Map 20A-1-16).[82] In 2018, the owner was the Inn at Little Washington LLC. This property contained 0.5603 acre and was a gravel parking lot shielded by tall shrubbery and wooden fencing.

Lot 7 - Tax Map 20A-1-17A (437 and 443 Main Street)

The first owner of Lot 7 in 1798 was John Collins who paid 40 pounds for the lot.[83] The original log house on this lot may have been built in the early 1800s; in 1836 the house was valued at $200. The logs are now covered in weatherboard.

In 1833, Lewis Fossett acquired the lot from Richard Tutt. In 1841, Fossett leased the building on this lot for five years to Robert M. Heterick, who used the building as his law office.[84] Heterick was clerk of the Town of Washington Board of Trustees in 1839[85] and was a member of the Board of Trustees in 1855.[86] He was also the Rappahannock County Court Clerk from 1860 to 1881. Lewis Fossett continued to own Lot 7 in 1850, when the lot was valued at $50 and the building on the lot was valued at $250. In that year, Fossett was age 77 years and was a farmer; he owned several farms in Rappahannock County where he lived.[87] He died in 1854, and in 1860, 1870, and 1880, the owners were Martha and Hetty Scroggins; in 1890 the owner was Francis Scroggins.[88] A Chancery Suit next ensued, titled Compton and wife vs. Scroggins et al., and a public auction of the half-acre property was conducted by the Rappahannock County Court. William M. Stuart purchased the property in 1905, and in 1910 F. W.

---

[79] Rappahannock County Will Book 27, page 474
[80] *Rappahannock News*, 4 February 1988
[81] In June 2019 the Rappahannock County Health Department was moved from 491 Main Street to Dr. Jerry Martin's former medical office at 338-A Gay Street (*Rappahannock News*, 27 June 2019)
[82] Rappahannock County Deed Book 179, page 514
[83] Culpeper County Deed Book T, page 374
[84] Rappahannock County Deed Book D, page 138
[85] Minute Book, Town of Washington Board of Trustees, 3 June 1839
[86] Minute Book, Town of Washington Board of Trustees, 5 August 1855
[87] 1850 U.S. census
[88] Rappahannock County Land Books

Young was living in the house.[89] The lot was valued at $15 and the building on the lot was valued at $250. Stuart sold the property to Vance Keeler and Nellie Hampton in 1946.[90]

There were three log cabins on Lot 7. The log house closest to Main street on the south side of the lot was probably built in the early 1800s. It was 1½ stories, with a living room below and a sleeping room above. Typical of early 1800s construction, the chimney of this building was built away from the house proper after clearing the second-floor fireplace, for fire prevention. The arched brick chimney caps are also unusual. A log kitchen house was located to the rear, connected to the other house by a covered passage. At some point before the 1940s, these two building were joined by a hallway where the original logs were still exposed. In 1965 the potter, June Jordan, purchased the lot.[91] With her husband Wayne Jenkins, she began restoring the buildings and added a large slate patio in the rear of the building.

Jordan was a native of Mount Crawford, Virginia. She lived in the first two log buildings and established her "Fodderstack Pottery" shop in the adjacent third cabin on Lot 7. This building had earlier served as a tanner's shop, cobbler's shop, butcher's shop, and antique shop.[92] In the early 1990s, a bookstore called "Cabin Fever Books" was housed in the cabin. In 1995, the Ragged Mountain Resource Center, the home base for the Rappahannock League for Environmental Protection (RLEP) was located here. This organization coordinated educational and recreational activities focusing on sustainability of the Blue Ridge mountain ecosystem.

In 1985, Dean and Linda Morehouse purchased the property.[93] He became a mayor of the town of Washington, and she was an interior designer who restored and remodeled the old structures that made up their home.[94] With the assistance of Peter Kreyling, a local skilled artisan-carpenter, a contemporary two-story bedroom and loft were added to the rear beyond the kitchen, with care taken to maintain the character of the older parts with exposed beams and other details. The main part of the residence was the clapboard-covered 1½-story log house which contained the living room and an upstairs bedroom. On the north wall was the large fireplace whose exterior chimney still stood. Joined to this was the other log house which was converted to a kitchen dominated by a large stone fireplace. The Morehouses sold the property to Patrick O'Connell and Reinhardt Lynch in 1998.[95]

---

[89] Rappahannock County Deed Book X, page 41, and Deed Book Z, page 251
[90] Rappahannock County Deed Book 48, page 12
[91] Rappahannock County Deed Book 84, page 319
[92] *Rappahannock News*, 3 March 1966, quoted in the 26 July 2018 edition of the newspaper
[93] Rappahannock County Deed Book 152, page 566
[94] *Rappahannock News*, 13 October 1988
[95] Rappahannock County Deed Book 230, page 372

In 2018, the owner of Lot 7, designated as Tax Map 20A-1-17A and containing 0.25 acre, was the Inn at Little Washington LLC which renovated and remodeled the structures on the property. The front of the building, facing on Main Street, became overnight accommodations for Inn guests and was called "The Mayor's House," located at 437 Main Street. Described as "one of the oldest structures in town, it was at one time the residence of a mayor of the Town of Washington. The house has a formal sitting area with a gas fireplace. The bedroom features a king-sized four-posted bed and a massive fieldstone wood burning fireplace. The bathroom is decorated in blue and white hand-painted Portuguese tile and has a double vanity, jacuzzi tub, and separate shower. There is a private walled garden, perfect for afternoon tea, a small wedding ceremony, or any type of celebration."[96] The rear of the building was remodeled to become separate overnight lodging and was called "The Gamekeeper's Cottage," located at 443 Main Street.

Lot 8 - Tax Map 20A-1-18 (439 Main Street)

The first owner of Lot 8 in 1798 was George Calvert, who paid 49 pounds for Lots 8, 42, and 43.[97] Calvert was one of the three men who petitioned the General Assembly of Virginia to establish the town of Washington in 1796. George was descended from the Maryland Calverts, including the 1st Lord Baltimore. His father George moved to Prince William County, Virginia, and established his farm there; in the late 1700s son George moved to what was then Culpeper County, later Rappahannock County. He established his home was at "Horseshoe Farm" located on Fodderstack Road north of the town of Washington between Fodderstack Mountain and Big Mulky Mountain.[98] He married Lydia Beck Ralls and they had 14 children.[99] In 1802, George Calvert sold Lot 8 to his niece Anne Coxe, the daughter of George's brother John Calvert and his wife Helen (Bailey) Calvert. Anne had married Capt. David J. Coxe in 1799. In 1803, Anne received a license to establish an "ordinary" (an inn or tavern) at this site,

[96] http://www.theinnatlittlewashington.com/mayors-house.shtml
[97] Culpeper County Deed Book T, page 398
[98] Culpeper County Deed Book H, page 525
[99] Ella Foy O'Gorman, compiler, *Descendants of the Virginia Calverts*, Higgenson Book Co., Salem, Massachusetts, 1947

so the building that still exists on this site was probably constructed in the very early 1800s.

The main floor was used to serve meals; upstairs were several small private rooms that were rented to lady travelers and to more affluent gentlemen and a large common room where lodgers rented space – often just a space on a bed that was shared with other travelers or even space on the floor.[100] In 1833, the commissioners charged with determining the most appropriate place for the county seat of the new county of Rappahannock met at Anne's tavern. This building was also where the county government held its meetings in 1833-1834 before the Courthouse was built on Lot 45. The bell on the upper balcony of today's building is believed to have been used to call the justices to meeting and customers to dinner. An 1833 plan of the town shows Mrs. Coxe's Tavern located on Lot 8.[101]

A mercantile store abutting the north side of the tavern was built later for Mrs. Coxe's nephew.[102] In 1838 Anne sold this building to James Jett and John G. Lane; it was described as a storehouse and warehouse.[103] In 1843, Lane sold his interest in the property to Jett; the storehouse and warehouse were occupied by the firm of Jett & Green.[104]

Anne Coxe was the owner of the tavern until her death in 1850, when the lot was valued at $100 and the building on the lot was valued at $1700. A chancery suit ensued to settle Anne's estate and the Rappahannock County Court declared that the tavern should be sold.[105] At a public auction, the highest bidder was Peter Ruffner at the sum of $1255. The Court substituted Amos Dear for Ruffner, because Dear had executed his bonds covering the sale price with security. These bonds were fully paid by 1850, when a deed was issued to Dear.[106] The deed conveyed "all of that part of Lot 8 not owned by James Jett" (i.e., it excluded the mercantile store) upon which stood "the tavern and other buildings owned by Mrs. Ann Coxe at the time of her death." After Dear acquired the property, the building became known as Dear's Hotel.

In the 1850 census, Amos was age 38 years and was listed as a tavern keeper. Present with him in the building on Lot 8 at the time that the census was taken were his wife Phebe and their three children; Tamar Spiller; Walter Hackley and

---

[100] Recollections of Mrs. Edna Walker, owner of "Washington House", in Daphne Hutchinson and Theresa Reynolds, *On the Morning Side of the Blue Ridge*, a compilation of articles published in the *Rappahannock News* in 1983, page 50

[101] Rappahannock County Deed Book A, page 189

[102] *Rappahannock News*, 20 May 1976, quoted in the 30 July 2015 issue of this newspaper; also, testimony by Fran Eldred, granddaughter of John Edward Thornton

[103] Rappahannock County Deed Book A, page 288

[104] Rappahannock County Deed Book E, page 334

[105] Rappahannock County Chancery Suit, Nicklin and Calvert vs. Calvert et al.

[106] Rappahannock County Deed Book H, page 421

Robert Spindle, both lawyers; Benjamin F. Kinsey, a physician; John Payton, a merchant clerk; and John W. Barneyels, a road contractor. All of these individuals were probably living in the hotel at the time of the census. Amos Dear was a member of the Town of Washington Board of Trustees in 1855.[107] His building became known as Washington House during the latter half of the 1800s. In 1881, the Board of Trustees of the town of Washington voted to have the public well near the hotel covered over with a guard and substantial framework.[108]

After the death of the Dears, two chancery suits were instigated to settle their estate.[109] As a result of these suits, in 1903 a commissioner of the Circuit Court of Rappahannock County conveyed to John Edward Thornton for $1725 "the house known as Washington House with two acres and thirty-two poles attached" (the Dears owned additional land on the west side of Lot 8).[110] In 1933, the hotel, an apple evaporating plant, and other buildings were located on this 2.2-acre property.[111] The property remained in the Thornton family, being passed down through several generations. In 1950, the owner was Margaret B. Thornton, widow of John Edward Thornton. The lot was valued at $100; the buildings on the lot were valued at $700.[112] Margaret died in 1962; she willed the property to her two daughters, Hilda Levesque and Edna T. Walker.[113] The former tavern and hotel was next owned by Charles and Frances (Walker) Eldred who operated a restaurant named Washington House in the building. Frances was the daughter of Edna (Thornton) Walker and the granddaughter of John Edward and Margaret Thornton.

The storehouse adjacent to and north of Coxe's Tavern, built originally as a mercantile building for Anne Coxe's nephew (above), was inherited by William Jett at the death of his father, James, and in 1874 this was sold by grandson James Jett to James W. Stonestreet.[114] The storehouse was again acquired by the Jett family in 1887 and then sold to William M. Stuart in 1912; it remained in the Stuart family until 1946 when it was purchased by Vance Hite Keeler.[115] The land was described by metes and bounds as being adjacent to the Hotel, with 50.2' along the north-south boundaries and 18.8' along the east-west boundaries.

In 1969, Edna Walker (daughter of John Edward Thornton) and her husband Paul purchased the storehouse building and land,[116] and in 1976 her daughter Frances

---

107 Minute Book, Town of Washington Board of Trustees, 5 August 1855
108 Minute Book, Town of Washington Board of Trustees, 13 May 1881
109 Rappahannock County Chancery Suits Dear vs. Dear and Dear vs. Cook
110 Rappahannock County Deed Book W, page 71
111 Rappahannock County Deed Book 37, page 235
112 1950 Rappahannock County Land Records
113 Rappahannock County Will Book T, page 389
114 Rappahannock County Deed Book N, page 321
115 Rappahannock County Deed Book R, page 165; Deed Book Z, page 251; and Deed Book 48, page 12
116 Rappahannock County Deed Book 96, page 24

Eldred and husband Charles restored the old mercantile building attached to their restaurant and opened a new business there called "The Washington House of Reproductions."[117] The shop included many handsome gift items but the main feature was lighting fixtures of all types, modern and traditional. The business named "Eldred Handcrafted Solid Brass Lighting" which provided lighting restoration services was located within the building. During restoration of the building, corncobs were found within the walls, a legacy of the upstairs room where corn had been stored. On 26 December 1986 the building was partially destroyed by fire, and Eldred discovered an original back wall and determined that the structure had been two separate buildings. Eldred's plans for restoration included raising the roof in the rear of the building to gain a full second floor over the back room, adding several windows on the north side and at the back of the building, and finishing the front with an antique stain rather than painting it white as it was then. The back of the building remained white to continue the appearance of two separate buildings.[118] After the death of Charles Eldred, the building was rented to Carolyn Hallissey, who opened Pockernocker's Reproduction Lighting and Wares in May 1998. This business was primarily a lighting shop with items made from tinware, wrought iron, brass, glass, crystal, and wood.[119]

In 2002 Frances Eldred sold Lot 8, containing the original Mrs. Coxe's tavern and the mercantile building designated as Tax Map 20A-1-18 (439 Main Street) and containing 0.6648 acre, to Patrick O'Connell and Reinhardt Lynch, owners of the Inn at Little Washington.[120] The buildings underwent major renovation and restoration and were converted for use as gift shops on the main floor and storage areas in the upper floor.[121] In 2015, the Town of Washington transferred

---

[117] *Rappahannock News*, 20 May 1976, quoted in the 30 July 2015 issue of this newspaper.
[118] *Rappahannock News*, 28 May 1987
[119] *Rappahannock News*, July 1998 (day unknown)
[120] Rappahannock County Instrument 020000388; plat in Rappahannock County Deed Book 136, page 33
[121] *Washington Post*, 16 October 2002

ownership of the northern half of the Middle Street "stub street" containing 0.0586 acre to the Inn at Little Washington LLC, to be combined with Tax Map 20A-1-18.[122]

Lot 9 - Tax Map 20A-1-37A (371 Main Street) and Tax Map 20A-1-37 (389A Main Street and 389B Main Street)

The first owner of Lot 9 in 1798 was Thomas Thatcher who paid 17 pounds 10 shillings for the lot.[123] John McNeale purchased the lot from Jeremiah and John Strother in 1817, but in 1822 he was forced to sell the lot because of debts; William Porter Jr. was the purchaser at the price of $875.[124] Given this large purchase price, the house on the lot as probably built in about 1800-1820; in 1836 the buildings on the lot were valued at $600. Daniel Mason was the next owner (William Porter Jr.'s brother-in-law); he was a member of the Washington Town Board of Trustees in 1839.[125] In 1840 Mason went bankrupt and all his properties were sold at public auction.[126] This included Lot 9 which was sold to James W. Porter, the younger brother of William Porter Jr.[127] In 1844, James Porter sold the lot to Oliver Perry Smith.[128] The owner of Lot 9 in 1850 was James F. Strother who had acquired the lot, containing a dwelling house and accessory buildings, from Turner A. Jones in 1848 for $600.[129] The lot was valued at $50 and buildings on the lot were valued at $1200. Given this valuation, there was a substantial house on the property.

In 1855 John and Frances Carter acquired Lot 9 and converted the building to a hotel and tavern.[130] In the 1850 census John Carter was age 46 years and was a tavern keeper. Present with him in the building on Lot 9 at the time that the census was taken were his wife Frances and their seven children; John Holland, a bar keeper; and Lewis Oden and George L. Richards, both wheelwrights.[131] A map drawn during the time of the Civil War shows that the building, located on the southwest corner of Main and Middle streets, was a hotel called "Mansion House." The Carter's son, William Hamilton Carter, became the owner of the property. His daughter Saintie married Francis Dudley, son of William Dudley who was the clerk of Mount Salem Church, and the Dudleys lived in the "Carter House" on Lot 9 where they raised four daughters.

[122] Rappahannock County Instrument 150000512
[123] Culpeper County Deed Book T, page 399
[124] Copy of Culpeper County deed in Rappahannock County Chancery Case #354
[125] Minute Book, Town of Washington Board of Trustees, 3 June 1839
[126] Rappahannock County Deed Book C, page 506, and Book D, page 62
[127] Rappahannock County Deed Book D, p. 224
[128] Rappahannock County Deed Book E, page 418, and Deed Book F, page 148
[129] Rappahannock County Deed Book G, page 527
[130] Rappahannock County Deed Book R, page 81
[131] One of their sons was French Pendleton Carter, who became the owner of "Tranquility" on Lot 19.

In 1900, Saintie Carter Dudley was the owner of Lot 9; the lot was valued at $50 and the building on the lot was valued at $600. Photographs of the house by the Works Progress Administration in about 1936 show that the house was a very large two-story building located at the southwest corner of Main and Middle streets. In 1944, L. V. Merrill acquired Lot 9 and 2.5 acres adjacent to the west for $6000.[132] He had the house moved to the south end of Lot 9, and changed the interior of the house from a single-family home to apartments. The back wing of the house and the small building beside it were moved to the back of the lot and made into a rental house.[133] It was reputed to be a house of prostitution. The telephone office was located on the first floor of the Carter House during the time before a dial system was instituted; an operator was on duty 24 hours a day.[134]

On the land at the corner of Main and Middle streets where the Carter House originally stood, L. V. Merrill constructed a new brick building to house his car dealership in 1945.[135] (Earlier, Merrill had rented Thornton's Garage on Lot 24.) With this new construction and the existing Carter House, the buildings on Lot 9 were valued at $9000 in 1950. Merrill's Motor Company was a Ford dealership with a car display window in the front of the building. By this post-war time, traffic was increasing on Lee Highway, which ran through the town, as vacationers traveled to the Skyline Drive and the Shenandoah National Park. In 1976 Merrill conveyed Lot 9 to his granddaughter, Nina Merrill Norman.[136] When it closed in 1979, Merrill's Ford was one of the oldest car dealerships in America from the standpoint of continuous existence.

Northern Part of Lot 9 (389A and 389B Main Street): The building where Merrill's car dealership was located was purchased by Werner Krebser M.D. in 1979.[137] He renovated the building and rented it to four businesses – Nature's Foods, Hayseed Antiques, the Beauty Box, and photographer Pali Carolyn Delevitt.[138] In 1981 the Washington post office was relocated from Lot 14 to the northern part of the building[139] and remained there through 2018. A series of short-lived restaurants occupied the southern part

[132] Rappahannock County Deed Book 45, page 45
[133] Information from Marilyn (Merrill) Bailey, November 2015
[134] Information from Marilyn (Merrill) Bailey, November 2015
[135] Rappahannock County Deed Book 45, page 45; Rappahannock County Plat Book 3, page 13
[136] Rappahannock County Deed Book 119, page 635
[137] Rappahannock County Deed Book 133, page 607; Krebser was a partner in Little Washington Assoc., Inc.
[138] *Rappahannock News*, 26 November 2015
[139] Personal communication from Carol Miller, former postmistress, 2018

of the building from March 1985 to December 1989. These were the Brambles Cafe, operated by John and Ilene Shipman; a renovated Brambles Cafe operated by Richard and Elaine Vigurie, who lived on Gay Street, serving "good healthy food" under the management of Mel Davis; and the Village Cafe managed by Marque and Ann Kolack and Lois and Arthur Neufeld.[140] Finally, in December 1989 the restaurant was reopened as The Country Cafe by David Huff, who remained the manager in 2018.[141]

In 1992, Werner Krebser sold his part of Lot 9 to Patrick O'Connell and Reinhardt Lynch.[142] In 2015, the Town of Washington transferred ownership of the southern half of the Middle Street "stub street" containing 0.0586 acre to the Inn at Little Washington LLC, to be combined with the property on the northern part of Lot 9.[143] In 2018 the property, designated as Tax Map 20A-1-37, contained a brick building that housed The Country Cafe (389A Main Street), which featured homestyle cooking and was a favorite dining establishment among locals, and the U.S. post office (389B Main Street). The owner of the property was the Inn at Little Washington LLC.

Southern Part of Lot 9 (371 Main Street):
In 1990, Nina Merrill Norman and her husband John sold the Carter-Dudley home on the southern part of Lot 9 to J. Stewart and Evelyn Willis.[144] The building housed an antique shop called "Rare Finds" which sold an eclectic assortment of antique and new items.[145] In 2005, the building and land were purchased by the Inn at Little Washington.[146] The house underwent a major restoration by Joseph Keyser Construction Company of Washington in 2017, with the collaboration of Annapolis architect Wayne Good and Peter Post Restoration of Richmond, and was converted to overnight accommodations for guests of the Inn.[147] While the tin roof of the house was being removed, centuries-old poplar and chestnut

[140] *Rappahannock News*, 28 March 1985, 22 May 1986, and 10 December 1987
[141] *Rappahannock News*, 7 December 1989
[142] Rappahannock County Deed Book 193, page 199
[143] Rappahannock County Instrument 150000512
[144] Rappahannock County Deed Book 178, page 389
[145] *Rappahannock News*, 9 January 1992
[146] Rappahannock County Instrument 050000068
[147] *Rappahannock News*, 21 December 2017

were uncovered, as well as hand-wrought nails shaped on a blacksmith's forge. In 2018 the property, designated as Tax Map 20A-1-37A (371 Main Street) and containing the Carter-Dudley home on 0.4235 acre, was owned by the Inn at Little Washington LLC.

Lot 10 - Tax Map 20A-1-38 (341 Main Street, 349 Main Street, and 353 Main Street)

The first owner of Lot 10 in 1798 was Nathan Dyke who paid 9 pounds 15 shillings for the lot.[148] Apparently Dyke did not build on Lot 10, as required by the 1796 Act forming the town, and the lot was forfeited to the town trustees. In 1822 the trustees sold the lot to Daniel Mason for $50.[149] In 1840, Mason went bankrupt and all his properties were sold at public auction; this included Lot 10 which was sold to Henry Johnson, a cabinet-maker.[150] One year later, Johnson sold part of the lot to James Brereton Jones, whose home was across Main Street on Lot 26.[151] In 1850, Johnson's part of Lot 10 was valued at $35 and the buildings on the lot were valued at $350; Jones' part of Lot 10 was valued at $15 and the buildings on the lot were valued at $200.

By 1880, the sole owner of Lot 10 was Eliza Jones, widow of James B. Jones. The property was inherited by Annie Jones Clopton Wood, the daughter of James and Eliza, and then by her son Edward Clopton. In 1950 the lot was valued at $60 and the buildings on the lot were valued at $350. In 1983, John Dobrisky acquired Lot 10 from Peter Kramer,[152] and Dobrisky sold the lot to Jean F. Goodine in 1991.[153] The lot was designated as Tax Map 20A-1-38 and contained 0.5176 acre. Goodine was the owner of Lot 10 in 2018.

Three buildings were located on Lot 10 in 2018. At the west side of the lot (349 Main Street) was a 1½-story frame single-family house, constructed in about 1850 and formerly located on the west side of Lot 25. Peter Kramer moved the house to the rear of Lot 9 and later to the western part of Lot 10. The house was enlarged by Kramer in about 1978 by adding

[148] Culpeper County Deed Book T, page 392
[149] Culpeper County Deed Book OO, page 346
[150] Rappahannock County Deed Book C, page 506; Deed Book D, page 62; and Deed Book D, page 236
[151] Rappahannock County Deed Book D, page 243; Minute Book, Town of Washington Board of Trustees, 3 June 1839, 1 June 1842
[152] Rappahannock County Deed Book 158, page 647
[153] Rappahannock County Deed Book 185, page 831

a small building formerly located on Lot 9.[154] On the northeast part of the lot was a frame 1½-story building constructed in about 1995 by Butch Zindel (353 Main Street).[155] It housed the business variously called Chris' Shop, The Silver Hammer, and Goodine's Gold and Silver; this business sold jewelry fashioned in gold or silver created by Christopher Goodine.[156] In 2018 it was the location for the business called "Wine Loves Chocolate" which featured hard-to-find small-batch wines, cigars, and exquisite artisan chocolates. On the southeast corner of Lot 10 was a small frame 1-story building constructed in about 1980 by Peter Kramer (341 Main Street).[157] The building housed the Geneva Welch Gallery which featured Welch's limited-edition prints, note cards, and original paintings along with gift items of jewelry and hand painted items. Geneva Welch is a nationally known artist who specialized in watercolors and oil paintings of animals and country scenes.

Lot 11 - Tax Map 20A-1-39 (329 Main Street) and Tax Map 20A-1-40 (307 Main Street)

The first owner of Lot 11 in 1798 was Courtney Norman who paid 7 pounds for the lot.[158] Apparently Norman did not build on Lot 11, as required by the 1796 Act forming the town, and the lot was forfeited to the town trustees. In 1822 the trustees sold the lot to Samuel Evans, together with forfeited Lot 28, for $38.50.[159] The 1833 plan of the town shows that 'Dr. Drake' was located on Lot 11; Francis T. Drake was one of the two physicians who were residents of the town at that time.[160] The value of the buildings on the lot in 1836 was $300. By

---

[154] National Register of Historic Places, Washington Historic District, 1975 nomination and 2006 Update; information from Peter Kramer, 2019

[155] National Register of Historic Places, Washington Historic District, 2006 Update

[156] Information from Jean Goodine, February 2019

[157] National Register of Historic Places, Washington Historic District, 2006 Update

[158] Culpeper County Deed Book T, page 377

[159] Culpeper County Deed Book PP, page 247

[160] Rappahannock County Deed Book A, page 189; Joseph Martin, compiler, *The 1835 Gazetteer of Virginia and the District of Columbia*, reprinted by Willow Bend Books, 65 East Main Street, Westminster, Maryland, 2000, pp. 276-277

1841, the owner of Lot 11 was Horatio G. Moffett.[161] He was an attorney, maintaining a private practice and also serving as prosecuting attorney for the Virginia Commonwealth, and was a member of the Town of Washington Board of Trustees.[162] In 1850 and 1860, Moffett was still the owner, with the buildings on the lot valued at $350. In 1880 through 1910, John and Lucy Cooper were the owners of Lot 11; he is believed to have had a saddler shop on the lot.[163]

Northern Part of Lot 11 (329 Main Street):
By 1920, the northern part of Lot 11 was owned by George E. and Louella Cary, where they resided.[164] This was also the location of *The Blue Ridge Guide* newspaper office, in a small frame building fronting on Main Street. This newspaper was the successor to the original *Rappahannock News*, *The Call*, and *The Blue Ridge Echo*. Publication of *The Blue Ridge Guide* was under the capable management of George E. Cary from 1889 to 1936.

In 1950, the owner of the northern part of Lot 11 containing the Cary home was Edward B. Cary, son of George and Louella; the lot was valued at $20 and the buildings on the lot were valued at $500. Edward lived in the house on this property until his death in 1970. He willed his property to Joe Ellen Crane, Mary Lee Goff, and Libby Jane Pullen.[165] In 1996, the owner of the property was Libby Jane Pullen, and in 2018 the owner was Ridge III LLC c/o Abdo Development of Washington DC. The two-story frame Cary home fronted by a first-floor porch was located on the property, designated as Tax Map 20A-1-39 (329 Main Street).

Southern Part of Lot 11 (307 Main Street):
In the 1930s, the Carys constructed a two-story frame building on the southern part of Lot 11 for recreational purposes. A poolroom serving beer was in the basement. The private Rappahannock Club had Saturday night dances, dancing lessons, and children's parties on the main floor; there were apartments above.[166] In 1950, the owner of this part of Lot 11 was Louella Cary; the lot was valued at $50 and the building was valued at $1100. The property had multiple owners

---

[161] Rappahannock County Deed Book D, page 243
[162] Minute Book, Town of Washington Board of Trustees, 3 June 1839
[163] Rappahannock County Land Records
[164] Rappahannock County Deed Book T, page 39
[165] Rappahannock County Will Book Y, page 320 and Deed Book 103, page 34
[166] Elisabeth B. and C.E. Johnson Jr., *Rappahannock County, Virginia, A History*, Green Publishers, Orange, VA, 1981, p. 144

during 1985 to 1997.[167] Located in the building in the 1980s was the business called "La Galerie Des Beaux-Arts" with emphasis on European paintings from the 18th to early 20th centuries. The business was owned and operated by Jane Krebser. In 1993 the business called "Country Heritage" occupied the building. It sold antiques and reproductions, pottery, folk art, quilts, dried flowers, and gifts. In 1998 the building housed R.H. Ballard Fine Art which sold original art prints, and antique and new Persian, Caucasian, Turkish, and Afghan rugs.[168] Robert and Joan Ballard purchased the property in 2004[169] and remained the owners in 2018. The property, located at the northwest corner of Main and Jett streets (307 Main Street) and designated as Tax Map 20A-1-40, contained 0.090 acre. On this property was the store, R. H. Ballard Shop and Gallery, which sold fine art, rugs, table linens, and gift items, with a rental apartment on the second floor.

Lot 12 - Tax Map 20A-1-41 (291 Main Street) and 20A-1-42

The first owner of Lot 12 in 1798 was William Porter who paid 25 pounds 18 shillings for Lots 12, 13, 14, and 47.[170] Porter was one of the four men who petitioned the General Assembly of Virginia in 1797 to include part of his land in the new town of Washington.[171]

In 1833, William's widow Sarah purchased Lot 12 (as well as Lots 13, 14, and 15)[172] and then sold the lot to Henry Johnson.[173] Johnson was a member of the Town of Washington Board of Trustees in 1839 and 1843.[174] In about 1837 Johnson began construction of a 16' by 32' two-story frame house for himself and his bride, Eliza Ann Grove. He also constructed an ice house on the property. In 1850 the house was valued at $250. Johnson remained the owner of Lot 12 until

---

[167] Rappahannock County Deed Book 151, page 178; Deed Book 179. page 219; Deed Book 195, page 618; and Instrument 970000750

[168] *Rappahannock News*, 11 November 1998, quoted in the 26 July 2018 edition of the newspaper

[169] Rappahannock County Instrument 040000297

[170] Culpeper County Deed Book T, page 371

[171] George Calvert, James Jett Jr., James Wheeler, and William Porter, Culpeper County, 1 December 1797, Legislative Petitions Digital Collection, Library of Virginia, Richmond, VA, Record number 000154073; Legislative Petitions of the General Assembly, 1776-1865, Accession Number 36121, Box 58, Folder 71.

[172] Rappahannock County Deed Book A, page 157

[173] Rappahannock County Deed Book A, page 146

[174] Minute Book, Town of Washington Board of Trustees, 3 June 1839, 1 June 1842

1851, when he sold the lot to James B. Jones & Co.; from 1854 to 1907 the property was owned by Walker and Mary Holland.[175] In 1900, Lot 12 was valued at $50 and the buildings on the lot were valued at $300. Walker Holland was a tailor who maintained his business in his home on Lot 12. He was also the Washington postmaster, and the post office was located on his property, probably in his home. After Holland's death, the post office was moved and Lot 12 was sold to D. Cleveland Updike in 1910. The house was expanded at the back, sides, and front and gained a distinct colonaded "manor house" appearance. Updike's wife Margaret Updike established a tourist guest house business in the home, and substantial improvements were made to the building to serve this business; in 1920 the buildings on the lot were valued at $750. The Updike's daughter, Kathleen Updike Scudere acquired the property in 1952,[176] and P.W. Scudere's Garage was located on the property.

It is believed that the ice house was moved closer to Main Street at this time. In about the 1970s the businesses Nature's Foods and Ice House Crafts, selling homemade bread, gifts, furniture, and Christmas decorations were located in this small building.

There were multiple owners subsequently, and in 1985 the property was acquired by James and Nancy Thomasson who established a bed and breakfast business in the former Holland home, as well as an antiques and crafts shop, crafts studio, and restoration workshop in the house and outbuildings. James was a professor of theology at Georgetown University and Nancy was a weaver and quilter who also managed the antiques shop. In 1991, Francis and Jean Scott acquired Lot 12, and their bed and breakfast establishment received a 3-diamond rating by the American Automobile Association in 1993. The Scotts sold the property to Harry Carlip in 1998, who conveyed it to Piedmont Partners and Gary and Michelle Schwartz in 2004-2006; the charming manor house and land were renamed "Heritage House."[177] In 2014, the building and 0.2843 acre were sold to The Inn at the Ridge LLC which

175 Rappahannock County Deed Book I, page 54, and Deed Book I, page 451

176 Rappahannock County Deed Book 58, page 108

177 Rappahannock County Deed Book 233, page 823; Rappahannock County Instruments 040000847, 050000199, and 060002277; Rappahannock County Instruments 050000199 and 060002277

retained the bed and breakfast function and renamed the building as "The White Moose Inn;" in 2016 the remaining 0.2098 acre was sold to Ridge 35 LLC.[178] The colonnaded inn on the property was described as "a hip, modern approach to the historic country Inn, built circa 1837, combining calm with luxury. Features include a large terrace with mountain views, rooms with vaulted ceilings, and crisp clean designs." The property is designated as 20A-1-41 (291 Main Street) and Tax Map 20A-1-42.

Lot 13 - Tax Map 20A-1-43 (261 Main Street) and Tax Map 20A-1-44 (249 Main Street) and Lot 14 - Tax Map 20A-1-45 (233 Main Street) and Tax Map 20A-1-45A (211 Main Street)

The first owner of Lot 13 and Lot 14 in 1798 was William Porter who paid 25 pounds 18 shillings for Lots 12, 13, 14, and 47.[179] Porter was one of the four men who petitioned the General Assembly of Virginia in 1797 to include part of his land in the new town of Washington.[180]

In 1833, William's widow Sarah was the owner of Lot 13 and 14.[181] She sold Lot 13 to Henry Johnson[182] and Lot 14 to George Abernathy.[183] There were no buildings on either property in 1836. However, by 1841, Henry Johnson had constructed a home on Lot 13. The building was a two-story brick house with porches on the first and second floor. It was often described as one of the most beautiful homes in the town of Washington. Also on the lot were a smokehouse and other outbuildings; the value of these buildings and the home was $1200 in 1841. In that year, J.Y. Menefee acquired Lot 13 from Johnson and in 1857 he acquired Lot 14 from George Nicol.[184]

For the next 70 years these two lots were the home of J. Y. Menefee, his family, and his descendants. He was a distinguished lawyer, the county Commonwealth Attorney in the 1850s, and a member of the Town of Washington Board of Trustees in 1855.[185] The Menefees raised eleven children in their home. In 1893 Dora, Nita, and Jennie Menefee were the owners of the property.[186] Nita died in 1900, Jennie died in 1930, and Dora died in 1936, and in 1937 two of their heirs -- Mary S. Gibbons and Dora M. Sangster -- purchased the interest of the other

---

[178] Rappahannock County Instruments 120000812 and 160000879

[179] Culpeper County Deed Book T, page 371

[180] George Calvert, James Jett Jr., James Wheeler, and William Porter, Culpeper County, 1 December 1797, Legislative Petitions Digital Collection, Library of Virginia, Richmond, VA, Record number 000154073; Legislative Petitions of the General Assembly, 1776-1865, Accession Number 36121, Box 58, Folder 71.

[181] Rappahannock County Deed Book A, page 157

[182] Rappahannock County Deed Book A, page 146

[183] Rappahannock County Deed Book A, page 147

[184] Rappahannock County Deed Book H, page 501, and Deed Book K, page 154

[185] Minute Book, Town of Washington Board of Trustees, 5 August 1855

[186] Rappahannock County Deed Book S, page 424

heirs in the two lots.[187] Only Lot 13 appeared to have a house on it, although there may have been outbuildings on Lot 14.[188] Mary and Dora sold the lots to Charles Keyser in 1936-1937, who sold the properties to Jessie Cox in 1946, who sold them in the same year to Harold Geest.[189] The Menefee home on Lot 13 had been severely weakened when Main Street was macadamized and widened during construction of Lee Highway through the town in the 1930s. Large cracks appeared in the house, and the home was dismantled in the 1940s. Harold Geest, a resident of Culpeper County, divided Lot 13 and Lot 14, beginning in 1946:

Northern part of Lot 13 (261 Main Street):

In 1946, Geest sold the northern part of Lot 13, with 50' of frontage on Main Street and on which there were no buildings, to Marion Gray Watts.[190] A plain 1½-story brick building was constructed on this property. The building was occupied by the Watts' Barbershop and Bertha's Diner. In 1996, the owner of

the property was Hook & Crook Associates. More recently, the businesses called The Hair Gallery owned by Kimberly Nelson and The Little Washington Wellness & Spa owned by Jackie Meuse were located in the building. In 2018, the building housed the business called The Little Washington Spa and the owner of the property, designated as Tax Map 20A-1-43 (261 Main Street) and containing 0.188 acre, was First Markin Group LLC c/o Joseph Meuse of Warrenton, Virginia.

[187] Rappahannock County Deed Book 40, pages 385 and 402
[188] Rappahannock County Land Books, 1850-1950
[189] Rappahannock County Deed Book 46, page 442, Deed Book 47, page 279, and Deed Book 48, page 120
[190] Rappahannock County Deed Book 49, page 159

Southern Part of Lot 13 (249 Main Street):

This property was formerly the location of the Menefee family home. Harold Geest sold this then-vacant land to Lucy Catherine Bowie in 1950.[191] A plain 1½-story concrete block building was constructed, and the building was occupied by the *Rappahannock News* office, which remained in the building until 2013. In 1996, the owner of the property was Arthur Arundel who was also the owner of the *Rappahannock News*. In 2018 the property, designated as Tax Map 20A-1-44 (249 Main Street) and containing 0.2259 acre, was owned by Ridge 249 LLC of Washington, D.C.

Lot 14 (211 and 233 Main Street):

In 1951, Harold Geest leased Lot 14 to the Town of Washington for use as a recreation area for a period of five years, and the town playground was developed on this property.[192] After this, he sold the southern half of Lot 14 to W. Arthur Miller in 1955,[193] on which was constructed a concrete block building. This was used by the W.A. Miller-John Caskie Real Estate company on the south side of the building and the Washington Post Office, from April 1956 to 1981, on the north side. The Rappahannock Health Department was also located in the building and Mrs. John M. Barber Jr. opened a beauty shop in the building.[194] Douglas Baumgardner purchased the building in 1982 for his law office and added ground and upper levels in the rear. Dr. W. Neal Mayberry of Luray opened a dental office in the rear ground level on 3 June

[191] Rappahannock County Deed Book 54, page 127
[192] Rappahannock County Deed Book 56, page 448; *Rappahannock News*, 12 July 1952
[193] Rappahannock County Deed Book 64, page 299
[194] *Rappahannock News*, 12 April 1956

1982, seeing patients on Thursdays.[195] In 1987, the rear lower level was the site of Washington Video Rentals, owned by Susan Kauffman and Rae Haase, which sold and rented video tapes. When Baumgardner retired in 2014, Miller Building LLC (Eve Willis, daughter of Arthur Miller) acquired the property.[196] The south side of the building was converted to an antique/gift shop called "Rare Finds"; the north side of the building housed the law office of Michael Brown of the Walker-Jones legal firm. In 2018, Rare Finds occupied the main floor of the building. The offices of Hampton Title Agency were on the rear lower level. In 2018, the owner of the property, designated as Tax Map 20A-1-45A (211 Main Street), was Miller Building LLC (J. Stewart Willis).

Geest sold the northern half of Lot 14 to Marion and Nell Watts in 1965.[197] On this property was constructed a one-story concrete block building with a basement level[198] that was a 6-unit apartment building in 2018, with units on the

eastern Main Street side and lower-level units on the western side of the lot. In 2018, the owner of the property, designated as Tax Map 20A-1-45 (233 Main Street), was T&M Properties of Rappahannock LLC.

Lot 15 - Tax Map 20A-1-61 (199 Main Street and 195 Main Street)

The first owner of Lot 15 in 1798 was John O'Neal who paid 8 pounds 2 shillings for the lot.[199] In 1833, Sarah Porter was the owner of the lot which she sold to John F. Carter.[200] There were no buildings on Lot 15 in 1836. In 1850, the lot was valued at $40 and the buildings on the lot were valued at $400. Carter sold Lot 15 to Howard Compton in 1855; at that time, there was a wagon-makers shop on the lot.[201] In 1860 through 1892, the lot was owned by Elias Compton; it was purchased by John W. Clark in 1893.[202] In 1900, Lot 15 was valued at $25 and the building on the lot was valued at $100.

---

[195] *Rappahannock News*, 27 May 1982
[196] Rappahannock County Instrument 140000753
[197] Rappahannock County Deed Book 84, page 138
[198] *Rappahannock News*, 4 November 1965
[199] Culpeper County Deed Book T, page 407
[200] Rappahannock County Deed Book A, page 157 and page 166
[201] Rappahannock County Deed Book J, page 309
[202] Rappahannock County Deed Book S, page 397

Clark began a jitney service named the Front Royal & Washington Motor Transportation Company that was chartered in 1916. He constructed a second building on Lot 15, adjacent to and south of his home, which served as the bus station. He and his wife Alice sold Lot 15 and the bus company to Walker B. Jenkins in 1920 for $1000.[203] He renamed the company as the Walker B. Jenkins Bus Line, which provided daily bus service from Culpeper to Winchester via Washington and Front Royal, and later from Sperryville to Fredericksburg via Washington and Culpeper.[204] In the mid-1950s Jenkins sold the line to the Virginia Trailways Bus Company. (See Chapter 14 for more details.)

Two of Walker Jenkins' four daughters, Mary and Ruby, did not marry and resided in the house on Lot 15 for many years. Mary was a local first grade teacher, and Ruby was secretary for the Virginia Extension Service. In 2018 the owner of the property, located at the southwest corner of Main and Porter streets and designated as Tax Map 20A-1-61; was Winsor Properties LLC. Deborah Winsor had restored the property. She applied for and was granted permission to use the house as an occasional tourist home (199 Main Street). In the former bus station building was the shop known as August Georges (195 Main Street).

Lot 16 - Tax Map 20A-1-62 (189 Main Street and 191 Main Street) and Lot 51 - Tax Map 20A-1-63

The first owner of Lot 16 in 1798 was Henry Menefee who paid 8 pounds 2 pence for the lot.[205] The first owner of Lot 51 in 1798 was John Vince who paid 6

[203] Rappahannock County Deed Book 30, page 357
[204] Daphne Hutchinson and Theresa Reynolds, compilers, *On the Morning Side of the Blue Ridge*, articles from the Rappahannock News of 1983, page 28
[205] Culpeper County Deed Book T, page 385

pounds 9 shillings for the lot.[206] Apparently neither Menefee nor Vince built a house on their lots, as required by the 1796 Act forming the town, and both lots was forfeited to the town trustees. In 1822 the trustees sold the two adjacent lots to Francis Carey for $62.[207] By 1836, a house worth $300 had been built on Lot 16, but there was no structure on Lot 51. In 1845, George Ficklin sold both lots to George Nicol, a blacksmith, who sold them to Henry Foster in 1857 for $375.[208] Henry Foster was a shoemaker and was a member of the Washington Town Board of Trustees in 1855.[209]

In 1862, Lot 16 and Lot 51 were purchased by George M. Cary from Henry and Hetty Foster for $390.[210] Cary sold the two half-acre lots to John A. Compton in 1863 for $450.[211] The two lots remained in the Compton family for the next 85 years, being passed down through several generations until 1948. Through this time, the buildings on Lot 16 increased in value from $300 to $1500, but there were no buildings on Lot 51.

Northern Part of Lot 16 (191 Main Street):

In 1948 Eugene and Hetty Wagner purchased the northern part of Lot 16, containing 0.3445 acre, from the Compton heirs, and in 1950 they sold this land to William and Elizabeth Buntin.[212] The Buntins built a brick home on the property. William was appointed sheriff of Rappahannock County in 1976 and retired in 1984. Elizabeth taught at the high school and served as director of Rappahannock County Social Services.[213] In 2018, Elizabeth was the owner of the northern part of Lot 16, designated as Tax Map 20A-1-62 (191 Main Street). She had lived in the town of Washington for 68 years and she celebrated her 102nd birthday with her daughter Nancy on 1 November 2018.

[206] Culpeper County Deed Book T, page 383
[207] Culpeper County Deed Book PP, page 250
[208] Rappahannock County Deed Book F, page 215 and Deed Book L, page 251
[209] Minute Book, Town of Washington Board of Trustees, 5 August 1855
[210] Rappahannock County Deed Book L, page 252
[211] Rappahannock County Deed Book L, page 283
[212] Rappahannock County Deed Book 50, page 190, and Deed Book 54, page 250
[213] *Rappahannock News*, 31 August 1978 and 8 November 2018

Southern Part of Lot 16 and Lot 51 (189 Main Street):

Edna Updike was the next owner of these properties and held them until Patrick Foster and Camille Harris purchased them in 1981.[214] Patrick was a renovation specialist and decorative painter who brought charm back into the old Victorian house formerly owned by the Compton family, and he and Camille opened a bed and breakfast there known as the Foster-Harris House. In 1992, Phyllis Marriott purchased the property and retained the bed and breakfast business and the name of the Foster-Harris House. In 2008 the owners were John and Diane MacPherson.[215] In 2018, the owner of the property designated as Tax Map 20A-1-63 (189 Main Street) and containing 0.6534 acre was Peters Hospitality Management LLC.[216] On the property was the Foster-Harris House, a 5-bedroom bed and breakfast establishment that sponsored the "Tour d'Epicure" by which patrons could bicycle to various sites. The Foster Harris House Bed & Breakfast also served five-course dinners on weekends to its overnight guests as well as to the public in an intimate 10-seat dining room.

Lot 17 - Tax Map 20A-1-125a

The first owner of Lot 17 in 1798 was David Lansdown who paid 31 pounds 15 shillings for Lots 17, 19, 20, 45, and 46.[217] By 1843, the owner of Lot 17 was Mrs. Anne Coxe. She was the daughter of John Calvert, a brother of George Calvert who was one of the founders of the town of Washington. In 1850, the owner of Lot 17 was the estate of Anne Coxe, deceased; the lot was valued at $25 but there was no valuation for any building on the lot.[218] Indeed, Rappahannock County land records indicate that no buildings have ever been constructed on this lot.

The owner of Lot 17 in 1920 and 1930 was Henrietta Carter, and African American. In 1996 the owner was the Rappahannock County Citizens League, a group composed of African Americans who were members of the First Washington Baptist Church. In 2011, Sidney and Mary Catherine Worley sold

[214] Rappahannock County Deed Book 140, page 55
[215] Rappahannock County Instrument 080001185
[216] Rappahannock County Instrument 170000090
[217] Culpeper County Deed Book T, page 372
[218] 1850 Rappahannock County Land Records

the lot to Jerry and Cynthia Hodges of Clifton, Virginia.[219] The owners in 2018 were Godfrey and Jeanne Kauffmann; the property contained 0.6701 acre.

Lot 18 - Tax Map 20A-1-141, Tax Map 20A-1-142 (309 Wheeler Street), and Tax Map 20A-1-143 (225 Wheeler Street)

The first owner of Lot 18 in 1798 was George Yates who paid 5 pounds 15 shillings for the lot.[220] In 1815, Yates sold the one-half acre lot to James Yates and John Miller for "the benefit of the public and on which is erected a house for public worship."[221] An 1833 plan of the town of Washington showed that a meeting house was located on Lot 18[222] and an 1843 list of owners of Washington lots showed that it was "the Meeting House Lot." By 1880, the Church lot was considered to be abandoned and the trustees of Old Church, who were James O'Neale, Middleton Miller, James L. Powers, John Jett, and Adolphus W. Reid, relinquished all claim to the lot and gave the lot, known as "the Old Church Lot" to the Reformed Episcopal Church.[223] Willie Jett was the minister.

In 1914, trustees of the Reformed Episcopal Church petitioned the Rappahannock County Court for permission to sell Lot 18 to Eugenia F. Dudley, who had offered $250 for the property. The trustees explained that the property had been used for a number of years by the congregation of the Reformed Episcopal Church, but that some years ago the congregation had become extinct and ceased to use the property as a place of worship. The Council of the Reformed Episcopal Church authorized the trustees to sell the property and to use the proceeds to erect a parsonage for the Antioch Reformed Episcopal Church in Essex County, Virginia. The trustees -- D. B. Phillips, Joshua T. Hopper, and E. C. Heterick -- sold the lot to Eugenia Dudley.[224] Nothing is left of the church except possibly part of a foundation wall.[225]

The next owner was Frank Jones, who built two Dutch-colonial houses there. The 1½ story house at 225 Wheeler Street and its exact duplicate, the home at 309 Wheeler Street, were both constructed in about 1927.[226] In 2018, the owner of the western part of Lot 18, designated as Tax Map 20A-1-143 (225 Wheeler Street), was Dorothy B. Hawkins, who served on the All-Women Town Council elected in 1950. The owner of the central section of Lot 18 in 1996, designated as Tax Map 20A-1-142 (309 Wheeler Street) and containing 0.2724 acre, was Clarence Ashby Wayland; in 2018 the owner was Lisa Leftwich. The owner of

---

[219] Rappahannock County Instrument 110001057
[220] Culpeper County Deed Book T, page 397
[221] Culpeper County Deed Book HH, p. 288
[222] Rappahannock County Deed Book A, page 189
[223] Rappahannock County Deed Book Q, page 327
[224] Rappahannock County Deed Book 27, page 204
[225] Information from Dorothy Hawkins, in M. Elizabeth Buntin, *Mission: A Study of the Churches of Bromfield Parish*, pages 46, files of Trinity Episcopal Church
[226] National Register of Historic Places, Washington Historic District, 2006 Update

the southeastern corner of Lot 18 in 2018, designated as Tax Map 20A-1-141 and containing 0.0340 acre, was Fredette S. Engle of McLean, Virginia.

225 Wheeler Street (front view)

309 Wheeler Street (side view)

Lot 19 - Tax Map 20A-1-140 (567 Gay Street) and Tax Map 20A-1-140A (593 Gay Street)

The first owner of Lot 19 in 1798 was David Lansdown who paid 31 pounds 15 shillings for Lots 17, 19, 20, 45, and 46.[227] Apparently Lansdown did not build a dwelling on the property, as required by the 1796 Act forming the town, and the lot was forfeited to the town trustees. In 1823, the trustees sold Lot 19 to Harvey Evans for $10.[228] In 1835, the lot was owned by Samuel Evans and Benjamin Hesser and had to be sold because of debts; it was purchased by Daniel Mason.[229] The lot had no value for buildings in the 1836 Rappahannock Land Book. When Mason went bankrupt, all his properties were sold at public auction in 1841 and the attorney William J. Menefee purchased the lot, on which there was a house.[230] The house was thus apparently constructed between 1836 and 1841; the buildings on Lot 19 were valued at $700 in 1850.

William J. Menefee was a member of the Washington Town Board of Trustees in 1839 and 1843.[231] He was also the Rappahannock County Court Clerk from 1833 to 1858. In 1850, the lot was valued at $50 and the building on the lot was valued at $700. It is believed that the house was used by Union forces during the War Between the States. In 1879 "Tranquility," as it was then known, was purchased by French Pendleton Carter. He brought his bride Judith Terrier Miller of Poplar Shade to this home, and they raised a family of seven children. He was born in Washington in 1845 and died there in 1920. He was a member of Company G, 12th Regiment, Virginia Cavalry, became an attorney and served as Commonwealth's Attorney from 1870-1879 and as Examiner of Records for the 26th Judicial District, and was a representative of the Senatorial District in the

[227] Culpeper County Deed Book T, page 372
[228] Culpeper County Deed Book PP, page 248
[229] Rappahannock County Deed Book B, page 166
[230] Rappahannock County Deed Book C, page 506, and Deed Book D, page 62 and 233
[231] Minute Book, Town of Washington Board of Trustees, 3 June 1839, 14 April 1843

Virginia State Senate.[232] One of the Carter daughters, Louemma, married William Francis Moffett. In 1900, the lot was valued at $100 and the buildings on the lot were valued at $1000. Lot 19 stayed in the Carter family, being passed down several generations until Peter Kramer purchased it. Kramer, a well-known local carpenter and cabinet maker, remodeled the home in 1973, keeping intact the woodwork and pine floors. Kramer sold the home to William and Joan Frizzel. The eight-room house has six working fireplaces, a full finished basement, and a full attic.

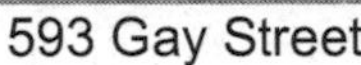

593 Gay Street

567 Gay Street

Lot 19 was divided into two parts. In 2018, the owner of the northern part of Lot 19, designated as Tax Map 20A-1-140A (593 Gay Street), was Fredette S. Engle of McLean, Virginia; a frame house was located on the property, fronting on Gay Street. This home might have been slave or servant quarters for Tranquility.[233] The owner of the southern part of Lot 19, designated as Tax Map 20A-1-140 (567 Gay Street) and known as "Tranquility," was John W. Kilgore, trustee, Ernest Helms III. A frame house was located on the property, fronting on Gay Street.

Lot 20 - Tax Map 20A-1-139 (537 Gay Street)

The first owner of Lot 20 in 1798 was David Lansdown who paid 31 pounds 15 shillings for Lots 17, 19, 20, 45, and 46.[234] Lansdown did not build on Lot 20, as required by the 1796 Act forming the town, and the lot was forfeited to the town trustees. In 1822, the trustees sold Lot 20 to Armistead Hesser for $22.50.[235]

---

[232] Mary Elizabeth Hite, *My Rappahannock Story Book*, Dietz Press, Richmond, Virginia, 1950, page 177

[233] National Register of Historic Places, Washington Historic District, 2006 Update

[234] Culpeper County Deed Book T, page 372

[235] Culpeper County Deed Book PP, page 8

In 1835, Lot 20 owned by Samuel Evans and Benjamin Hesser had to be sold because of debts; it was purchased by Daniel Mason.[236] When Mason went bankrupt, all his properties were sold at public auction in 1841.[237] This included Lot 20 which was sold to William J. Menefee, the Rappahannock County Court Clerk from 1833 to 1858.[238] He continued to own Lot 20 in 1850, when the lot was valued at $50; there was no valuation for any building on the lot. Indeed, the Rappahannock Land Books showed no value for buildings on Lot 20 until 1900, when the buildings value was only $25.

In 1900, the owner of Lot 20 was French Pendleton Carter who owned the adjacent Lot 19. It is believed that Lot 20 served as the garden for the house named "Tranquility" located on Lot 19 until the late 1920s. At that time, William Francis Moffett purchased Lot 20 and a brick home was constructed on the property by Rappahannock native Charles Hawkins in 1929.[239] Moffett was the son of Horatio Gates Moffett Jr.; his wife, Louemma Lee Carter Moffett, was the daughter of French Pendleton Carter. Their son, William Francis Moffett Jr., followed in his father's footsteps as Virginia Commonwealth Attorney and later as a judge. In 1950, the owner of the property was Louemma C. Moffett. In 1957, the owner was Mrs. Jean Moffett, widow of W. F. Moffett Jr. When she died in 2015, her children inherited the house.[240] The Moffetts were owners of Lot 20, designated as Tax Map 20A-1-139 (537 Gay Street), in 2018.

Lot 21 - Tax Map 20A-1-138 (510 Main Street)

The first owner of Lot 21 in 1798 was David Engler who paid 16 pounds 8 shillings for Lots 3 and 21.[241] The lot was acquired by Peter Priest who sold the lot to Ferdinand Gourdon of Baltimore, Maryland, who sold the lot to Daniel Mason in 1833.[242]

An 1833 plan of the town shows that a jail was located on Lot 21.[243] The town "lock-up" was located there, in a small log building, before the new jail was built

236 Rappahannock County Deed Book B, page 166
237 Rappahannock County Deed Book C, page 506 and Deed Book D, page 62
238 Rappahannock County Deed Book D, p. 233
239 National Register of Historic Places, Washington Historic District, 2006 Update
240 Rappahannock County Will File 150000030
241 Culpeper County Deed Book T, page 379
242 Rappahannock County Deed Book B, page 5
243 Rappahannock County Deed Book A, page 189

on Lot 45. Prisoners were held in leg irons, and four large chains still hang on the wall of the log building that was incorporated into the current house on Lot 21. During the day, debtors were allowed work release, but felons could work no more than a block away.

In 1836, the buildings on Lot 21 were valued at $385, indicating that a substantial house had been constructed on the property. In 1837, Daniel Mason sold the lot to James Leake Powers.[244] Powers was born in Charlottesville in 1799. There is no information about his life between 1799 and 1836. However, because he was a resident of Charlottesville and was a carpenter, he probably worked on the buildings of the University of Virginia when the University was constructed during 1817-1826. He emerged from obscurity in 1837 when he purchased Lot 21 and married Martha Ann Nicklin, a daughter of Dr. Joseph Nicklin and his wife Elizabeth Calvert, who were residents of the town.[245] In all likelihood, Powers had been brought to the town of Washington by Malcolm Crawford to help in Crawford's construction of the Rappahannock County courthouse and Clerk's office during 1833-1834. Powers was later the architect of Trinity Episcopal Church on Lot 25, the Presbyterian Church on Lot 22, and several homes in Rappahannock County.

Powers and his wife Martha Ann Nicklin had three daughters while they lived in the home on Lot 21 – Elizabeth, Lavinia, and Martha Ann. It was at the birth of daughter Martha Ann that Mrs. Powers died on 25 March 1843. Powers sold the home to Dr. Adolphus W. Reid and his wife Mary in 1848.[246] Dr. Reid was retained in a medical capacity annually for a stipulated sum by local families. He was also chairman of the Washington Board of Trustees in the 1880s.[247] In 1885, the property was acquired by Lyle and Susie Millan and then by Thomas Hayward who was Clerk of the Rappahannock County Court during 1892 to 1902.[248] The Fox family lived there next and it served as the first central telephone office, with Mrs. Daisy Fox Partlow as the only operator. In the 1920s, the owners were Katherine Fox Hurst and then Randolph G. Jenkins.[249] The first

[244] Rappahannock County Deed Book C, page 111
[245] ancestry.com/genealogy/records/james-leake-powers_7584913; www.geni.com/people/James-Powers/6000000001075408642; Rappahannock Historical Society Powers family file
[246] Rappahannock County Deed Book G, page 505; 1850 Rappahannock County Land Records
[247] Minute Book, Town of Washington Board of Trustees, 27 July 1880
[248] Rappahannock County Deed Book Q, page 443, and Deed Book V, pages 34, 293, and 362
[249] Rappahannock County Deed Book 31, page 283, and Deed Book 34, page 64

major renovation and modernization was made by Mr. and Mrs. N.B.T. Coleman in 1927.[250] Mrs. Coleman, nee Corrie F. Peyton, opened an antique shop, and the house became known as Peyton House. The *Front Royal Record* of 3 November 1932 stated that Mrs. Coleman, proprietress of the Antique Shop, was having an auction sale of all her antiques. The property remained in the Peyton family for 30 more years.[251] In 1963 it was purchased by Mrs. Martha (Mattie) Ball Fletcher, wife of William Meade Fletcher.[252] On 12 September 1996, Mrs. Fletcher passed away at the age of 107. She had been the oldest living relative of Mary Washington, mother of the first president. Her great-grandfather married Martha Dandridge, a granddaughter of Charles Washington, brother of George Washington.

In 2018, the owner of Lot 21, designated as Tax Map 20A-1-138 (510 Main Street), was Caroline Anstey. Sited on the western end of the lot was a stucco house and garage.

Lot 22 - Tax Map 20A-1-136 (485 Gay Street) and Tax Map 20A-1-137 (492 Main Street)

The first owner of Lot 22 in 1798 was John Miller I who paid 11 pounds 2 shillings for the lot.[253] John, who lived at "Mountain Green," was the son of Henry Miller I and Susannah Sibler. He was married to Nancy Hitt, daughter of Peter Hitt and Sarah James of Fauquier County, Virginia. In 1804, John and Nancy sold the lot to Michael Nicol for 25 pounds.[254] Nicol was the husband of John's niece, Sarah ("Sally") Miller. In 1807 Nicol sold the lot to John Resor and the Lot remained in the Resor family until the 1830s when the Spiller family acquired the property. The wood frame house at the southeast corner of Calvert and Main streets probably dates from the 1830s; the 1836 Rappahannock County Land Book shows that the buildings on Lot 22 were valued at $285 at that time. Elizabeth Spiller bequeathed the lot to her daughter Tamar in 1844, and in 1856 Tamar Spiller sold the lot to Robert Deatherage and Robert S. Bell for $350.[255]

The Eastern Half of Lot 22:
The deed from Spiller to Deatherage and Bell specified that the eastern half of the lot, measuring 132' along Gay Street by 82.5' along Calvert Street, should be held by Deatherage and Bell in their capacity as trustees of the Presbyterian Church of Washington, for the purpose of establishing "a house of worship for the use and benefit of the said Church." James Leake Powers designed and constructed the Washington Presbyterian Church on the eastern half of Lot 22 in

---

[250] Rappahannock County Deed Book 41, page 366
[251] Rappahannock County Will Book Q, page 339
[252] Rappahannock County Deed Book 79, page 348 and Deed Book 83, page 273
[253] Culpeper County Deed Book T, page 370
[254] Culpeper County Deed Book Z, page 207
[255] Rappahannock County Will Book 3, page 169, and Deed Book J, page 414

1856-1858. It was constructed of brick in the Doric architectural style. The Presbyterian Church continued until 1891, when only two active church members remained, and the church building was officially closed the following year.[256] During the next half century, shrubs and trees grew wild, eventually hiding the building from view. In 1939, the lot and building were purchased by Franklin Clyde Baggarly, the owner of Avon Hall adjacent to the town and a former attorney for the town.[257] After he was declared incompetent in 1959,[258] his wife Frances Trott Bagggarly sold the lot in 1960 to the trustees of the County Free Library System, who were Q. D. Gasque (Superintendent of Public Schools), Elisabeth Johnson, Freer Wilson, T. J. Pillar, and Virginia Miller.[259] This group of dedicated Rappahannock County residents rescued the old building and turned it into a public library which was dedicated in 1963. The fact that the building

was still sound after nearly 75 years of disuse and neglect is a tribute to Mr. Power's construction ability. In 1983 a 100-year time capsule in the shape of a pyramid was constructed by Edward Bailey and installed on the grounds of the library. A sealed copper box containing artifacts and messages was placed in a concrete water-tight vault in the stone-faced capsule. The vault was sealed in a special ceremony on July 4, 1983 to be opened on July 4, 2083. The library remained in the old church building until the end of 1989, when it was moved into a newly erected building on Lee Highway just outside of the town. The building and land were sold to the Town of Washington in 1989[260] and it was converted to serve as the Washington Town Hall, which had been located in the former Washington Methodist Church building on Lot 43 since 1980.[261] Pews from the Methodist church were purchased by Peter and Joyce Kramer and were moved to the building, and ladder-back chairs from an early stage of the Inn at Little Washington were donated.[262] Eve Willis, an interior decorator and spouse of Mayor J. Stewart Willis, created the cushions and draperies for the building.[263] Fawn Evenson donated rugs for the floors. Many books were donated by Mayor John Fox

---

[256] Elisabeth B. and C. E. Johnson Jr., *Rappahannock County, Virginia, A History*, Orange, VA, Green Publishers, 1981, page 155

[257] Rappahannock County Deed Book 44, page 177

[258] Rappahannock County Chancery Case #2292, Frances Trott Baggarly vs. Franklin Clyde Baggarly

[259] Rappahannock County Deed Book 71, page 595

[260] Rappahannock County Deed Book 175, page 298

[261] Rappahannock County Deed Book 136, page 710

[262] Information from Laura Dodd, the Town's administrative Assistant, 2018

[263] Information from J. Stewart Willis in an interview given to the Rappahannock League for Environmental Protection, 2018

Sullivan to fill the former library shelves. An office for the Town's administrative assistant was created in the former church balcony.

In 2018, the owner of the eastern part of Lot 22, designated as Tax Map 20A-1-136 (485 Gay Street), was the Town of Washington. The lot contained 11,373 square feet and the building on the lot served as the Washington Town Hall.

The Western Half of Lot 22:

In 1889, there was a public auction sale of the western half of Lot 22. The ¼-acre lot and house were then occupied by Byrd Kendall.[264] In 1893, pursuant to a decree by the Rappahannock County Chancery Court, John F. Lillard acquired the western half of Lot 22 and the house on this land for $275.[265] James Oden purchased the property from Lillard one year later[266] and it remained in the Oden family until 1952. The deed of sale specified numerous improvements to the property to be made by Lillard, including "to have all necessary woodwork and plastering completed in a workmanlike manner … to build a front porch of eight by ten feet … to enclose the lot on the west and north sides with a neat and substantial picket plank fence." In 1900, the land of this part of Lot 22 was valued at $50 and the building was valued at $250. Annie Miller Almond purchased the house and lot from Sarah and Clarence Oden in 1952.[267] In 1984, Reinhardt Lynch and Patrick O'Connell, owners of the Inn at Little Washington, acquired the property from Rayner Snead, who was a judge in the County.[268] The property was designated as Tax Map 20A-1-137 (492 Main Street) and contained 0.2568 acre. The Inn at Little Washington LLC was the owner in 2018.

Lot 23 - Tax Map 20A-1-135 (448 Main Street)

The first owner of Lot 23 in 1798 was James Wheeler paid 174 pounds for Lots 23 and 24.[269] Wheeler was one of the three men who petitioned the General Assembly of Virginia to establish the town of Washington in 1796. Wheeler sold Lot 23 to another of the town's founders, William Porter, in 1811, and died in

---

264 Rappahannock County Chancery Case No. 939
265 Rappahannock County Deed Book Q, page 170; Chancery Case Deatherage vs. Bell; Deed Book S, p. 447
266 Rappahannock County Deed Book T, page 3
267 Rappahannock County Deed Book 58, page 123
268 Rappahannock County Deed Book 148, page 202
269 Culpeper County Deed Book T, page 387

that year.[270] At Porter's death in 1815, his son Tilmon inherited the lot.[271] In 1843, the owner of Lot 23 was Mrs. Elizabeth Dorsey, who sold the property to John T. Corder in 1850. The lot was valued at $50 and the building on the lot was valued at $250. During this time, Calvert & Holland had a tailor's shop and John T. Corder had a saddlers shop on the lot.[272]

In 1880 the lot was owned by William A. Lillard. The buildings on the lot were destroyed by fire in about 1890.[273] Lillard constructed a substantial house on the lot; the buildings on Lot 23 were valued at $700 in 1900. The Lillard family owned the property until 1944, when it was sold to Irving and Eunice Sisk.[274] In 1989, the Sisk heirs sold the property, designated as Tax Map 20A-1-135 (448 Main Street) and containing 0.4568 acre, to Patrick O'Connell and Reinhardt Lynch, owners of the Inn at Little Washington.[275] Before the Inn purchased the property, much of it was a junkyard. Now the beautiful Inn gardens, open to the public, are located on this property as well as the Lillard house which is adjacent to the Inn restaurant and serves as offices for Inn staff.

Lot 24 - Tax Map 20A-1-133 (335 Middle Street), Tax Map 20A-1-134 (309 Middle Street), and Tax Map 20A-1-134A (325 and 325A Middle Street)

The first owner of Lot 24 in 1798 was James Wheeler who paid 174 pounds for Lots 23 and 24.[276] Wheeler was one of the three men who petitioned the General Assembly of Virginia to establish the town of Washington in 1796. On these lots was probably Wheeler's storehouse, which was mentioned in the deed in which he acquired 2 acres from William Porter in 1792; these 2 acres were within the town boundaries when the town was formed in 1796-1797.[277] Wheeler sold the eastern part of Lot 24 to Gabriel Smither for 100 pounds in 1804.[278] He sold the western part of the lot to William Porter in 1811 and died in that year.[279]

---

270 Culpeper County Deed Book EE, page 181, and Will Book F, page 263
271 Maureen I. Harris, "The Lost Will of William Porter, Culpeper County, 1815," *Magazine of Virginia Genealogy*, Vol. 50, No. 4, pp. 320-324
272 Rappahannock County Deed Book G, page 534
273 Notation from the 1890 Rappahannock County Land Book
274 Rappahannock County Deed Book 45, page 34
275 Rappahannock County Deed Book 172, page 551
276 Culpeper County Deed Book T, page 387
277 Culpeper County Deed Book R, page 35
278 Culpeper County Deed Book Y, page 369
279 Culpeper County Deed Book EE, page 181, and Will Book F, page 263

Eastern Part of Lot 24 (Tax Map 20A-1-133):

Gabriel Smither purchased the eastern part of Lot 24 for 100 pounds in 1804. Given this high price, there must have been a considerable building on the property at that time. This building may have been Wheeler's storehouse, and a "storehouse" was stated to be located on the property in 1853 (below). Smither died in about 1822, and his widow Getty Smither went into debt and had to surrender her properties to the Sheriff of Rappahannock County; John Jett acquired the property which he sold in 1841 to Nancy and Sarah Reid.[280] In 1850 the buildings on the property were worth $325. Frances Whitescarver purchased the property from the Reids in 1853 and sold the lot to William F. Anderson and Samuel J. Spindle in 1867; the property included a "storehouse."[281] Spindle had been elected Treasurer of Rappahannock County in 1870 but he failed to properly collect taxes and was sued by the County. The property was placed in trust and sold to Edward Cary in 1873;[282] a building described as a "Store House" was located on the property. The building and lot remained in the Cary family for 30 years and was sold in 1903 to Giles E. Bywaters.[283] It remained in the Bywaters family until 1944 when Alice Verner purchased the property;[284] the building was valued at $600 in 1950. The property was sold to Virginia Miller in 1966, to Charles Henry Cannon in 1971, and to Patrick O'Connell and Reinhardt Lynch in 2001.[285] In 2018 the owner of the eastern section of Lot 24, designated as Tax Map 20A-1-133 (335 Middle Street) and containing a two-story frame house, was the Inn at Little Washington LLC; the lot contained 0.2197 acre.

Western Part of Lot 24 (Tax Map 20A-1-134) and Tax Map 20A-1-134A:

At William Porter's death in 1815, his son Tilmon inherited the western part of Lot 24.[286] A log building located at the southwest corner of the lot was the site of the post office in 1815, with Tilman Porter as postmaster. An 1837 plan of the town shows the post office located at this site.[287]

[280] Rappahannock County Deed Book D, page 217
[281] Rappahannock County Deed Book I, page 350, and Deed Book M, page 8
[282] Rappahannock County Deed Book P, page 161
[283] Rappahannock County Deed Book W, page 150
[284] Rappahannock County Deed Book 45, page 148
[285] Rappahannock County Deed Book 86, page 331; Deed Book 101, page 722; and Instrument 010000531
[286] Maureen I. Harris, "The Lost Will of William Porter, Culpeper County, 1815," *Magazine of Virginia Genealogy*, Vol. 50, No. 4, pp. 320-324
[287] Rappahannock County Deed Book C, page 71

In 1833, the property was owned by Francis S. Browning; by 1841, the property was owned by Oliver P. Smith who was a tailor.[288] In the late 1840s the lot contained a dwelling used by John Sills and the shoeshop of Edwin Whitney. In 1849 Smith sold the property for $224 to James B. Jones and Middleton Miller, trading under the name of James B. Jones & Co.[289] On the lot at this time was Albert Holland's cabinet-maker shop and Henry Foster's shoe-maker shop; Foster was a member of the Washington Town Board of Trustees in 1855. During 1850-1861, Lewis D. Massie acquired the house and land, together with Foster's adjacent 20-foot square building.[290]

In 1870 David Lloyd purchased, from the estate of Lewis D. Massie, "the house and lot opposite the hotel of Mrs. Dear, known as the Corner House" together with "the shop known as the Foster shop," i.e., the western part of Lot 24, for $800.[291] The house had recently been occupied by Henry Foster. In the 1870 census, Lloyd was listed as being a "mulatto" and his occupation was a "confectioner;" in the 1880 census, he was a "hotel keeper." The house and shop buildings together were worth $750.[292] The Rappahannock County supervisors had the authority to grant licenses to merchants, and there were strict regulations in regard to selling alcoholic beverages. In 1874, such a license was issued to David Lloyd for Lloyd's Hotel in Washington. Apparently Lloyd had converted the "Corner house," which had been the post office in 1815, into a hotel. From later deeds, it is known that this 1½-story building was constructed of logs and measured 18' x 24'.

In 1904, John Edward Thornton purchased Lloyd's property for $2100,[293] on which he constructed a one-story weatherboarded frame garage. He appears to have moved the log "Corner house" to the east, where it later became the Middle Street Gallery. The new garage was located on the northeast corner of Main and Middle streets opposite the former Mrs. Coxe's Tavern/Dear's Hotel on Lot 8 which Thornton then owned and operated as "Washington House." Thornton's Garage complemented his hotel business by providing parking space for carriages. He added an additional 1½ stories to the garage, reportedly to appease his wife who wanted rowdy card games, partying, and dancing removed from Thornton's hotel.[294] The expansive upper space in the building evolved into the town's first community entertainment and recreational center. Over time, there

[288] Rappahannock County Deed Book A, page 13, Deed Book B, page 387, Deed Book D, page 221, Deed Book C, page 71, Deed Book D, page 231; Deed Book C, page 495
[289] Rappahannock County Deed Book G, page 534
[290] Rappahannock County Deed Book H, page 236, Deed Book K, page 43, and Deed Book M, page 47
[291] Rappahannock County Deed Book M, page 285
[292] Rappahannock County Land Books
[293] Rappahannock County chancery suit, Lloyd vs. Lloyd's Administrator; Deed Book X, page 140
[294] Recollections of Mrs. Edna Walker, owner of "Washington House", in Daphne Hutchinson and Theresa Reynolds, *On the Morning Side of the Blue Ridge*, a compilation of articles published in the *Rappahannock News* in 1983, page 50-51

was a barroom, poolhall, poker and card games, dance hall, basketball court, and a theater to show movies. In the 1920s, L.V. Merrill moved to the town of Washington from his home in Wisconsin and rented Thornton's Garage. After the introduction of the automobile, the garage offered the convenience of servicing motor cars with gas, tires, and repairs.

In 1929, Thornton mortgaged his property to secure payment of debts totaling $5785. He defaulted in payment of the debts and the property was sold at public auction, at which his daughter Edna Walker was the highest bidder. She acquired Thornton's property on Lot 24, which was stated to be one-fourth acre and to contain a garage, butcher shop, blacksmith shop, and a dwelling.[295] An Amoco gas station was located at the garage in the 1940s.

According to Edna Walker, there was a shoeshop next to the garage and behind it, a wheelwright's shop and a blacksmith's shop. The little block also had a butcher shop squeezed in. In the 1940s the butcher shop made way for a sandwich shop (the Washington House Sandwich Shoppe) that was later destroyed by fire.[296]

In 1950, the owner of the property was Margaret B. Thornton, wife of John Edward Thornton; her part of Lot 24 was valued at $150 and buildings on the lot were valued at $1200. When she died in 1959, she willed the property jointly to her daughters Edna Walker and Hilda Levesque.[297] Edna sold her interest to her sister in 1963 and in 1966 Hilda sold the property to William Carrigan (who was the owner of Avon Hall).[298] He refurbished the two-story former garage, adding a columned portico to the front, and installed an antiques shop in the building.

Carrigan sold the property to Louise Sagalyn of Washington, D.C., in 1972.[299] A plat of the property showed that it was 0.3691 acre and contained a large building at the west side of the property (formerly Thornton's garage) and a 18' x 24' building at the east side of the property (formerly the log post office/hotel).[300] The large building became the home of "The Country Store" in 1976, managed by Peter Kramer. This business featured an array of quality goods, both new and old, handcrafted merchandise, and unique country items. It was also an antique shop and a craft shop for a short time. The log building became the Middle Street Gallery. Sagalyn divided the property in 1978 into a western parcel of 0.2740

---

[295] Rappahannock County Deed Book 35, page 215, and Deed Book 37, page 235

[296] Recollections of Mrs. Edna Walker, owner of "Washington House", in Daphne Hutchinson and Theresa Reynolds, *On the Morning Side of the Blue Ridge*, a compilation of articles published in the *Rappahannock News* in 1983, page 51

[297] Rappahannock County Will Book T, page 389

[298] Rappahannock County Deed Book 80, page 545 and Deed Book 87, page 595

[299] Rappahannock County Deed Book 103, page 606

[300] Rappahannock County Deed Book 129, page 643; files of the Rappahannock Commissioner of Revenue

acre adjacent to Main Street containing the large building and an adjacent eastern parcel of 0.0951 acre containing the log building.

The Western Sagalyn Parcel: In 1978 Louise and Arnold Sagalyn rented part of the building on the western parcel to Patrick O'Connell and Reinhardt Lynch and then sold the whole property to them in 1979.[301] This became the Inn at Little Washington restaurant. (See Chapter 10.) In 1985-1986, the upstairs was converted to eight overnight guest rooms and two bilevel suites; an expanded kitchen was added in 1999.[302] Over time, the Inn garnered international awards including America's first Five Star, Five Diamond Inn for both its dining room and its lodgings, the highest rated establishment in the Zagat U.S. hotel survey in all categories, a member of Relais and Chateaux, and selection as one of the ten best restaurants in the United States. The property, designated as Tax Map 20A-1-134 (309 Middle Street) and containing 0.3151 acre, was owned by the Inn at Little Washington LLC in 2018.[303]

The Eastern Sagalyn Parcel:
In 1980, Sagalyn constructed an addition measuring 24' x 40' onto the rear of the 18' x 24' log building and installed a metal gable roof.[304] Dan Lewis, a native of Washington D.C., founded a for-profit art gallery featuring local artists in the basement of the Clopton House on town Lot 25 in 1981. He moved his business in 1983 to Sagalyn's building. The art gallery was not profitable, and in 1987 he converted it to a non-profit artist's cooperative and the building was named the Middle Street Gallery.[305] This venture remained in the building through 2013, featuring museum quality painting, photography, and sculpture. In 2014 the Gallery moved out of the building, and the building was occupied by the store called "Antiques At Middle Street." This shop was a conglomeration of beautiful and interesting finds in the world of collectibles. The front room was filled with vintage furniture and other unique pieces surrounded by a display of art. The porcelain collection included Limoges pieces and pieces from Czechoslovakia, Germany, Japan and England. Displays of Chinese artifacts and depression glass were lighted by lamps artfully placed among the treasures. The back room held

---

[301] Rappahannock County Deed Book 132, page 93
[302] Information from the Inn at Little Washington LLC
[303] See separate chapter in this book for a more extensive history of the Inn at Little Washington
[304] Files of the Rappahannock County Commissioner of Revenue
[305] *Rappahannock News*, 29 August 1991 and 13 December 2018

another treasure trove including lovely primitives, kitchen collectibles, toys, knickknacks, interesting works of art, and a collection of old clocks, from small to wall clocks. In the winter of 2017-2018, the Middle Street Gallery returned and occupied the rear part of the Middle Street building, with Antiques at Middle Street remaining in the front part of the building.[306] In 2018, the owner of this part of Lot 24, designated as Tax Map 20A-1-134A (325 and 325A Middle Street) and containing the business Antiques at Middle Street and the artists' cooperative Middle Street Gallery, was the Sharon M. Labovitz Trust; the lot contained 0.095 acre.

Lot 25 - Tax Map 20A-1-108 and Tax Map 20A-1-109 (379 Gay Street)

The first owner of Lot 25 in 1798 was James Jett Jr. who paid 185 pounds for the lot.[307] Jett was one of the three men who petitioned the General Assembly of Virginia to establish the town of Washington in 1796. On this lot was Jett's store, which was mentioned in the deeds in which he acquired 2 acres of William Porter's land in 1795.[308] In 1803, Jett sold the half-acre lot to Gabriel Smither for 100 pounds; at that time, John Strother was renting the building on the lot.[309] By 1835, Lot 25 had been divided. John Jett acquired the western part in 1835 and sold this to James B. Jones.[310] The owner of the eastern part was Daniel Mason; when he went bankrupt in 1840, all his properties were sold at public auction.[311] This included his part of Lot 25, which was sold to John Jett.[312]

Eastern Part of Lot 25 (Tax Map 20A-1-109, 379 Gay Street):

In 1857, John G. Lane purchased the eastern part of Lot 25,[313] which he conveyed to Trinity Episcopal Church. However, this deed was never recorded. In 1956, this omission was recognized by trustees of the Church who were D.D. Miller, W.A. Miller, C.J. Menefee Jr., J.D. Keyser, James M. Settle, E.L. Brown, and T.C. Lea. They instituted a chancery suit in Rappahannock County Court, which clarified the title to the 0.175-acre property that the church building now resides

[306] *Rappahannock News*, 23 November 2017
[307] Culpeper County Deed Book T, page 406
[308] Culpeper County Deed Book R, page 333 and Deed Book S, page 278
[309] Culpeper County Deed Book Y, page 107
[310] Rappahannock County Deed Book B, page 249
[311] Rappahannock County Deed Book C, page 506 and Deed Book D, page 62
[312] Rappahannock County Deed Book D, p. 229
[313] Rappahannock County Deed Book K, page 301

on, fronting on Gay Street.[314] The church also acquired from Edward Jones Clopton a 15' strip of land, running east-west from Gay Street, at the south edge of its property in 1952.[315]

The Trinity Church building (379 Gay Street) was constructed by James Leake Powers. The cornerstone was laid on 30 May 1857, by the Masonic Lodge of Washington, Virginia. According to Masonic records, the cornerstone contains a copper box into which were inserted copies of the Book of Common Prayer, the journal of the 61st annual convention of the Protestant Episcopal Church of Virginia, the Episcopal Recorder, the Southern Churchwoman, the Masonic Mirror, and a small book titled "Dew Drops" by J. E. Dow, a teacher at "the Academy" on Lot 34. Masons and other townsfolk tossed in the following coins of the day – seven 5-cent pieces, two ten-cent pieces, one 25-cent piece, one 50-cent piece, and one gold dollar (donated in the name of the Grand Orient of France). Construction of the church was completed within the year at a total cost of $1,800. The original facade was board and batten.

The church was modified later. The steeple and stained-glass windows were added, as was the pebbledash stucco finish. In daylight, the memorial stained glass windows softly illuminate the interior and ceiling. The cross at the front was made from old boards by Philip Strange, a local cabinetmaker and Vestry member. The parish hall attached to the church was built in 1957 at the south side of the church, using plans submitted by the Charlottesville architect firm of Johnson, Craven, and Gibson, with Charles W. Hawkins as the local builder. The hall was added to in 1985, and was renovated in 2016. The church building, in the style known as "country Gothic," is considered one of the finest examples of American village church architecture in Virginia. For 42 years, the rector of the church was the Rev. Jennings W. Hobson III, who retired in 2015.

Western Part of Lot 25 (Tax Map 20A-1-108):

This part of Lot 25 was owned by John G. Lane in 1857 and contained a storehouse; in 1880 it was sold to James Morrison.[316] In 1887, Julia Parnell

---

[314] Rappahannock County Chancery Case 2222; Rappahannock County Deed Book 65, page 183
[315] Rappahannock County Deed Book 59, page 59
[316] Rappahannock County Deed Book M, page 298

acquired the property and sold it in 1901 to Clarence T. Owen.[317] Oral history indicates that a store was located here managed by Owen, Tom Lake, Charlie Blake, and Giles Eldridge Bywaters. In 1920, Owen sold the property to Bywaters and in 1928 Bywaters sold the property to the Marean, Hughes, Meigs Motor Company Inc.[318] On this western part of Lot 25 was located a gas station, a garage, and a store and restaurant known as "The Cherry Tree and Hatchet," all constructed in the early 1930s.[319] In 1949, the store building became the office of *The Rappahannock News* for one year until the office was moved to the southern part of Lot 13. On 1 July 1950 Mr. and Mrs. Charlie Jenkins opened the "Washington Cafe" on this western part of Lot 25, serving regular meals, short orders, and sandwiches.[320] A poolroom was located downstairs. Harold S. Marean was the owner of the property in 1950, and the buildings on the lot were valued at $1500.

In 1957 the property, containing 6771 square feet, was purchased by the Quarles Oil Company, which sold it to Trinity Episcopal Church in 1962.[321] The many small buildings on this property were torn down, and a parking lot for the church was constructed on the land.[322] In 2014, the Inn collaborated with Trinity Church to improve the church's parking lot, which the Inn leased from the Church and which was adjacent to one of the entrances of the Inn's newly renovated building named "The Parsonage" which was formerly the home of the Jones/Clopton family on Lot 26. The Inn paid for improvement to the parcel, including paving the parking lot and installing hardscaping and landscaping.[323] It was estimated to cost $180,000, and the Town of Washington contributed $20,000 towards this cost.[324]

Lot 26 - Tax Map 20A-1-107 (360 Main Street) and the Northern Part of Lot 27 - Tax Map 20A-1-107A (337 Gay Street) and Tax Map 20A-1-107B (322 Main Street)

The first owner of Lot 26 and Lot 27 in 1798 was Edward Pendleton; he paid 18 pounds for the two properties.[325] He was born in 1770, the son of Henry and Ann Thomas Pendleton. Henry was the owner of a large plantation at the fork of the Hazel and Thornton rivers, was a Gentleman Justice of Culpeper County in 1763-1764, and was a member of the Culpeper Committee of Safety and of the Patriot

[317] Rappahannock County Deed Book R, page 247, and Deed Book V, page 274
[318] Rappahannock County Deed Book 30, page 195, and Deed Book 34, page 243
[319] M. Elizabeth Buntin, *Mission: A Study of the Churches of Bromfield Parish*, pages 78-82, files of Trinity Episcopal Church
[320] *Rappahannock News*, 19 May 2016, quoted in the 29 June 1950 edition of the newspaper
[321] Rappahannock County Deed Book 67, page 408, and Deed Book 77, page 48
[322] Photograph and caption for the western part of Lot 25, *Rappahannock News*, 13 December 1962, reprinted in the 4 September 2008 edition of the newspaper
[323] Rappahannock County Instrument 140000455
[324] *Rappahannock News*, 26 March 2015
[325] Culpeper County Deed Book T, page 320

Convention in 1775-1776. Edward married Sarah Strother, a daughter of Capt. John Dabney Strother of the Wadefield plantation in 1794. He died in 1802 and directed in his will that all his properties should be sold, with half the proceeds going to Sarah and half to his daughter Nancy.[326] In 1803, a public auction of Lots 26 and 27 was held, and Sarah was the highest bidder at a price of 335 pounds.[327] Because of this high price, it can be concluded that a substantial house and other buildings had been constructed between 1798 and 1803.

In 1822, William Pendleton mortgaged Lot 26 because of debts; he failed to pay the debts and the mortgage holder auctioned the lot, at which Bailey Buckner was the highest bidder.[328] Bailey and Helen Strother exchanged properties in 1831, with Helen obtaining Lot 26 on which was located "the Yellow House;" she sold the lot to Charles Miller in 1832, and at his death the lot became the property of John Miller Sr.[329]

In 1836, John Miller Sr. and his wife Nancy (Hitt) Miller conveyed the one-half acre property with the Yellow House to James Brereton Jones, whose wife Eliza was the daughter of John and Nancy.[330] The house on the property was still painted yellow in 1973.[331] In 1858, Jones added to his property by purchasing the northern part of Lot 27 from Oliver P. Smith.[332] On the western part of this land was the log cabin now designated as 322 Main Street; on the eastern part he constructed a frame mercantile building now designated as 337 Gay Street. Also associated with the Yellow House were three dependencies consisting of a kitchen with sleeping quarters above, a dairy, and a brick smoke house/root cellar.[333] Several reasons are given for an exterior kitchen: it did not add to the heat in the main house; it kept cooking odors out of the main house living areas; and, probably most important, it reduced the chance of fire in the main house. There was a large fireplace situated in the basement of the Yellow House that would have been suitable for cooking, and it is possible that the exterior kitchen may have been used only in warm weather.

James Brereton Jones (born in 1804, died in 1865) was the son of James Jones, a Revolutionary War soldier. He was a merchant and a member of the Washington Town Board of Trustees in 1839 and 1843. James and his wife Eliza (born 1811, died 1899) had two children, Edward Thompson Jones (born 1831, died 1920) and Ann A. (born 1839, died 1858 at age 19 years, from diptheria). The Jones family lived in the Yellow House for their entire lives. Edward was an attorney,

[326] Culpeper County Will Book D, page 430
[327] Culpeper County Deed Book Y, page 142
[328] Culpeper County Deed Book OO, page 158; Deed Book QQ, page 147; and Deed Book QQ, page 503
[329] Rappahannock County Deed Book B, page 246, page 312, and page 313
[330] Rappahannock County Deed Book C, page 51
[331] Information from Peter and Joyce Kramer, 2019
[332] Rappahannock County Deed Book K, page 302
[333] Information from Peter Kramer, 2019

was the Rappahannock County Clerk in 1860, and served as a quartermaster sergeant in the Confederate forces during the Civil War. He married Eliza Edmonia Miller (born 1840, died 1905) in 1860 and they had five children – Edward Barton (born 1861), John Brereton (born 1864), Annie Washington (born 1867), Jessie F. (born 1870), and James T. (born 1873).

In 1892 Annie Washington Jones, the daughter of Edward T. and Eliza E. Jones, married Reverend Samuel Cornelius Clopton Jr. He was born in Canton, China in 1847 and was descended from a long line of ministers. He and his mother moved to Virginia after the death of his father. He graduated from Columbian College and was a Baptist preacher in Richmond and Smithfield, Virginia. After their marriage, Samuel and Annie moved to Alabama where Reverend Clopton had taken a position as pastor in a Baptist church. They had two children, Edward Jones Clopton (born 1896) and Eliza Clopton (born 1902). After Reverend Clopton's death, Annie and her two children returned to her father's home on Lot 26.

Annie's mother died in 1905 and her father died in 1920. In his will, her father gave her "The Yellow House."[334] Annie died in 1944, and she willed the 0.75-acre property to her two children who sold it to Peter and Joyce Kramer in 1973.[335] By this time, the home was known as "The Clopton House." The property included the home, the cluster of three dependencies, a log house fronting on Main Street, and the Jones' mercantile building fronting on Gay Street; both of the latter were located on the northern part of Lot 27.

In 1974, cabinet maker and builder Peter Kramer and his wife Joyce remodeled the three dependencies into a single house in which they lived, joining the smoke house to the dairy with a sky-lighted hall and the dairy to the kitchen through the addition of a living room on the east side. The dairy was converted to a bathroom and the smoke house to a bed/sitting room and office. To the latter, Kramer added a greenhouse wall, making a solarium. Outside the living room was a fenced patio shaded by large old trees that surrounded the entire complex. The kitchen was dominated by a large fireplace whose hearth was made of huge stones. The bed/sitting room/office was on three levels with the root cellar serving as an office. The second or main level was the sitting room; several feet above this was the bedroom loft.[336] This custom-built home was dismantled by David Cole to whom the Kramers sold the property in 2000, and the dairy building was removed and the smokehouse was modified.[337]

[334] Rappahannock County Will Book H, page 378
[335] Rappahannock County Will Book K, page 498, and Deed Book 108, page 640
[336] "A Taste for Tradition," *Better Homes and Gardens Country Home*, March/April 1984, pages 21-36
[337] Rappahannock County Deed Book 180, page 466, and Instrument 000000013; information from Peter Kramer, 2019

Division of the Property:

In 1978, 0.3565-acre on which the Clopton House was located was purchased by Eileen M. Dwyer[338] and the building became the site of Eileen M. Day Realtors. The business called Country Heritage, managed by Nan Thomasson, was also located here. In 1991 Piedmont Fine Arts opened in the Clopton House; this business sold an eclectic mix of painting, photography, sculpture, and furniture. In the 1990s Ochs Delikatessen (sometimes called the "Ochs Box") was also located on Lot 26. The property was sold to Pan Pacific Ventures, to Sunnyside Farms LLC, and to Joseph and Jacqueline Meuse; the letter owner used the house as an office building.[339]

In 2012, the 0.3565-acre property designated as Tax Map 20A-1-107 (360 Main Street), was sold by the Meuses to The Clopton House LLC, c/o the Inn at Little Washington LLC, for $900,000.[340] This acreage was augmented by 0.1839 acre in 2015 when The Clopton House LLC purchased the 0.3115-acre property adjacent to the south (formerly part of the Jones/Clopton land) from Sunnyview LLC and sold 0.1276 acre of this to Bradams Ridge LLC.[341] The former Jones/Clopton house was renamed "The Parsonage" because of its location adjacent to Trinity Episcopal Church. Extensive interior renovations and exterior improvements were performed to convert the 6000 square foot Victorian home for use as overnight lodging. The building was modified to create six luxurious guest rooms with fireplaces and bay windows overlooking the town. London designer Joyce Conway Evans collaborated with Chef and Proprietor Patrick O'Connell to develop the ambiance of an enchanting house in the countryside full of surprise and whimsy. The Parsonage's interiors reflect a lighter, more modern interpretation of The Inn at Little Washington's beloved English Country House aesthetic.

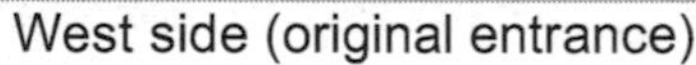

West side (original entrance)

North side (current entrance)

[338] Rappahannock County Deed Book 128, page 6
[339] Rappahannock County Instrument 990001093, Instrument 000000150, and Instrument 050001929
[340] Rappahannock County Instrument 120000273
[341] Rappahannock County Instrument 150000150 and Instrument 150000328

Included in part of the 0.3115-acre property retained by The Clopton House LLC was the dismantled home of Peter and Joyce Kramer that had been based on the three dependencies originally associated with the Yellow House of the Jones family. The Clopton House LLC purchased this property from Sunnyview LLC in 2015; a Town ordinance directed that it be incorporated into Tax Map 20A-1-107 after the eastern 0.1276 acre was sold to Bradams Ridge LLC.[342]

The 0.1276-acre property sold by The Clopton House LLC to Bradams Ridge LLC contained a building on the northeastern part of Lot 27 that is believed to have been the store owned and operated by James Brereton Jones when he was a merchant and living on Lot 26 in the "Yellow House." This building has traditionally been a general store and a gathering place for local residents. It served for a time as a bus station, with twice-daily bus service between the District of Columbia and New Market, Virginia; the south part of the building was a garage for buses. This service was still available during the 1950s and 1960s. It was possible to order a pair of shoes from a store in Washington D.C. and have them delivered by bus that afternoon to Washington, Virginia. It has also served as an art gallery, craft shop, and book store. In the 1980s and 1990s it was the location of "The Rush River Company" owned by Peer and Joyce Kramer, which was a gallery that featured a variety of unique American crafts and art by many artists and artisans. Stoneyman Gourmet Farmer, a gourmet grocery store and cafe, occupied the building in 2011-2015. In 2015 the Clopton House LLC acquired 0.3110 acre at the southern part of Lot 26 and northern part of Lot 27;[343] the Jones mercantile building and 0.1276 acre on which it stands was sold to Bradams Ridge LLC (Tax Map 20A-1-107A, 337 Gay Street).[344] After renovations, the former store became the art gallery and studio for the artist Kevin Adams.

The remaining part of the 0.75-acre Jones/Clopton property was 0.0850 acre located on the northwestern part of Lot 27. The small log building on this parcel (322 Main Street) is probably what some of the original buildings in the town of Washington looked like in the early 1800s. The 1796 Act of the Virginia General Assembly that established the town required that on each lot of the town be built "a dwelling house, sixteen feet square at least, with a brick or stone chimney, to be furnished fit for habitation." According to Wayne Baldwin, Wade Fletcher's

[342] Rappahannock County Instrument 150000150 and 150000328
[343] Rappahannock County Instrument 150000150
[344] Rappahannock County Instrument 150000328

grandmother Jeanie Robinson lived in the building at one point and his aunt Lucy lived in the structure over 100 years ago. The house stands on property formerly owned by Roy Pullen Sr. whose parents, Clyde Pullen and Lillie Dwyer Pullen, gave the cabin to him. Clyde and Lillie had purchased it from Lillie's father, Thomas Booten Dwyer, who had bought it from Jim and John Jones, who had obtained it from John and Mollie Monroe Fincham. Mollie's father, Silas J. Monroe bought it from William and Elizabeth L. Scott in July 1875. Elizabeth had inherited the house from her great-grandfather, James L. Green Sr. in 1844. The last person to live in the cabin was Bob Scott.[345]

At some point in time, the building was extended to the east and a cat-slide roof was constructed over this new part of the building. In the 1970s the building was restored by Peter Kramer and Wayne Jenkins. In the 1980s the building was the site of "Country Heritage Antiques and Crafts," owned by Nan and Jim Thomasson which specialized in American Folk art, quality hand-crafts, country and primitive furniture, and fine antiques. In the 1990s it was the location of the business "Windflower Gallery" which featured the art of Tanya M. Richey. In 1995 the property was acquired by Edmund and Bridget Kavanagh and was the location of Edmund's Jewelry shop.[346] In 2018 it was the location of the real estate offices of Washington Fine Properties, Inc., formerly Armfield, Miller, and Ripley Realty Company. The owner of the northwestern part of Lot 27 in 2018, designated as Tax Map 20A-1-107B (322 Main Street) was Edmund P. Kavanagh.

Southern Part of Lot 27 - Tax Map 20A-1-106 (311 Gay Street) and Tax Map 20A-1-105 (309 Jett Street)

The first owner of Lot 27 in 1798 was Edward Pendleton who paid 18 pounds for Lots 26 and 27.[347] Lot 27 was forfeited to the town trustees, and in 1823 the trustees sold the lot to John Baylis for $10.[348] In 1836 the buildings on the lot were valued at $835 and a brick store stood on the property; this apparently was built between 1823 and 1836. The lot was acquired by Daniel Mason who went

[345] Undated letter to the editor of *The Rappahannock News* by Wayne Baldwin, in files of Rappahannock Historical Society, detailing previous owners and occupants of the log building
[346] Rappahannock County Deed Book 214, page 517;*Rappahannock News*, 17 December 1997,28 April 1999
[347] Culpeper County Deed Book T, page 320
[348] Culpeper County Deed Book PP, page 433

bankrupt in 1840 and the property was sold to Peter Mason, then Pleasant Houston, and then Oliver P. Smith in 1848.[349] Smith was a member of the Washington Town Board of Trustees in 1843 and in 1855.[350] In the 1850 census he was listed as a merchant, age 34 years, with wife Margaret and children Mary and John. In that year, the buildings on the lot were valued at $1450. In 1858, Smith sold the northern part of Lot 27 to James Brereton Jones;[351] in 1870 he sold the southern part of the lot containing the brick storehouse for $1200 to James Wayman, N.B. Wayman, and James A. Templeman, merchants and partners, trading under the name of Wayman and Templeman.[352]

In the early part of the 1900s, Luther T. Partlow's General Store was located on the southeastern part of Lot 27 in the old brick storehouse, at the corner of Jett and Gay Streets, fronting on Gay Street. It was a large, 2-story brick building that extended along Gay Street with a lower level along Jett Street. The building had a varied and colorful career having contained the mercantile store, a barroom, drug store, Felbert Green's barber shop, and a restaurant in the basement owned by Lucy "Jennie" Roberts, a member of a local African-American family. The restaurant served a delicious meal for 25 cents (35 cents on special days).[353] There was also a Delco electric plant in the basement of Partlow's store which furnished electricity to many of the residents of the town.

During 1917-1925, D.C. Updike acquired all of the southern part of Lot 27.[354] He divided the property into two parts:

Southeastern part of Lot 27 (311 Gay Street, Tax Map 20A-1-106):

In 1929, Updike sold the southeastern part of Lot 27 to W.B. Lea, L.L. Lea, J.P. Lea, and T.C. Lea for $6400. This property contained "a Brick Store House and other outbuildings."[355] The building was destroyed by fire, and a new building was constructed on the site in 1933-1934.[356] The new building contained one story on Gay Street and a basement level along Jett Street. T.C. Lea moved his Lea Brothers Store from Lot 6 to this new building. He came from a family of storekeepers; his father J. P. Lea and his two uncles W. B. Lea and L. L. Lea were in the mercantile business. From 1938 to 1941, T. C. Lea served as the fire chief of the Rappahannock Volunteer Fire Department. In 1942 he served as chairman of the Panel War Price and Ration Board of the county and in the late

---

[349] Rappahannock County Deed Book C, page 506; Deed Book D, page 62; Deed Book F, page 133; and Deed Book G, page 376

[350] Minute Book, Town of Washington Board of Trustees, June 1843, and 5 August 1855

[351] Rappahannock County Deed Book K, page 302

[352] Rappahannock County Deed Book M, page 466.

[353] Caption for a 1909 photograph of Partlow's store in 1909, Rappahannock Historical Society files

[354] Rappahannock County Deed Book 28, page 465, Deed Book 30, page 202, and Deed Book 32, page 409

[355] Rappahannock County Deed Book 35, page 330

[356] *Rappahannock News*, 19 January 1950 and 3 March 1966; National Register of Historic Places, Washington Historic District, 2006 Update

1940s he served on the school board. Lea began the Rappahannock Insurance Agency in 1941. He served on the Washington Town Council for a number of years and was treasurer of the Rappahannock Red Cross.[357]

In 1950 the lot was valued at $80 and the building was valued at $3000. Lea operated his store until his death in 1957, after 38 years of doing mercantile business in the town. His widow continued the business until 1964 and then sold it to her son T. Carlyle Lea Jr. He was an attorney and judge for the Rappahannock County Court.[358] On 19 December 1968 an IGA food store opened in the building; the store was owned and operated by Mr. and Mrs. Wayne Sophia.[359] However, this enterprise was short-lived; the building housing the store and the contents of the building were sold at public auction in 1970.[360] On 7 February 1976 an auction house and furniture store was opened in the building by John Walker Jenkins.[361] Jenkins had been an auctioneer for many years and formerly had an auction house in Sperryville. The building was remodeled to have a rustic atmosphere, paneled with apple wood. The front windows displayed glassware, copper, brass, and novelty items. The auction auditorium provided room for comfortable seating and the front area was used for furniture display. The building also contained a snack bar.

In 1984, the building and lot containing 12,395 square feet (0.28 acre) were purchased by Peter and Joyce Kramer.[362] He added 1½ stories to the building and renovated the interior. In the 1990s, this large building on the southeastern part of Lot 27 was named the "Washington Arts Building" but was generally known as "the Kramer Building." It contained several businesses: Peter Kramer, cabinetmaker, who created hand-crafted furniture; Talk of the Town, a shop filled with imaginative gifts and accessories, such as hand-crafted jewelry and puppets; The Buyers Agency, which specialized in representing the buyers in real estate transactions; Minuteman Printers, the Washington office of Bob Naylor Sales & Graphics; Tree Works, the office of forester and arborist Lyt Wood offering all kinds of tree care; and Hospitality Design, which

[357] *Rappahannock News*, 19 January 1950, quoted in the 3 March 2016 edition of the newspaper

[358] *Rappahannock News*, 3 March 1966, quoted in the 26 July 2018 edition of the newspaper

[359] *Rappahannock News*, 12 December 1968, quoted in the 20 April 2017 edition of the newspaper

[360] Auction sale advertised in *Rappahannock News*, 12 February 1970; plat recorded in Deed Book 80, page 631, 9 January 1964

[361] *Rappahannock News*, 7 February 1976, quoted in the 2 February 2017 edition of the newspaper

[362] Rappahannock County Deed Book 148, page 298

designed commercial interiors for hotels and restaurants. Mazie's Daisies, a full-service florist shop managed by Patricia Bartholomew, opened in the lower level of the building in 1998.[363] The property, designated as Tax Map 20A-1-106 and containing 0.28 acre, was sold by Peter Kramer to Kramer Building LLC (Ken Thompson) in 2010 and was sold in 2015 to 311 Gay Street LLC (attorney Mark Allen and journalist John McCaslin, editor of *The Rappahannock News*).[364]

In 2018, this building located at 311 Gay Street housed several establishments. Tula's Off Main, a delightful bistro serving breakfast, lunch and dinners was located here at the corner of Gay and Jett streets, fronting on Gay Street. Adjacent to Tula's on Gay Street was the realty firm of Rappahannock Real Estate Resources Inc., owned by Louis G. (Butch) Zindel. On the second floor were several telework "virtual" offices. At the back of the building were the Rappahannock County Zoning office, Building Inspector's office and Emergency Services office.

Southwestern Part of Lot 27 (309 Jett Street, Tax Map 20A-1-105):

D.C. Updike sold this part of Lot 27 to Ben and Jessie Cox in 1925; the property measured 55' along Jett Street and an unstated distance along Main Street, meeting the land to the north owned at that time by Eliza Jones.[365]

The two-story frame building on this parcel in 2018 was formerly located on Lot 29 (Tax Map 20A-3-89) where it had been the home of John Jett Sr. in 1835.[366] In the last quarter of the 1800s the building had been used as a drugstore, a saloon, and a barroom.[367] In 1900 the building was converted into a branch of the Farmers and Merchants Bank; in 1903 the property was purchased by the Rappahannock National Bank which continued to use the building on Gay Street as a bank.[368] The building was moved to its present location on Lot 27 several years later; there it served as the Rappahannock National Bank until a new brick bank building was constructed on Lot 29 in 1914-1915.[369] The building was then used as the Washington Post Office until the mid-1950s. The building's entrance was originally on Main Street, and a porch was constructed across the Main Street side of the building. When Main Street was widened after World War I, the porch was removed and the entrance was moved to Jett Street. The exterior of

---

[363] *Rappahannock News*, 11 November 1998, quoted in the 26 July 2018 edition of the newspaper
[364] Rappahannock County Instrument 100000095 and Instrument 150000856
[365] Rappahannock County Deed Book 32, page 430, and Deed Book 33, page 576
[366] Rappahannock County Deed Book B, page 319, and Deed Book G, page 438
[367] Rappahannock County Deed Book O, page 73; Deed Book Q, page 426; Deed Book U, page 111
[368] Rappahannock County Deed Book V, page 62, and Deed Book W, page 95; Kathryn Lynch, *Images of America, Rappahannock County*, Arcadia Publishing, Charleston SC, 2007, cover photograph
[369] Postcard cancel-stamped in 1906 showing 'Bank' above the Main Street door of the building, Rappahannock Historical Society files; the construction date of 1914-1915 is based on information from Rappahannock County Land Books which show that the value of the building on the Gay Street property increased from $380 in 1914 to $1950 in 1915.

the building was pebble-dashed in the 1920s. The property was purchased in 1961 by Mary H. Lea,[370] who made major renovations and restored the building as a residence. In the 1970s the building housed "Country Cupboards," a cabinet

and restoration shop. Eugene and Clarissa Leggett owned the building in the 1990s; he was a mayor of the town of Washington. In the 1990s, the building was the site for Hospitality Design Inc., which was a business for commercial space planning, interior design, and project management for hotels, inns, and restaurants. In 2013 it became the offices of the local newspaper, the *Rappahannock News*. Lucy Catherine Bowie and Bruce Bowie had started publishing this newspaper in 1949, as a successor to *The Blue Ridge Guide* which had gone out of business in 1936. Fronting on Main Street adjacent to the building in 2018 was the establishment called "Artifacts on Main," an outdoor commercial sculpture gallery. This business was owned by Robert H. Ballard. In 2018, the owners of the southwestern part of Lot 27, designated as Tax Map 20A-1-105 at the corner of Main and Jett streets (309 Jett Street), were John and Beverly Sullivan; he was the mayor of the town of Washington during 2011-2018.

Lot 28 - Tax Maps 20A-3-86 (291 Gay Street), 20A-3-87, 20A-3-88, 20A-3-102, 20A-3-103, and 20A-3-104
Lot 29 - Tax Maps 20A-3-89 and 20A-3-90 (239 Gay Street), 20A-3-91, 20A-3-92, 20A-3-99, 20A-3-100 (250 Main Street), and 20A-3-101 (262 Main Street)
Lot 30 - Tax Maps 20A-3-93, 20A-3-94, 20A-3-95, 20A-3-96, 20A-3-97 (218 Main Street), and 20A-3-98

The first owner of Lot 28 in 1798 was John Strother who paid 20 pounds 10 shillings for the lot.[371] Apparently Strother did not build on Lot 28, as required by the 1796 Act forming the town, and the lot was forfeited to the town trustees. In 1822 the trustees sold the lot, together with forfeited Lot 11, to Samuel Evans for $38.50.[372] It was owned by Dr. Francis T. Drake in 1836 and then by William A. Lane who sold the lot to John Jett Jr. in 1848; Dr. Benjamin F. Kinsey

[370] Rappahannock County Deed Book 74, page 97
[371] Culpeper County Deed Book T, page 384
[372] Culpeper County Deed Book PP, page 247

purchased the lot in 1850.[373] At that time, the lot was valued at $50 and the building on the lot was valued at $100.

The first owner of Lot 29 in 1798 was Thomas Estes who paid 9 pounds 18 shillings for the lot.[374] Estes did not build on Lot 29, and the lot was forfeited to the town trustees who sold the lot to Harvey Evans for $6 in 1826.[375] Alexander H. and Adaline G. Spilman were the next owners, and in 1836 there was substantial house on the Spilman property that was valued at $700. In 1835, the Spilmans had sold a 30' by 50' parcel located at the northeast part of the lot, fronting on Gay Street, to John Jett Sr.; this parcel had a dwelling house located on it;[376] it eventually became Tax Map 20A-3-89 (see below). The remainder of the lot was sold to Daniel Mason, then to William A. Lane in 1837, to John Jett Jr. in 1848, and to Benjamin F. Kinsey, a physician, in 1850.[377] The small house (250 Main Street) next to the large house built by Spilman (262 Main Street) was possibly built by Kinsey.

The first owner of Lot 30 in 1798 was Thomas Walters who paid 9 pounds 6 shillings for the lot.[378] Walters did not build on Lot 30, and the lot was forfeited to the town trustees who sold the lot to Elijah Amiss in 1833.[379] William A. Lane was the owner of the half-acre lot with a building in 1837.[380] The owner in 1843 was Thomas Hughes; the building on the lot was valued at $50.

Lots 28, 29, and 30 (except the part of Lot 29 that had been sold to John Jett Sr. in 1835) were owned by Benjamin F. Kinsey at his death in 1870. His personal estate was insufficient to pay his debts, and his wife Ann V. Kinsey petitioned the Court to sell her husband's lands and invest the money to support her children. On 10 October 1877, she made a contract with the trustees of St. Paul's and Trinity Episcopal Churches to purchase the lots. This contract described several commercial buildings on the lots. A blacksmith shop operated by Ben Cliffen was located at the southeast part of Lot 30 and a stable was located on the northeast part of Lot 28; a drug store was located along Gay Street in the house that had belonged to John Jett Sr..[381] In 1880, the Rappahannock County Court conveyed the three lots (less the part of Lot 29 that had belonged to John Jett Sr.), to the trustees of Trinity Episcopal Church, who were James W. Fletcher, John A. Browning, H.S. Menefee, and John T. Fletcher.[382] The lots were acquired by Trinity Church for use by the ministers of St. Paul's and Trinity

[373] Rappahannock County Deed Book G, page 438, and Deed Book H, page 377
[374] Culpeper County Deed Book T, page 393
[375] Culpeper County Deed Book TT, page 408
[376] Rappahannock County Deed Book B, page 319
[377] Rappahannock County Deed Book C, page 59; Deed Book G, page 438; and Deed Book H, page 377
[378] Culpeper County Deed Book T, page 380
[379] Rappahannock County Deed Book A, page 85
[380] Rappahannock County Deed Book C, page 59
[381] Rappahannock County Chancery Case 728
[382] Rappahannock County Deed Book P, page 303

Episcopal Churches, located in Woodville and Washington, respectively. The three lots were known as "the Rectory Lots" and the Spilman/Kinsey house on Lot 29, originally built in the 1830s and valued at $1025 in 1880, was used by the ministers of the churches. The small house adjacent to the Spilman/Kinsey house may have been used as a school by the Church.

In 1921, W.M. Stuart, John J. Miller, and P.H. O'Bannon, trustees of St. Paul's and Trinity Episcopal churches, sold Lots 28, 29, and 30 to W.C. Armstrong for $5000 (less the part of Lot 29 that had been sold to John Jett Sr. in 1835 and was then owned by the Rappahannock National Bank).[383] Armstrong was the Rappahannock County Court Clerk from 1902 to 1922. The three lots were divided into nineteen parcels, with nine lots along Main Street and ten lots along Gay Street. In 2018, the owners of the parcels were as shown below.

Lot 28:
Tax Map 20A-3-86, The Theatre at Washington, Virginia LLC (Nancy Raines)
Tax Map 20A-3-87, 257 Gay Street LLC – vacant lot
Tax Map 20A-3-88, 257 Gay Street LLC – vacant lot
Tax Map 20A-3-102, Robert L. Weinberg – vacant lot
Tax Map 20A-3-103, Robert L. Weinberg – vacant lot
Tax Map 20A-3-104, Patricia Weinberg – vacant lot

In the 1930s to the 1950s, J.A. Swan of Culpeper owned multiple parts of Lot 28, and on days when the Rappahannock County Court was in session, he would bring his new machinery, tools, and wares to his empty lots for people to see. Children were even let out of school for this event.[384] Much of Lot 28 remains vacant land in 2018.

Tax Map 20A-3-86 is the location of The Theatre at Washington, Virginia LLC (291 Gay Street). The building also houses the Court Row Offices, including the offices of Kohler Realty Co. (Real Estate III), managed by Rick and Kaye Kohler, and the Rappahannock League for Environmental Protection. W.C. Armstrong, who purchased the rectory lots in 1921, sold this parcel of land, measuring 50' along Gay Street by 86' along Jett Street, to William M. Stuart two years later.[385] There was a barn on the property, and a harness shop next door.[386] His widow, Lucy M. Stuart, sold the property to Buford Roy Armel in 1945.[387] After Armel's death in 1967, the property devolved to his son, Beverly Roy Armel; it was then

[383] Rappahannock County Deed Book 30, page 466
[384] Recollections of Jack Miller, who lived in the town of Washington all his life, in Daphne Hutchinson and Theresa Reynolds, *On the Morning Side of the Blue Ridge*, a compilation of articles published in the *Rappahannock News* in 1983, page 100-101
[385] Rappahannock County Deed Book 31, page 249
[386] Recollections of Jack Miller, who lived in the town of Washington all his life, in Daphne Hutchinson and Theresa Reynolds, *On the Morning Side of the Blue Ridge*, a compilation of articles published in the *Rappahannock News* in 1983, pages 100-102
[387] Rappahannock County Deed Book 46, page 279

sold to James Respress in 1976, Douglas Baumgardner in 1977, and Patricia (Wendy) Weinberg in 1983.[388]

Information from Rappahannock County Land Books indicates that the theater on the property was constructed by Armel in 1947-1948, when the value of the building on the property increased from $0 to $3500. In a 1950 deed, the property was described as "the Theater Lot owned by B.R. Armel."[389] It was originally used as a movie theater and also as a venue for community plays by local citizens and schoolchildren. During the early film years, the theater was packed almost every night of the week, hot dogs and hamburgers were sold from what is now the box office, and what is now the office section of the building was an apartment lived in by the building's owner and his family.[390] The building acquired the name "The Gay Street Theater." The theater was owned and managed beginning in 1983 by Patricia W. (Wendy) Weinberg.[391] The building underwent extensive renovation, including repainting and wall papering the entire interior, retiling and carpeting the floor, installing new stage lights and stage flats, reupholstering seats, installing air-conditioning, and upgrading the

heating system.[392] Weinberg developed the theater into a venue for a wide variety of musical and dramatic performances, usually on weekends and often for one or two performances only. The Theatre became known for its professional musical performances, including the noted Smithsonian at Little Washington chamber music series, and featured many well-known classical instrumental and vocal artists. The Theatre also presented professional chamber music, recitals, jazz, and a variety of other light music, humor and drama. The Rappahannock Association for the Arts and the Community (RAAC), a local

---

[388] Rappahannock County Deed Book 119, page 760; Deed Book 120, page 757; Deed Book 125, page 21; Deed Book 125, page 40; Deed Book 143, page 590; Deed Book 143, page 593; and Deed Book 146, page 536

[389] Rappahannock County Deed Book 53, page 271

[390] Personal communication from Wendy Weinberg, 2019

[391] Margaret Ralph, Clerk of the Court, recalls that, in the 1980s, her husband John W. Ralph would pick up movie films in Washington, D.C., and bring them to be shown at the theater by Richard H. ('Freeman') Allen, the projectionist.

[392] Personal communication from Wendy Weinberg, 2019

nonprofit volunteer organization promoting local artists, also used the theater before relocating their performance venue to the former Methodist Church building on Lot 43, but the film series sponsored by RAAC continues in the Theatre. In 2014, Weinberg sold this enterprise to The Theatre at Washington, Virginia LLC (Nancy Raines), which continued the tradition of high-quality performances developed by Weinberg.[393]

Tax Map 20A-3-102 and Tax Map 20A-3-103 were acquired by Robert and Patricia Weinberg in 1981 from Mary Updike, who had purchased them from the Rappahannock National Bank.[394]

Lot 29:
Tax Map 20A-3-89, 257 Gay Street LLC
Tax Map 20A-3-90, 257 Gay Street LLC
Tax Map 20A-3-91, 257 Gay Street LLC
Tax Map 20A-3-92, Rappahannock County
Tax Map 20A-3-99, Robert L. Weinberg
Tax Map 20A-3-100, Robert L. Weinberg
Tax Map 20A-3-101, Robert L. Weinberg

In 1835, John Jett Sr. purchased from Alexander H. Spilman a 30' by 50' parcel with a dwelling house located at the northeast corner of Lot 29, fronting on Gay Street.[395] This is now Tax Map 20A-3-89. The property was owned in 1876 by James Leake Powers, the architect of Trinity Episcopal Church and the Presbyterian Church, and his third wife Margaret. They sold the parcel to Dr. Adolphus W. Reid in that year.[396] The building was used as a drug store, and the store and land were purchased from Reid by John Dulin in 1885.[397] Dulin turned the building, located opposite the courthouse on Gay Street, into "Dulin's Saloon;" after moving to California, he sold the property in 1897 to George G. Bywaters.[398] He also maintained a barroom on the property. In 1900 Bywaters sold the property to C.J. Rixey for $500, who converted the building into a branch of the Farmers and Merchants Bank; Rixey sold the property in 1903 to the Rappahannock National Bank.[399] The president of this new bank was H.M. Dudley, and the bank had received authorization to commence business the prior year.[400] The 2-story frame building on the property was the site of the bank for several years, until the building was moved to the northeast corner of Jett and

---

393 Rappahannock County Instrument 140001081

394 Rappahannock County Deed Book 140, page 119, and Deed Book 135, page 658

395 Rappahannock County Deed Book B, page 319, and Deed Book G, page 438

396 Rappahannock County Deed Book O, page 73

397 Rappahannock County Deed Book Q, page 426

398 Rappahannock County Deed Book U, page 111

399 Rappahannock County Deed Book V, page 62, and Deed Book W, page 95; this property became Tax Map 20A-3-89

400 Treasury Department certificate No. 6443 authorizing the bank to commence business, dated 29 September 1902, copy in Rappahannock Historical Society files

Main streets on Lot 27; there it continued to serve as the bank[401] until a new bank building made of brick was constructed on the original parcel of land on Gay Street. Information from Rappahannock County Land Books indicate that the new bank building was constructed in 1914-1915, when the value of the building on the property increased from $380 to $1950. During 1940-1980, the Bank purchased additional land on Lots 28 and 29 along Gay Street and made additions to the bank building.[402] The bank business was purchased by Union First Market Bank (later Union Bank and Trust), the property was purchased by Peter and Sharon Luke in 2002,[403] and the bank offices were moved to a new site on Route 211. In 2018, the building on Tax Map 20A-3-89 and 20A-3-90 (257 Gay Street) housed Rappahannock Title LLC, Wheelock Web Works (Toby and Jennifer Wheelock), the law office of Alan Dranitzke, and the law office of Michael Brown of the Walker-Jones legal firm, who also served as Rappahannock County Commissioner of Accounts.

Tax Map 20A-3-92 was sold by W.C. Armstrong to Dr. E. W. Brown in 1923; subsequent owners during 1923-1940 were Mary Partlow, J. T. Rowles, and Warner Miller.[404] In 1940, Miller sold the lot to the Town of Washington.[405] On the lot was constructed the cinderblock Washington Fire Department building, which was set back from the street and had large bays for entrance and exit of the fire trucks. The fire department moved to a new larger building on Warren Avenue in the 1970s, and in 1980 the town of Washington conveyed this parcel and the building to Peter and Sharon Luke.[406] In May 1981 the Washington Fire Company siren was moved to the newly acquired Washington town hall, formerly the

[401] Undated photograph of the building at the corner of Main and Jett streets, with the word "Bank" above the door, Rappahannock Historical Society files

[402] Rappahannock County Deed Book 42, page 462; Deed Book 113, page 783; Deed Book 135, page 161; Deed Book 135, page 165; these properties were Tax Map 20A-3-87, -88, -89, and -90

[403] Rappahannock County Instrument 020001966

[404] Rappahannock County Deed Book 31, page 315 and page 316; Deed Book 40, page 127 and page 336

[405] Rappahannock County Deed Book 43, page 139

[406] Rappahannock County Deed Book 136, page 558

Methodist Church, on Gay Street.[407] The Lukes sold the lot and building to Rappahannock County in 2012,[408] and the building became the offices of the Commonwealth Attorney and the Rappahannock County Attorney (239 Gay Street).

In 2018 there were two buildings on the parcels designated as Tax Map 20A-3-99, -100, and -101. A stuccoed house, facing Main Street, was located on the parcel designated as Tax Map 20A-3-101 (262 Main Street). This house was built by Alexander Spilman in the 1830s and was the home of Benjamin and Ann Kinsey until the property was sold in 1880. It next served as the rectory for Trinity Episcopal Church, and Reverend Tellinghest and Rev. Claybrook lived there. In the 1900s it was the home of Mrs. W. H. Massie Jr. Adjacent to it was a 1½-story frame house (250 Main Street) possibly built in the late 1800s that may have served as a school for the rectory; a small kitchen was added in 1980.[409] The three properties were acquired by Robert and Patricia Weinberg in 1981.[410]

Lot 30:

In 1972, James and Mary Garwood purchased the six parcels of Lot 30, denoted by their tax map numbers 20A-3-93, 20A-3-94, 20A-3-95, 20A-3-96, and 20A-3-97, and 20A-3-98. On these parcels is located the home called "Stonehaven," fronting on Main Street at its junction with Porter Street. The 2½-story stone home on town Lot 30 at 218 Main Street was constructed in 1930.[411] The Garwoods remained the owners in 2018.

Lot 31 and Lot 32 - Tax Maps 20A-1-67, 20A-1-68 (171 Gay Street), 20A-1-68A, 20A-1-69 (198 Main Street), and 20A-1-70 (330 Porter Street)

The first owner of Lot 31 in 1798 was John Wheeler who paid 20 pounds 10 shillings for the lot.[412] In 1836, the owner was John Strother. In 1845, John F. Carter purchased the lot from Alexander H. Hansbrough of Orange County; the

[407] *Rappahannock News,* 7 May 1981, quoted in the 25 February 2016 edition of the newspaper
[408] Rappahannock County Instrument 120000873
[409] National Register of Historic Places, application for the Washington Historic District, 1975
[410] Rappahannock County Deed Book 140, page 119
[411] National Register of Historic Places, Washington Historic District, 2006 Update
[412] Culpeper County Deed Book T, page 375

lot was valued at $40 and the building on the lot was valued at $60 in 1850.[413] Carter sold the lot, containing a house, to Howard Compton in 1855.[414] In 1870, 1880, and 1890, the lot was owned by Elias Compton and the buildings on the lot were valued at $350.

The first owner of Lot 32 in 1798 was Charles Yates who paid 6 pounds 8 shillings for the lot.[415] James Pickwell was the next owner and in 1803 he sold Lot 32 to James Stonestreet. In 1843, Lot 32 was owned by James Stonestreet; the lot was occupied by James Hamrick.[416] John F. Carter purchased the lot with a house on it from Butler Stonestreet in 1847.[417] In 1850, Lot 32 was valued at $50 and the building on the lot was valued at $70.[418] Carter remained the owner in 1860. In 1870, 1880, and 1890, the lot was owned by Elias Compton; there were no buildings of any value on the property.

John W. Clark purchased Lot 31 and Lot 32 in 1893.[419] He lived in the building on Lot 31 and there operated Clark's Tavern with his wife Alice until he died in 1922. Two years later, Alice began dividing and selling Lot 31 and Lot 32. She sold the northeastern portion to John F. Kinsey (Tax Map 20A-1-70).[420] She sold most of the remaining part of Lot 31 and Lot 32 (Tax Maps 20A-1-69, -68, and -68A) to Walker B. Jenkins in 1926.[421] In 1956, Walker and his wife Anna conveyed their properties to their daughters Ruby and Mary.[422]

Lot 31 and Lot 32 have been divided into five parcels:

Northeastern section of Lot 31 (Tax Map 20A-1-70, 330 Porter Street):

On this part of Lot 31 was located John and Washington Clark's blacksmith shop, livery stable and stage coach stop. On one terrible night in March 1916, the livery stable caught fire. The fire was so intense that the livery stable was destroyed, several horses lost their lives, and the facade of the Baptist church across Gay Street was scorched by the flames.[423] In the 1920s F. Downing Wood purchased the property and constructed an apple packing facility; the Wood family owned the farm called "Sunnyside" adjacent to the town of Washington on which there

---

[413] Rappahannock County Deed Book E, page 277, and Deed Book F, page 422; 1850 Rappahannock County Land Records
[414] Rappahannock County Deed Book J, page 309
[415] Culpeper County Deed Book T, page 373
[416] Rappahannock County Deed Book E, page 277
[417] Rappahannock County Deed Book G, page 277
[418] 1850 Rappahannock County Land Records
[419] Rappahannock County Deed Book S, page 397
[420] Rappahannock County Deed Book 32, page 213
[421] Rappahannock County Deed Book 34, page 562
[422] Rappahannock County Deed Book 65, page 456
[423] Recollections of Jack Miller, who lived in the town of Washington all his life, in Daphne Hutchinson and Theresa Reynolds, *On the Morning Side of the Blue Ridge*, a compilation of articles published in the *Rappahannock News* in 1983, page 100-102

were extensive apple orchards. The lot was sold by Alice Wood to Peter and Joyce Kramer in 1973.[424] Peter renovated the building and converted it to be used as a business office for his building company and as a shop for his original woodworking creations and furniture restoration.[425] Joyce Kramer and June Jordan established an arts and crafts gallery in the building. In 1987 the building was the site for two businesses -- the Washington Antiques Center managed by Donna Fisher and Franklin Photography owned by Franklin Schmidt. In 1991 the building housed the office of the Rappahannock Association for the Arts and the Community (RAAC). Later in the 1990s the building was the site of the Washington Thrift Store which sold used clothes and household items for the benefit of the Washington Fire Department. Also in this building was the office of Thomas L. Zumwalt, specializing in residential interior design and re-creation of historic interiors. The old frame building on this parcel has also served as a studio for artist Kevin Adam, as the art gallery called the "Packing Shed Gallery," and as the store for Cinema Paradiso which sold and rented movie videos. In 2018, JPC Designs Woodworking was the only business in the building.

This deteriorating building is an historic landmark in the town of Washington. The gambrel-roofed core and wraparound wings bear influence of the evolution of barns and houses in the Lancaster and Shenandoah valleys. The building retains many original materials and characteristics of its evolution. Weatherboard frame with butterfly hinges accent two single leaf doors. In 2018, the owner of this northeastern part of Lot 31 (Tax Map 20A-1-70, 330 Porter Street) was Jeff Akseizer.

Northwestern section of Lot 31 (Tax Map 20A-1-69, 198 Main Street):

On the northwestern part of Lot 31, facing Main Street, was a large three-story hotel with porches on the first and second floors known as Long House, owned during 1893 until the mid-1920s by Washington Clark and then by his son John, both of whom operated Clark's Tavern. Meals were served in the late 1800s for 50 cents and people would line up from the courthouse down to this building to be served. Later, the building also housed a shoe shop and Frank Kendall's carpentry shop; Kendall lived on the second floor and Sam Atkins lived on the first floor. Buggies from the livery stable nearby were stored at the back of the house.[426] When Main Street was widened and paved after World War I, it was

[424] Rappahannock County Deed Book 180, page 266
[425] *Rappahannock News*, 15 February 1973, quoted in the 24 January 2019 edition of the newspaper
[426] Caption for an undated photograph of the three-story building, Rappahannock Historical Society files

necessary to remove both the front porch and the second-story porch of the tavern. Subsequently, the two top floors were also removed, leaving only the single-story structure that is evident in 2018. The removed material was used in construction of part of a house on Piedmont Avenue.[427]

Alice Clark sold this northwestern part of Lot 31 to Walker B. Jenkins in 1926.[428] He used the building primarily for storage. In 1956, Walker and his wife Anna conveyed the property to their daughters Ruby and Mary.[429] In the building, Ruby created the "First Washington Museum." The museum consisted of a reproduction of an 18th century tavern kitchen with copper kettles, kerosene lamps, and samplers. She also recreated a one-room school and a large historic room filled with the history of Rappahannock County and the town of Washington.[430] The contents of her museum were dispersed after her death. In 2002, Marcia Nagle and Joyce Kramer purchased the property.[431] In 2018, the owner of this part of Lot 31, designated as Tax Map 20A-1-69 at the southeastern corner of Porter and Main streets (198 Main Street), was Ridge 198 LLC.

Southern Section of Lot 31 and Northern Section of Lot 32 (Tax Map 20A-1-68, 171 Gay Street):

The log building on this parcel of land was constructed in 1986 by a local craftsman. The logs were once part of a barn in Harris Hollow belonging to James DeBergh's great-great-grandfather. In 1993 it was the site of the office of the "Harris Hollow Frozen Food Company" owned by DeBergh. A lean-to was added to the building to give the office additional space. The company brokered frozen fruit in the United States and abroad. In 2018 the owner of this 0.55-acre property (171 Gay Street) was J&B Virginia LLC.

---

427 Oral history from Maude Roy to Bill Metcalfe, as related to the Rappahannock Historical Society in 2015
428 Rappahannock County Deed Book 34, page 562
429 Rappahannock County Deed Book 65, page 456
430 The museum was featured in an article in *Southern Living*, February 1978, page 64.
431 Rappahannock County Instrument 020012191

Southern Section of Lot 32 (Tax Map 20A-1-67 and Tax Map 20A-1-68A):

The southern part of Lot 32 has been divided into two parcels. The eastern parcel, designated as Tax Map 20A-1-67 and containing 0.1512 acre, was sold by Robin Kevis to the Gay Street Inn LLC in 2005; in 2013 the property was sold to GSI Properties LLC; and in 2016 it was acquired by Douglas and Margaret Baumgardner.[432] The western parcel (Tax Map 20A-1-68A) was purchased by the Baumgardners in 1983. A small brick house constructed in 1963 is located on this parcel.[433] The Baumgardners remained the owners of the two parcels in 2018.

Lot 33 - Tax Map 20A-1-125c

The first owner of Lot 33 in 1798 was Richard Jackson who paid 18 pounds, 14 shillings for Lots 1, 33, and 44.[434] Other early owners included James Yates and Thomas Stonestreet. In 1843 the owner was Anne Coxe; the lot was purchased by James Jett in 1850. The lot was valued at $25; there was no valuation for any building on the lot.[435] In 1950, the owner of Lot 33 was James Fincham. The lot was valued at $80 and the building on the lot was valued at $100.[436] The Rappahannock County Citizens League owned the lot in 1996. In 2011, Jerry and Cynthia Hodges of Clifton, Virginia purchased the lot from Sidney and Mary Catherine Worley (together with the adjacent Lot 17).[437] Godfrey and Jeanne Kauffmann were the owners of the lot in 2018, designated as Tax Map 20A-1-125c. The lot contained 0.7692 acre and incorporated the land that had been the north end of Gay Street. There were no buildings on the lot.

Lot 34 - Tax Map 20A-1-126 (598 Gay Street)

The first owner of Lot 34 in 1798 was James Yates who paid 6 pounds 1 shilling for the lot.[438] Apparently Yates did not build on Lot 34, as required by the 1796 Act forming the town, and the lot was forfeited to the town trustees. In 1822 the trustees sold the property (together with forfeited Lot 35) to James Yates for

---

[432] Rappahannock County Instrument 050002277; Instrument 130000563; and Instrument 160000111
[433] Files of the Rappahannock County Commissioner of Revenue
[434] Culpeper County Deed Book T, page 381
[435] 1850 Rappahannock County Land Records
[436] 1900 Rappahannock County Land Records
[437] Rappahannock County Instrument 110001057
[438] Culpeper County Deed Book T, page 386

$5.50.[439] In 1835, Lot 34 owned by Samuel Evans and Benjamin Hesser had to be sold because of debts; it was purchased by Daniel Mason who went bankrupt.[440] The lot was sold at public auction in 1840 to James Jett.[441] In 1850, the owner of Lot 34 was John Jett Jr.; the lot was valued at $50 and the building on the lot was valued at $400.

In 1834, at the very beginning of education in Rappahannock County, the Academy was established on Lot 34. The Academy was incorporated in 1837 under the supervision of George W. Grayson, assisted by James Dow, a graduate of Union College in New York.[442] The school was housed in a brick building of two rooms with a fireplace in each room. When the building was renovated in the early 1960s, it was found that the walls of the building were constructed of homemade bricks, three deep, so that the walls are 21 inches thick. On the front side of the building was a small porch, two doors, and two windows; on the back side of the building were four windows.[443] There were 26 pupils in the first year of the school and 45 pupils in the second year, of whom 15 were girls. The building was beloved by students and townspeople, who affectionately called it "the Rabbit Gum" because of its resemblance to a rabbit box, the two-compartment trap used to catch rabbits. This academy existed as a private institution before public education was instituted. With the formal establishment of the public school system in 1871, it became Washington's public school. The building may have been used by Union forces during the War Between the States. The school served as somewhat of a town hall for the community, a place for dances, prayer meetings, lectures, and parties.[444]

In 1908, the Hampton School Board deeded the property to F. Pendleton Carter; in 1930 and 1940 the owner was his wife, Judith Carter. In 1950, the owner of Lot 34 was James Fincham.[445] In the early 1960s Lot 34 was acquired by Thomas and Edith Rees of Vienna, Virginia. They added a 12' sunroom to the house and a 20' garage, shop, and utility room. They also removed the old wall between the

[439] Culpeper County Deed Book OO, page 50
[440] Rappahannock County Deed Book B, page 166
[441] Rappahannock County Deed Book D, page 230
[442] Elisabeth B. and C. E. Johnson Jr., *Rappahannock County, Virginia, A History*, Orange, VA, Green Publishers, 1981, page 201
[443] *Rappahannock News*, 8 July 1965
[444] Recollections of William E. Compton, articles in *The Rappahannock News* in 1956
[445] 1950 Rappahannock County Land Records

old and new parts of the living room. Lot 34 was owned for many years by Diane Bruce, who served as Clerk of the Rappahannock County Court from 1977 to 2010. In 2018, the owner of Lot 34, designated as Tax Map 20A-1-126 (598 Gay Street) and containing 0.5246 acre, was George H. Eatman.

Lot 35 and Lot 36 - Tax Map 20A-1-123 and 20A-1-127 (558 Gay Street)

The first owner of Lot 35 and Lot 36 in 1798 was Levy Garwood who paid 12 pounds 6 shillings for the two lots.[446] Levy was the son of John Garwood, who owned several parcels of land near the town of Washington and was a leader of the Quaker Church community in the county. In 1800, he sold these two lots to Nathaniel Tobin for 17 pounds. Because no building was constructed on Lot 35, the lot was forfeited to the town trustees; in 1822, the trustees sold the lot to James Yates for $5.50.[447]

In 1835, Lot 35 was owned by Samuel Evans and Benjamin Hesser and had to be sold because of debts; it was purchased by Daniel Mason.[448] He went bankrupt in 1840 and all his properties were sold at public auction.[449] This included Lot 35, which was sold to William J. Menefee and Robert M. Heterick.[450] Menefee was the Rappahannock County Court Clerk from 1833 to 1858, and Heterick was the Clerk from 1860 to 1881. In 1850, Lot 35 owned by Heterick and Menefee was valued at $50 and the building on the lot was valued at $100. They remained the owners in 1860.

Lot 36 was owned by George Connard in 1836 and had a substantial building worth $265. In 1850 and 1860 the owner was John Jett Jr.[451] The lot was valued at $25 and the building on the lot was valued at $250. In 1870, Lots 35 and 36 were owned by William J. Menefee and A.Y. Menefee; in 1880, the owner of both lots was F. Pendleton Carter.

In 1890 through 1940, H. M. Dudley and his wife Eugenia owned Lot 35 and Lot 36. Lot 35 appeared to have no buildings on it, but the building value for Lot 36 increased from $250 in 1890 to $1000 in 1900, indicating significant

---

446 Culpeper County Deed Book T, page 394
447 Culpeper County Deed Book OO, page 50
448 Rappahannock County Deed Book B, page 166
449 Rappahannock County Deed Book C, page 506 and Book D, page 62
450 Rappahannock County Deed Book D, page 234
451 1850 Rappahannock County Land Records

improvement to the buildings on Lot 36. Dudley was a councilman on the first Washington Town Council in 1894, was an attorney, and was a County judge. Morgan and Christine Johnson owned the two lots in 1950.[452] Lloyd and Susan Feller were owners in 1996. In 2004, 0.3293 acre at the north end of Lot 35 was merged with land adjacent to the east, was designated as Tax Map 20A-1-123, and was sold to Pleasant View of Rappahannock LLC.[453] The remainder of Lot 35 and Lot 36, designated as Tax Map 20A-1-127 (558 Gay Street), contained 0.5505 acre. In 2018, Pleasant View of Rappahannock LLC owned both properties.

Lot 37 - Tax Map 20A-1-128 (532 Gay Street) and Tax Map 20A-1-129 (353 Calvert Street)

The first owner of Lot 37 in 1798 was George Wheeler who paid 6 pounds 12 shillings for the lot.[454] George was a brother of James Wheeler, and George Wheeler's wife was Lydia Calvert, a daughter of George Calvert and his wife Lydia Beck Ralls. Thus George Wheeler was related to two of the three men who petitioned the General Assembly of Virginia to establish the town of Washington in 1796. The lot was acquired by Martin Slaughter who sold it to Daniel Mason in 1834. Mason sold the lot to Lucy A. Calvert, Lydia B. Calvert, and Martha P. Calvert in the same year; these three women were daughters of Ralls Calvert and Mary Wade Strother (who lived on Lot 40)[455]. In 1836, the buildings on the lot were valued at $285.

In 1844, Lucy A. Calvert married James Leake Powers, who would become the architect and builder of Trinity Church and the Presbyterian Church in the town of Washington and several homes in the County. Powers' first wife was Martha Ann Nicklin, daughter of Dr. Joseph and Elizabeth (Calvert) Nicklin, by whom he had three daughters – Elizabeth, Lavinia, and Martha Ann. After Martha died in 1843, he married Lucy Calvert who was Martha's cousin. Powers and his three daughters moved to Lot 37 at that time. Lucy (Calvert) Powers died in 1848, and James Leake Powers married his third wife, Margaret Cary, in 1853. They remained on Lot 37 until his death in 1889 at the age of 89 and her death in 1900. The house

[452] 1950 Rappahannock County Land Records

[453] Rappahannock County Instrument 040000566

[454] Culpeper County Deed Book T, page 395

[455] Rappahannock County Deed Book A, page 340

was made of logs, and the "pebble dash" facade of the house was probably added in the 1930s. There is a "hump" in the line of the long rear roof, indicating that an addition was probably added at some unknown date.

The southern part of Lot 37, containing the James Leake Powers home on 0.239 acre, was acquired by Charles and Erma Jenkins in 1948.[456] By a Deed of Gift, Erma conveyed the property, designated as Tax Map 20A-1-129 (353 Calvert Street), to Jeffrey and Oxana Butler in 2011.[457] They remained the owners in 2018.

The northern part of Lot 37 containing 0.462 acre, was inherited in 1975 by Clarence (Skippy") Giles Jr. from his father, Clarence Giles Sr.[458] The property contained a 1½ story brick house, estimated to have been built in 1954.[459] Giles and his wife Patricia were the owners of this property, designated as Tax Map 20A-1-128 (532 Gay Street), in 2018.

Lot 38 - Tax Map 20A-2-130 (480 Gay Street)

The first owner of Lot 38 in 1798 was Daniel Covington Brown who paid 13 pounds 8 shillings for Lots 38 and 39.[460] In 1834, Jacob Nicol purchased Lot 38; in 1836 the buildings on the lot were valued at $235. The 1850 census showed that Jacob was age 75 years and was a gunsmith. His wife Abigail was age 60 years. Living with them were five children – Mary age 35 years, Susan age 30 years, Ann B. age 25 years, Napolean age 24 years, and his twin sister Morjean. Napolean was a blacksmith and had his blacksmith shop, shoeshop, and wagon repair shop on Lot 38 until his death in 1892. His obituary stated "He had been a perfect stand-by in the repair of guns and machinery. He had been a Justice of the Peace and Supervisor of this District." The Nicol family owned Lot 38 until the late 1890s. The house on this lot is believed to have been destroyed by fire.[461]

In 1900, the owner of Lot 38 was Dr. E.W. Brown. Dr. Brown built the house on Lot 38; the buildings value increased from $200 when the Nicol family owned the lot in 1890 to $1200 when Brown owned the lot in 1900. Brown was the son of Whitfield Brown, owner of Brown's Store in Culpeper County. He received

---

[456] Rappahannock County Deed Book 50, page 161
[457] Rappahannock County Instrument 110001060
[458] Rappahannock County Will Book 27, page 474
[459] National Register of Historic Places, the Washington Historic District, 2006 Update
[460] Culpeper County Deed Book T, page 404
[461] Oral history, Rappahannock Historical Society files

his M.D. degree from the University of Virginia, married Rappahannock County native Elizabeth Eastham, and practiced medicine in Rappahannock County for over 60 years. His office was located in a small building at the southwest corner of Lot 38; this building was moved to Lot 39 in the 1950s. Brown was an active Mason, a member of the Baptist church, and was appointed to the first Washington Town Council in 1894. He died on 2 June 1950 at the age of 92 years.

In 1957 the owner of Lot 38 was John Davis. By 1996, the owner was Elaine Viguerie. In 2018, the owner of Lot 38, designated as Tax Map 20A-2-130 (480 Gay Street), was Jeffrey and Veronika Benson. The lot contained 0.52 acre.

Lot 39 and Lot 40 - Tax Map 20A-2-131 (456 Gay Street), 20A-2-132 (430 Gay Street), and 20A-2-132A (408 Gay Street)

The first owner of Lot 39 in 1798 was Daniel Covington Brown who paid 13 pounds 8 shillings for Lots 38 and 39.[462] Apparently Brown did not build on Lot 39, as required by the 1796 Act forming the town, and the lot was forfeited to the town trustees. In 1834 the trustees sold Lot 39 to Daniel O'Neale.[463] There were no buildings of any value on the lot for many decades.

The first owner of Lot 40 in 1798 was Ralls Calvert who paid 10 pounds 19 shillings for the lot.[464] Ralls (born in 1767, died in 1815) was the third postmaster of Washington, Virginia, and was the son of George Calvert, one of the founders of the town of Washington, and his wife Lydia Beck Ralls (see Lot 8). Ralls Calvert married Mary Wade Strother in 1790 and they raised a family of twelve children. Their youngest child, Lucy, married James Leake Powers in 1844 (his second wife); she died in 1848 (see Lot 37). In 1811, Ralls Calvert sold Lot 40 to Daniel O'Neale for $500.[465] In 1836, the buildings on Lot 40 were valued at $435, indicating that a substantial house was located on the property. In 1850, Lot 40 was valued at $50 and the buildings on the lot were valued at $550.

---

[462] Culpeper County Deed Book T, page 404
[463] Rappahannock County Deed Book A, page 248
[464] Culpeper County Deed Book T, page 389
[465] Culpeper County Deed Book EE, page 206

Daniel O'Neale had married Sarah Jennings on 15 January 1807. Their children were E. Catherine, who married George M. Cary, son of Francis Cary; Mary Ann who married Thomas Fogg; Susan Ellen who married Edward Cary; Mildred Elizabeth who married Charles B. Cary; James R.; John R.; Sarah Jane who married William A. Lillard; Charles Henry; and William Edward. Daniel O'Neale was a member of the Washington Town Board of Trustees in 1837, 1839 and 1843.[466] The 1850 census showed that Daniel was age 63 years and was a millwright and Sarah was age 56 years. Two children were living with them at that time – Catherine age 18 years and Ellen age 15 years.

The O'Neale family remained the owner of Lot 39 and Lot 40 until the 1870s. During this time, Rappahannock County Land Books indicate that there were no buildings on Lot 39, but the valuation for the buildings on Lot 40 was about $500. It can be surmised that the O'Neale family lived on Lot 40. At Daniel's death, his estate was in debt to James B. Jones & Co., Walter B. Hackley, and James Jett. In 1879 Lots 39 and 40, containing the O'Neale home and one acre of land, were sold at auction for $600 to the highest bidder who was George M. Cary, in trust for his wife Catherine Cary, a daughter of Daniel O'Neale.[467] (Three of Daniel O'Neale's daughters married Carys.) In the northeast corner of Lot 39 is located a graveyard containing the graves of Susan Ellen Cary (born 1835, died 1903), Edward Cary (1827-1898), George Michael Cary (1823-1894), and Daniel O'Neale Cary (1873-1875).[468] In 1900, the owner of Lot 39 and Lot 40 was George M. Cary, trustee for his wife Catherine. There were still no buildings on Lot 39; the valuation of the buildings on Lot 40 was $400.

In 1905, Catherine Cary sold Lot 39 to Dr. E.W. Brown for $300, retaining for herself the Cary graveyard located in the northeast corner.[469] Two years later, Dr. Brown conveyed this property to his wife, Elizabeth Eastham Brown.[470] Catherine Cary, who was the widow of George M. Cary and had no children, willed Lot 40 to Sarah Jane (O'Neale) Lillard who sold the property to Elizabeth E. Brown in 1914.[471] With this sale, Elizabeth owned both Lot 39 and Lot 40 (as well as Lot 38).

When Elizabeth died in about 1955, her executor divided Lots 39 and 40 into several parts.[472] The executor sold the northern part of Lot 39 (0.384 acre) to Guy Burke for $2500.[473] A contingency of the sale to Burke was that Dr. Brown's office building, located at the southwest corner of Lot 38, be moved to this

---

[466] Minute Book, Town of Washington Board of Trustees, 3 June 1839, 1 June 1842, 14 April 1843
[467] Rappahannock County Deed Book P, page 92
[468] Rappahannock Historical Society cemetery records
[469] Rappahannock County Deed Book X, page 14
[470] Rappahannock County Deed Book X, page 403
[471] Rappahannock County Will Book H, page 206, and Deed Book 27, page 147
[472] Rappahannock County Will Book L, page 495
[473] Rappahannock County Deed Book 65, page 74

northern part of Lot 39. On 31 January 1963, Guy Burke resigned as custodian of the jail, having served in this capacity since 1 May 1940. He and his wife had lived at the jail and cared for and fed the numerous prisoners there.[474] They moved to their home, called the "Pill Box" which they had built on the northern part of Lot 39. Their home was a simple frame, 4-room dwelling. The property was acquired by Byrd G. Jones in 1979 who added two rooms and a second bath to the house.[475] In 1990, Patrick O'Connell and Reinhardt Lynch, owners of the Inn at Little Washington, purchased the property.[476]

They began renovations on the house but more and more of the original building was removed because of deteriorated conditions; by the end of 1991 virtually nothing was left of the original building except the foundation and some of the framework.[477] A new house was built on the property and, for a time, this served as the home of O'Connell and Lynch. In 2007 the building was remodeled into a house with multiple rooms and several porches and bathrooms. With interior decoration and landscaping the building became an elegant overnight residence for guests of the Inn. The house was renamed "The Claiborne House" in honor of Craig Claiborne, food journalist for the New York Times newspaper. The house was described as "a 3600 sq.ft. cottage, just a stone's throw from The Inn's main building. Overlooking a newly created herb and cutting garden, the residence features two bedrooms, 2½ baths, a living room, dining room, media room and library. A two-story veranda overlooking a private garden in the rear offers additional space for outdoor entertaining." Dr. Brown's office on the northern part of Lot 39 adjacent to the Cary cemetery was converted to be the main wine cellar for the Inn At Little Washington. The property is designated as Tax Map 20A-2-131 (456 Gay Street) and contains 0.384 acre.

In 1956, the remaining small southern part of Lot 39 and the adjacent northern half of Lot 40 were sold by the executor of Elizabeth Brown to T. Morgan Johnston and Christine T. Johnston for $3500.[478] The Johnstons sold this property to Earl W. and Hilda Burke; in 1992 the property was purchased by

---

[474] *Rappahannock News*, 7 February 1963, quoted in the 30 June 2016 edition of the newspaper

[475] Rappahannock County Deed Book 132, page 635; Records of the Commissioner of the Revenue for Tax Map 20A-2-131

[476] Rappahannock County Deed Book 182, page 30

[477] *Rappahannock News*, 14 November 1991

[478] Rappahannock County Deed Book 65, page 83

Patrick O'Connell and Reinhardt Lynch.[479] The small building on the property, designated as Tax Map 20A-2-132 (430 Gay Street) and containing 0.301 acre, was converted for use as storage, work space, and a maintenance shop. This building is a log house that has been covered with siding. In 2018, The Inn at Little Washington LLC was the owner of the property.

The southern part of Lot 40 was owned by the Pauline Bruce Trust in 1996. The house on this land, that was formerly the home of the Cary family, underwent restoration in the mid-1990s. It was found that the sills were hewn and the floor joists were sawn by a vertical saw; this construction method suggested that the building was constructed in about 1800. During the restoration, it was discovered that all four corner posts of the house and the two corner posts of the back kitchen (formerly the porch) are solid trees, squared off and cornered to support the house. Both inside and outside walls are brick, mortared with mud, called "Brick Noggin," an 18th century form of insulation. In 2018, the owner of this parcel, designated as Tax Map 20A-2-132A (408 Gay Street) and containing 0.326 acre, was Carrol P. Beard.

Lot 41 - Tax Map 20A-1-110, Tax Map 20A-1-111, Tax Map 20A-111A, and Tax Map 20A-1-112 (370 Gay Street)

The first owner of Lot 41 in 1798 was John Farrow who paid 10 pounds 4 shillings for the lot.[480] In the early 1800s, Lot 41 was owned by Gabriel Smither and his wife Getty. Their children were Gabriella (who married George W. Abernathy), Emilina, Lucy (who married Robert Rudacilla), Ann (who married Nathaniel B. Ralls, owner of Lot 1), Richard, and John. Gabriel died in 1815 and the lot was inherited by Getty who declared herself to be an "insolvent debtor;" she surrendered her properties to Philip Slaughter, sheriff of Culpeper County. From the 1830s until the 1880s, Lot 41 was the home of John Groves and his

[479] Rappahannock County Deed Book 71, page 314; Rappahannock County Deed Book 191, page 634
[480] Culpeper County Deed Book T, page 391

descendants.[481] Groves was the town collector in the early days of Washington.[482] In 1850, the lot was valued at $50 and the buildings on the lot were valued at $550.

In 1881, Benjamin Cliffen, an African American, purchased the lot for $735 and had his home and a blacksmith shop on the property; in 1893, Patsey Cliffen acquired the property.[483] A building on the lot is believed to have been the location of the Washington Female Institute, with the Misses Janie and Julie Chapin as principals. The first annual commencement celebration for the school was held on 4 June 1896.[484] Cliffen sold a 20' by 36' parcel of land located on the northeast corner of the lot to the House of Ruth, Order of Oddfellows, on which was constructed a building worth $100 in 1930.[485]

In 1908, Patsey Cliffen sold a 35' by 136' parcel at the south end of the lot to Phelbert Scott Green.[486] Green constructed a house on his property and also a small building at the rear of the land which served as Green's Barbershop; his buildings were valued at $450 in 1920 and 1930. In his old age, Phelbert Scott Green moved to the Arlington, Virginia, home of Dorothy Scott. When he died in 1964 he bequeathed money to his sisters and brothers but gave his property on Lot 41 to Dorothy because she "brought me to her home to live as a member of the family and for many other acts of kindness."[487] The Green property was sold to Walter and Anna Payne in 1974, to Barbara Wood in 1981, and to Roger Batchelder in 1987.[488] The craft and antique store "Rare Finds" was located in Green's house, and in the early 1990s "Mountainside Market" managed by Ray Haase was located there. This shop sold gourmet and natural foods including a wide assortment of specialties from fruit juices and vitamins to kitchen gadgets and toiletries and imported and Virginia wines. In 1998 Batchelder sold the property, containing 0.1093 acre, to the trustees of Trinity Episcopal Church,[489] which retained the frame house that now serves as the church office, "Trinity House" (Tax Map 20A-1-112, 370 Gay Street).

[481] Information from the Rappahannock County Land Books
[482] Minute Book, Town of Washington Board of Trustees, 3 June 1839
[483] Rappahannock County Deed Book P, page 398; Rappahannock County Deed Book U, page 171
[484] Rappahannock Historical Society school files
[485] Rappahannock County Deed Book Y, page 181
[486] Rappahannock County Deed Book Y, page 30
[487] Rappahannock County Will Book W, page 257
[488] Rappahannock County Deed Book 113, page 713, Deed Book 140, page 61, and Deed Book 165, p. 471
[489] Rappahannock County Instrument 980001684

Patsey Cliffen willed her home and remaining land to her son, Richard Cliffen, in 1925 and to her grandchildren at his death.[490] The Cliffen and House of Ruth parcels were conveyed to C. Carlyle Lea through a Chancery suit, and Lea conveyed these two parcels to Trinity Episcopal Church on 17 November 1969.[491] The parcels were designated as Tax Map 20A-1-110, Tax Map 20A-1-111 and Tax Map 20A-1-111A. Over the years, the Cliffen home and the House of Ruth building fell into disrepair. Trinity Episcopal Church razed these buildings and created a parking area and children's play area on the northern part of Lot 41.[492] The Church also razed Green's barbershop, leaving only Green's home (Trinity House) on the Church property.

Lot 42 and Lot 43 - Tax Map 20A-1-113 (338, 354, and 360 Gay Street), Tax Map 20A-1-113B (328 Gay Street), Tax Map 20A-113A (320 Gay Street), and Tax Map 20A-1-114 (310 Gay Street)

The first owner of Lot 42 and Lot 43 in 1798 was George Calvert who paid 49 pounds for Lots 8, 42, and 43.[493] Calvert was one of the three men who petitioned the General Assembly of Virginia to establish the town of Washington in 1796. In 1801, Calvert sold Lot 42 and Lot 43 to his son, Ralls Calvert (who lived on Lot 40). Ralls held Lot 42 and Lot 43 for a year and then sold them in 1802 to his first cousin, Elizabeth Calvert, and her new husband Dr. Joseph Nicklin whom she married in 1802.[494]

In 1821, Nicklin sold Lots 42 and 43 to Abner Carter who quickly sold them to John Resor. Resor and his wife Mary had six children – Jacob, Ann G. (wife of Frosty English), John P., Montgomery P., Elisha W., and William H. An 1833 plan of the town shows that "Mrs. Resor's house" was located on the lots.[495] John Resor died in 1833 and Mary Resor's dower inheritance was the two lots, on which were located a stable and the Resor house where Mary resided and kept a tavern.[496] The property stayed in the Resor family until 1835 when John William

---

[490] In 1940 Blanche Cliffen Fletcher, granddaughter and heir of Patsey Cliffen, sold a 60' wide strip at the east side of the lot to F. C. Baggarly (Rappahannock County Deed Book 422, page 459, Tax Map 20A-1-111B); in 1996 this parcel was owned by Werner Krebser and Jerry Martin who owned Tax Map 20A-1-113

[491] Rappahannock County Chancery Case #2521, Rappahannock County Deed Book 96, page 623

[492] Caption for an undated photograph of the razed buildings, Rappahannock Historical Society files

[493] Culpeper County Deed Book T, page 398

[494] Elizabeth was a daughter of John Calvert, a brother of George Calvert, one of the founders of the town of Washington. A daughter of Elizabeth and Joseph Nicklin was Martha Ann, born in 1809, who married James Leake Powers (the architect and builder) in 1837; she died in 1843.

[495] Rappahannock County Deed Book A, page 189

[496] Rappahannock County Chancery Case #5, Resor vs. Resor; Rappahannock County Deed Book A, p. 384

Jett[497] purchased part of Lot 42, all of Lot 43, and 4.1 acres to the east of the two lots;[498] in 1844, Jett purchased the remainder of Lot 42 from the Resor family.[499]

An 1837 plan of the town shows that Thorn's Tavern fronted on Gay Street on Lot 42 and part of Lot 43.[500] A merchant's license had been issued to George Thorn in 1834 and an ordinary license had been issued to him in 1836, and Thorn presumably rented the former Resor tavern from Jett. In 1849, the Washington Academy was established in the building, founded by George W. Grayson (born in Kentucky) and H. W. Maertens (born in Germany).[501] Tuition ranged from $16 to $30. Needlework and drawing were taught, in addition to the basics; music and language lessons were available for an extra charge. Board was available for a 10-month session at $85 per month. One of the teachers was Annie Powers, a daughter of James Leake Powers who had directed the construction of the Presbyterian Church on Lot 22, Trinity Church on Lot 25, and several Rappahannock County homes.

In 1850, the owner of Lot 42 was John Bailey Jett. The lot was valued at $80 and the buildings on the lot were valued at $50.[502] Jett also owned Lot 43; this lot was valued at $60 and the buildings on the lot, formerly Thorn's Tavern and then housing the Washington Academy and also serving as a boarding house, was valued at $1100.[503] Residents of the building in 1850 included Grayson, a teacher, with his wife and children and mother; Maertens, a teacher; Reuben, Maria, and Mary Long; Mary Hitt; and Ida Carter.[504] In 1866, Jett sold the two lots to Baldwin Bradford Baggarly for $2255, who converted the old tavern and school building into his home. [505] Baggarly and his wife Emma had two sons: Franklin Clyde Baggarly who became an attorney in Washington D.C. and president of the Washington Bar Association; and Carroll Baggarly who became a physician in Richmond and died at age 38 years.

In 1889, Baggarly and Emma gave a parcel measuring 61' x 37' located at the southwest corner of Lot 43 to the Washington Methodist Episcopal Church South, to be used as a place of divine worship subject to authorizations by the

---

[497] John William Jett had married Hannah Calvert in 1793. Hannah was the daughter of John Calvert (a brother of George Calvert) and was a sister to Elizabeth (Calvert) Nicklin (above). John and Hannah Jett had three known children: James W. Jett who married Julia Mason Lane, Lavinia Jett who married John Green, and John Bailey Jett.

[498] Rappahannock County Deed Book B, page 200 and page 249

[499] Rappahannock County Deed Book F, page 15; Jett also acquired land to the east of these lots from the Resor family in 1838 (Rappahannock County Deed Book C, page 245)

[500] Rappahannock County Deed Book C, page 71

[501] Elisabeth B. and C. E. Johnson Jr., *Rappahannock County, Virginia, A History*, Orange, VA, Green Publishers, 1981, page 201

[502] 1850 Rappahannock County Land Records

[503] 1850 Rappahannock County Land Records

[504] 1850 U.S. census of Rappahannock County

[505] Rappahannock County Deed Book L, page 464; Jett also sold property to the east of the lots to Baggarly

General Conference of the Church.[506] Through many fundraisers and solicited contributions, $4,000-$5,000 was raised for construction of the church. The cornerstone of the church was laid by Washington Lodge No. 78, Ancient Free and Accepted Masons, in the northeast corner of the foundation, as required by Masonic tradition. The inscription on the stone reads "M. E. Church South, September 5, 1889." The building was erected by John A. Cannon of Manassas, Virginia, and was completed during 1890. The Church retained the property until 1980, when trustees of the United Methodist Church sold the property to the Town of Washington.[507] The Washington Fire Department Ladies Auxiliary Thrift Store operated in the building after this. The building was used only sporadically and in 1990 the Town of Washington sold the lot and building to Rappahannock County for use as a public facility.[508] The lot had the dimensions of 56' by 32' together with a space of 5' around the church lot for the purpose of repairing the church. In the 1990s it became the Ki Theater; it then became the theater of the Rappahannock Association for the Arts and the Community (RAAC). The RAAC Community Theater presents plays, readings, poetry coffee houses and workshops. For more than 25 years, RAAC has been a focal point for the arts in Rappahannock County. Its mission is to create the opportunity for all residents of Rappahannock County to enrich their lives through exposure to the arts. RAAC sponsors workshops, dances, programs, concerts, school events, cinema, and other activities that enhance the community's artistic well-being. In 1996, Werner Krebser and Jerry Martin sold a parcel located adjacent to and east of the former Church property to Rappahannock County.[509] The County retains ownership of the two parcels, containing 0.0797 acre, designated as Tax Map 20A-1-114 (310 Gay Street).

In 1900, the owner of Lot 42 and the remainder of Lot 43 was B. B. Baggarly. Lot 42 was valued at $100 and the building on the lot was valued at $1200. The remainder of Lot 43 was valued at $15 and the building on the lot was valued at $50.[510] In 1913, B. B. Baggarly died at the age of 88 years and his only surviving son, Franklin Clyde Baggarly, inherited his land.[511] An old photograph of the buildings on Lot 42 and 43 shows that the Baggarly home fronted on Gay Street

[506] Rappahannock County Deed Book R, page 475
[507] Rappahannock County Deed Book 136, page 710
[508] Rappahannock County Deed Book 179, page 774
[509] Rappahannock County Deed Book 220, page 416
[510] 1900 Rappahannock County Land Records
[511] Quoted from Rappahannock County Will Book Q, page 245

and was a large manor house with a verandah. There were also several outbuildings located on Lot 43 south of the manor house. A stone wall at the front of Lots 42 and 43 encompassed the entire Baggarly home property. In 1931 Franklin Clyde Baggarly moved the house from Gay Street to the hill east of the town above a pond, enlarged the building, added a two-story portico with full height columns, and renamed it Avon Hall.

In 1959, Baggarly's wife Frances Trott Baggarly petitioned the Rappahannock County Court to permit her to take over her husband's business affairs because of his mental incompetence.[512] The next year, Frances sold a parcel containing 5625 square feet, located on Gay Street adjacent to the Methodist Church lot, to the Virginia Telephone & Telegraph Company.[513] A brick building was constructed on this parcel that was completed on 17 January 1963 and was placed in service as the central equipment office in May 1963.[514] The building, designated as Tax Map 20A-1-113A (320 Gay Street), housed the Century Link telephone services owned by the Virginia Telephone & Telegraph Company in 2018.[515]

Frances Trott Baggarly sold Lot 42 and the remainder of Lot 43, containing 0.871 acre, to Edward Scroggins.[516] He retained this land until 1966, when he sold the property to Ray and Ruby Cannon who sold it to Werner Krebser M.D. and Jerry Martin M.D. in 1974.[517] In that year, Krebser and Martin obtained permission from the Washington Town Council to build a full-time medical clinic on Lot 42 and, in January 1975, the new brick building housing the Rappahannock Medical Clinic was opened.[518] In 1999, Jerry Martin M.D. became sole owner[519] and in 2018 he was the owner of this clinic housing his medical offices, located at 338 Gay Street and designated as Tax Map 20A-1-113.[520]

---

[512] Rappahannock County Chancery Case #2279 and Case #2286, Baggarly vs. Baggarly
[513] Rappahannock County Deed Book 72, page 496
[514] *Rappahannock News*, 17 January 1963
[515] *Rappahannock News*, 17 January 1963
[516] Rappahannock County Deed Book 71, page 333
[517] Rappahannock County Deed Book 87, page 65; Rappahannock County Deed Book 111, page 190
[518] *Rappahannock News*, 9 January 1975, quoted in the 20 January 2019 edition of the newspaper
[519] Rappahannock County Instrument 990000074
[520] Martin retired from medical practice in early 2019; in June 2019 the Rappahannock County Health Department was moved from 491 Main Street to Martin's former medical office at 338-A Gay Street (*Rappahannock News*, 27 June 2019)

Two other buildings are located on the Martin property, at the northern end of Lot 42. The small building on the northwest side, fronting on Gay Street, was the office of the Roger Batchelder Realty Company in the 1990s. In 2018 it was the office of Country Places Realty (360 Gay Street). In 1986, Krebser and Martin constructed an office building on the northeast part of the lot.[521] The Rappahannock County Department of Social Services was located in this building in 2018 (354 Gay Street).

360 Gay Street

354 Gay Street

On the parcel of land purchased by the Virginia Telephone and Telegraph Company in 1960 was a very old building, one of the outbuildings to the Baggarly manor house. This brick two-story building is believed to be one of the earliest brick structures in the town of Washington. The building saw service as a temporary office for the County Treasurer sometime between 1871, when Samuel Spindle was elected as the first County treasurer, and 1875, when the Treasurer's office was completed on Lot 44. The building is also believed to have been used as a law office, Jimmie Jewell's shoe shop in the 1920s, and a barroom. The Telephone Company planned to raze this building but when approached by concerned citizens, they agreed to give the building to the Rappahannock Historical Society, providing that the building be moved. There was no lot to move onto, so they agreed to deed 2250 square feet of their land to the Society in 1965.[522] Shortly thereafter, a moving contractor was contacted, a basement dug, foundation poured, and the building was placed on the donated lot, at a cost of $2750 for moving and an additional $2750 for landscaping. In 1974, the building underwent renovation, including repairs to the foundation, roof, and

[521] Rappahannock News, 28 November 1985
[522] Rappahannock County Deed Book 86, page 519

floors at a cost of $7419.[523] In 2000 the building was moved closer to Gay Street and an addition was constructed at the back which approximately doubled the size of the building. The Rappahannock Historical Society continues to own the brick building located at 328 Gay Street and designated as Tax Map 20A-1-113B. The building contains the Society's offices, research library, museum, and gift shop.

Lots 44, 45, and 46 - The Rappahannock County Courthouse and County Offices

The first owner of Lot 44 in 1798 was Richard Jackson who paid 18 pounds, 14 shillings for Lots 1, 33, and 44.[524] After Jackson's death in 1820, Lot 44 was conveyed to David Miller who sold it to Jacob Nicol in 1822. The first owner of Lot 45 and Lot 46 in 1798 was David Lansdown who paid 31 pounds 15 shillings for Lots 17, 19, 20, 45, and 46.[525] Clayton Johnson acquired Lot 45 and sold this lot to Jacob Nicol in 1820. Apparently no building was constructed on Lot 46, as required by the 1796 Act forming the town, and the lot was forfeited to the town trustees. In 1822 the town trustees sold this lot to Jacob Nicol for $3.[526]

On 18 May 1833, Jacob and Abigail Nicol sold Lots 44, 45, and 46 to the Justices of Rappahannock County for $800.[527] These three lots comprise the land on which are located the Rappahannock County Courthouse, Treasurer's office, Commissioner of Revenue's office, Court Clerk's office, and Sheriff's office, jail, and a small frame building that formerly served as the County Administrator's office.

Lot 44:
Vacant small building – 290 Gay Street
Rappahannock County Treasurer's office – 274 Gay Street
Lot 45:
Rappahannock County Commissioner of Revenue office – 262 Gay Street
District Courthouse – 250 Gay Street
Lot 46:
Rappahannock County Court Clerk's office – 238 Gay Street
Rappahannock County Sheriff's office and jail – 383 Porter Street

Before the courthouse was constructed, court was held in the Free Meeting House on Lot 6.[528] On 2 April 1833, the Court of Rappahannock County appointed

---

[523] Elisabeth B. and C. E. Johnson Jr., *Rappahannock County, Virginia, A History*, Orange, VA, Green Publishers, 1981, page 73
[524] Culpeper County Deed Book T, page 381
[525] Culpeper County Deed Book T, page 372
[526] Culpeper County Deed Book PP, page 185
[527] Rappahannock County Deed Book A, page 18
[528] Rappahannock County Minute Book A, page 4

William A. Lane, Daniel Mason, and Henry R. Menefee as commissioners to form a plan of the dimensions and construction of the public buildings for the county.[529] They submitted their report four days later; the report described the dimensions and arrangement of and the materials needed to build the jail and the jailor's house, the courthouse, and the court Clerk's office, with estimates for the cost of building these structures.[530]

Rappahannock County Deed Book A, page 12

"Pursuant to an order of the County Court of Rappahannock made on the 2nd day of April, 1833 appointing us the undersigned commissioners for the purpose of forming a plan of the dimensions of the public buildings of the said county, we have, after consulting with contractors, who have been exclusively engaged in erecting public buildings, come to the following conclusions.
First in regard to the Jail: The dimensions of this building is believed by us to be of sufficient size to answer the purpose of Jail and Jailor's house, if built forty-six feet long, and twenty-six feet wide, the Jail to be twenty-one feet long with a passage between the Jail and Jailor's house seven feet wide; leaving eighteen feet for the Jailor's house, which we believe should be divided into two rooms below, and two above, with a chimney so built as to give a fireplace to each room below. The Jail to be divided into two rooms or cells below for criminals, and two above for debtors – to be well secured with iron bars, bolts and locks – the walls of the lower room to be two feet thick – those above, with the part designed for the Jailer to be of the usual thickness of other buildings, the whole room to be well painted together with the inside of the Jailer's house – for greater security of the criminals the walls of the cells to be lined with thick oak plank or bars of iron (the difference of cost not differing materially). For warming the prisoner's cells, a stove is thought to be the best suited, so fixed upon the wall dividing the cells as to heat each cell, and be heated from the passage. The debtors room, we supposed can be warmed from one chimney – this building we believe can be contracted for, and commenced immediately at about the sum of twenty-five hundred dollars payable in three or four payments, the first to be made the first of December next.
Signed - William A. Lane, Daniel Mason, Henry Menefee

The foregoing report was filed the 6th day of May 1833. On the motion of William A. Lane, sheriff of Rappahannock County, Armistead Hesser was appointed the first jailor of the County.

For the courthouse and Clerk's office, the three commissioners had originally believed that a courthouse similar to that in Culpeper would be appropriate, with a detached Clerk's office. However, they believed that this would be too expensive and they suggested a plan similar to that used in Luray, 40' square with

[529] Rappahannock County Deed Book A, page 12
[530] Rappahannock County Deed Book A, page 12

an office at each of the front ends of the building measuring 20' by 15'. The jail and courthouse were to be constructed of brick, with stone foundations of 18" above ground and slate roofs. The cost of the courthouse and clerk's office was estimated to be $5000. They recommended that a bell not be housed in a cupola because of the cost.

Some of the commissioner's recommendations for the courthouse were obviously not followed, since the courthouse was constructed during 1833-1835 as a separate building from the Clerk's office and a cupola was placed on the building.

On 6 May 1833, William Lane, Daniel Mason, Henry R. Menefee, William Slaughter, and Gabriel Parks were appointed as commissioners to contract for erection of the public buildings.[531] Malcolm F. Crawford was given the contract to construct the courthouse and Clerk's office, at a cost of $4500, payable in three installments of $1500 each. The third and final payment to Crawford was authorized at the June 1836 Court meeting, to be paid on 1 December 1836.[532]

On 13 October 1834, Lane, Mason, and Menefee were authorized to purchase a bell for the courthouse.[533] In 1835, Duff Green was paid $123.60 for the bell.[534] In 2014, during restoration of the exterior of the courthouse, a photograph was taken of the bell in the building's belfry. The bell had the date "1834" on it, indicating that it was the original courthouse bell. Built of brick, the courthouse has double front doors and deep recessed windows. Some of the windows are false to give the building a more uniform appearance from the outside. Originally, the entire first floor was the courtroom with a second story balcony containing two jury rooms; later, the courtroom was moved to the second story and offices were constructed on the ground level.

---

531 Rappahannock County Minute Book A, page 17
532 Rappahannock County Minute Book A, pages 241, 248-249; Minute Book B, page 3
533 Rappahannock County Minute Book A, page 221
534 Rappahannock County Minute Book A, page 316

Construction of the jail was performed by Stafford County carpenter John W. Fant. The County Court Commissioners signed a $2,000 contract with him in June, 1833. The next October, the commissioners approved a change from stone to brick for the foundations of the jail. The jail was completed in June of 1836, when the Court appointed Fant as commissioner to procure a stove for the criminal room.[535]

It was not until 1921 that the Commissioner of Revenue had his own office, but this was only a rented room in the Rappahannock National Bank located on Lot 29.[536] A brick outbuilding to the Baggarly home on Lot 42, that now houses the Rappahannock Historical Society, served as a temporary office for the County Treasurer sometime between 1871, when the first County treasurer was elected, and 1875, when the Treasurer's office with a fireproof vault was constructed by John J. Hawkins on Lot 44.[537] On 6 December 1875, the construction was certified by James Leake Powers.[538] Prior to the establishment of the office of the Treasurer, the sheriff had the responsibility for collecting taxes from which he received a commission of 5%.

In 1885, an addition was made to the rear of the Clerk's office and a fireproof vault was installed. This building eventually proved inadequate for the business of the Court, and in 1978 a new Clerk's office was built on Lot 46 by the Lanz Construction Company, with Pryer, Faulkner, and Wanderpool as architects at a cost of $145,000 and an architect

[535] National Register of Historic Places, the Washington Historic District, 2006 Update, Section 8, page 30
[536] Elisabeth B. and C. E. Johnson Jr., *Rappahannock County, Virginia, A History*, Orange, VA, Green Publishers, 1981
[537] Board of Supervisors Book 1, page 80; Elisabeth B. and C. E. Johnson Jr., *Rappahannock County, Virginia, A History*, Orange, VA, Green Publishers, 1981
[538] Board of Supervisors Book 1, page 92

fee of $15,000.[539] The building was designed in the same style as the older brick buildings of the courthouse complex. The former Clerk's office was renovated and converted to the office of the Commissioner of Revenue.

The small frame building at the northwest corner of Lot 44 was constructed in 1857. In that year J.Y. Menefee, who was Commonwealth Attorney, received approval from the Rappahannock County Justices to construct a building there, "not to be larger in size than eighteen by twenty six feet with only one door which must front the street" and to be used only as a law office.[540] This building was apparently used as the office of the Commonwealth Attorney by J.Y. Menefee (1858-1870), F.P. Carter (1870-1879), H.G. Moffett Jr. (1879-1916), and W.F. Moffett (1916-1941).[541] It was also used by W.F. Moffett Jr. as a law office in 1956-1958. The building served as the County Extension Office and the Home Demonstration Agent office during the 1970s and then as the Rappahannock County Administrator's office until 2018.

Significant repairs and renovations to the county's public buildings have been conducted over the years.[542] In 1859, repairs to the buildings were commissioned, including a shingle roof on the courthouse and jail and a tin roof on the clerk's office, at a cost not to exceed $350.[543] In 1876, a woodyard was created between the new Treasurer's office and the old Clerk's office. In 1877, a new roof was put on the courthouse. A porch was constructed on the jail and other repairs were made in 1876 for the sum of $150. In 1882, a gate to the courthouse grounds was constructed. A fireproof vault was added to the Clerk's office in 1884. In 1885, an addition was built onto the Clerk's office at a cost of $3 per 1000 bricks. In 1900-1902, repairs were made to the jail and the courthouse belfry and a new floor of tongue-and-groove heart pine was installed in the Clerk's office. In 1916, an icehouse was dug on the jail lot. In 1921, lights and a water system were installed in the jail. In 1922, a new oil stove was purchased for the Clerk's office. In 1924, a cement walk was constructed in front of the courthouse yard. In 1932, $1270 was expended for an addition and repairs

---

[539] Elisabeth B. and C. E. Johnson Jr., *Rappahannock County, Virginia, A History*, Orange, VA, Green Publishers, 1981

[540] Rappahannock County Minute Book G, page 125

[541] Rappahannock County Minute Book 5, page 379; letter dated 25 May 1960 to the Board of Supervisors from Commonwealth Attorney George H. Davis Jr.

[542] Many of these repairs and renovations are detailed in the Board of Supervisors Book #1

[543] Elisabeth B. and C. E. Johnson Jr., *Rappahannock County, Virginia, A History*, Orange, VA, Green Publishers, 1981

to the courthouse, a new floor was laid at the cost of $659, and a pipeless furnace was installed for $483. In 1933, a heating plant was installed in the Clerk's office. In 1938, a fireproof room in the Treasurer's office was constructed. In 1945, $15,000 was set aside for renovating the courthouse. In 1947, the jail was condemned and $15,000 was allocated for repairs. The courthouse was remodeled in 1947 at a cost of $18,000. In 1961, an oil heater was installed in the small frame building, which was being used as a Civil Defense office. In 1964, local contractors were asked to determine the cost of converting this building into an office; a toilet, supply room, mimeograph room, and septic system were added. In 1965, repairs and renovations were again conducted on the courthouse.

In 1990, an addition was made to the jail to accommodate the sheriff's office, deputy and dispatcher offices, new jail cells, and a prisoner dayroom. Another addition to the jail was made in 2012. In 2014, the County became part of a regional jail system and all prisoners were moved to the Rappahannock-Shenandoah-Warren Regional jail.

Many improvements to the water and sanitary facilities of the courthouse complex have been made. A privy was constructed on the courthouse lot sometime before 1837. A well was dug on the courthouse grounds in 1839. In 1879, a windlass was purchased for the well for $2. In 1897, the Sheriff was instructed to have a blind erected in the lower corner of the courthouse lot near the stable of B. B. Baggarly for the purpose of urinating behind; in 1900 Thomas Hayward, the Clerk of the Court, was instructed to have the privy moved and blinds put around it. In 1900, a pump was installed in the well. In 1932, a lavatory was installed in the Clerk's office and the Treasurer's office. In 1932, an electric pump was installed in the well. In 1934, a septic tank was installed for the jail. In 1935, a sanitary drinking fountain was installed on the courthouse lot. A sewer system was installed in the jail and toilets in the courthouse in 1936 through use of Works Project Administration (WPA) labor. In 1947, a toilet was installed for the Clerk and the Treasurer. An electric water cooler was installed in the courthouse for $250 in 1949. In 1957, because the top of the courthouse well was rotting, a concrete top was installed.

One of the most significant residents of the jail was the slave Kitty Payne who was the daughter of her owner, Samuel Maddox. Kitty and Robert Payne, a free black, had four children. Maddox died in 1837, leaving the slaves to his wife Mary, who emancipated them in 1843 and moved them to Gettysburg, Pennsylvania, where Robert Payne died in 1844. However Maddox's nephew, Samuel Maddox Jr., alleged that Mary Maddox was not the rightful heir and was not entitled to Payne and her children. On 24 July 1845, he and five accomplices kidnapped them and returned them to Rappahannock County. While Payne fought Maddox's allegations in the Rappahannock County courthouse, the judge confined Kitty and her children in the jail for their safety; a year later, after complex court proceedings, she regained her freedom. In November 1846, Payne and her children left Virginia with the aid of Quakers and returned to Gettysburg. A Civil War Trails marker on Lot 45 commemorates the ordeal of Kitty Payne, and the site has been designated as part of the Underground Railroad Trail to Freedom.

At the north end of Lots 44-46 is the Confederate Monument, which was erected in 1900 through the efforts of the local chapter of the Daughters of the Confederacy to honor the men from Rappahannock County who served their cause in the War Between the States. The monument is a 24-foot tall column of marble on a red sandstone base, decorated with recessed panels that show the profiles of Gen. Robert E. Lee, the Confederate Army commander, Col. Robert S. Mosby, a famous cavalry commander, and other decor including a drum and trumpet. Names of local Confederate regiments are carved into the stone, along with soldiers' names. The list of names is only partial, as the County sent over 1000 men to the Civil War. Underneath the obelisk are listed four major battles, a motto, and a list of names of companies. These are: Chancellorsville with the motto "Sacred Martyrs," Manassas with the motto "Heroes of Rappahannock", Cold Harbor "Hallowed Names," and Wilderness "Deathless Dead." A Civil War Trails marker, erected adjacent to the monument in 2013, lists the names of the soldiers who are on the monument.

In 1950, the Ladies Auxiliary of the American Legion was given permission to place a plaque inside the courthouse honoring the county's veterans of WWII.

Lot 47 - Tax Map 20A-1-71 (180 Gay Street)

The first owner of Lot 47 in 1798 was William Porter who paid 25 pounds 18 shillings for Lots 12, 13, 14, and 47.[544] Porter was one of the four men who petitioned the General Assembly of Virginia in 1797 to include part of his land in the town of Washington. In 1834, Dr. Joseph Nicklin purchased the lot from Thomas Smith.[545] In 1850, the lot was valued at $50 and the building on the lot was valued at $50.[546] After Dr. Nicklin died in 1853 his son-in-law, James Leake Powers, held the lot until 1874 when he sold it to Mary Long, a longtime member of Mount Salem Baptist Church who was then living in Baltimore, Maryland.[547] In the same year, she deeded part of the lot to the trustees of the Baptist Society of Christians and the Washington Masonic Lodge 78 for the purpose of erecting a Baptist church.[548] Since both the Baptists and the Masons were looking for

[544] Culpeper County Deed Book T, page 371
[545] Rappahannock County Deed Book B, page 12
[546] 1850 Rappahannock County Land Records
[547] Rappahannock County Deed Book N, page 268
[548] Rappahannock County Deed Book N, page 434

places to meet at the time, they collaborated on constructing a building, with the Masons owning the top floor and the Baptists owning the rest.[549] This relationship still exists today, with both sharing in the upkeep of the building. The Washington Masonic Lodge was chartered on 15 December 1841 by the Grand Lodge of Virginia.[550]

The Washington Baptist Church building was constructed in 1875 by Corbin L. Proctor, a carpenter from Shenandoah County, Virginia.[551] The 2½-story 7-course American brick building with a gable roof and belfry is an impressive example of Renaissance revival Italianate style architecture.[552] The church was built to serve the inhabitants of Washington and environs because the parent church, Mount Salem Baptist Church, was some miles distant and was difficult to reach in winter. In 1885, the remainder of Lot 47, which had been willed to F. L. Slaughter by Mary Long, was conveyed by Slaughter to the Baptist Church.[553]

In 1927, four Sunday school rooms were added, two on each side of the church, and in 1953 an addition for educational purposes was added to the back of the church. In 1962, 0.37 acre adjoining the church property on Mt. Salem Avenue was given by Judge Rayner Snead (a member of the Church) and his wife Lois (a member of Trinity Episcopal Church), and their son William constructed a brick parsonage there in 1979.[554] In 1999-2000 there was construction of a handicap-accessible building with a large fellowship hall, offices, a new kitchen, and restrooms. The monument in the churchyard honors the Reverend Barnett Grimsley (1807-1885), pastor of the parent Mount Salem Baptist Church. An oil portrait of Reverend Grimsley and a portrait of his wife are in the museum of the Rappahannock Historical Society.

The church property is designated as Tax Map 20A-1-71 (180 Gay Street) and the rectory as Tax Map 20A-1-72A (432 Mount Salem Avenue).

---

[549] Elisabeth B. and C. E. Johnson Jr., *Rappahannock County, Virginia, A History*, Orange, VA, Green Publishers, 1981, page 172

[550] Mary Elizabeth Hite, *My Rappahannock Story Book*, The Dietz Press, Richmond, Virginia, 1950, page 175

[551] National Register of Historic Places, the Washington Historic District, 2006 Update, Section 8, page 31

[552] National Register of Historic Places, 1975 Washington Historic District nomination application, and 2006 resurvey

[553] Rappahannock County Deed Book R, page 26

[554] Rappahannock County Deed Book 78, page 364; Elisabeth B. and C. E. Johnson Jr., *Rappahannock County, Virginia, A History*, Orange, VA, Green Publishers, 1981, page 173

Lot 48 - Tax Map 20A-1-72 (160 Gay Street)

The first owner of Lot 48 in 1798 was William Smith who paid 5 pounds for the lot.[555] In 1843 the owner was William A. Lillard, and in 1850 the owner was the estate of Daniel Mason, deceased; the buildings on the lot were valued at $100. In 1895 Thomas Hayward purchased the lot with a house for $505;[556] the buildings on the lot were valued at $775 in 1900. The markedly increased value for the buildings reflects the construction of a house on Lot 48. Hayward was Clerk of the Rappahannock County Court during 1892-1902. In 1901, Charles Keyser bought the property and the home was enlarged. In 1973, Peter and Joyce Kramer purchased the property, restored the home, and converted it to a bed and breakfast establishment which it has remained ever since.[557] Subsequent owners have been Robin Kevis and Donna Dalton, the Gay Street Inn LLC (Jay Ward Brown and Kevin Adams), and GSI Properties LLC (Gary and Wendy Aichele).[558] In 2018, the owner of the Gay Street Inn, designated as Tax Map 20A-1-72 (160 Gay Street) and containing 0.3706 acre, was DB&DH LLC (Drew Beard and Deb Harris).[559]

Lot 49 and Lot 50 - Tax Map 20A-1-65 (132 Gay Street) and Tax Map 20A-1-66

The first owner of Lot 49 in 1798 was David Johnston who paid 6 pounds 3 shillings for the lot.[560] In 1823, Johnston and his wife Sarah sold the one-half acre lot to Abner Sims for $350.[561] One year later, Sims sold the property and an adjoining parcel of 2¼ acres to Robert Dearing for $500.[562] A log cabin appears to have been located on Lot 49 at this time and a wagon makers shop was located on the larger parcel of land. In 1833, Dearing and his wife Mary (Thorn) Dearing were in debt and mortgaged Lot 49, where they lived, and the adjoining land on which Dearing had a blacksmith shop.[563] Dearing mortgaged the land again in

[555] Culpeper County Deed Book T, page 403
[556] Rappahannock County Deed Book T, page 210
[557] Rappahannock County Deed Book 108, page 317, *Rappahannock News*, 19 April 1984
[558] Rappahannock County Deed Book 164, page 271; Instrument 050002277; Instrument 130000563
[559] Rappahannock County Instrument 170000337
[560] Culpeper County Deed Book T, page 390
[561] Culpeper County Deed Book PP, page 411
[562] Culpeper County Deed Book RR, page 86
[563] Rappahannock County Deed Book A, page 65

1838.[564] Mary died in 1837, and Robert died in 1846 in Jefferson County, Virginia. The house and lot were acquired by Margaret Whitehead who adopted the Dearing children – John S., Elizabeth C., George, and William R.[565]

The first owner of Lot 50 in 1798 was Fielding Scandland who paid 6 pounds 15 shillings for the lot.[566] There appears to have never been a house constructed on the lot.

In 1848, Middleton Miller acquired Lot 49 and Lot 50 from John S. Hughes, together with adjoining land to the south on which he built the home "The Maples."[567] He is believed to have lived in the Dearing home while he was constructing "The Maples." He was a member of the Washington Town Board of Trustees in 1843[568] and in 1855.[569] He died without a will in 1893; his many properties, located in Loudon, Culpeper, and Rappahannock counties, were valued at $34,300.[570] The Rappahannock County properties were inherited by two of Miller's children, Howell M. Miller and Clarence J. Miller. Howell died intestate and Clarence acquired his share of the land of their father. Clarence was a councilman on the first Washington Town Council in 1894 and was Commissioner of Revenue for Rappahannock County from 1895 until his death in 1929. In 1900, the lots were valued together at $50 and the buildings on the lots were valued at $200.[571] In 1933, after Clarence's death, the land was forfeited because of debts and sold at public auction; Clarence J. Miller Jr. was the highest bidder.[572] In 1946, Clarence and his wife, Achsah D. Miller, sold 70.58 acres of land, including Lots 49 and 50, to Louise M. Price.[573] Subsequently, there were multiple owners of Lots 49 and 50.

In about 1960, the house on Lot 49 was owned by J. Newbill Miller, a descendant of Middleton Miller. He renovated and restored the house, which became the home of Miller's aunt, Mrs. Harry Hurtt. In 1986, the owner was Truman Kessey who sold Lot 49 to Raymond L. Gooch.[574] In 1960, the owner of Lot 50 was Dan Price; subsequent owners were Howard Berger, Newbill Miller, and Raymond L. Gooch.[575] Gooch sold Lots 49 and 50 to John and Beverly Sullivan in 2003, and in 2013 the Sullivans sold the two lots back to Gooch.[576]

---

[564] Rappahannock County Deed Book C, page 207
[565] Rappahannock County Will Book C, page 425
[566] Culpeper County Deed Book T, page 378
[567] Rappahannock County Deed Book G, page 468
[568] Minute Book, Town of Washington Board of Trustees, June 1843
[569] Minute Book, town of Washington Board of Trustees, 5 August 1855
[570] Rappahannock County Deed Book U, page 145
[571] 1900 Rappahannock County Land Records
[572] Rappahannock County Deed Book 40, page 53
[573] Rappahannock County Deed Book 48, page 493
[574] Rappahannock County Deed Book 157, page 30
[575] Rappahannock County Deed Book 72, pp. 275 and 396; Deed Book 92, p. 527; Deed Book 230, p. 298
[576] Rappahannock County Instrument 030000675 and Instrument 130001299

In 2018, the owner of Lot 49, designated as Tax Map 20A-1-65 (132 Gay Street), was Raymond L. Gooch; the lot contained 0.50 acre. Gooch also owned Lot 50, designated as Tax Map 20A-1-66; the lot contained 0.50 acre. In 1998, Gooch acquired a conservation easement on Lot 50, which was termed the "132 Gay Street Pasture." He granted a deed of easement to the Virginia Board of Historic Resources of the Commonwealth of Virginia to preserve the scenic open-space property on Lot 50.[577]

Lot 49 contains two log houses, joined originally by a breezeway or covered porch. The smaller of two log cabins is believed to have been built first, probably by the Dearings in the 1830s; the value of the buildings on Lot 49 was $235 in 1836. The second cabin was probably built in the 1860s, when the value of the buildings was $400. At some time the two cabins were connected by a breezeway, which became an enclosed room in the 1900s. The cabins were sometimes called "the Roy House" because the Roy family rented the home. The well in front of this old house is one of the original town wells shown in an 1833 plan of the town of Washington.

Lot 51 - Tax Map 20A-1-63

See Lot 16 and Lot 51, above.

Homes Outside the Original Boundaries of the Town of Washington

There are several notable buildings that are outside of the original 1797 plan of the town but are within the current town corporate limits.

Avon Hall[578]

The Avon Hall house began its history as Mary Resor's tavern and then as Thorn's Tavern on Gay Street on Lot 42 and part of Lot 43.[579] It also served as the Washington Female Academy and in 1866 was purchased by Baldwin Bradford Baggarly and converted to his home.[580] (See Lot 42 and Lot 43, above.) The property on which the Avon Hall house is sited was acquired by the Baggarly

---

[577] Rappahannock County Instrument 980001962
[578] For a detailed discussion of the history of Avon Hall, see Maureen Harris, "History of the Avon Hall Property, Washington, Virginia," Rappahannock Historical Society, 2014
[579] Rappahannock County Deed Book C, page 71
[580] Rappahannock County Deed Book L, page 464

family during 1866-1954 in multiple parcels, totaling 12.452 acres.[581] In 1931 Franklin Clyde Baggarly moved the home from Gay Street to the hill east of the town above a pond, enlarged the building, added a two-story portico with full height columns, and renamed it Avon Hall.

In 1959, Baggarly's wife Frances Trott Baggarly successfully petitioned the Rappahannock County Court to permit her to take over her husband's business affairs because of his mental incompetence.[582] She sold the Avon Hall property to William and Ramona Carrigan in 1960.[583]

In 2002, the Town purchased the Avon Hall property and adjacent land owned by Carrigan for $920,000.[584] Four years later, the Town sold 4.0 acres to Rappahannock County for $400,000.[585] In 2009-2010, the Town constructed the Wastewater Treatment facility on the southern part of the Avon Hall property (Tax Map 20A-1-80), with access to this via a 50-foot right of way from Warren Avenue along Leggett Lane. In 2016 the Town sold two adjacent parcels of the land to Avon Hall LLC (William Fischer and Drew Mitchell) for $750,000.[586] The first parcel, designated as Tax Map 20A-1-115, was 7.5584 acres and contained the Avon Hall mansion, the pond, a two-story cottage, and a small frame building. The second parcel, designated as Tax Map 20A-1-116 and located east of the first parcel, was 1.5289 acres and contained a frame building. Certain restrictions were included in the deed, including that the Avon Hall mansion should be preserved in its current appearance and be used only for a single-family residence, that the two parcels could not be subdivided, and that a 50-foot wide wooded buffer zone be maintained to separate the first parcel from view of the Wastewater Treatment facility. These restrictions were to be in place for a period of 40 years. The Town still owns the Wastewater Treatment facility (Tax Map 20A-1-80), and 1.0665 adjacent acres (Tax Map 20A-1-144).

---

[581] Rappahannock County Deed Book L, page 464, Deed Book V, page 294, Deed Book Y, page 85, Deed Book Z, page 281, Deed Book Z, page 282, Deed Book 28, page 377, Deed Book 28, page 478; Deed Book 29, page 254; Deed Book 42, page 459, and Deed Book 61, page 107

[582] Rappahannock County Chancery Case #2279 and Case #2286, Baggarly vs. Baggarly

[583] Rappahannock County Deed Book 72, page 378

[584] Rappahannock County Instrument 020001760

[585] Rappahannock County Instrument 060001175

[586] Rappahannock County Instrument 160000598

The Meadows[587]

The Meadows is located at the west end of Porter Street. In 1781 William Porter was given 247 acres of land by his father-in-law Samuel Porter; on this land William and his wife Sarah built their home and raised a family of 13 children.[588] The home and part of the land remained in the Porter family until 1871. The home had its beginning, as did many structures in the county, as a log cabin but it has been greatly expanded several times. It is believed to have been used as a field hospital during the Civil War and those who died there were buried in the yard behind the house. Among the stones in the retaining wall behind the house is one carved with initials, probably a headstone from the grave of a soldier. Visible for many years, graffiti was written on the walls of the attic by recuperating soldiers and bloodstained floorboards bespoke its Civil War service. When the house was remodeled, this was painted over.

In 1871, Judge James French Strother purchased The Meadows. The house was said to be haunted and Judge Strother is reported to have had difficulty keeping servants. To solve this problem, he let it be known that he had shot all the ghosts with silver bullets and he was able to keep help once again. Judge Strother married Mary Botts and they had seven children. Both of their sons became lawyers, and Andrew Botts Strother became Rappahannock County Juvenile Court Judge. One of James and Mary's daughters, Belle, held her dancing classes at The Meadows. She inherited the property and retained it until 1946. There have been several owners since then – Charles Keyser, Edwin Benton, Willis B. Snell, and Edward and Martha Barton. In 2018 the property was owned by the mayor of the town of Washington, John Fox Sullivan, and his wife Beverly.

Mount Prospect[589]

Mount Prospect is located on a small knoll on the west side of Main Street about ¼ mile south of the center of town. The property was part of the original 1735

---

[587] For an expanded discussion of the history of The Meadows, see Maureen Harris, "History of The Meadows," Rappahannock Historical Society, 2012

[588] Samuel Porter had acquired 447 acres of the western land from Robert Shirwood in 1773 (Culpeper County Deed Book G, page 276); he gave the northern part of this land to his son-in-law William Porter in 1791 (Culpeper County Deed Book Q, page 387) and the southern part of this land to his son-in-law Edward Burgess in 1795 (Culpeper County Deed Book S, page 194)

[589] For an expanded discussion of the history of Mount Prospect, see Maureen Harris, "History of Mount Prospect," Rappahannock Historical Society, 2017

land grant to the Kennerlys on which the town of Washington is located. The Mt. Prospect land was acquired by William Porter in 1781, and the land remained in the Porter family for many years.

In 1872 Daniel Webster Mason (son of Daniel Mason and Sarah Porter, grandson of William Porter) sold 12.7 acres of Porter land to Walter Hackley.[590] Three years later, Hackley acquired an additional 30.2 acres of Porter land.[591] The Mount Prospect home, a Victorian-Italianate red brick residence, was probably built by Walter Hackley and his wife Betty Ellen Jordan after they purchased the 12.7-acre parcel. It is believed that the brick was produced on the property. Surrounded and shaded by large oaks, maples, and walnuts, its high-ceiling rooms, which are typical of the period, made it a cool retreat in hot summers.

The home was used as a small private school by Miss Mary Betsy Jordan, niece of Betty Hackley, who in 1922 at age 56 years married Robert Eastham, a former Mosby ranger who was then age 80 years. Mary lived at Mt. Prospect until her death in 1939 when it became the property of Arthur and Emily Miller.[592] He was a foxhunter and was Master of the Rappahannock Hounds. Restoration and modernization began and the home is an example of how great care can result in the elegance that the home retains today. The property passed to the Miller's daughter, Evelyn, who had married Colonel J. Stewart Willis in 1983.[593] He was a mayor of the town of Washington. They restored the exterior to what is believed to be its original appearance. An octagonal porch on the left rear overlooks a swimming pool, the original well, the Jordan family cemetery, and the Blue Ridge Mountains. In 2003, the Willises sold Mount Prospect to Jeff B. Franzen and his wife for $1.59 million.[594] In 2014, the 41-acre property was sold to Charles and Deanna Akre for $2.3 million.[595] They conducted an extensive renovation of the house and property, with an enlargement of the house.

---

[590] Rappahannock County Deed Book N, page 25

[591] Rappahannock County Deed Book F, page 265; Rappahannock County Deed Book M, page 49; information from Rappahannock County Deed Book Q, page 149

[592] Rappahannock County Chancery Case 1869; Rappahannock County Deed Book 42, page 429

[593] Rappahannock County Deed Book 137, page 423 and page 625

[594] Rappahannock County Instrument 030001689

[595] Rappahannock County Instrument 140000217

The Middleton Inn

The Middleton Inn, formerly known as The Maples, is located at 176 Main Street, almost directly across Main Street from Mount Prospect. The home was constructed on land that was one of the early farms of Henry Miller I. It is a Federal-style house built in the mid-1800s by Middleton Miller, and it was named The Maples because of the many mature maple trees in the front yard of the property. The architecture is similar to that of the Rappahannock County courthouse, and the bricks were kilned on the property. The smoke house and servant's quarters were built at the same time as the main house. While the house was being built, the Millers are believed to have lived in the log house located on Lot 49.

Miller owned a woolen mill just outside the county near Waterloo where he made the wool fabric used for Civil War uniforms in the color known as "Confederate Grey." The Millers raised a family of four children: Josephine who married Col. P. Henry O'Bannon; Fannie Helen who married Robert Menefee; Howell who was Superintendent of Public Schools and lived at The Maples; and Clarence Jackson who was Rappahannock County Commissioner of Revenue for 33 years, married Sallie Hunt Strother of The Meadows, and raised his family at The Maples.

The Maples remained in the Miller family for almost 140 years. During this time, a solarium was added to the right side of the house. In 1960 the property was purchased by Dr. Howard Berger of Falls Church, Virginia, who changed the name to "Clairmonte" and added a left wing as a garage. The Bergers sold the home in 1968 to J. Newbill and Carol Miller; he was a descendant of Henry Miller I. In 1994, the Millers sold two adjacent tracts, containing 3.0245 acres and 2.6181 acres, to Mary Ann Kuhn for $500,000.[596] These tracts extended along Main Street adjacent to and south of town Lots 49 and 50. Kuhn converted the residence into a bed and breakfast establishment and renamed it The Middleton Inn, after the name of the original owner. The Inn has received AAA's Four Diamond Award, and the house is listed on the Virginia Landmarks Register. The property is designated as Tax Map 20A-1-64 and 20A-1-64A.[597]

---

[596] Rappahannock County Deed Book 189, page 537 (plat), and Deed Book 208, page 582 (deed)

[597] In 2019, the property was sold to Luis A. Vinhas Catao for $1.5 million.

The Campbell House

The Campbell House, located at 490 Mt. Salem Avenue, was designed and built in about 1920 by William Curtis Campbell when he returned from World War I. He had come to Rappahannock County in 1914 to supervise the convict crews building the macadam roads going through the town of Washington, and he met Mayes Dudley shortly after arriving here. They soon became engaged before he left for the war and were married when he returned.[598] According to the oral history of Mayes, many of the girls in Rappahannock County found husbands in the road crew. Mayes and William had twins when she was 33 years old: William Jr. and Mary. William Jr. was killed in action during World War II in Anzio, Italy. Campbell died in 1969 and Mayes died in 1990 at age 99 years. In 2007, a conservation easement was placed on the property with the Virginia Board of Historic Resources.[599] In 2017, the property designated as Tax Map 20A-1-74 was purchased by Justin and Gail Swift.[600]

The Heterick House

The Heterick House is located at 417 Middle Street behind Lot 40. Robert Mackey Heterick purchased a lot containing 1¼ acres in 1850 for $15 from Sarah Booker of Wayne, Indiana. This property has remained in the Heterick/Critzer family to the present. Robert was born in Frederick County, Virginia, in 1810. He moved to Rappahannock County in 1834 where he practiced law for 25 years. He also served as Commissioner of the Schools, and during the Civil War he served as a colonel of "The Home Guard." He and his wife Mary Elizabeth Cary, whom he married in 1853, raised a family of five children. In 1860 he was elected Clerk of the Rappahannock County Court and served in this position until 1881 when he retired from public life. Edward Cary Heterick, his son, succeeded his father as Clerk of the Court from July 1881 to January 1892; an extreme illness took his life at age 38.

When Robert died in 1892, the Heterick House was inherited by his son Robert Bruce Heterick who married Lillie Frances Parnell in 1882. They also had five children. He was a carpenter, cabinet maker, and an apiarist and served as the town sergeant (constable) of the town of Washington. When James Leake Powers died, he willed his carpenter tools and carpentry supplies to Heterick.[601]

---

598 Information from Rappahannock Historical Society files

599 Rappahannock County Instrument 070001831

600 Rappahannock County Instrument 170000913

601 Rappahannock County Will Book F, page 414

Roberta Lee Heterick (known as Robbie) inherited Heterick House and married John Wallace Critzer in 1920. John was sheriff of Rappahannock County for 11 years, retiring in 1962. In 1950, Robbie was one of the six women elected on the all-women slate for town council which defeated an all-male ticket. Robbie and John had only one child, Wallace Heterick Critzer. John died in 1962 and Robbie died in 1983 at the age of 86 years; both are buried in the Masonic Cemetery adjacent to the town of Washington. Heterick House became the property of Wallace Heterick Critzer who had two sons, Bruce Lee Critzer and Steven Owen Critzer. In 2018 the home belonged to Steven Critzer.

Chapter 12. Schools in the Town of Washington

William Porter's Schools

In 1793, William Porter sold 2 acres of land to James Jett Sr. and John Jett[1] that became part of the town of Washington when it was founded in 1796. The southeast corner of this parcel of land was marked by "a red oak stump near a schoolhouse." Apparently Porter had built a school on his land at some time prior to 1793. After this land was taken to form the town, Porter donated ½ acre adjacent to the northwestern border of the town to trustees John Miller, Gabriel Smither, George Calvert, and Ralls Calvert, to erect a school "for educating youth of both sexes" and for "the promotion of science and dissemination of useful knowledge."[2] When the First Washington Baptist Church congregation purchased a lot of land on Main Street north of the town in 1880, the lot was described as being adjacent to "the old school house lot."[3] It appears that the school which Porter founded had lasted here for a significant period of time.

The Academy ("Rabbit Gum")

In 1834, at the very beginning of education in Rappahannock County, the Academy was established on town Lot 34. It was incorporated in 1837 under the supervision of George W. Grayson, originally from Kentucky, assisted by James Dow, a graduate of Union College in New York.[4] The school was housed in a brick building of two rooms with a fireplace in each room. When the building was renovated in the early 1960s, it was found that the walls of the building were constructed of homemade bricks, three deep, so that the walls were 21 inches thick. On the front side of the building were two doors and two windows; on the back side of the building were four windows.[5] There were 26 pupils in the first year of the school and 45 pupils in the second year, of whom 15 were girls. At one time only reading, writing, and arithmetic were taught, but later Latin was added to the curriculum. John S. Gibson, W.A.L. Jett, W.W. Moffett (later a judge), Mr. Warden, Margaret Compton, Ida Wood, and Miss Bell were some of the teachers in this school.[6]

The building was beloved by students and townspeople, who affectionately called it "the Rabbit Gum" because of its resemblance to the two-compartment

---

[1] Culpeper County Deed Book R, page 333
[2] Culpeper County Deed Book Z, page 202
[3] Rappahannock County Deed Book P, page 416
[4] Elisabeth B. and C. E. Johnson Jr., *Rappahannock County, Virginia, A History*, Orange, VA, Green Publishers, 1981, page 201
[5] *Rappahannock News*, 8 July 1965
[6] Rappahannock Historical Society school files, based on information from William E. Compton, Elmira Dulin, and Mrs. George Cary, who all went to school at The Academy.

trap used to catch rabbits. This academy existed as a private institution before public education was instituted. With the formal establishment of the public school system in 1871, it became Washington's public school. The school was just for primary grades; older children went to private schools, most with just a handful of students, scattered around the County until the high school was established in Washington in 1908.[7] The building may have been used as a hospital by Union forces during the War Between the States. In 2018, it was a private residence owned by George H. Eatman, located on town Lot 34 and designated as Tax Map 20A-1-126 (598 Gay Street).

The Washington Academy

The 1837 map of the town shows that Thorn's Tavern fronted on Gay Street on Lot 42 and Lot 43[8] (see Chapter 4). In about 1849, the Washington Academy was established in this building, which was owned by John Bailey Jett. The Academy was founded by George W. Grayson (born in Kentucky) and Henry W. Maertens (born in Germany).[9] Tuition ranged from $16 to $30. Needlework and drawing were taught, in addition to the basics; music and language lessons were available for an extra charge. Board was available for a 10-month session at $85 per month. One of the teachers was Annie Powers, a daughter of James Leake Powers who had directed the construction of the Presbyterian Church on Lot 22, Trinity Church on Lot 25, and several county homes. In 1850, the building housed the Washington Academy and was also being used as a boarding house; Grayson and his family and Maertens were among those living there.[10] Sometime before 1866, the Academy was discontinued and John Bailey Jett sold the property to Baldwin Bradford Baggarly for $2255.[11] In 1931 Baggarly's son, Franklin Clyde Baggarly, moved the building to the hill east of the town and converted it to the home named "Avon Hall."

Washington Female Institute

In 1893, Patsey Cliffen acquired Lot 41.[12] A building on this lot is believed to have been the location of the Washington Female Institute, with the Misses Janie and Julie Chapin as principals. The first annual commencement celebration for the school was held on 4 June 1896.[13] The building is no longer in existence.

---

[7] Recollections of Mayse Dudley Campbell, who was born in 1890 and grew up in the Carter-Dudley house on Lot 9 in the town of Washington, in Daphne Hutchinson and Theresa Reynolds, *On the Morning Side of the Blue Ridge*, a compilation of articles published in the *Rappahannock News* in 1983, page 31

[8] Rappahannock County Deed Book C, page 71

[9] Elisabeth B. and C. E. Johnson Jr., *Rappahannock County, Virginia, A History*, Orange, VA, Green Publishers, 1981

[10] 1850 Rappahannock County Land Records; 1850 U.S. census of Rappahannock County

[11] Rappahannock County Deed Book L, page 464

[12] Rappahannock County Deed Book P, page 398; Rappahannock County Deed Book U, page 171

[13] Rappahannock Historical Society school files

Big Branch School

Before the 1920s, African-American children attended a school housed in the Odd Fellows Hall, located just north of the town of Washington, or the Big Branch School, located on Main Street near the stream named "Big Branch." Both schools were taught by Anna Green and her husband P. S. Green, who was later a barber in a building on Lot 41 in the town of Washington.[14] In 1922 the Trustees for Hampton School District No. 3, who were D. Lyle Miller, F. R. Slaughter, and Howell M. Miller, petitioned the Circuit Court and requested that the school property be sold at public auction. At the auction, Clarence J. Miller was the purchaser, at the price of $360.[15]

Washington Graded School on Piedmont Avenue

During the early 1920s, African-Americans in Rappahannock County's Hampton District organized the Parent's Civic League to aid the School Board in erecting a Public Colored Free School building to further their children's education.[16] In 1922, this League purchased a two-acre lot west of the town of Washington on Piedmont Avenue from R. B. Heterick for $350 and conveyed this to the School Trustees of the Hampton School District, who were D. Lyle Miller, F.R. Slaughter, and Howell M. Miller.[17] The school received financial help from the Julius Rosenwald fund.[18]

The one-story frame school was constructed as a two-classroom building with a concrete foundation, weatherboard siding, metal roof, and two porches attached to the separate classroom vestibules. A central brick chimney accommodated two coal-burning stoves, one for each classroom. The front of the school housed the Industrial Room, a common feature of Rosenwald schools. In the late 1950s an addition at the rear of the building housed a boy's bathroom and a girl's bathroom, replacing two outside privies. Two water fountains were also added. There was a hand-dug stone and concrete well. Later in its history, a kitchen was added so that students could have a hot lunch.

---

[14] Rappahannock Historical Society school files; Recollections of Marilyn Price, in Daphne Hutchinson and Theresa Reynolds, *On the Morning Side of the Blue Ridge*, a compilation of articles published in the *Rappahannock News* in 1983, page 67

[15] Rappahannock County Deed Book 31, page 87

[16] Rappahannock Historical Society school files

[17] Rappahannock County Deed Book 31, page 84; Heterick had acquired this land in 1895 from John A. Heterick (Deed Book T, page 205)

[18] Julius Rosenwald was the president of Sears Roebuck Company and was a philanthropist. He was persuaded by Booker T. Washington to help fund the construction of six schools for African Americans in Alabama. When these proved successful, he initiated a program that eventually constructed 5,357 rural schools for African Americans in fifteen southern states, at a time when there was little to no public money being put toward education of blacks. The Rosenwald Fund provided partial funds that had to be matched by the community and by a county school board appropriation.

The school served eight grades in two rooms. Children attended who lived near the town of Washington, as well as children who lived in the nearby hollows. Dedicated teachers provided subjects for the students in addition to their regular curriculum, some giving training in music and voice. While Mrs. Anna Green (who had taught at Big Branch School) was supervisor of the school, she taught industrial arts, instructing students in caning, basket weaving, and sewing. Because of the large area that it served, there were sometimes as many as 100 students in the two-room school.[19] There were only a few teachers, although at times the older students helped instruct the younger children.

Children attended this school until 1963.[20] In 1968, the school was sold at public auction[21] and converted into two apartments (267 Piedmont Avenue, Tax Map 20A-1-50). In 2018 the school was listed on the National Register of Historic Places[22] and was owned by William Metcalf.

Washington High School

After the Civil War, a State Board of Education was created and charged with the responsibility for instituting mandatory public education. The first public schools in Rappahannock County were for the primary grades, leaving secondary and advanced education to private schools or tutors. After the turn of the century, however, more stress was put on higher education. The State Board was authorized to give $250 to any school district that would provide $250 from local sources for administering a high school. The high school in Washington was established in 1908 in response to this. Land consisting of 3 acres on the north side of Mt. Salem Avenue was purchased from F. Pendleton Carter to serve as the academic campus.[23] The 4-year high school building was constructed at a cost of $12,500 and had four rooms downstairs and one room and an auditorium upstairs.[24] In 1929, an eighth grade was added to the school and students from Flint Hill and Amissville were transported to the school. Consequently, more

---

[19] Recollections of Marilyn Price, in Daphne Hutchinson and Theresa Reynolds, *On the Morning Side of the Blue Ridge*, a compilation of articles published in the *Rappahannock News* in 1983, page 67

[20] Rappahannock Historical Society school files

[21] Rapppahannock County Chancery Cases #2530 and #2533

[22] Virginia Department of Historic Resources, National Register of Historic Places, Washington Graded School, Rappahannock County, #078-5187; Rappahannock News, 5 July 2018, page B2

[23] Rappahannock County Deed Book Y, page 493

[24] Elisabeth B. and C. E. Johnson Jr., *Rappahannock County, Virginia, A History*, Orange, VA, Green Publishers, 1981, page 209-210; this reference also states that the auditorium was used for "many dances enjoyed not only by Rappahannock people but by guests from surrounding counties."

space was needed for classrooms, and during the 1930s the auditorium was converted to classrooms and a new auditorium was added to the rear. A vocational agriculture shop room and three additional classrooms were also added. In 1946 a lunchroom was installed; lunches initially cost 20 cents, with some free lunches provided to children who could not pay for them. Additional land consisting of 2.10 acres on the south side of Mt. Salem Avenue was acquired from C.J. Miller in 1936; this served as the school athletic fields.[25]

During this time there was also a high school in Sperryville, and it became apparent that the two high schools were too small to be efficient, since each school was graduating only 10 to 12 students each year. Beginning in 1950, all high school grades were being taught at the Washington school, which also taught primary school students. However, plans had already been made to create a new school, serving only high school students, which led to establishment of the current high school located outside the Washington town limits on Route 211. Construction of the new school was completed on 24 August 1960.[26]

In October 1969 the Rappahannock County School Board adopted a resolution to sell the Washington High School property. The Rappahannock County Circuit Court approved the proposed sale, which occurred on 28 October 1969. Col. Earl E. Holmes of Flint Hill was the purchaser, at a cost of $20,500. The property consisted of 3 acres with school buildings located on the north side of Mt. Salem Avenue and 2.1 acres on the south side of Mt. Salem Avenue.[27] In 1974, William and Ramona Carrigan acquired the 3-acre property;[28] they were also the owners of the adjacent Avon Hall.

In 1999, the guardian of the estate of William Carrigan, carrying out Carrigan's wishes, donated the 3 acres of the Washington School property to the Child Care

[25] Rappahannock County Deed Book 40, page 55

[26] Elisabeth B. and C. E. Johnson Jr., *Rappahannock County, Virginia, A History*, Orange, VA, Green Publishers, 1981, page 214. Land totaling 19.35 acres was purchased and the firm of Eubank and Caldwell of Roanoke, Virginia, was asked to prepare architectural drawings for the new school, which was estimated to cost $225,000. Funds and loans were requested from the Battle Fund and the State Literary Fund and a tax of $10 was placed on all cars and trucks and $3 on motorcycles. In 1959, the Baughan Construction Company of Luray was the low bidder to construct the new high school, at a bid of $264,756, plus $5,401 for a sewage plant and two added classrooms at $12,468.

[27] Rappahannock County Chancery Case #2569; Rappahannock County Deed Book 96, page 510 and Deed Book 98, page 191

[28] Rappahannock County Deed Book 113, page 575

and Learning Center (CCLC), together with an adjacent 0.772 acre.[29] For the prior three years, the school building had housed the After School Club of the CCLC, providing a recreational program for 40-50 children after the school day and full time during the summer.[30] In 2013, CCLC sold the bulk of the property (2.533 acres) to Rappahannock Investment Partners.[31]

---

[29] Rappahannock County Instrument No. 990001141

[30] *Rappahannock News*, 14 July 1999, quoted in the 21 December 2017 edition of the newspaper.

[31] Rappahannock County Instrument No. 130000476

Chapter 13. Churches in the Town of Washington

The Old Church Meeting House

In 1815, James Yates and John Miller purchased town Lot 18 on Wheeler Street containing one-half acre for "the benefit of the public and on which is erected a house for public worship."[1] An 1833 plan of the town of Washington showed that a meeting house was located on this Lot and an 1843 list of owners of Washington lots showed that it was "the Meeting House Lot."[2] The "Old Free Church" was the center of the community's religious life for many years. It was nondenominational and was used by the Presbyterians, Episcopalians, Baptists, and Methodists until they built their own separate places of worship.[3] In 1867, the Rappahannock County Court appointed James M. O'Neale, Middleton Miller, James L. Powers, John Jett, and Adolphus Reid as trustees.[4] By 1880, the Church lot was considered to be "abandoned by all of the Christian denominations for whose benefit the lot was originally given who have thereby surrendered their right to use the lot as a church lot and place of worship."[5] The trustees of the Old Church, listed above, relinquished all claim to the lot and transferred the property to the Reformed Episcopal Church.[6]

In 1914, trustees of the Reformed Episcopal Church petitioned the Rappahannock County Court for permission to sell Lot 18. The trustees explained that the property had been used by the congregation of the Reformed Episcopal Church, but that some years ago the congregation had become extinct and had ceased to use the property for a place of worship. The Council of the Reformed Episcopal Church authorized the trustees to sell the property and to use the proceeds to erect a parsonage for the Antioch Reformed Episcopal Church in Essex County, Virginia. The trustees -- D. B. Phillips, Joshua T. Hopper, and E. C. Heterick -- sold the lot to Eugenia Dudley.[7] It subsequently became a residential lot (Tax Maps 20A-1-141, -142, and -143).

First Baptist Church of Washington

The First Baptist Church is historically significant for its construction in 1881 for the African-American religious community and for the Oddfellows use of the

---

[1] Culpeper Deed Book HH, p. 288

[2] See Chapter 4 for the 1833 town plan; Rappahannock County Deed Book A, page 189

[3] Mary Elizabeth Hite, *My Rappahannock Story Book*, The Dietz Press, Richmond VA, 1950, page 177; M. Elizabeth Buntin, *Mission: A Study of the Churches of Bromfield Parish*, pages 43-46, files of Trinity Episcopal Church

[4] Rappahannock County Order Book C, page 207

[5] Rappahannock County Deed Book Q, page 327

[6] Rappahannock County Deed Book Q, page 327

[7] Rappahannock County Deed Book 27, page 204

second floor. The church was organized in 1876 by Reverend George W. Horner. The congregation began with 45 members who were all baptized in the Rush River on the same day that they joined.[8] Because there were no negro churches in the town, the congregation met in the Old Church Meeting House building on town Lot 18. In 1877, the Dear family sold a lot containing 1.25 acres to Howard Cliffen, James F. Jordan, James Banks, James Roy, and Joseph L. Grayson who were trustees of "an association of colored persons known under the name of The Washington Benevolent Society." The purchase price was $56.25, and the deed specified that the land was to be used as a burial place and church for the Society. The property was located along the Fodderstack Road near the Rush River.[9]

In 1880 the congregation purchased another small lot of land on Main Street, just north of the original boundaries of the town of Washington and adjacent to "the old school house lot", from the Dear family for $50. The trustees of the congregation of Colored Christians of the Regular Baptist Church[10] at this time were James Banks, Lewis Barbour, Milton Cliffin, John Gillis, Charles Roy, and Lewis Carter.[11] The church construction was soon started, with one-third of the cost being borne by the Rising Hope Lodge Grand United Order of Odd Fellows who maintained an Assembly hall above the church sanctuary.[12] The cornerstone was laid in 1881 in a ceremony that drew a large crowd of well-wishers. The architectural work was done by Mr. V. Veers. The church building was constructed as a 1½ story wood frame building with a gable roof and two exterior side chimneys.[13]

The building was pebble-dashed (stuccoed) in the 1920s. Additional land was acquired to enlarge the yard surrounding the church building. The church was lengthened 10 feet; a pastor's study, choir room, choir stand and a vestibule were added; and bell tower was constructed and a 1400-pound bell was installed. A loan financed these improvements, paid in large part by the Gold Star Mothers

---

[8] Much of the history of the Church in this section is drawn from P.H. Green, Church Clerk, "First Baptist Church, Washington, Virginia," copy in the files of the Rappahannock Historical Society

[9] Rappahannock County Deed Book O, page 359

[10] Confusion existed for some time regarding the names Regular Baptist Church and First Baptist Church. In 1969 this was clarified and the name First Baptist Church was codified (Rappahannock County Deed Book 96, page 371)

[11] Rappahannock County Deed Book P, page 416

[12] Elisabeth B. and C. E. Johnson Jr., *Rappahannock County, Virginia, A History*, Orange, VA, Green Publishers, 1981, page 174

[13] National Register of Historic Places, 1975 Washington Historic District nomination application, and 2006 resurvey

Club organized by the church organist, Anna W. Green. As the church grew, other improvements such as cathedral windows and an electric organ were installed and modern conveniences including plumbing and restrooms. During high winds in 2018, the bell tower was blown off the church but this was reconstructed by John McCoy of Woodville.

Subsequent pastors after George W. Horner included Rev. Davenport, Rev. James G. Fields, Rev. James S. Woodson, Rev. D.H. Banks, Rev. Isadore D. Richards, Rev. R.C. Davis and Rev. Kenneth Coleman. The pastor in 2018 was James M. Kilby. The church celebrated its 100th anniversary in 1976 with a special bicentennial program. Other activities that have been sponsored by the Church include an annual Homecoming and "Friends and Family Day."

The church building is located on Tax Map 20A-1-4 (687 Main Street) and the Church also owns the 0.5 acre of land designated as Tax Map 20A-1-125B.[14]

Washington Methodist Church

In 1866, Baldwin Bradford Baggarly purchased town Lots 42 and 43 from John Bailey Jett for $2255.[15] In 1889, Baggarly and his wife Emma gave a parcel measuring 61' x 37' located at the southwest corner of Lot 43 to the Washington Methodist Episcopal Church South, to be used as a place of divine worship subject to authorizations by the General Conference of the Church.[16] Many fundraisers were conducted to raise money for construction of the church building. A "Ladies Sewing Society" made ladies wear and household goods and donated the proceeds. A "Dinner Committee" prepared and served meals to judges, lawyers, juries, and others attending the monthly County Court sessions. There was also a weekly "Oyster Supper." Through these fundraisers and solicited contributions, $4,000-$5,000 was raised for construction of the church.

The cornerstone of the church was laid by Washington Masonic Lodge No. 78, Ancient Free and Accepted Masons, in the northeast corner of the foundation, as required by Masonic tradition; the inscription on the stone was "M. E. Church South, September 5, 1889." The building was erected by John A. Cannon of Manassas, Virginia, and was completed during 1890; the

[14] Rappahannock County Deed Book 209, page 5
[15] Rappahannock County Deed Book L, page 464
[16] Rappahannock County Deed Book R, page 475

dedication sermon was by Reverend J.R. Griffith. The church was constructed as a 1½ -story wood frame building in the Gothic Revival style, with a gable roof and belfry and Gothic arch shape in each window and the front doors. There were many donations to the church: the walnut chancel rail was a gift of the Warrenton Methodist Church; a bible stand was given by Emma Baggarly; the walnut pews came from the Washington Presbyterian Church which was no longer active; and the weather vane on the spire was contributed by the contractor, Mr. Cannon. The bell was hung in the belfry in 1895 and the organ was purchased in that year.[17]

Ministers who served the Church included Charles H. McGee, M.A. Davidson, W.A.S. Conrad, Richard Ferguson, R.T. Clarke, H.J. Brown, T.G. Pullen, P.M. Bell, A.P. Williams, W.A. Osser, C.C. Jones, J.K. Holman, C.L. Salmon, J.H. Abernathy, D.L. Hager, L. Yowell, S.W. Wilkinson, L.C. Vaughan, O.W. Lynch, E.E. Henley, and W. Flythe.

The Church retained the property until 1980, when the congregation had so significantly decreased that the trustees of the United Methodist Church sold the property to the Town of Washington.[18] The church pews were moved to the Washington Town Hall on Lot 22. The Washington Fire Department Ladies Auxiliary Thrift Store operated in the building for some time. The building was used only sporadically and in 1990 the Town sold the land and building to Rappahannock County for use as a public facility.[19] In the 1990s it became the Ki Theater and then the theater of the Rappahannock Association for the Arts and the Community (RAAC).

The County retains ownership of the property, designated as Tax Map 20A-1-114 (310 Gay Street).

Washington Baptist Church[20]

The Baptist congregation in and near Washington originally met at the Old Free Church on Lot 18; this building was used by several different Christian congregations. Reverend Barnett Grimsley, pastor of Mount Salem Baptist Church, preached in the Old Free Church once a month in 1870. In 1874 Mary

---

[17] History of the Methodist Church, files of the Rappahannock Historical Society; Elisabeth B. and C. E. Johnson Jr., *Rappahannock County, Virginia, A History*, Orange, VA, Green Publishers, 1981, page 194; National Register of Historic Places, 1975 Washington Historic District nomination application, and 2006 resurvey

[18] Rappahannock County Deed Book 136, page 710

[19] Rappahannock County Deed Book 179, page 774

[20] Much of the information about the Washington Baptist Church was derived from "Washington Baptist Church History," written in 1953 by Mrs. J. Frank Jones, copy in the files of the Rappahannock Historical Society; *The Shiloh Stories*, the Shiloh Baptist Association, Culpeper, Virginia, 2007; Rob Hewitt, *Seeds of Faith*, Shemaya Inc., Afton, Virginia, 1996; and Elisabeth B. and C. E. Johnson Jr., *Rappahannock County, Virginia, A History*, Orange, VA, Green Publishers, 1981.

M. Long, a longtime member of Mount Salem church, purchased Lot 47 in the town from James Leake Powers, architect of Washington Presbyterian church and Trinity Episcopal church.[21] In the same year, she deeded part of the lot to the trustees of the Baptist Society of Christians and the Washington Masonic Lodge 78 for the purpose of erecting a Baptist church.[22] The church was intended to serve the inhabitants of Washington and environs because the parent church, Mount Salem Baptist Church, was some miles distant and was difficult to reach in winter. Since both the Baptists and the Masons were looking for places to meet at the time, they collaborated on constructing a building, with the Masons owning the top floor and the Baptists owning the rest. This relationship still exists today, with both sharing in the upkeep of the building.

A Building Committee for the church had been established in 1873. Members representing the Baptists were Dr. A.W. Head, James A. Templeton, James Kemper, B.F. Miller, and F. L. Slaughter, and representing the Masons were Thomas B. Massie, Baldwin B. Baggarly, Robert L. Menefee, Napolean B. Nicol, and John A. Compton. The 2½-story 7-course American brick building with a gable roof and belfry was constructed in 1875 by Corbin L. Proctor, a carpenter from Shenandoah County, Virginia. It is an impressive example of Renaissance revival Italianate style architecture.[23]

The set of Bylaws and Ordinances were adopted by the Town of Washington Board of Trustees in 1877. One of the provisions was "that there shall be no Horse Racks upon any public thoroughfares except in the alleys, but any person may by permission of the Board upon application made to it, erect a horse rack upon the streets for the convenience of customers." In 1881, the Baptist Church was allowed to erect horse racks on the east side of Gay Street and on the south side of Porter Street near the church.[24] In 1885, the remainder of Lot 47, which had been willed to F. L. Slaughter by Mary Long, was conveyed by Slaughter to the Baptist Church trustees, who were Middleton Miller, William H. Carter, and Stonewall J. Wood.[25]

---

[21] Rappahannock County Deed Book N, page 268
[22] Rappahannock County Deed Book N, page 434
[23] National Register of Historic Places, 1975 Washington Historic District nomination application, and 2006 resurvey
[24] Minutes of the 10 June 1881 meeting of the Town Trustees
[25] Rappahannock County Deed Book R, page 26

A Sunday School was organized two months after the church was built. During this first year of the Church, when the membership numbered only 24 persons, there were 94 individuals enrolled in Sunday School, and this meant much for the spiritual welfare of the community.[26] For years, it was the only Sunday School in the town. John W. Kemper was Sunday School superintendent for 40 years, followed by Judge Rayner Snead. The Covenant of Organization occurred on 10 January 1882, and the Church was admitted into the Shiloh Baptist Association in August 1882. A chapter of the Women's Missionary Union was organized in 1884, with Eliza Jones as president, and the Church hosted the Shiloh Meeting Association in 1896.

The Church has had many different pastors during its 135-year history and was without a pastor for various periods during this time. James F. Kemper preached the first few months after the church was established; the first regular pastor was L.R. Steel, followed by Ashby Jackson Fristoe and Hugh Goodwin through 1892. After that, R. Atwell Tucker, S.C. Clopton, Stockton Wharton Cole, M.R. Sanford, J.F. Kemper, W.J. Reynolds, and A.S. McFadden served as pastors through 1916. Stockton Wharton Cole returned to the Church and served until 1929, followed by John A. St. Clair, Lewis Brougham, M.E. Sliger, Gilbert M. Proffitt, John Divers, Warren Wilbur, Arnold L. Sorrells, and Ray Williams. During 1968-1977, the Church was without a regular pastor, but in 1977 David Moore was chosen for this position. At that time, there were 85 members of the Church, but only 60 were residents of Rappahannock County. Full of energy and enthusiasm, Moore reinvigorated the Church. He organized a youth choir, a Sunday School class for young adults, and a nursery. Under his leadership, the first woman deacon was ordained. Steve Scoggin replaced Moore in 1981, and he established a strong ecumenical youth group. Larry Hovis and Darrell Bare served next, and in 1996, Rev. Phillip Bailey became pastor. He served the church for many years until his retirement in 2013.

Some improvements and new construction have been made to the church. In the 1910s, the side aisles were closed and the center aisle repaired, the choir stand was made level with the pulpit, and gas and electric were installed. In the 1920s, four Sunday School rooms were added, two on each side of the church. In 1939 new electric light fixtures were installed; in 1949, a central heating plant was installed; and in 1953 an addition was made to the back of the church in which four Sunday School and educational rooms, two restrooms, and a small kitchen were built. In 1999-2000 there was construction of a handicap-accessible building containing a large fellowship hall, offices, a new kitchen, and restrooms.

In 1962, 0.37 acre on Mt. Salem Avenue adjoining the church property was given by Judge Rayner Snead (a member of the Church) and his wife Lois (a member

[26] Minutes of the Shiloh Baptist Association, 1882

of Trinity Episcopal Church), and their son William constructed a brick parsonage there in 1979.[27]

The monument in the churchyard honors the Reverend Barnett Grimsley (1807-1885), pastor of the parent Mount Salem Baptist Church. An oil portrait of Reverend Grimsley and a portrait of his wife are in the museum of the Rappahannock Historical Society. The church property is designated as Tax Map 20A-1-71 (180 Gay Street) and the parsonage as Tax Map 20A-1-72A (432 Mount Salem Avenue).

Washington Presbyterian Church

This building is located on the eastern half of the original Town Lot 22. On 12 May 1856, Tamar Spiller sold all of Lot 22 to Robert Deatherage and Robert S. Bell, trustees of the Presbyterian Church of Washington, for $350.[28] The deed specified that the eastern half of the lot, measuring 132' along Gay Street by 82.5' along Calvert Street, should be held by Deatherage and Bell in their capacity as trustees of the Presbyterian Church of Washington, for the purpose of establishing "a house of worship for the use and benefit of the said Church." Construction occurred during 1856-1858 under the direction of James Leake Powers, financed in part by collections taken up in all congregations in the Presbytery. The 1½-story 5-course American brick building is in the Doric architectural style.

During her lifetime, Lucy A. Kirk attempted to raise funds to acquire the western half of Lot 22 to provide a manse for the church minister. She was unsuccessful but, after her death, her funds and additional money that was collected amounted to $200 which was sufficient in 1883 to purchase Bell's one-half interest in the western half of Lot 22.[29] However, the Chancery case of Deatherage v. Bell ensued, and by a decree of the Rappahannock County Chancery Court, John F. Lillard purchased the western half of Lot 22 and the house on this land for $275.[30]

[27] Rappahannock County Deed Book 78, page 364
[28] Rappahannock County Deed Book J, page 414
[29] Rappahannock County Deed Book Q, page 170
[30] Rappahannock County Deed Book Q, page 170; Chancery Case Deatherage vs. Bell; Deed Book S, page 447

The minister during 1853-1866 was Thomas S. Witherow but after that time it appears that only lay individuals ministered to the congregation. Over time, church membership declined. The Church continued until 1891, when only two active church members remained, and the church building was officially closed the following year.[31] During the next half-century, shrubs and trees grew wild, eventually hiding the building from view. The Presbytery of the Potomac directed Charles W. Warden, T. E. Bartenstein, and Alfred Thomason, Trustees of the Church, to petition the Rappahannock County Court for permission to sell the property "since attendance made it impractical to maintain the building and there was no hope to revive or reestablish membership within the town." In 1939, the lot and building were purchased by Franklin Clyde Baggarly who was the owner of Avon Hall adjacent to the town and a former attorney for the town.[32] After he was declared incompetent in 1959,[33] his wife Frances Trott Bagggarly sold the lot in 1960 to the trustees of the County Free Library System, who were Q. D. Gasque (the Superintendent of Public Schools), Elisabeth Johnson, Freer Wilson, T. J. Pillar, and Virginia Miller.[34] This group of dedicated Rappahannock County residents rescued the old building and turned it into a public library which was dedicated in 1963. The fact that the building was still sound after nearly 75 years of disuse and neglect is a tribute to Mr. Power's construction ability. Except for repairs, no changes were made to the exterior of the church building; bookcases were installed in the interior but the original pulpit was retained. The library remained in the old church building until the end of 1989, when it was moved to a newly erected building on Lee Highway just outside of the town. The church building and land were sold to the Town of Washington.[35]

In 2018, the church building served as the Town Hall and the office of the Town Clerk of the Town of Washington. The property was designated as Tax Map 20A-1-136 (485 Gay Street).

Trinity Episcopal Church

Trinity Episcopal Church is located within Bromfield Parish, which was created by the Virginia General Assembly in 1752 from the western part of St. Mark's Parish; it includes the present counties of Rappahannock and Madison.[36] The parish was named for the Culpeper family chapel at Leeds Castle in England. The church building, constructed in the style known as "country Gothic" with an

---

[31] Elisabeth B. and C. E. Johnson Jr., *Rappahannock County, Virginia, A History*, Orange, VA, Green Publishers, 1981, page 155

[32] Rappahannock County Deed Book 44, page 177

[33] Rappahannock County Chancery Case #2292, Frances Trott Baggarly vs. Franklin Clyde Baggarly

[34] Rappahannock County Deed Book 71, page 595

[35] Rappahannock County Deed Book 175, page 298

[36] An excellent history of Bromfield Parish can be found in M. Elizabeth Buntin, *Mission: A Study of the Churches of Bromfield Parish*, files of Trinity Episcopal Church

exterior originally of board and batten, is considered to be one of the finest examples of American village church architecture in Virginia. The building is located on the eastern part of the original town Lot 25. In 1857 John G. Lane conveyed this land to the Church but the deed was never recorded. This omission was recognized in 1956 by the trustees of the Church who were D. D. Miller, W. A. Miller, C. J. Menefee Jr., J. D. Keyser, James M. Settle, E. L. Brown, and T. C. Lea. They instituted a chancery suit in Rappahannock County Court, which clarified the title to the 0.175-acre property that the church building now resides on, fronting on Gay Street (379 Gay Street).[37] The Church also acquired from Edward Jones Clopton a 15' strip of land, running east-west from Gay Street, at the south edge of the church property in 1952.[38] Ten years later, 0.15 acre of the western part of Lot 25 was sold by Quarles Oil Company to the Church.[39] Multiple small buildings on this property were torn down, and a parking lot for the Church was constructed on the land.[40]

The cornerstone for the church building was laid on 30 May 1857, by the Masonic Lodge of Washington, Virginia. According to Masonic records, the cornerstone contains a copper box into which were inserted copies of the Book of Common Prayer, the journal of the 61st annual convention of the Protestant Episcopal Church of Virginia, the Episcopal Recorder, the Southern Churchwoman, the Masonic Mirror, and a small book titled "Dew Drops" by J. E. Dow, a teacher at the Academy ("Rabbit Gum") on Lot 34. Masons and other townsfolk tossed in the following coins of the day – seven 5-cent pieces, two ten-cent pieces, one 25-cent piece, one 50-cent piece, and one gold dollar (donated in the name of the Grand Orient of France).[41] The first church rector was Rev. William Thomas Leavell, who served the Church until the Civil War.[42] Many rectors served the church over the years, but there were multiple times when no rector was present to minister to the congregation.[43]

Construction of the church building under the supervision of James Leake Powers was completed within the year at a cost of $1,800. The original facade was board and batten and the windows were of clear glass. There was neither a bell nor a tower and the front door was where the Green Memorial window is now located.

---

[37] Rappahannock County Chancery Case 2222; Rappahannock County Deed Book 65, page 183

[38] Rappahannock County Deed Book 59, page 59

[39] Rappahannock County Deed Book 77, page 48

[40] Photograph and caption for the western part of Lot 25, *Rappahannock News*, 13 December 1962, reprinted in the 4 September 2008 edition of the newspaper

[41] Elisabeth B. and C. E. Johnson Jr., *Rappahannock County, Virginia, A History*, Orange, VA, Green Publishers, 1981, pages 189-190

[42] Mary Elizabeth Hite, *My Rappahannock Story Book*, Richmond VA, The Dietz Press, 1950, page 228

[43] M. Elizabeth Buntin, *Mission: A Study of the Churches of Bromfield Parish*, pages 135-140, files of Trinity Episcopal Church

For 48 years, there were no modifications to the building. In 1905 the bell tower and vestibule were constructed by Bob Eastham, a local carpenter. By 1924 the board and batten siding had deteriorated; Mark Reid of Front Royal was contracted with for $850 to cover the exterior with a stucco, pebble-dash finish. In the mid-1930s stained glass windows were installed; in daylight, these memorial windows softly illuminate the interior and ceiling.[44] The cross at the front was made from old boards, taken from the church, by Philip Strange, a local cabinet maker and Vestry member. The parish hall attached to the church was built in 1957 at the south side of the church, using plans submitted by the Charlottesville architect firm of Johnson, Craven, and Gibson, with Charles W. Hawkins as the builder. The hall was enlarged and the Bromfield meeting room was added in 1985 and was renovated in 2016. The memorial garden at the Gay Street entrance was developed in 1990, and the garden along the Middle Street side of the church was created in 1999.[45]

(Left) Trinity Episcopal Church as it was originally constructed in 1857 by James Leake Powers but after it was stuccoed in the mid-1920s (photo courtesy of the Church). (Right) Trinity Episcopal Church in 2018

In addition to the property on Lot 25, the church also acquired land on the east side of Gay Street on town Lot 41. In 1969, T. Carlyle Lea gave 0.28 acre in two tracts to the Church trustees, who were Harry Stephenson, James E. Yates, Fred W. Schaeffer, W.A. Miller, D.D. Miller, J.D. Keyser, and R.L. Brown.[46] This was converted to a parking area, playground, and natural area. In 1998, the Church acquired the adjacent 0.1093 acre on which stood a two-story frame

[44] M. Elizabeth Buntin, *Mission: A Study of the Churches of Bromfield Parish*, pages 74, 91-93, files of Trinity Episcopal Church

[45] www.trinwash.org

[46] Rappahannock County Deed Book 96, page 623, and Rappahannock County Chancery Case No. 2521

house with a front porch that was originally the home of Phelbert Scott Green[47] and which had many subsequent uses.[48] In 2018 the building served as the church office, "Trinity House."

Trinity House, the offices of Trinity Episcopal Church

The original church rectory was located in a stuccoed house facing Main Street, on the parcel now designated as Tax Map 20A-3-101 (262 Main Street) on town Lot 29. Reverend Tellinghest and Rev. Claybrook lived in this house and served the church. Lots 28, 29, and 30 (except for a small parcel of Lot 29) had been owned by Benjamin F. Kinsey at his death in 1870. His personal estate was insufficient to pay his debts, and his wife Ann V. Kinsey petitioned the Court to sell her husband's lands and invest the money to support her children. On 10 October 1877, she made a contract with the trustees of St. Paul's and Trinity Episcopal Churches to purchase the lots. A chancery suit next ensued, termed Kinsey's Guardian vs. Kinsey.[49] In 1880, Thomas Kinsey, commissioner of the Rappahannock County Court for this chancery suit, conveyed the three lots (without the small parcel) to the trustees of Trinity Episcopal Church, who were James W. Fletcher, John A. Browning, H. S. Menefee, and John T. Fletcher.[50] The property was known as "the Rectory Lots." In 1921, W. M. Stuart, John J. Miller, and P. H. O'Bannon, trustees of St. Paul's and Trinity Episcopal churches, sold the property to W. C. Armstrong for $5000.[51] Between 1921 and 1937 the Church did not own a rectory.

In 1937, David D. Miller and his wife Etta offered a lot of land on Mount Salem Avenue to the Church. The Church building committee received approval to use the full amount of the Rectory Building Fund, $7500, to construct a new rectory on this lot.[52] The building was completed in 1937, and the next year the trustees of Bromfield Parish, who were D. D. Miller, W.M. Stuart, E. M. Greene, W.A. Miller, W.L. Yancey, W. Meade Fletcher, Harry A. Trescott, and Robert Menefee, formally acquired from Miller the lot of land containing 0.40 acre with a dwelling.[53] The deed stipulated that if the Church sold the land or mortgaged it, the Church trustees would have to pay Miller $750. The deed further stipulated

---

[47] Rappahannock County Deed Book Y, page 30
[48] Rappahannock County Instrument No. 980001684
[49] Rappahannock County Chancery Case #728
[50] Rappahannock County Deed Book P, page 303
[51] Rappahannock County Deed Book 30, page 466
[52] Trinity Episcopal Church, brochure on "Rectory Blessing and Open House," 11 June 2016
[53] Rappahannock County Deed Book 34, page 313, and Deed Book 41, page 269

that if the rectory house was destroyed and not replaced, the land would revert to Miller. These restrictions were removed in 1962.[54]

The Church rectory is a 2½-story three-bay stretcher-course brick home in the Colonial Revival style. It has a standing-seam metal gable roof and two exterior end brick chimneys.[55] During 2016 extensive renovation of the building and the grounds was accomplished.[56] Ten rectors have lived in the house between 1938 and 2015. The longest staying resident was the Rev. Jennings 'Jenks' W. Hobson III who resided in the home with his family for 42 years from 1973 to 2015. The Church's rector in 2018 was H. Miller Hunter, Jr., and about 250 parishioners belonged to the Church. Trinity Church has been involved in many community activities over the years. Some of these are described in Chapter 7.

In 2014, the Inn at Little Washington collaborated with Trinity Church to improve the church's parking lot located at the southeast corner of Main and Middle streets, which the Inn leased from the Church and which was adjacent to one of the entrances of the Inn's newly renovated building named "The Parsonage." The Inn paid for improvement to the parcel, including paving the parking lot and installing hardscaping and landscaping.[57] It was estimated to cost $180,000, and the Town of Washington contributed $20,000 towards this cost.[58]

The land on which the church building is located is designated as Tax Map 20A-1-109 (379 Gay Street); the church parking lot as Tax Map 20A-1-108; "Trinity House" and adjacent parcels as Tax Map 20A-1-110, 20A-1-111, 20A-1-111A, and 20A-1-112 (370 Gay Street); and the church rectory as Tax Map 20A-1-82 (423 Mount Salem Avenue).

Biography of James Leake Powers[59]

James Leake Powers was the architect of both the Washington Presbyterian Church in 1856-1858 and the Trinity Episcopal Church in 1857. He is also credited with construction of the Ben Venue mansion and slave quarters.

Powers was born in Charlottesville, Virginia, on 10 June 1799, one of the five children of Norborne Powers and Mildred Leake. There is no documentation regarding his life between 1799 and 1836. However, because he was a resident of Charlottesville, he probably worked on the buildings of the University of

---

[54] Rappahannock County Deed Book 76, page 569
[55] National Register of Historic Places, 1975 Washington Historic District nomination application, and 2006 resurvey
[56] Trinity Episcopal Church, brochure on "Rectory Blessing and Open House," 11 June 2016
[57] Rappahannock County Instrument 140000455
[58] *Rappahannock News*, 26 March 2015
[59] Maureen Harris, "Will the Real Courthouse Architect Please Stand Up," *Rappahannock News*, 4 June 2017 (Part 1) and 17 June 2017 (Part 2)

Virginia when the University was constructed during 1817-1826. He would have learned the craft of building construction in the Jeffersonian tradition during this period. He emerged from obscurity in 1837 when he purchased Lot 21 in the town of Washington[60] and married Martha Ann Nicklin.[61] In all likelihood, Powers had been brought to the town of Washington by Malcolm Crawford after their work on the University of Virginia to help in Crawford's construction of the Rappahannock County courthouse and Clerk's office during 1833-1834.

Martha Ann Nicklin, the first wife of James Leake Powers, was born on 18 December in 1809, one of the six children of Dr. Joseph Nicklin and Elizabeth Calvert who were residents of the town.[62] Nicklin was a well-known physician and served as a surgeon in the War of 1812. He was president of the Town of Washington Board of Trustees in 1839 and 1843 and was a member of the Virginia House of Delegates. He owned several lots in the town, including Lots 42 and 43 on Gay Street between Middle and Jett Streets that he acquired in 1802 from Ralls Calvert, son of George Calvert and first cousin of Nicklin's wife Elizabeth. Elizabeth Calvert (1777-1833) was a daughter of John and Helen (Bailey) Calvert; John was a brother of George Calvert, one of the founders of the town of Washington.[63]

James Leake Powers and Martha Ann Nicklin had three daughters while they lived in the home on Lot 21 – Elizabeth Nicklin Powers (1838-1882); Lavinia Green Powers (1840-1909); and Martha Ann (Annie) Powers (1843-1928).[64] Elizabeth married Capt. W. C. Sheerer, [65] but the other two girls remained single throughout their life.[66] It was at the birth of daughter Martha Ann that Mrs. Powers died on 25 March 1843 at age 33 years.

The next year, Powers married Lucy Calvert (1815-1848) who was a cousin of his first wife Martha Ann Nicklin. Lucy was the last of the twelve children of Ralls Calvert and Mary Wade Strother. Ralls, who became a postmaster in the town of Washington, was the first of the fourteen children of George Calvert (1744-1821) and Lydia Beck Ralls (1749-1830). George's brother, John Calvert, was the grandfather of Martha Ann Nicklin.[67]

In 1848, Lucy died. Powers sold Lot 21 to Adolphus Read and purchased Lot 37 in the town of Washington from George and Eliza Calvert of Fauquier County.[68]

---

[60] Rappahannock County Deed Book C, page 111, 3 October 1837

[61] www.ancestry.com/genealogy/records/james-leake-powers_7584913; www.geni.com/people/James-Powers/6000000001075408642; Rappahannock Historical Society Powers family file

[62] Rappahannock Historical Society Nicklin family file

[63] Ella Foy O'Gorman, compiler, *Descendants of Virginia Calverts,* Higgenson Pub. Co., 1947

[64] 1850-1900 U.S. censuses; Rappahannock Historical Society Powers family file

[65] www.thekingealogy.com/tng/getperson.php?personID=I50151&tree=tree1

[66] U.S. censuses for Lavinia and Martha Ann Powers

[67] Ella Foy O'Gorman, compiler, *Descendants of Virginia Calverts,* Higgenson Pub. Co., 1947

[68] Rappahannock County Deed Book G, page 505, and Deed Book H, page 13

The Powers family, including James, his three daughters, his sister Mary, and Joseph Nicklin (father of James' first wife) moved to Lot 37 at this time.[69] The lot is located on the northeast corner of Gay and Calvert Streets. In 1853, James Leake Powers married his third wife, Margaret Cary, who was then age 34 years. She was the daughter of Francis and Chloe Cary who lived in the town of Washington; Francis was a tanner by trade.[70] One of Margaret's brothers was Alexander Cary, a merchant in Flint Hill.[71]

In 1856, Margaret gave birth to a daughter. In 1860, when Margaret was age 41 and James was age 61, Margaret gave birth to another daughter. Both children died shortly after their births.[72] James and Margaret continued to live in the house on Lot 37 until his death in 1889 and her death in 1900.[73] Both were buried in the Heterick cemetery in the town of Washington and were reinterred in Evergreen Cemetery in Luray, Virginia.[74] In Powers' will, he gave "the house and lot on which he then lived" and most of his personal property to his wife Margaret and daughters Annie and Lavinia.[75] His carpenter tools and carpentry supplies were bequeathed to Bruce Heterick.

Photograph of James Leake Powers, date unknown, photo courtesy of the Rappahannock Historical Society

In the 1850-1880 U.S. censuses in which information on occupation was collected, James Leake Powers consistently described himself as a "carpenter." During his life, in addition to his building profession, Powers was a trustee of the "Old Church" located on Lot 18 on Wheeler Street between Main and Gay streets.[76] He was also appointed as "Supervisor of the Streets" in 1839 by the Town of

[69] 1850 U.S. census of Rappahannock County
[70] U.S. census of Rappahannock County; Rappahannock Historical Society Cary family file
[71] Rappahannock County Will Book G, page 368
[72] Rappahannock County birth and death records
[73] www.ancestry.com/genealogy/records/james-leake-powers_7584913; Rappahannock County Will Book G, page 368
[74] Rappahannock Historical Powers family file
[75] Rappahannock County Will Book F, page 414
[76] Rappahannock County Deed Book Q, page 327

Washington Board of Trustees.[77] His duties were to ensure that residents of the town worked to maintain the streets, although individuals could be exonerated from this duty by paying 75 cents per day of work. In 1843, the year of the death of his wife Martha Ann, he resigned this position. Powers also purchased other lots in the town of Washington, including the one-half acre Lot 47 (now the Washington Baptist Church lot) from the estate of his father-in-law, Joseph Nicklin, in 1854 and a 50' by 30' part of Lot 29 fronting on Gay Street across from the Courthouse in 1874.[78]

[77] Minute Book for 1839, Town of Washington Board of Trustees
[78] Rappahannock County Deed Book J, page 150; Rappahannock County Deed Book N, page 308

Chapter 14. Roads and Transportation

The first identification of a road through the land that became the town of Washington comes from a purchase of part of the Kennerly land grant by Robert Strother in 1769.[1] The western boundary of this purchase was termed "the main road" in the purchase deed. This "main road" was located on the roadbed of today's Main Street, extending from Big Branch south for 1221', where it intersected with the road from Thornton's Gap. In all likelihood, this "main road" was part of the road north to Chester's Gap.[2] Based on deeds of sale of the Kennerly land during 1770-1799, this road continued north from Big Branch along the high point of the land, which was the border between the farms of William Porter and George Calvert and was approximately the roadbed of today's Gay Street.[3] The road crossed the Rush River at a ford east of today's bridge, followed the roadbed of today's Fodderstack Road and Dearing Road to an area near Wakefield Manor, and then continued to Chester's Gap.

Main Street did not exist at this time. It was directed to be created in 1794 when William Porter sold 6 acres of his land to George Calvert.[4] This parcel of land was a rectangle oriented 15 degrees east of north measuring 165' on the north and south sides and 1584' on the east and west sides. The eastern side of this long rectangle was designated as "a new road to be cut." The location of this 6 acres was at the western border of the land that became the town of Washington, and the "new road" became today's Main Street after the founding of the town.

During the time that the Kennerlys owned the land, they built a mill on the Rush River, on the site of the current Washington Mill, and they constructed a road to the mill, creating what is now Old Mill Road.[5] This became part of the main road to the town from the east and, together with today's Middle Street and Main Street, was part of Lee Highway in the 1930s.

The town of Washington was created on 14 December 1796 by an Act of the Virginia General Assembly in response to a petition from George Calvert, James Jett Jr., and James Wheeler.[6] These three men and William Porter petitioned the General Assembly again in 1797, asking that part of Porter's land be added to the

[1] Culpeper County Deed Book E, page 696

[2] This was Chester's Road, named for Captain Thomas Chester who owned land west of the Gap that bears his name

[3] Maureen Harris, "History of the Land That Became the Town of Washington, Virginia, 1735-1833," Rappahannock Historical Society, 2014

[4] Culpeper County Deed Book S, page 99

[5] Culpeper County Deed Book B, page 132.

[6] Samuel Shepherd, *The Statutes at Large of Virginia, from October Session 1792 to December Session 1806, Inclusive, in Three Volumes, (New Series), Being a Continuation of Hening*, New York, AMS Press, Inc., 1836, Volume II, page 29-32

town.[7] A plan of the proposed streets of the town and 51 lots was attached to this second petition (see Chapter 2). The original grid and the names of two north-south streets and five cross streets as shown in the plan submitted in 1797 are still maintained in the core of the town of Washington today. While the naming of Main Street and Middle Street is obvious, and Calvert, Wheeler, Jett and Porter gave their names to four cross streets, the origin of the name Gay Street is unknown. It was shown on the 1797 plan; the name must have originated from one or more of the four founders, for reasons unknown.[8] No Gay family could be identified who lived in the vicinity of the town in the 1700s or 1800s. The street occupies the ridge that runs north-south through the town and was probably the site of the early road to Chester's Gap.

When Rappahannock County was created in 1833, the commissioners appointed to select the County seat chose the town of Washington, but noted that even though "it is not situated on any leading thoroughfares, it is accessible by good public roads from any point of the county."[9] An 1833 plan of the town shows the same streets and lots as designated and named in the 1797 plan submitted with the second petition.[10]

An 1837 plan shows the same street grid and lots and also shows the names of roads leading out of the town. These were designated by their destinations: Hopper's Mill (today's Harris Hollow Road), Amissville (today's Warren Avenue, but then leading east along today's Old Mill Road), Rock Mills (today's Mt. Salem Avenue), and Sperryville (the south end of today's Main Street).[11]

Early in the town's history, male residents were required to maintain the streets of the town. The Supervisor of the Streets was one of the offices appointed by the town's Board of Trustees. In 1839, the Board declared that residents of the town were required to work on maintaining the town's streets on a schedule of days, but could be exempt from this duty by paying 75 cents per day for each day they were scheduled. If a resident obstructed the streets of the town, a fine was levied in the amount of 25 cents per day.[12] In 1843, the Board reduced the amount for being exonerated from working on the streets from 75 cents per day to 50 cents per day.[13] The Board adopted a set of Bylaws and Ordinances in 1877.[14]

---

[7] George Calvert, James Jett Jr., James Wheeler, and William Porter, Culpeper County, 1 December 1797, Legislative Petitions Digital Collection, Library of Virginia, Richmond, VA, Record number 000154073; Legislative Petitions of the General Assembly, 1776-1865, Accession Number 36121, Box 58, Folder 71.

[8] A theory exists that Gay Street was named for Gay Fairfax who lived in the Tidewater region of Virginia in the 1700s. However, there is no evidence to support this theory. See Appendix 4.

[9] Rappahannock County Deed Book A, page 24.

[10] Rappahannock County Deed Book A, page 189; See Chapter 4 for town plan

[11] Rappahannock County Deed Book C, page 71; See Chapter 4 for town plan

[12] Minutes of the 6 July 1839 meeting of the Town Trustees

[13] Minutes of the 22 May 1843 meeting of the Town Trustees

[14] Minutes of the 16 June 1877, 12 July 1877, 17 July 1877, and 21 July 1877 meeting of the Town Trustees; See Chapter 5 for full text of the 1877 ordinances

Items 2 and 3 of this document stated "Be it further enacted and ordained that it shall be the duty of the Overseer of the Streets to call out all hands subject to work on the streets, for the purpose of working them according to law not to exceed six days in a year, giving them at least nine days previous notice thereof, and every person warned as aforesaid may be excused from working on the streets by paying to the said Town Collector before such day seventy-five (75) cents for each day, to be appropriated by said Town Collector to the hiring of other hands to work on the streets on such day. And be it further enacted and ordained that every person failing to work on the streets is to pay seventy-five cents for each day as provided for in the preceding section (and the oaths of the Overseer of the Streets and the Town Collector shall be evidence of the fact) and shall be returned by the said Overseer to the Trustees of the Town or one of them, as a defaulter. And upon their or his direction the same Collector shall proceed to make the fines without delay."

At this early time, transportation was by foot, by horseback, or by horse-drawn wagon or carriage. Item 18 of the 1877 Ordinance pertained to this: "And be it further enacted and ordained that there shall be no Horse Racks upon any public thoroughfares except in the alleys, but any person may by permission of the Board upon application made to it, erect a horse rack upon the streets for the convenience of customers to new places of business provided that such rack be not erected upon the side walk or the side of the street which has been or may be curbed for the use of foot passengers, and such rack when so erected shall be constructed so as to prevent horses being fastened to it from wetting upon the sidewalk. The location of such rack to be designated in the order of permission under this section. And no horses are to be tied or hitched to the fences or in the streets (except to racks) within the limits of the Corporation. And if any person tie or hitch a horse to the fences of the lots within the Corporation he shall be fined fifty cents." Item 8 prohibited horse racing: "And be it further enacted and ordained that no person shall ride a race through the streets or shall strain a horse through the streets, and if any person or persons shall offend against the provisions of this section they shall incur a fine of one dollar for each offence."

In regard to Item 18, Richard Morrison was given permission to hitch horses at the platform in front of his storehouse.[15] Also, W. W. Moffett was granted permission to erect a horse rack for the benefit of the *Blue Ridge Echo* newspaper office.[16] J.B. Cooper was permitted to construct a horse rack to be used by visitors to his house and shop.[17] And the Baptist Church was allowed to erect horse racks on the west side of Gay Street and on the south side of Porter Street near the church.[18]

---

[15] Minutes of the 21 July 1877 meeting of the Town Trustees
[16] Minutes of the 17 July 1880 meeting of the Town Trustees
[17] Minutes of the 27 July 1880 meeting of the Town Trustees
[18] Minutes of the 10 June 1881 meeting of the Town Trustees

Most of the traffic in the town was horses in this era, either ridden or pulling wagons, carriages, or buggies. Horses required accommodations and support from businesses, enterprises that made up a considerable portion of the town's commercial activity. Some of these have been documented:

- In the early 1800s Robert Dearing had a blacksmith shop adjacent to town Lot 49.[19] Butler Stonestreet operated his wheelwright and wagonmaker business on Lots 2 and 3; his son James was a blacksmith there; and David Nicol operated a blacksmith shop on a small part of Lot 3.[20] There was a wagonmakers shop on Lot 15.[21] John T. Corder operated a saddler's shop on Lot 24.[22]
- In the later 1800s, Napolean Nicol was a blacksmith and had his blacksmith shop, shoeshop, and wagon repair shop on Lot 38 until his death in 1892.[23] A blacksmith shop operated by Ben Cliffen was located at the southeast part of Lot 30 and a stable was located on the northeast part of Lot 28 in the late 1800s.[24] In 1881, Cliffen purchased Lot 41 and had his home and a blacksmith shop there.[25] In 1882, the blacksmith shop on the south part of Lot 3 was occupied by Haden Stonestreet.[26]
- In the early 1900s, a livery stable and blacksmith shop were operated by George Washington Clark on town Lot 31; a barn and a harness shop were located on Lot 27; and a wheelwright's shop and a blacksmith's shop were located on town Lot 24.[27]

When the town was incorporated in 1894, the Act of the General Assembly specifically addressed the issue of maintenance of streets in the town. The Town Council was instructed to "keep in order the streets, alleys and walks of said town; and it may require the male inhabitants over sixteen years of age to work on the same. The inhabitants of the said town shall not be required to work on the county roads, nor shall the real and personal property in said town be subject to taxation for county road purposes."[28] The Town Council was also given jurisdiction for condemning lands for streets, alleys, and sidewalks of the town and for preventing the "cumbering" of streets, sidewalks and alleys.

On 27 March 1848, the General Assembly of Virginia authorized a road through Rappahannock County to be called the Sperryville and Rappahannock Turnpike.

---

[19] Rappahannock County Deed Book A, page 65
[20] 1850 U.S. census; Rappahannock County Deed Book E, page 277
[21] Rappahannock County Deed Book J, page 309
[22] Rappahannock County Deed Book G, page 534
[23] U.S. censuses of Rappahannock County
[24] Rappahannock County Chancery Case No. 728
[25] Rappahannock County Deed Book P, page 398
[26] Rappahannock County Deed Book R, page 276
[27] Daphne Hutchinson and Theresa Reynolds, compilers, *On the Morning Side of the Blue Ridge,* articles from the Rappahannock News of 1983, recollections of Jack Miller, page 101, and of Mrs. Edna Walker, owner of "Washington House," page 51; Rappahannock County Deed Book 35, p. 215, and Book 37, p. 235
[28] Acts of the General Assembly of Virginia, Chapter 228. An act to incorporate the town of Washington, in the county of Rappahannock. Approved February 12, 1894.

The road was expected to cost $50,000 to construct. Financing of the road occurred by selling shares in the Sperryville and Rappahannock Turnpike Company at $50 per share; most of the subscribers were Rappahannock County farmers. John G. Lane was the Turnpike president. The road was designed to be 40' wide, lined by 2' ditches. It was completed in October 1852.[29] A deed in 1857 described Lot 14 in the town as being bounded on the east not by Main Street but by the Sperryville and Rappahannock Turnpike.[30] This was a macadamized road, consisting of crushed rock packed tightly in thin layers, with a top surface of layers of finely crushed stone. The road extended from Sperryville east to the town of Washington, passed through the town on today's Main and Middle streets and Warren Avenue, proceeded east along today's Old Mill Road, and then extended to the Rappahannock River. The final miles of the road were along today's Waterloo Road, and the road crossed the river through a ford, later a bridge, at the current site of the Waterloo Bridge. (The roadbed of Lee Highway, constructed in the 1930s, followed the general bed of the Sperryville and Rappahannock Turnpike.) Funds for maintenance of the road came from tolls paid at toll houses placed along the route. The old log Toll House on today's Route 211 between Washington and Sperryville is an example of such a building. It was even used as a toll house during the construction of Route 522 from Chester Gap to Sperryville via Massie's Corner in 1912-1916, when the toll for cars was 25 cents per ticket.[31] This building has seen many uses and many owners during its existence.

Toll Ticket for the Sperryville and Rappahannock Turnpike Company

Toll collections were generally insufficient to provide adequate maintenance of the road and were never enough to pay operating and maintenance costs. For most of Virginia's turnpike companies, the Civil War was the final blow from which they could not recover. The tolls roads suffered from neglect during the war, more so than actual destruction by opposing military forces, as occurred for railroads and bridges. Maintenance of roads reverted to the counties.

---

[29] Eugene M. Scheel, *Culpeper, A Virginia County's History Through 1920*, Green Publishers Inc., Orange, Virginia, 1982, pp. 139-140

[30] Rappahannock County Deed Book K, page 154

[31] *Rappahannock News*, 29 June 1978, quoted in the 8 November 2018 edition of the newspaper

In 1906, the Virginia legislature recognized the need for State support of roads and created the first State Highway Commission. While the counties still had responsibility for actually making improvement to its roads, they now had a new State agency to which they could turn for help. By 1908, the need for better roads had reached the point that the legislature made its first appropriation for road construction purposes. Also, a State law directed the counties to levy a road tax of up to 40 cents for each $100 in value on real estate and personal property, with the revenue to cover the counties' share of improvements and to buy road equipment.

Automobiles began to appear on Rappahannock County roads shortly before World War I; by 1929 there were 387,205 in the whole State.[32] In this era, Trinity Episcopal Church purchased its first automobile for the rector's use; in 1925 the Church purchased a new Ford coupe for the rector. Multiple minutes of the Church vestry mention dollar outlays for repairs. Many streets were still unpaved in the town, but with the advent of the automobile many of these were tarred and graveled during the 1920s.[33] U.S. Highway 21 (today's Route 211) was improved and rebuilt as a macadam road through the town and a concrete bridge was constructed over the Rush River on the part of the highway that is now Old Mill Road.[34]

The Commonwealth of Virginia took over maintenance of all primary and secondary roads in the 1930s. At that time, the State Highway Commission was constructing Lee Highway through Virginia. At the Town Council's request, this highway was run through the town, along today's Main and Middle streets and Old Mill Road. The Council's request was to create a better road through the town, but also to have maintenance of the road become the responsibility of the State rather than the town government. The request was probably also in anticipation of the benefits to the town of increased tourism from the planned new Shenandoah National Park. In the later 1930s there was economic recovery from the Depression, and cars of tourists began visiting the town of Washington on their way to Skyline Drive.[35]

During construction of the highway through the town, Main Street was macadamized and widened. Unfortunately, some of the town's residences were severely weakened by this construction. One of these was the two-story brick home built on Lot 13 in the mid-1800s for J.Y. Menefee, a distinguished lawyer.

---

[32] Elisabeth B. and C.E. Johnson Jr., *Rappahannock County, Virginia, A History*, Green Publishers, Orange, VA, 1981, p. 59-60

[33] Elisabeth B. and C.E. Johnson Jr., *Rappahannock County, Virginia, A History*, Green Publishers, Orange, VA, 1981, p. 140-141; Rappahannock County Deed Book 28, page 387 and Deed Book 30, page 357; Laura A. Matthews, *A Ramble Through Rappahannock*, Scribblers Inc., Warrenton, Virginia, 2000, page 20

[34] Rappahannock County Deed Book 30, page 357

[35] Daphne Hutchinson and Theresa Reynolds, compilers, *On the Morning Side of the Blue Ridge*, articles from the Rappahannock News of 1983, page 13

The building had porches on the first and second floor and was often described as one of the most beautiful homes in the town of Washington. It was valued at $1000 in 1900.[36] The highway construction weakened the house, large cracks appeared, and the house had to be dismantled in the 1940s. Another damaged building was Clark's Tavern on the southeast corner of Main and Porter streets (Lot 31); the front porches and second and third stories of this building had to be removed because of structural instability.

In 1930, the State Highway Department widened Middle Street, east of Main Street. The Washington Town Council petitioned Trinity Church to give up 4½ feet of land on the Middle Street side of the Church property so that a new sidewalk could be laid there, adjacent to the widened road. The Church agreed to this, with the stipulation that the Town would reset the iron fence in concrete and build a sidewalk on the Gay Street side of the church property also.[37]

For those who did not have automobile transportation, John W. Clark began a jitney service named the Front Royal & Washington Motor Transportation Company that was chartered in 1916. A building adjacent to his home on town Lot 15 served as the station for his bus service. Busses departed at 6am and 4pm; the fare to Front Royal was 90 cents one-way and $1.44 roundtrip and the trip took from one hour 10 minutes to one hour 30 minutes.[38] The route connected the town of Washington with the Southern Railway trains at Front Royal and permitted people to travel by railroad to Washington D.C., Harrisonburg, Hagerstown, or Roanoke. The busses were "the most modern and up-to-date

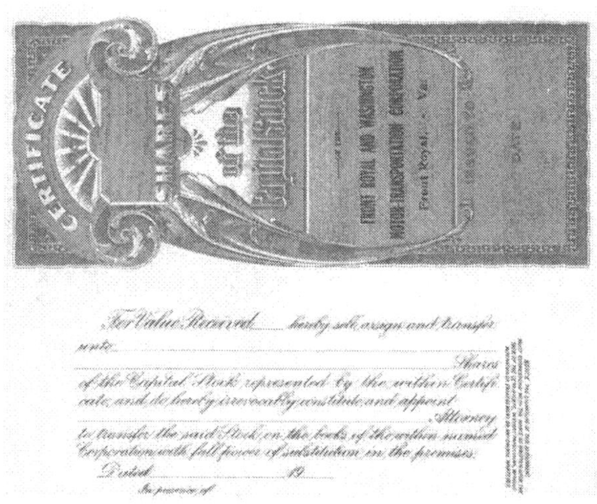

Stock Certificate for the Front Royal and Washington Motor-Transportation Corporation

[36] 1900 Rappahannock County Land Records

[37] M. Elizabeth Buntin, *Mission: A Study of the Churches of Bromfield Parish*, page 77, files of Trinity Episcopal Church

[38] Schedule of the Front Royal & Washington Motor Transportation Corporation, Rappahannock Historical Society files

pneumatic-tired motor busses, which are large, clean, cool, and comfortable, with a carrying capacity of from fifteen to twenty passengers." The busses traversed "the most beautiful section of Virginia, via Flint Hill, Huntly, Reager, and U.S. Remount Station, over a new macadam turnpike. The entire route is rich in magnificent scenery, fresh air, and pure water. The view at Chester's Gap, where the route crosses the Blue Ridge, is considered one of the most beautiful in America."

John W. Clark and his wife Alice sold the half-acre Lot 15 and the bus facilities to Walker B. Jenkins in 1920 for $1000,[39] and Jenkins renamed the company as the Front Royal and Washington Motor-Transportation Company. It provided daily roundtrip bus service from Winchester and Front Royal, through Washington, and then south to Culpeper and Fredericksburg, until the mid-1950s. The bus routes also connected with railroad service in Richmond and the Shenandoah Valley. The 7-passenger vehicles were purchased from Dick Weaver Buick in Culpeper.[40]

Travel by Motor Bus Between
FREDERICKSBURG, CULPEPER,
FRONT ROYAL, WINCHESTER

CONVENIENT
COMFORTABLE
Motor Bus Service

Fredericksburg-Winchester Bus Line
Washington, Virginia

Buses Stop by Signal Along Route

For information call Union Bus Terminal, Winchester; Princess Ann Hotel, Fredericksburg; Waverly Hotel, Culpeper; Jenkins Service Station, Washington; Lee Highway Hotel, Sperryville; Strickler House and Afton Inn, Front Royal, Va.

Jenkins made two round trips a day, giving Rappahannock residents without transportation a chance to spend a day shopping in the cities and meeting appointments. Ruby Jenkins, his daughter, remembered when people anywhere between Culpeper and Winchester could stand along the road and wave the Buick

[39] Rappahannock County Deed Book 30, page 357

[40] Daphne Hutchinson and Theresa Reynolds, compilers, *On the Morning Side of the Blue Ridge*, articles from the Rappahannock News of 1983, page 28

to stop.[41] The Jenkins bus service also aided those who were unable to do errands in person. The drivers would be given a list of notes and would pick up medicine, groceries and supplies for those on their list. In 1928, the fare from Washington to Front Royal was 75 cents, to Winchester was $1.75, to Culpeper was $1.25, and to Fredericksburg was $2.50.[42]

Jenkins sold his company to the Virginia Trailways Bus Company in the 1950s. The expanding automotive industry and increased highway building caused a decline in bus passengers and the service was discontinued shortly thereafter. It was a sad day when it was abandoned for the many citizens who counted on reliable bus service.

The dawn of the automobile age and the creation of Shenandoah National Park influenced the construction of commercial and residential garages in the town. Two substantial commercial garages appeared at the busy intersection of Main and Middle streets. In about 1900, John Edward Thornton built a one-story weather-boarded frame garage on the northeast corner of Main and Middle streets on Lot 24 opposite the former Mrs. Coxe's Tavern on the northwest corner, which he then owned. Thornton's Garage complemented his hotel business by providing parking space for carriages and then for new motor cars while offering the additional convenience of servicing the latter with gas, tires, and repairs. In the 1920s, L.V. Merrill moved to the town and rented Thornton's garage for many years. In the 1930s, a gas station and garage were constructed on the western part of Lot 25, where the Trinity Church parking lot was located in 2018.[43]

Critzer's Service Station was built in the 1940s on the north side of Middle Street, east of the Heterick House. This gas station sat below J.W. Clark's two tourist cabins on the northeast hillside, one of which remains behind the residence at 485 Middle Street. Another gas station was located on town Lot 13, built there after the Menefee home was dismantled.[44] In 2018, the only garage in the town was the Washington Motor Works on town lot 37.

During the Second World War, rationing was instituted throughout the nation to ensure that items in short supply would be available for the war effort. Gasoline was one of the rationed commodities.[45]

---

[41] Rappahannock News, 28 July 1983, page 8
[42] Rappahannock News, 28 July 1983, page 8
[43] M. Elizabeth Buntin, *Mission: A Study of the Churches of Bromfield Parish*, pages 74-78, files of Trinity Episcopal Church
[44] Mary Elizabeth Hite, *My Rappahannock Story Book*, The Dietz Press, Richmond, 1950, page 170
[45] Daphne Hutchinson and Theresa Reynolds, *On the Morning Side of the Blue Ridge*, a compilation of articles published in the *Rappahannock News* in 1983, page 88

L.V. Merrill purchased town Lot 9 at the southwest corner of Main and Middle streets in 1944 and constructed a new brick building there in 1945.[46] Merrill's Motor Company was a Ford dealership with a car display window in the front of the building. By this post-war time traffic was increasing on Lee Highway, which ran through the Town, as vacationers traveled to the newly finished Skyline Drive and the Shenandoah National Park. The highway speed limit at this point in town was 15 miles per hour.[47] Merrill's Motor Company thrived until its closing in 1979.[48]

To complement the need for tourist services, The Black Kettle Motel and Restaurant was constructed on land adjacent to the Avon Hall property and a wayside store was constructed near the Washington Mill on the east side of the part of the old highway that is now Old Mill Road. The wayside sold sandwiches, drinks and souvenir items. Both of these establishments suffered when the Virginia Department of Highways rerouted the new Route 211 out of the town and converted the old highway through Warren Avenue, Middle Street, and Main Street to Route 211 Business. Both the motel and the wayside were abandoned and are in considerable disrepair.

In 1953, the town's name had been put on highway markers stating the number of miles to Washington, Virginia.[49] In 1954, the Virginia Department of Highways presented its plans to resurface the town's roads; the town's streets were part of the Virginia State secondary road system. Also in that year, the Town Council approved the Department's proposal to change the speed limit in town to 35 miles per hour.[50] There was considerable congestion on Gay Street from parked cars; in 1965 the Town succeeded in having the County create an employee parking lot in back of the courthouse complex buildings.[51]

In 1965, The Town prevailed on the State Highway Department to install 12' of pipe in a drainage culvert which passed under Main Street at Piedmont Avenue. Ice and snow had accumulated in this area, presenting a dangerous situation for automobiles.[52] In the late 1960s, the Highway Department had planned to destroy the bridge over the Rush River east of town, on today's Old Mill Road, but the Town Council prevailed on the Department to retain this bridge.[53]

The minutes of the Washington Town Council during the 1950s-1990s are replete with complaints about the volume of traffic through the town, speeding, and

---

[46] Rappahannock County Deed Book 45, page 45, and Plat Book 3, page 13
[47] *Rappahannock News*, 12 September 1963, reprinted in the 22 December 2016 edition of the newspaper
[48] Rappahannock County Deed Book 193, page 199
[49] Minutes of the Washington Town Council, 13 April 1953
[50] Minutes of the Washington Town Council, April and June 1954
[51] Minutes of the Washington Town Council, January 1966
[52] *Rappahannock News*, 23 December 1965, quoted in the 28 June 2018 issue of the newspaper
[53] Minutes of the Washington Town Council, October 1967 and February 1968

dangerous intersections. Of particular concern was speeding near the high school school, and in 1965 a 25 mile per hour speed limit was imposed for traffic on Mount Salem Avenue.[54]

Most of the highway through Rappahannock County was widened in the 1970s to become the four-lane divided highway Route 211, although the western part to Sperryville was not completed until the late 1980s.[55] The expanded highway provided direct four-lane access from Washington DC to "the sleepy quaint village of Washington, Virginia."[56] With this construction, the highway proceeded directly east-to-west and no longer ran through the town. Instead, the road through the town along Warren Avenue, Middle Street, and Main Street was converted to a new designation as "Route 211 Business." The new four-lane road and a surge in interest in outdoor activities in Shenandoah National Park at this time resulted in increased access to the town of Washington and a growing tourist population. In 1990, the Virginia Department of Transportation reported 1,540 vehicles a day on Business 211 through the town.[57]

In March of 2003, the Virginia Regional Transportation Association began the Rappahannock Express bus service in Rappahannock County, with stops located in the town of Washington. This was a free service, funded on a trial basis by $21,760 from the County general fund. The County Board of Supervisors had agreed with interested citizens that a bus service could offer people an opportunity to meet their needs by having a bus that connected the various villages in the County and also traveled to Warrenton, Culpeper, and Front Royal. However, ridership was only 848 passengers during the first six months, and many busses traveled with no passengers. In September 2003 the Board voted to discontinue funding the bus service.[58] There was no public transportation servicing the town of Washington after that.

In 2014, new wooden street signs appropriate to the historic nature of the town were constructed by Scott Schlosser's students at Rappahannock High School. William Griffis and Jerry Goebel, the town treasurer, installed the set of signs.[59]

In 2018, the Virginia Department of Highways and Transportation owned and maintained the streets of the town. In that year, the Department milled and repaved two streets in the town, Mount Salem Avenue and the part of Main Street located north of Middle Street.

---

[54] Minutes of the Washington Town Council, May and June 1965
[55] *Rappahannock News*, 3 November 1988, quoted in the 14 January 2016 edition of the newspaper
[56] *Richmond Times-Dispatch*, 11 June 1978
[57] Town of Washington Comprehensive Plan, 2012, page 34
[58] *Rappahannock News*, 20 March 2003 and 11 September 2003
[59] *Rappahannock News*, 4 December 2014

Chapter 15. The Town of Washington in 2018

The town of Washington, founded in 1796,[1] is an historic village in the northern Piedmont area of the Commonwealth of Virginia in the foothills of the Blue Ridge mountains, close to Shenandoah National Park. It is a safe and quiet community within the rural agricultural environment of Rappahannock County, for which it is the County seat. The town combines a mixture of open spaces, residences, village commerce, tourism facilities, historic buildings, cultural offerings, and local government activities.

Washington still has the same grid of streets and the same street names shown in the town plan submitted in 1797 by the four men who petitioned the Virginia General Assembly to approve enlarging the boundaries of the town.[2] Four of the streets still bear their names -- Wheeler, Calvert, Jett, and Porter. However, the 51 original lots have been subdivided extensively and the boundaries of the town have been significantly enlarged, from an original 25 acres to 182.0171 acres.[3]

Many of the homes and other structures from the earliest period of the town survive today. The log cabin at 322 Main Street conforms to the original requirement by the General Assembly of Virginia in 1796 that the purchaser of a town lot was "subject to the condition of building on each, a dwelling house, sixteen feet square at least, with a brick or stone chimney, to be furnished fit for habitation." Many other structures built during the early 1800s through the Victorian Era are still in use in the town. Some examples include Mrs. Coxe's Tavern, now the Inn at Little Washington Tavern Shops at the corner of Main and Middle streets. Avon Hall, the mansion on a hill overlooking the town, was originally a tavern and then a school located on Gay Street in the early 1800s. The County courthouse, Clerk's office, and jail are government buildings constructed in 1834-1836 that still serve their original purpose.[4]

Washington is a community without large commercial businesses or any heavy industry. There is no public transportation available and there are no public restrooms in the town. There are also no recreational facilities in the town other than a small playground and natural area adjacent to Trinity House on Gay Street on town Lot 41. Much of the land contained within the corporate boundaries of

---

[1] Acts of the Virginia General Assembly, Chap. 21. – An Act to establish several towns (passed 14 December 1796), in Samuel Shepherd, *The Statutes at Large of Virginia, from October Session 1792 to December Session 1806, Inclusive, in Three Volumes, (New Series), Being a Continuation of Hening*, New York, AMS Press, Inc., 1836, Volume II, page 29-32

[2] George Calvert, James Jett Jr., James Wheeler, and William Porter, Culpeper County, 1 December 1797, Legislative Petitions Digital Collection, Library of Virginia, Richmond, VA, Record number 000154073

[3] Rappahannock County Instrument 990001042

[4] See Chapter 5 for a listing of the buildings in the town during the early 1800s, and Chapter 6 for a discussion of buildings in the town during the late 1800s

the town is open-space land devoted to fields, gardens, orchards, and pastures.[5] However, there are many governmental activities and businesses in the town, primarily along the original core streets. In the courthouse complex on Gay Street are located the courthouse serving the Twentieth Judicial Circuit Court, the General District Court, and the Juvenile and Domestic Relations Court. Other County offices in the courthouse complex are the offices of the Court Clerk, the Treasurer, the Commissioner of Revenue, the Voting Registrar, and the Sheriff. Across Gay Street are the offices of the Commonwealth Attorney and the County Attorney. Other governmental offices in the town include Zoning, Building Inspection, Emergency Services, Food Stamp and Welfare, Cooperative Extension, Health and Social Services, and a U.S. post office. A wide range of businesses in the town include the world-renowned Inn at Little Washington, bed and breakfast establishments, restaurants, shops, art and craft galleries, realty offices, law offices, personal services, small consulting firms, two performance theaters, three churches, a medical office, and the *Rappahannock News* office.[6] The town particularly benefits from having the world-famous Inn at Little Washington being located in the town, as this has fostered many of the businesses in the town. Because the meals and lodging tax is the town's primary source of revenue, restaurants and overnight lodging are especially important to the town.[7]

Many activities occur in the town. The Theatre at Washington, Virginia is a venue for cultural, music, and movie presentations. The RAAC Theater stages community-based plays and other cultural offerings. Educational presentations often occur in the Town Hall. Some of the other activities are a Sunday fresh air market sponsored by the Inn during late spring, summer, and fall; the 10K Fodderstack race that finishes in front of the courthouse; the Trinity Church annual house tour; the annual RAAC Artist Tour; 4th of July concerts at Avon Hall; and the annual Christmas in Little Washington parade.[8]

The town was recognized as an Historic District by the Virginia Historic Landmarks Commission in 1975 and was also placed on the National Register of Historic Places in that year. The town has developed a strong commitment to preserving the architectural and historical integrity of the residential homes and commercial structures within the town, while also acknowledging its responsibilities as the Rappahannock County seat and dealing with the commerce of modern tourism. New construction and renovation of existing structures are guided by the Historic District Design Guidelines, the Historic District Ordinance, the Zoning Ordinance, and the Architectural Review Board.

---

[5] Town of Washington Comprehensive Plan, 2017, page 16

[6] The medical office of Jerry Martin closed at the end of 2018. See Appendix 7 for a list of businesses located in the core of the town of Washington

[7] Washingtonva.gov/Meals & Lodging Tax Ordinance 2014

[8] The final year for the Inn's market and the Trinity House Tour was 2018.

The town is led by a seven-member elected Town Council composed of a mayor, a treasurer, and five other members, all of whom serve four-year terms. A vice-mayor is selected by a vote of the Town Council members from its membership.[9] Prior to 2018, elections were held on the first Tuesday in May. This changed in 2018 when the Town Council approved moving the election date to coincide with State and national elections on the first Tuesday in November. Elected on 6 November 2018 were Frederic F. Catlin as mayor; Gail K. Swift as Treasurer; and Mary Ann Kuhn, Katherine Weld Leggett, Patrick J. O'Connell, Bradley C. Schneider, and Joseph J. Whited as Council members. They were sworn in on 10 December 2018.[10] The Town's administrative assistant and Town Clerk, Laura Dodd, has served in this position for 16 years.[11]

The Council is guided by the town's Comprehensive Plan, zoning ordinance, subdivision ordinance, historic district guidelines, Planning Commission, Architectural Review Board, and Board of Zoning Appeals, together with focus groups composed of town citizens and consultants. General goals and objectives stated in the 2017 Comprehensive Plan included, for example, continuing to be an attractive destination with a culture of hospitality for visitors and new residents; creating a larger and more diverse mix of residents and businesses; enhancing a safe, user-friendly town environment for residents and visitors; preserving the historic character of the town; providing more employment opportunities and reasonably priced housing; ensuring the financial stability of the town; and protecting the open spaces that surround the town. The Plan acknowledged the issue of a decreasing population and the challenges of providing community services to an ever-smaller number of residents. In the U.S. census of 2010, there were 135 people who were residents of Washington. The estimate for 2018 was 125 residents.

The Town owns six properties:

- The Town Hall, located at 485 Gay Street on 11,373 square feet of land, which was built as a Presbyterian Church in 1856, became the first County library in 1960, and was purchased by the Town in 1989[12] (Tax Map 20A-1-136)
- A 0.5853-acre property on Warren Avenue containing a 2½-story frame house which is formerly part of the Avon Hall property sold by the Town in 2016.[13] The condition of the house is very poor due to age and neglect, and the Town has considered removing the house and relocating the U.S. post office to this site (Tax Map 20A-1-119)

---

[9] See Chapter 7, in which the town was rechartered in 1985

[10] *Rappahannock News*, 1 November 2018, 8 November 2018, and 13 December 2018

[11] Ms. Dodd announced her resignation in 2019, to take effect at the end of August, 2019

[12] Rappahannock County Deed Book J, page 414; Deed Book 71, page 595; Deed Book 175, page 298

[13] Rappahannock County Instrument 160000598

- 5.2824 acres, also formerly part of the Avon Hall property, on which was constructed the Wastewater Plant Laboratory and Control Room Building and a gravel road for access to the facility from Warren Avenue. The deed of sale of the Avon Hall property required that a 50-foot wide wooded buffer zone be maintained to separate it from view of the wastewater treatment facility (Tax Map 20A-1-80)
- 1.0665 acres adjacent to the southwest boundary of the 5.2824-acre property (Tax Map 20A-1-144)
- A 0.155-acre property acquired in 1988[14] measuring 25' by 270' along the north side of Piedmont Avenue (Tax Map 20A-1-33D)
- A 0.23-acre property (10,000 square feet) located adjacent to Route 622 (Harris Hollow Road) where it turns to meet the Rush River, acquired in 1981 from Clara Updike[15] and serving as the town well lot (Tax Map 20-11E)

The Town also owns easements associated with the water supply system:
- The Town had acquired 1 acre of land from the Cloptons in 1977 and an adjacent 1.0381 acres from the Berrys in 1981 for the purpose of town wells.[16] These two properties were conveyed to the Berrys in 2004, but the Town retained easements 5' on either side of the existing water pipes.[17]
- In 1991, in conjunction with the acquisition by the Town of the 10,000 square foot well lot, the Town also acquired a 20' wide by 2842' long easement across Updike's property adjacent to Route 622 leading toward the town[18]
- Also in 1991, the Town was granted a 20' wide by 2513' long easement by the Cloptons, extending from the well lot obtained in 1977 and intersecting with the waterline easement obtained from Clara Updike along Route 622[19]
- In 1993, three easements were obtained from Clara Updike at a cost of $4000.[20] These were a 5897 square foot enlargement of the 10,000 square foot parcel for the purpose of installation of a well house and wells for the public water supply; an adjacent 1532 square foot parcel for access to the well lot; and a 20' wide by 1388' long easement extending along Route 622 for laying waterline pipes adjacent to and parallel with the as-built water line. The distance from the end of this easement to Main Street was 1050'.
- In 2001, the existing reservoir was located on land owned by Nels Parson (Tax Map 19-62), adjacent to land owned by Sidney Berry (Tax Map 19-62A). Berry granted a 50' diameter easement for construction of a new reservoir and a 25' wide by 1055' long easement from the new reservoir to the well lot that Clopton had conveyed in 1977, adjacent to Piedmont Avenue (Tax Map 19-73).[21] In

[14] Rappahannock County Deed Book 168, page 538
[15] Rappahannock County Deed Book 139, page 624
[16] Rappahannock County Deed Book 126, page 389 and Plat Book 2, page 73; Rappahannock County Deed Book 138, page 605
[17] Rappahannock County Instrument 040002083
[18] Rappahannock County Deed Book 139, page 624
[19] Rappahannock County Deed Book 139, page 815
[20] Rappahannock County Deed Book 199, page 400
[21] Rappahannock County Instrument 010001390 and Instrument 010001391

2006, the waterline easement from the reservoir for a distance of 323.97' was relocated.[22]

The Town relies on two key elements to support its economy. One is its role as the County seat, which attracts economic activity associated with the judicial courts and the County government and other related activities that benefit from being located in the County seat. The second is the tourist industry, which is supported by the historic architectural character of the town, the scenic and historic landscape of the surrounding County including Shenandoah National Park, and the significant benefits of the town's restaurants and lodging facilities. These two base "industries" provide the foundation for the Town's economy.[23]

The Town budget for FY2019 was $852,250, divided into three parts -- General Operating Fund ($364,700), Washington Water Works ($112,050), and Washington Wastewater Works ($375,500). The Town has a 2.5% meals and lodging tax, and more than 80% of the operating budget comes from this tax, which is derived primarily from the tourist industry. This tax was passed by resolution in preference to a real estate or personal property tax.[24] The balance of the operating budget comes from an electric power franchise tax, building permits, fines, and revenue from the Commonwealth of Virginia which includes sales taxes and Alcoholic Beverage Control Board profits.[25] A major accomplishment for the Town has been establishing a safe and reliable water supply and facilities to deal with wastewater. The town's water facilities are funded under a separate proprietary fund called the Washington Water Works. Revenues come from connection fees and water sales.[26] The wastewater facilities are also funded separately under a proprietary fund called the Washington Wastewater Works. Revenues come from customer's connection fees and usage of the wastewater system.

Streets in the town are maintained by the Virginia Department of Transportation. Rappahannock Electric Cooperative is the sole provider of electricity to the town; this entity maintains the street lights and power poles. Telephone service is provided by CenturyLink, which has an office on town Lot 43. Property owners in the town pay real and personal property tax and a fire levy tax to Rappahannock County, and pay sales tax and income tax to the Commonwealth of Virginia. In return, the town is provided with road maintenance, schools, solid waste disposal, law enforcement, County and District Court services and records maintenance, and health and welfare services.

---

[22] Rappahannock County Instrument 060000325
[23] Town of Washington Comprehensive Plan, 2006, page 12
[24] Town of Washington Comprehensive Plan, 2006, page 15
[25] Town of Washington Comprehensive Plan, 2006, page 16
[26] Town of Washington Comprehensive Plan, 2006, page 16, and 2017, page 20

As this book is a history of the town of Washington, it seems appropriate to end these chapters with the assessment of the town as described by the Virginia Department of Historic Resources: Washington is "the best preserved of county-seat communities in the Piedmont."[27]

[27] Calder Loth, editor, *The Virginia Landmarks Register, 4th edition*, University of Virginia Press, 1999, p. 418

Appendix 1. Land Grant to the Kennerlys, 1735

George the Second by the Grace of God of Great Britain France and Ireland King Defender of the Faith To all to whom these presents shall come Greetings. Know ye that for divers goods and considerations but more especially for and in Consideration of the Importation of Six Persons to Dwell within this our Colony and Dominion of Virginia whose names are Samuel Kennerly, Ellin Kennerly, Thomas Kennerly, Elizabeth Kennerly, James Kennerly and Catherine Kennerly As also for and in consideration of the sum of Seven Pounds Five Shillings of good and Lawful money for our aide paid to our Receivor General of our Revenues in this our said Colony and Dominion We have given granted and confirmed and by these presents for us our Heirs and Successors Do Give Grant and Confirm unto Thomas Kennerly, James Kennerly and Elizabeth Kennerly one certain tract or parcel of Land containing One Thousand Seven Hundred and fifty acres commonly known by the name of Delameres Forest Lying and being in the Parish of Saint Mark in the County of Orange between the mountains and the fork of the Rushy River and bounded as followeth (to wit) Beginning at three red oaks and a white oak in a large vale thence South Seventy Six Degrees east one hundred and ninety Poles to a Double Chesnut and a Single one on a little Hill South fifty eight Degrees east Fifty Six poles to a white oak a Chesnut and Locust South Seventy eight Degrees East thirty six poles to two white oaks South thirty seven Degrees East Seventy two Poles to a red oak and white oak on the top of a Ridge South fifty Degrees west Seventy Six Poles to two white oaks and a Pine South fifty two Degrees East one Hundred and Eighty eight Poles to a white oak a red oak and a Poplar North Eighty eight Degrees East Forty eight Poles to a white oak and two Pines on Piney Point North forty Degrees East two hundred and eighty eight Poles to a white oak and a Pine North twenty five Degrees west two hundred and sixty eight poles to a Spanish oak and two white oaks North five Degrees east One Hundred and Sixteen Poles to a white oak North Sixty five Degrees East One Hundred twenty Poles to a red oak North thirty seven Degrees west one hundred and fifty six Poles to a red oak and a Hickory North Eighty Six Degrees west Sixty Poles to a red oak North thirty one Degrees west one Hundred and forty four Poles to three Chesnut oaks West twenty four Poles to two Chesnut Oaks South forty nine Degrees west twenty four Poles to a Chesnut and Chesnut Oak South Seventeen Degrees west thirty six Poles to two Chesnuts and a Chesnut Oak North Sixty nine Degrees west forty Poles to a white oak South twelve Degrees west thirty six Poles to a Hickory North Eighty Degrees west Sixty eight Poles to two red oaks South eighty seven Degrees west Fifty Six Poles to a red oak white oak and Poplar South one Hundred Poles crossing the River to a red oak South Seventy three Degrees East one hundred Sixty eight Poles to two red oaks South three Degrees east fifty two Poles to two white oaks South Seventy Degrees west Sixty eight Poles to a red oak South eleven Degrees east Ninety two Poles to a Gum in a Poyson Field South Seventy seven Degrees west eighty eight Poles to a Large white oak and two small ones on a run thence South fifty three Degrees west one Hundred and ninety Poles to the beginning. With all woods underwoods Swamps Marshes Lowgrounds Meadows Feedings and their due share of all veins mines and Quarries as well discovered and not discovered within the bounds aforesaid and being part of the said Quantity of One Thousand Seven Hundred and Fifty acres of Land and the Rivers Waters and Water Courses therein contained together with the privileges of Hunting Hawking Fishing Fowling and all other profits commodities and Hereditaments whatsoever to the same or any part thereof belonging or in any wise appertaining To Have Hold possess and enjoy the said tract or parcel of Land and all other the before Granted Premises and every part thereof with their and every of their appurtenances unto the said Thomas Kennerly, James Kennerly and Elizabeth Kennerly and to their heirs and assigns forever To the only use and behoof of them the said Thomas Kennerly, James Kennerly and Elizabeth Kennerly their Heirs and assigns forever To Be Held of us our Heirs and Successors as of our manor of East Greenwich in the County of Kent in free and common soccage and not in capito or by Knights Service Yielding and Paying unto us our Heirs and Successors for every fifty acres of Land and so Proportionably for a Lessor or Greater Quantity than fifty acres the Fee Rent of one shilling yearly to be paid upon the Feast of Saint Michael the Archangel and also Cultivating and Improving three acres part of every fifty of the tract above mentioned within three years after the Date of these Presents Provided always that if three years of the said Fee Rent shall at any time be in arrear and unpaid or if the said Thomas Kennerly, James Kennerly and Elizabeth Kennerly their Heirs or Assigns do not within the space of three years next coming after the Date of these presents Cultivate and Improve three acres part of every fifty of the tract above mentioned Then the Estate hereby granted shall cease and be utterly determined and thereafter it shall and may be lawful to and for our Heirs and Successors to Grant the same Lands and Premises with the appurtenances unto such other Person or Persons as our Heirs and Successors shall think fit In Witness whereof we have caused these our Letters Patent to be made Witness our trusty and welbeloved William Gooch Esq. our Lieut. Gov. and Commander in Chief of our said Colony and Dominion at Williamsburg under the Seal of our said Colony the nineteenth day of June One Thousand Seven Hundred and thirty five in the ninth year of our Reign.

William Gooch

Source: Library of Virginia, Land Office Patents Book No. 15, 1732-1735, page 531

Appendix 2. Petition to Establish the Town, 1796

Petition from George Calvert, James Jett Jr., and James Wheeler to Establish the Town of Washington, 10 November 1796

To the Hon'ble Speaker and Gentlemen of the house of Delegates
of the Commonwealth of Virginia—
The Petition of George Calvert, James
Jett jun & James Wheeler inhabitants of Culpeper County humbly
sheweth— That your Petitioners are possessed of lands within the
said County contiguous to each other: that they conceive it would
be of public utility were there a Town established on their lands;
being situated in a fertile thick settled Country; which might
induce Mechanics to settle therein— They therefore pray that
a Law may pass to establish a Town by the name of Washington on twenty five Acres of
land of your said petitioners in the County aforesaid, and whereon
they have already made some improvements, the same to be
laid off in lots of half an Acre each, under such regulations, as
have been heretofore customary for your Hon'ble house to
prescribe in similar institutions; And your Petitioners as
in duty bound shall pray &c

Source: George Calvert, James Jett, & James Wheeler, Culpeper County, 10 November 1796, Legislative Petitions Digital Collection, Library of Virginia, Richmond, VA, Record number 000154065; also, Legislative Petitions of the General Assembly, 1776-1865, Accession Number 36121, Box 58, Folder 63.

Appendix 3. Petition to Add Porter's Land to the Town, 1797

Petition from George Calvert, James Jett Jr., James Wheeler, and William Porter to include the land of William Porter in the Town of Washington, 1 November 1797. A plan of the town of Washington accompanied this written text (See Chapter 2 and Appendix 4).

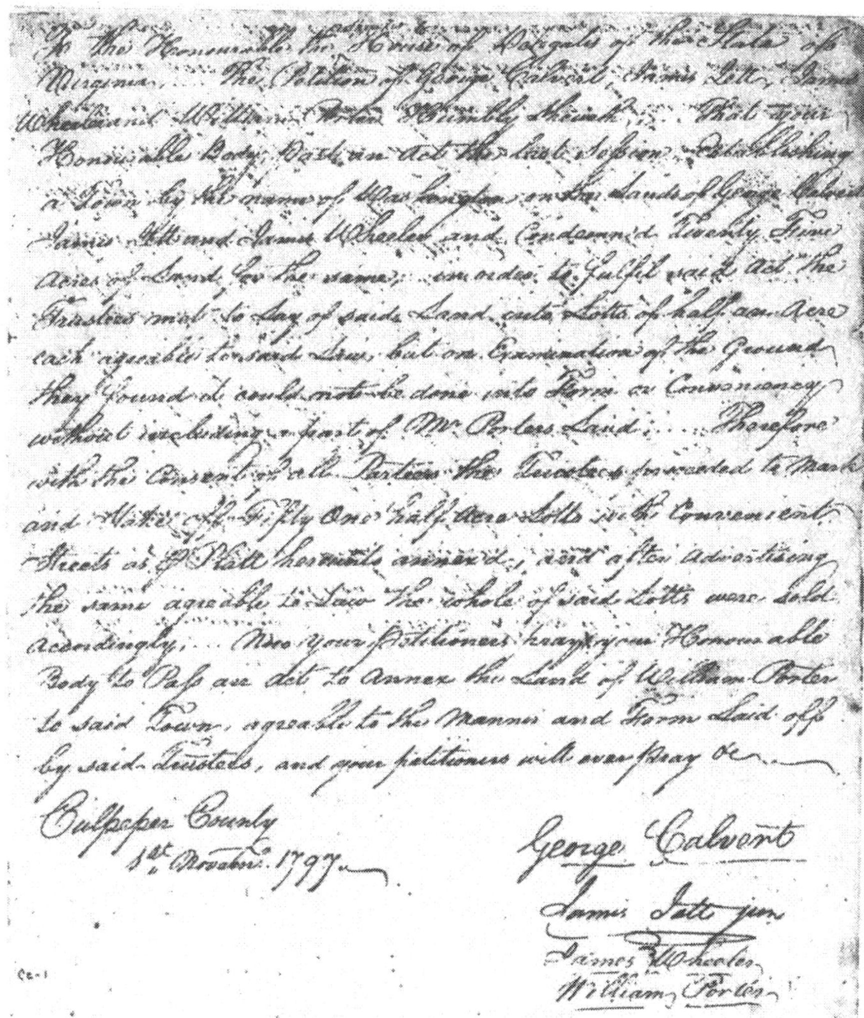

To the Honourable the House of Delegates of the State of Virginia. The Petition of George Calvert, James Jett, James Wheeler and William Porter Humbly Sheweth That your Honourable Body Hath in Act the last Session Establishing a Town by the name of Washington on the Lands of George Calvert James Jett and James Wheeler and Condemned Twenty Five Acres of Land for the same; in order to fulfil said Act the Trustees met to lay of said Land into Lotts of half an Acre each agreeable to said Law, but on Examination of the Ground they found it could not be done into Form or Conveniency without including a part of Mr. Porters Land. Therefore with the Consent of all Parties the Trustees proceeded to Mark and Make off Fifty One half Acre Lotts with Convenient Streets as p Platt herewith annexed, and after advertising the same agreeable to Law the whole of said Lotts were Sold accordingly. Now your Petitioners pray your Honourable Body to Pass an Act to Annex the Land of William Porter to said Town, agreeable to the Manner and Form laid off by said Trustees, and your petitioners will ever pray &c.

Culpeper County
1st November 1797

George Calvert
James Jett jun
James Wheeler
William Porter

Source: George Calvert, James Jett Jr., James Wheeler, and William Porter, Culpeper County, 1 December 1797, Legislative Petitions Digital Collection, Library of Virginia, Richmond, VA, Record number 000154073; also, Legislative Petitions of the General Assembly, 1776-1865, Accession Number 36121, Box 58, Folder 71.

Appendix 4. Franklin Clyde Baggarly and the Legend of George Washington

A legend exists that George Washington surveyed and drew a plan of the town of Washington on 24 July 1749.[1] While many authorities have questioned the validity of this legend,[2] it has existed for over 80 years and is firmly ensconced in local publications and websites, road markers, and a monument in the town.

This legend arose on 6 May 1932 when Franklin Clyde Baggarly presented to the Town Council of Washington his report titled "History of the Town of Washington, Virginia." The Town Council resolved that the report be recorded with the minutes of the Council meeting and in a Rappahannock County Court Clerk's office deed book.[3] The report was also published as a separate pamphlet.[4]

The report is quite lengthy and is written in an erudite style that is very persuasive. However, only two small parts of the report are directly pertinent to Baggarly's theory that Washington surveyed and prepared a plan of the town:

(1) "Landon published what he represents to be a verified copy of the survey made by Washington of the Barnes land in the county of Culpeper ... In connection therewith he [Landon] makes particular reference to an entry in Washington's handwriting preserved with his miscellaneous papers, in which Washington after referring to the Richard Barnes survey as having been made on 22 July 1749 continued his field record as follows: 'On the second day thereafter accompanied by John Lonem and Edward Corder, I journeyed one half day in a northwestern direction from Fairfax [then the name of the town of Culpeper] and in the Blue Ridge Mountains in Culpeper County I laid off a town.'" [At this time, the land that became Rappahannock County was part of Culpeper County.]

(2) "There is now preserved a plan of the town that was found in 1847 among the records of the Fairfax surveys and grants which purports to be, and from every appearance is, the original made by George Washington. This plan, which is in a fairly good state of preservation, contains not only the original boundaries, but the lot numbers are easily discernable and the names of the streets are clearly legible."

---

[1] In 1752, the English calendar was revised and 24 July 1749 became 4 August 1749.

[2] Clayton Torrence, Director, Virginia Historical Society, letter dated 5 August 1947 to Mrs. Edna T. Walker, owner of "Washington House" in the town of Washington; "George Washington's Professional Surveys, 22 July 1749-25 October 1752, *The Papers of George Washington, Colonial Series, 1748-August 1755*, University Press of Virginia, 1983; "George Washington's Professional Surveys," *Founders Online,* National Historical Publications and Records Commission of the National Archives, founders.archives.gov/documents/Washington/02-01-02-0004; Updated Nomination in 2006, Washington Historic District, Site #322-0011, National Register of Historic Places, Section 8, pages 35-36; Eugene M. Scheel, Culpeper, *A Virginia County's History Through 1920*, Green Publishers, Orange, VA, 1982, page 81-82; Eugene M. Scheel, "Putting Little Washington on the Map," *The Portolan Journal of the Washington Map Society*, No. 54, 2002, pages 37-39; Edward J. Redmond, a scholar at the Library of Congress and expert on the maps of George Washington, quoted in Eugene M. Scheel, "In Washington's Shadow, Little Town Has a Big Reputation, *Washington Post*, 17 February 2002, Loudoun Extra Section, pages 3 and 5; personal communication from Peter Luke, former County Attorney for Rappahannock County, 2017.

[3] Rappahannock County Deed Book 37, pages 3-16

[4] Rappahannock Historical Society files related to the town of Washington

Item 1

- No publication relating to George Washington authored by anyone named Landon has ever been identified.[5] According to Eugene M. Scheel, the noted historian and cartographer, Baggarly had declared in 1930, in connection with the development of the book of Washington's plats by the George Washington Bicentennial Commission, that he had in his possession the paper in which Washington stated he surveyed the town, but that this paper had burned in a fire in his office.[6] Thus, there is no tangible evidence that the statement about laying off a town had ever been made by Washington.
- The most comprehensive and complete of Washington's surveying records are his field books. The field book covering the year 1749 has five sheets torn out; however, two of these are at Cornell University and another is in the Dreer Collection of the Historical Society of Pennsylvania; there is no mention of a survey of the town of Washington. In the Washington Papers at the Library of Congress there is a small note book in which Washington copied finished versions of his 1749 surveys, apparently as a permanent record for his own reference. This notebook includes those surveys missing from the 1749 field book, although one of the notebook's sheets is torn out; that sheet is at the Pennsylvania Historical Society. There is no mention in the notebook of a survey for the town of Washington. No finished survey by Washington has been discovered for the 1749-1751 period which does not appear in his field books or his 1749 notebook.[7]
- Washington had been appointed at age 17 as surveyor of the newly-formed Culpeper County on 20 July 1749.[8] Two days later, he surveyed 400 acres of the land of Richard Barnes in Culpeper County.[9] This is the only survey he is known to have made in this county.[10] Thereafter, his surveys were almost entirely done in the Shenandoah and Cacopon valleys of Frederick County, west of the Blue Ridge. On 3 November 1750 Henry Lee officially replaced Washington as the surveyor for Culpeper County.[11]

---

[5] Personal communication in 2017 from Peter Luke, former County Attorney for Rappahannock County, based on his research and inquiries; Updated Nomination in 2006, Washington Historic District, Site #322-0011, National Register of Historic Places, Section 8, page 35

[6] Eugene M. Scheel, "Putting Little Washington on the Map," *The Portolan Journal of the Washington Map Society*, No. 54, 2002, pages 37-39; Eugene M. Scheel, "In Washington's Shadow, Little Town Has a Big Reputation, *Washington Post*, 17 February 2002, Loudoun Extra Section, pages 3 and 5

[7] "George Washington's Professional Surveys, 22 July 1749-25 October 1752," *Founders Online,* National Historical Publications and Records Commission of the National Archives and the University of Virginia, founders.archives.gov/documents/Washington/02-01-02-0004.

[8] Howe, Historical Collections of Virginia, page 237.

[9] Lawrence Martin, editor, *The George Washington Atlas*, U.S. George Washington Bicentennial Commission, Washington, D.C., A.H. Hoen & Co. publisher, Baltimore, 1932.

[10] The land that became Rappahannock County was part of Culpeper County at that time. "George Washington's Professional Surveys, 22 July 1749-25 October 1752," *Founders Online,* National Historical Publications and Records Commission of the National Archives and the University of Virginia, founders.archives.gov/documents/Washington/02-01-02-0004.

[11] "List of County Surveyors, *Virginia Magazine*, Vol. 50, pages 368-369.

Item 2

- Baggarly's wife found the purported plan of the town in her husband's papers after she had him declared legally incompetent in 1959.[12] She took the plan to the Rappahannock County Court Clerk on 5 June 1959, and the document is now secured in the Clerk's office. A copy of the plan is recorded in a Rappahannock County deed book.[13]
- The plan is virtually identical to the town plan submitted in 1797 in a petition to the Virginia General Assembly by George Calvert, James Jett Jr., James Wheeler, and William Porter in which they requested adding some of Porter's land to the land that formed the town in 1796.[14] The names of four of the streets on both plans are the surnames of these four men. However, none of these men were living or they were only children in 1749, the date Baggarly asserted Washington drew his plan, although there was a Jett family in Virginia.[15] Thus, it seems impossible that Washington could have selected street names that were identical to the names of the four men involved in laying out the town forty-seven years later in 1796-1797. Baggarly also proposed that Gay Street was named after Gay Fairfax, whom Baggarly stated was romantically involved with George Washington. However, nowhere in the many papers of Washington is the name Gay Fairfax mentioned.[16] It is well known, however, that Washington was passionate about Sally Fairfax who was the wife of his best friend, George William Fairfax.[17]
- Baggarly stated that the plan of the town "was found in 1847 among the records of the Fairfax surveys and grants." However, he does not explain by whom it was found or how he came to have it. Further, the land on which the town is located was not granted by Thomas Lord Fairfax, but by King George II in 1735 to Thomas, James, and Elizabeth Kennerly.[18] The land thus has no connection to the Fairfax surveys and grants. In his report, Baggarly made no mention of

---

[12] Rappahannock County Chancery Case #2279 and Case #2286, Baggarly vs. Baggarly; Rappahannock County Bond Book 10, page 100

[13] Rappahannock County Deed Book 36, two copies are located prior to page 1

[14] See Chapter 2. George Calvert, James Jett Jr., James Wheeler, and William Porter, Culpeper County, 1 December 1797, Legislative Petitions Digital Collection, Library of Virginia, Richmond, Record number 000154073; also, Legislative Petitions of the General Assembly, 1776-1865, Accession Number 36121, Box 58, Folder 71

[15] James Jett Jr. was born in 1763; he was the grandson of John Jett, who had acquired land in the Flint Hill area in 1749 (Culpeper County Deed Book A, page 188). The Calvert family lived in Prince William County; George Calvert was born there in 1744 and lived there until 1777 when he purchased land near Mulkey's Mountain (Culpeper County Deed Book H, page 525). The Porter family was from Fauquier County; William Porter was born there in 1749 and lived there until 1791 when his father-in-law gave him the land on which most of the town of Washington is now located (Culpeper County Deed Book Q, page 387). James Wheeler was born in about 1755 and acquired his first property, which was land near the Rush River, only in 1786 (Culpeper County Deed Book Q, page 366).

[16] Library of Congress, *The Papers of George Washington*; rotunda.upress.virginia.edu, digital edition of The Papers of George Washington, University of Virginia Press. A search of Washington's papers was made by Eugene M. Scheel, as reported in "In Washington's Shadow, Little Town Has a Big Reputation, *Washington Post*, 17 February 2002, Loudoun Extra Section, pages 3 and 5.

[17] Joseph J. Ellis, *His Excellency, George Washington*, Alfred A. Knopf, New York, 2004, pages 36-37

[18] Library of Virginia, Virginia Colonial Land Office Patent Book No. 15, 1732-1735, p. 531. The land grant was to the Kennerlys was for 1750 acres along the Rush River (see Chapter 1).

Plan of the town of Washington proposed by Franklin Clyde Baggarly to have been drawn by George Washington. The plan was given to the Court Clerk of Rappahannock County by his wife Francis Trott Baggarly in 1959. Source: Rappahannock County Deed Book 36, two copies are located prior to page 1.

Plan of the town of Washington submitted to the Virginia General Assembly in 1797 by George Calvert, James Jett Jr., James Wheeler, and William Porter with their written request to add land of William Porter to the 25 acres authorized by the Assembly in 1796. Source: George Calvert, James Jett Jr., James Wheeler, and William Porter, Culpeper County, 1 December 1797, Legislative Petitions Digital Collection, Library of Virginia, Richmond, VA, Record number 000154073; also, Legislative Petitions of the General Assembly, 1776-1865, Accession Number 36121, Box 58, Folder 71.

the land grant by King George II and was apparently unaware that this was the origin of the town land.

- Where did Baggarly's plan of the town come from? Eugene M. Scheel surmised that a plan should have been recorded in Culpeper County records when the town was formed in 1796-1797. When he investigated the plat books in the Culpeper

Court Clerk's office, he found that "someone had deftly razor-bladed the plan from Culpeper County Plat Book 1."[19] Although a recent search for this plat book has been made by Peter Luke and the Clerk of the Culpeper Court, it has not been found.[20]

- Finally, Washington's extant survey plats are typical of those drawn by a professional surveyor, with distances (e.g., 40 feet) and directions (e.g., North 67 West) shown on each line of the land's boundaries; survey monuments (e.g., a red oak tree) mark each corner where two boundary lines meet. If Washington had surveyed the town, particularly by bringing the chainmen Lonem and Corder with him, a proper survey plat would have been prepared by him, not the simple plan that Baggarly presented.

Eugene M. Scheel has made a thorough investigation of Baggarly's assertion that George Washington surveyed and drew a plan of the town. Scheel is an eminent historian and cartographer. He is the author of nine books on Virginia history and has researched and drawn over 50 historical maps, including that of Rappahannock County and each of the surrounding counties. Scheel first visited the town of Washington in 1962, at which time he noticed the monument at the east end of Jett Street referring to Washington surveying the town in 1749. This puzzled him, because he knew that 1749 was a very early date for a town in the Piedmont backwoods. For example, the important seaport town of Alexandria was only established in 1749, and Chapter 1 of this book provides evidence that in 1749 the area that is now the town was simply farmland owned by Thomas Kennerly. Nowhere in the papers of George Washington is the name Thomas Kennerly found.[21] It is highly improbable that Kennerly would have permitted the 17-year-old Washington to lay off a town on his private farmland and to name the town after himself.

Some years later, while Scheel was preparing his historical map of Culpeper County in 1776 (which then included the land that is now Rappahannock County), he queried residents of the town, and old-timers told him they had never heard that their town had been laid out by Washington until the Baggarly report was published. They also told him that, shortly before the publication of Baggarly's report, Baggarly had contacted the George Washington Bicentennial Commission requesting that the town plan which Baggarly had "found" be included in the atlas of Washington maps and surveys that the Commission was preparing. Lawrence Martin, the atlas' editor, sent a researcher to see Baggarly

---

[19] Eugene M. Scheel, "Putting Little Washington on the Map," *The Portolan Journal of the Washington Map Society*, No. 54, 2002, pages 37-39; Eugene M. Scheel, "In Washington's Shadow, Little Town Has a Big Reputation, *Washington Post*, 17 February 2002, Loudoun Extra Section, pages 3 and 5

[20] Personal communication from Peter Luke, 2017

[21] Library of Congress, *The Papers of George Washington*; rotunda.upress.virginia.edu, digital edition of The Papers of George Washington, University of Virginia Press. A search of Washington's papers was made by Eugene M. Scheel, as reported in "In Washington's Shadow, Little Town Has a Big Reputation, *Washington Post*, 17 February 2002, Loudoun Extra Section, pages 3 and 5.

in Washington. However, Baggarly told him that the entry in Washington's handwritten papers regarding the town survey had burned in a fire in his office, and the researcher had doubts that the plan was the work of Washington. Based on this, the plan was not included in the Washington atlas.[22]

Several residents of the town told Scheel that Baggarly was angered at this slight, so he wrote his report and also funded construction of the stone monument at the east end of Jett Street.[23] Scheel wrote "for several years, Baggarly promoted his theories and, as old-timers died, the town and county began to accept the honor. Upon pressure from the town, the state historical marker was erected which reads, in part, 'Washington, Virginia, the first of them all.'"

Franklin Clyde Baggarly was an imposing person in the town of Washington. He had been the Town's attorney in 1910-1918 and was a successful attorney for the federal government in Washington D.C.[24] He was the sole surviving child of Baldwin B. Baggarly who had moved to the town in 1850,[25] acquired what had been Thorn's Tavern and later the Washington Academy,[26] and converted this building into his home. In 1931 Franklin Clyde Baggarly moved it from Gay Street to the hill east of the town, enlarged the building, added a two-story portico with full height columns, and renamed it Avon Hall. His report on George Washington presented to the Washington Town Council in 1932 was written in a very erudite fashion and, given Baggarly's reputation and status, the report seems to have been persuasive to the Town Council members.

Baggarly's legend of George Washington was promulgated extensively by Dorothy Cox Davis, who was elected mayor of the Town in 1950 and was an amateur George Washington scholar. In an interview in that year, she stated "There is no doubt in my mind that George Washington surveyed this town," despite historian Douglas Freeman's inability to unearth information confirming Baggarly's claim.[27] She also stated that "We intend to put this town on the map," and perhaps the legend of George Washington was one means she undertook to do this during her 20-year reign as mayor of the town.

---

[22] Lawrence Martin, editor, *The George Washington Atlas*, U.S. George Washington Bicentennial Commission, Washington, D.C., A.H. Hoen & Co. publisher, Baltimore, 1932.

[23] The monument has the date of the survey as being August 4, 1749, rather than July 24, 1749, because of the revision of the English calendar in 1752

[24] Obituary of Franklin Clyde Baggarly, *Washington Post*, 19 October 1961

[25] 1850 U.S. census

[26] Rappahannock County Deed Book L, page 464

[27] Interview of Davis by Edwin B. Lockett, "She-Town," *Collier's Magazine*, 4 November 1950

Appendix 5. Mayors of the Town

Mayors of the Town of Washington Since Its Incorporation in 1894

Theodore L. Booten
Edward W. Brown
Edward T. Jones
John Clark
Albert J. Slaughter
Burrell T. Partlow
William E. Compton
William F. Moffett Jr.
Dorothy Cox Davis
Andrew Kozik
Virginia Miller
Peter H. Kramer
J. Newbill Miller
Dean Morehouse
J. Stewart Willis
Eugene Leggett
John Fox Sullivan
Frederic C. Catlin

Sources: Program for the installation of the all-women town council, 1 September 1950; Minutes of the meetings of the Washington Town Council

Appendix 6. Population Estimates

U.S. Census Bureau Estimates
for the Population of the
Town of Washington, Virginia

Year	Population
1880	254
1890	252
1900	300
1910	235
1920	233
1930	250
1940	245
1950	249
1960	255
1970	189
1980	247
1990	198
2000	183
2010	135
2018	125

Appendix 7. Businesses and Organizations in the Town,2018

Lodging
Foster Harris House Bed and Breakfast
Gay Street Inn Bed and Breakfast
The Inn at Little Washington (multiple sites)
Middleton Inn Bed and Breakfast
The White Moose Inn Bed and Breakfast

Restaurants
The Country Cafe
The Inn at Little Washington
Foster Harris House
Tula's Off Main

Attorneys
Michael T. Brown (Walker Jones PC)
Alan Dranitzke
Frank B. Reynolds Jr.

Shops
Antiques at Middle Street
Artifacts on Main
August Georges
Geneva Welch Gallery
Inn at Little Washington Tavern Shops
R.H. Ballard Shop and Gallery
Rare Finds
Wine Loves Chocolate

Art Galleries
Dwell Fine Art
Gay Street Gallery and Kevin Adams Studio
Middle Street Gallery

Realty Companies
Rappahannock Real Estate
Country Places Realty
Real Estate III
Washington Fine Properties

Personal Services
Little Washington Wellness and Spa

Theaters
Rappahannock Association for the Arts and the Community theater
The Theatre at Washington, Virginia

Other Businesses and Organizations
Century Link telephone services
JPC Designs Woodworking
Hampton Title Agency
Rappahannock Historical Society
Rappahannock League for Environmental Protection
Rappahannock Medical Center
Washington Metro Physical Therapy
The Rappahannock News
Rappahannock Title LLC
Telework offices on second floor of 311 Gay Street
Washington Motor Works

Governmental Offices
Town Hall
Twentieth Judicial Circuit Court
General District Court
Juvenile & Domestic Relations Court
Clerk of the Court
Commissioner of Revenue
Treasurer
Commissioner of Accounts
County Attorney
Sheriff
Zoning and Building Inspection
Emergency Services
Social Services
Voting Registrar
Virginia Commonwealth Attorney
Virginia Cooperative Extension Service
Virginia Health Department
U.S. Post Office

Index

Academy, The, 221, 252
Adams, Kevin, 90, 205
All-women Town Council, 1950, 82
Animals loose in town, 1880, 49
Animals loose in town, 1894, 65
Apple packing building, 74, 87
Architectural Review Board, 106, 120, 122
Armel, Buford Roy, 76, 98
Artists of Rappahannock art tour, 99
Automobiles, early 1900s, 278
Avon Hall, 111, 245, 284
Avon Hall, sale by town, 141
Baggarly, Baldwin B., 56, 61, 231
Baggarly, Franklin Clyde, 78, 111, 232, 294
Banks in the town, 72
Banks, James, 157
Basketball, 76
Baumgardner, Douglas, 88, 181
Bed and breakfast establishments, 92
Bertha's Diner, 180
Bicentennial celebration, 97
Big Branch, 16
Big Branch School, 254
Black Branch, 129
Black Kettle Motel, 92, 282
Blue Ridge Echo, 49, 71
Blue Ridge Guide, 69, 71
Blue Ridge mountains, 284
Board of Trustees, 1833-1894, 42
Boundaries of the town, 59, 110, 284
Bourgeois, John, 99
Bowie, Lucy Catherine, 71, 95, 181
Brack, Dennis, 95
Brown, Dr. E.W., 224
Browning, Francis S., 39
Building construction, 1865-1900, 52
Building house within 7 years, 32
Buildings constructed since 1950, 93
Buntin, William and Elizabeth, 95, 184
Businesses in the town, 285
Businesses in town, 2018, 302
Busses, 79
Bylaws and ordinances, 1877, 46
Bywaters' barroom, 46
Cabin Fever Books, 89, 166
Cabin Hill, 157
Calvert, George, 15, 17, 41, 162, 296
Calvert, Ralls, 41
Campbell House, 250
Caroline County courthouse, 28
Carrigan, William and Ramona, 97, 112
Carter, French Pendleton, 44, 53, 187
Carter, John F., 38
Carter-Dudley house, 80
Carter's hotel and tavern, mid-1800s, 45
Cary, George E. and Louella, 71, 176
Cary, George M. and Catherine, 226
Catlin, Frederic F., 286
Cherry Tree and Hatchet, 77, 87, 90, 201
Chester's Gap road, 16, 273
Christmas celebrations, 100
Christmas parade, 101
Christmas tree, 84
Church construction, 1800s, 50
Churches, 40, 258
Cinema Paradiso, 218

Civil War, 44
Civilian Conservation Corps, 77
Claiborne, Craig, 153, 227
Clark, John W., 79
Clark, Washington, 46
Clark's Tavern, 46, 56, 80, 217
Claudia Mitchell Fund, 99
Cliffen, Ben, 55, 276
Cliffen, Patsey, 229
Clopton House, 89, 203
Colonial Virginia Land Office, 12
Comprehensive Plans, 118, 286
Confederate flag, 85
Confederate Monument, 44, 58, 69, 241
Contamination of water supply, 1956, 133
Country Cafe, 90, 92, 173
Country Cupboards, 87, 210
Country Heritage Antiques and Crafts, 88, 206
Country Store, 86, 90, 143, 197
County employee parking lot, 1965, 282
Court Clerk's office, 93, 236, 238
Court Clerk's office, 30
Courthouse architecture, 28
Courthouse bell, 29
Courthouse construction, 25
Coxe, Anne, 24, 36, 38, 41, 167
Coxe's Tavern, 284
Coxe's Tavern, 41, 167
Crawford, Malcolm F., 26, 237
Critzer, Robbie, 82
Critzer's Service Station, 80, 281
Culpeper courthouse, 24
Culpeper plat books, 297
Davis, Dorothy Cox, 82, 299
Dear, Amos and Phebe, 52, 168
Dear's Hotel, 41, 45, 168
Dearing, Robert, 243
Delameres Forest, 11, 290
Delco electric plant, 74, 207
Dental office, 89
Department of Environmental Quality grant, 139
Department of Environmental Quality loan, 139
District 3, the Hampton District, 1870, 45
Districts formation, 1852, 43
Dodd, Laura, 286
Dowser to find water, 135
Drake, Dr. Francis T., 33, 38, 39, 42, 175
Drinking and gambling, 76
Drinking fountain, 129
Drought, 77
Drought in 1930s, 131
Drug store, late 1800s, 57
Drunkenness, fines, 49
Dudley, Francis, 171
Dulin's Saloon, 45, 76, 214
Easements for water lines, 287
Edmund's Jewelry shop, 206
Eldred, Charles, 145
Eldred, Frances, 83, 86, 170
Election date, 286
Environmental Protection Agency, 136
Fairfax, Gay, 296
Fairfax, Sally, 296
Fairfax, Thomas Lord, 12, 296
Fairfax, town of, 18
Fant, John W., 30, 238
Farmers and Merchants Bank, 72
Fire department, 78, 131, 215
Fire insurance, 131, 133
First Baptist Church, 258
First Friday Movie, 99
Fletcher, James W., 131
Fletcher, Mattie Ball, 144, 148, 191
Fodderstack Pottery, 87
Fodderstack Road, 273
Foster Harris House Bed & Breakfast, 92, 185
Fountain at Middle & Main Sts, 115

Four-lane divided highway, 1970s, 283
Fourth of July, 97, 99
Francis Asbury, Bishop, 31
Free Meeting House, 25, 235
Free Town Meeting House, 38, 163
Front Royal & Washington Motor Transportation Company, 79, 183, 279
Front Royal-Washington bus line, 280
Gardens of the Inn, 145
Gas lights, 68
Gay Street, 16, 273, 296
Gay Street Gallery, 105
Gay Street Inn, 243
Gay Street Theater, 99, 213
General Assembly of Virginia, 17, 19, 24, 32, 43, 45, 58, 67, 70, 107
Geneva Welch Gallery, 175
George II, King, 11, 290, 296
Giles, Clarence (Skippy) Jr., 164
Glenn Mills, 44
Goodine, Chris and Jean, 174
Government of the town, 117, 286
Grayson, George W., 40
Green, Phelbert Scott, 229
Green's barber shop, 74, 81, 207
Grimsley, Barnett, 242, 261
Groves, John, 228
Hansbrough Drug Store, 1880, 50
Harris Hollow Road, 138
Hawkins, Dorothy B., 82, 186
Hawkins, John J., 45, 238
Hayward, Thomas F., 161
Heritage House, 178
Heterick House, 250
Heterick, Robert M., 38, 46, 52
Highway 21, 79
Highway markers, 1953, 282
Historic District, 120, 285
Historic District Design Guidelines, 123
Historic District designation, 1975, 106
Historic District designation, 2006, 121
Historic District Ordinance, 1985, 120
Historic District Ordinance, 1991, 120
Historic District Ordinance, 2007, 122
Hog pens, 50
Holland, Walker, 38, 53, 178
Holschuh, Howard and Helen, 103
Home construction, early 1900s, 81
Homes converted to commercial establishments, 93
Horse racks, 49, 275
Horse-related businesses, early 1800s, 276
Horses, fines, 47, 49, 63
Ice House Crafts, 87
IGA food store, 85, 208
Incorporation of the town, 1894, 58
Indians, 9
Inn at Little Washington, 143, 198, 285
Inn's 25th anniversary, 146
Inn's 40th anniversary, 150
Inn's awards, 148
Inn's charitable work, 149
Inn's community activities, 148
Inn's first menu, 143
Inn's properties, 151
Innstock Culinary Festival, 150
ISO rating, 134
Jail condition, 1892, 50
Jail construction, 30, 236
Jail on Lot 21, 189
Jefferson, Thomas, 26, 32
Jenkins Auction House, 87, 208
Jenkins, Ruby, 82, 104
Jett Jr., James, 15, 16, 17, 23, 199, 296
Jett Sr., James, 15, 16

Jett Sr., John, 39, 214
Jett Street stub street, 114
Jett, John, 15
Johnson, Henry, 38, 177
Jones, Edward T., 45
Jones, James Brereton, 54, 202
Jordan, June, 166
Kavanagh, Edmund, 89, 206
Kennerly - Thomas, James, and Elizabeth, 11
Kennerly land grant, 11, 273, 290
Kennerly, Thomas, 290, 298
Ki Theater, 101
Kinsey, Dr. Benjamin F., 42, 210
Kramer, Peter, 85, 88, 106, 203
Krebser, Werner, 88, 105, 233
Kuhn, Mary Ann, 286
Lane, John G., 45
Lea Brothers Store, 74, 85, 164, 207
Lederer, John, 10
Lee Highway, 79, 273, 282
Leggett Lane, 112, 142
Leggett, Eugene, 141
Leggett, Katherine, 286
Lemonade stands, 1894, 63
Lewis, Dan, 104
Library, 101, 192
Library of Congress, 295
Licenses tax, 1894, 61
Lillard, John F., 193
Lillard, William A., 54, 194
Little Washington, 31, 144
Lloyd, David, 45, 196
Lloyd's Hotel, 196
Lloyd's Hotel, late 1800s, 45, 54
Long House, 56, 218
Lord Baltimore, 15
Luke, Peter, 298
Lynch, Reinhardt, 143
Madison county, 24
Madison County courthouse, 28
Main Street, 16, 273
Main Street was macadamized, 278
Maintenance of roads by State, 1930, 278
Maintenance of streets, early 1800s, 274
Maintenance of streets, late 1800s, 276
Manahoac, 9
Marean, Hughes, Meigs Motor Co., 201
Martin, Jerry, 105, 233
Martin, Lawrence, 298
Mayors of the town, 1894-2018, 300
McCaslin, John, 91, 92, 95, 209
Meadows,, 37
Meadows, The, 14, 247
Meals and lodging tax, 285
Meeting House Lot, 186, 258
Menefee, J.Y., 38, 53, 80, 179
Menefee, William J., 38, 39, 53, 187
Merchant's licenses, 1830s, 35
Merrill, L.V., 80, 88, 172
Merrill's garage, 143
Merrill's Motor Company, 76, 80, 88, 282
Methodist Church, 98, 101, 232, 260
Middle Street Gallery, 75, 104, 196, 197, 198
Middle Street stub street, 114, 146
Middleton Inn, 31, 44, 93, 157, 249, 302
Millan, Dr. Lyle J., 52, 164
Millennium Preservation Services, 121
Miller, Achsah Dudley, 82
Miller, Middleton, 44, 56, 244
Miller, W. Arthur, postmaster, 72
Moffett, Horatio G., 38, 45
Moffett, William Francis, 189
Monacan Indians, 9
Mount Prospect, 247
Mountainside Market, 89, 91, 229

Movie theater, 98, 143
Mt. Salem Avenue homes, 81
National Register of Historic Places, 106, 107, 120, 285
Nature's Foods and Cafe, 92
Newspapers, 57
Newspapers, 1900s, 95
Nicklin, Dr. Joseph, 42, 43, 163
Nicklin, Walter, 89
Nicol, George, 38, 184
Nicol, Jacob and Abigail, 25, 39
Nicol, Lucy and Mary, 52, 161
Nicol, Michael, 161
Nicol, Michael and Sarah, 161
Nicol, Napolean, 39, 46, 224, 276
No Ordinary People, 99
Northern Neck (Fairfax) Proprietary, 11
Northern Virginia Power Company, 73
O'Connell, Patrick, 143, 286
O'Connell, Patrick, books by, 150
O'Neale family, 226
O'Neale, Daniel, 56, 225
Ochs Delikatessen, 89, 92, 204
Oden family, 159
Oden, James, 193
Oden, John W., 160
Old Church Lot, 53
Old Church Meeting House, 38, 258
Old Free Church, 258
Old Mill Road, 14, 273
Ordinance, 1894, 61
Overseer of the Streets, 46, 275
Packing Shed Gallery, 105, 218
Page County courthouse, 28
Parent's Civic League, 254
Parsonage, The, 204
Partlow, Daisy Fox, 190
Partlow's General Store, 74, 207
Payne, Kitty, 44, 240
Petition to add Porter's land, 1797, 19, 293
Petition to establish Washington, 1796, 17, 292
Physicians, 42, 57, 105
Plan of the streets and 51 lots, 1797, 19
Plan of the town, 1833, 34, 274
Plan of the town, 1837, 36, 274
Plan of Washington in 1833, 33
Planning Commission, 118
Playground, 181
Playground on Lot 14, 96
Poll tax of $1.50, 1902, 69
Poolroom, 76, 77
Population and housing estimate, 1833, 33
Population and housing estimate, 1835, 35
Population of the town, 1880-2018, 301
Porter, Samuel, 14
Porter, Sarah, 14
Porter, Tilmon, 38, 41, 195
Porter, William, 14, 15, 16, 19, 37, 296
Post Office, 38
Post Office, 1837, 37
Post office, 1956-1981, 86
Post office, 2000s, 94
Post office, 2018, 286
Post office, early 1800s, 41, 195
Post office, early 1900s, 71, 209
Post office, late 1800s, 53
Post office, later 1900s, 94
Powers, James Leake, 38, 43, 56, 190, 223, 264, 266
Powers, James Leake, biography, 269
Powhatan confederacy, 9
Presbyterian Church, 101, 191, 264
Price, Louise Miller, 82
Privies, 128
Privies and hog pens, 66, 128
Privy on the jail lot, 129
Proctor, Corbin L., 262

Prohibition, 69
Property tax, 1898, 67
Public Colored Free School building, 254
Public transportation, 284
RAAC, 98, 285
Rabbit Gum, 39, 40, 56, 221, 252
Racer, Nellie Elizabeth, 82
Ralls, Lydia Beck, 41
Ralls, Nathaniel B., 38, 157
Rappahannock Association for the Arts and the Community, 98, 213
Rappahannock Club, 176
Rappahannock County Citizens League, 185
Rappahannock County creation, 1833, 24
Rappahannock County Land Books, 33, 155
Rappahannock Express bus service, 283
Rappahannock Historical Society, 102, 234
Rappahannock Medical Clinic, 105, 233
Rappahannock National Bank, 72, 91, 209, 214
Rappahannock News, 71, 90, 95, 210, 285
Rare Finds, 89, 91, 182, 229
Rechartering of the town, 1985, 107
Rectory Lots, 55, 212
Reid, Dr. Adolphus W., 38, 42, 49, 164
Renovation of buildings, 93, 107
Reservoir, 2006, 137
Resor, John and Mary, 230
Resor's tavern, 39, 230
Road tax, early 1900s, 278
Roosevelt's New Deal, 77
Route 211 Business, 283
Rural Development Administration loan, 137
Rush River, 14, 135, 273
Rush River Company, 87, 205
Sale of town lots, 1798, 22
Scheel, Eugene M., 295, 298
Schneider, Bradley C., 286
School of William Porter, 252
Schools, 40, 252
Scudere's Garage, 178
Second Friday Talk, 99
Septic systems, 138
Shenandoah National Park, 79, 92, 284
Shepherd, Cheryl H., 121
Sidewalks, 63, 71
Sisk, Irving and Eunice, 194
Skyline Drive, 282
Smith, Oliver P., 39
Smither, Gabriel, 39
Snead, Rayner V., 132
Speeding in town, 282
Sperryville and Rappahannock Turnpike, 276
Spiller, Tamar, 40, 191
Spilman, Alexander H., 211
Spotswood, Governor, 10
Springhouse, 129
Springs as water source, 129
State Highway Commission, 79, 278
Stonehaven, 216
Stonestreet, Butler, 38, 157, 158, 159
Stonestreet, Haden, 52
Stonestreet, James, 46
Stoneyman Gourmet Farmer, 90
Street maintenance, 2018, 288
Strother, Judge James French, 247
Stuart's Store and Bank, 72, 164
Stuart's Store and Bank, 74
Sullivan, John Fox, and Beverly, 14
Supervisor of the Streets, 43, 274
Swan, J.A., 76, 212

Swift, Gail K., 286
Task Forces of the town, 2018, 127
Tavern licenses, 1830s, 36
Tax rate, 1880, 50
Tax rate, 1894, 60, 61
Telephones, 69, 73
The Horseshoe, 15
The Maples, 44, 244, 249
The Meadows, 44
Theatre at Washington, Virginia, 98, 212, 285
Thorn, George, 36, 38
Thorn's Tavern, 37, 39, 41, 231
Thornton, John Edward, 169, 196, 281
Thornton's garage, 76, 80, 281
Thornton's garage, 75
Toilets in courthouse, 129
Toll houses, 277
Tour d'Epicure, 185
Town budget, 1976, 85
Town budget, 2019, 85, 288
Town Collector, 46, 48
Town Councilmen, 1894, 61
Town Hall, 102, 192
Town lots, resale of, 1822-1834, 33
Town Sergeant, 49
Town well, 37
Town-owned properties, 286
Tranquility, 44
Treasurer's office, 56
Treasurer's office, 1874, 45
Treaty of Albany, 11
Trinity Church house tour, 97
Trinity Church parking lot, 90, 115, 147, 201
Trinity Church rectory, 268
Trinity Episcopal Church, 200, 265
Trinity House, 229, 268
Tula's Off Main, 91, 92, 209, 302
Underground Railroad Trail to Freedom, 241
Union First Market Bank, 215
University of Virginia, 26
Vagrancy, 1894, 64
Virginia constitution, 1870, 45
Virginia Department of Historic Resources, 121
Virginia Historic Landmarks Commission, 106, 121, 285
Virginia Landmarks Register, 93, 120
Walker B. Jenkins Bus Line, 79, 183
Washington Academy, 40, 231, 253
Washington Arts Building, 90
Washington as County seat, 1833, 24
Washington Baptist Church, 242, 262
Washington Baptist Church parsonage, 264
Washington Cafe, 201
Washington Cash Store, 74, 86, 90, 97, 164
Washington D.C., 31
Washington Female Institute, 253
Washington Graded School, 254
Washington High School, 255
Washington House, 77, 91, 169, 196
Washington House of Reproductions, 86
Washington Masonic Lodge, 242, 260
Washington Methodist Church, 51
Washington Mill, 14
Washington Motor Works, 281
Washington Museum, 91, 104, 219
Washington Water Works, 129
Washington, George, 17, 294
Washington, George, Bicentennial Commission, 295, 298
Washington's plats, 295
Washington's field books, 295
Wastewater collection system, 2010, 139

Wastewater Treatment facility, 112
Water fountain, 132
Water pipes easements, 1935, 130
Water Policy Resolution, 1999, 138
Water reservoir, 129, 131, 137
Water shortage, 1977, 134
Water shortage, 1977-1980, 134
Water source - springs, 134
Water source - well, 132, 134, 135, 136, 138
Water supply, 113
Water supply system, 1964 description, 133
Water system bonds, 1935, 130
Water tap fee, 138
Water Works & Wastewater budget, 2018, 141
Water Works in receivership, 1942, 131
Water Works purchased by town, 1966, 133
Watts' barbershop, 180
Wayman and Templeman, 55, 207
Wayside store on Old Mill Road, 282
Weinberg, Patricia W., 98
Well near Dear's hotel, 50
Wells in the town, 128
Wheeler, George, 223
Wheeler, James, 15, 16, 17, 23, 37, 193, 194, 296
White Moose Inn, 92, 179, 302
Whited, Joseph J., 286
Willis, Eve, 102
Windflower Gallery, 206
Woodville, 18
Works Projects Administration (WPA), 77, 78, 129
Worley, Sidney and Mary Catherine, 121
Yellow House, 202
Zindel, Louis G. (Butch), 91
Zoning districts, map of, 125
Zoning ordinance, 1970, 123
Zoning Ordinance, 1986, 123
Zoning Ordinance, 2008, 124

Made in the USA
Lexington, KY
01 November 2019